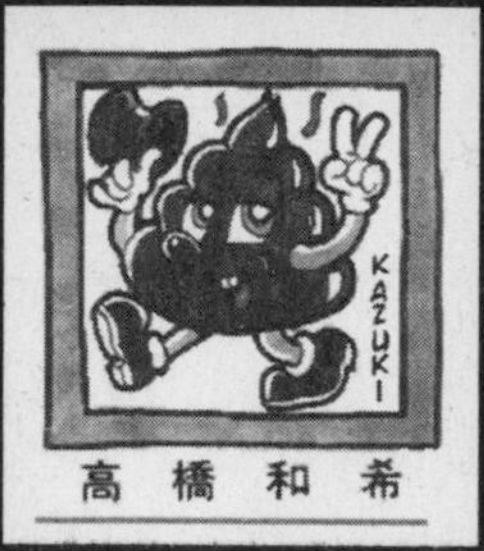
KAZUKI
高橋和希

THIS HAPPENED TO ME IN 7TH GRADE. MR. "W," MY HOMEROOM TEACHER, NEVER LIKED ME. ONCE HE SAID THIS IN FRONT OF THE WHOLE CLASS:

"TAKAHASHI! ALL YOU DO IS EAT, SLEEP AND POOP. YOU'RE A POOP-MAKING MACHINE!"

THE WHOLE CLASS ERUPTED IN LAUGHTER. I LAUGHED TOO, BUT I CLENCHED MY FIST AND THOUGHT TO MYSELF, "I COULD JUST PUNCH YOU RIGHT NOW!"

I WAS MAD. BUT I THOUGHT, A POOP-MAKING MACHINE CAN'T WRITE MANGA! THAT'S WHEN I DECIDED TO BECOME A MANGA ARTIST.

-KAZUKI TAKAHASHI, 2001

Artist/author Kazuki Takahashi first tried to break into the manga business in 1982, but success eluded him until **Yu-Gi-Oh!** debuted in the Japanese **Weekly Shonen Jump** magazine in 1996. **Yu-Gi-Oh!**'s themes of friendship and fighting, together with Takahashi's weird and wonderful art, soon became enormously successful, spawning a real-world card game, video games, and two anime series. A lifelong gamer, Takahashi enjoys Shogi (Japanese chess), Mahjong, card games, and tabletop RPGs, among other games.

YU-GI-OH!: DUELIST VOL. 21
The SHONEN JUMP Manga Edition

STORY AND ART BY
KAZUKI TAKAHASHI

Translation & English Adaptation/Joe Yamazaki
Touch-up Art & Lettering/Eric Erbes
Design/Andrea Rice
Editor/Jason Thompson

Managing Editor/Frances E. Wall
Editorial Director/Elizabeth Kawasaki
Editor in Chief, Books/Alvin Lu
Editor in Chief, Magazines/Marc Weidenbaum
Sr. Director of Acquisitions/Rika Inouye
Sr. VP of Marketing/Liza Coppola
Exec. VP of Sales & Marketing/John Easum
Publisher/Hyoe Narita

In the original Japanese edition, YU-GI-OH!, YU-GI-OH!: DUELIST and
YU-GI-OH!: MILLENNIUM WORLD are known collectively as YU-GI-OH!.
The English YU-GI-OH!: DUELIST was originally volumes 8–31
of the Japanese YU-GI-OH!.

Printed in the U.S.A.

Published by VIZ Media, LLC
P.O. Box 77010
San Francisco, CA 94107

SHONEN JUMP Manga Edition
10 9 8 7 6 5 4 3 2 1
First printing, June 2007

THE WORLD'S
MOST POPULAR MANGA

PARENTAL ADVISORY
YU-GI-OH!: DUELIST is rated T for Teen
and is recommended for ages 13 and
up. Contains fantasy violence.

www.viz.com

www.shonenjump.com

SHONEN JUMP MANGA

Vol. 21

DUEL THE LIGHTNING!

STORY AND ART BY
KAZUKI TAKAHASHI

THE STORY SO FAR...

**YUGI MUTOU/
YU-GI-OH**

When 10th grader Yugi solved the Millennium Puzzle, another spirit took up residence in his body...Yu-Gi-Oh, the King of Games, a dark avenger who challenges evildoers to "Shadow Games" of life and death!

YUGI FACES DEADLY ENEMIES!

Using his gaming skills, Yugi fights ruthless adversaries like Maximillion Pegasus, multimillionaire creator of the collectible card game "Duel Monsters," and Ryo Bakura, whose friendly personality turns evil when he is possessed by the spirit of the Millennium Ring. But Yugi's greatest rival is Seto Kaiba, the world's second-greatest gamer—and the ruthless teenage president of Kaiba Corporation. At first, Kaiba and Yugi are bitter enemies, but after fighting against a common adversary—Pegasus—they come to respect one another. But for all his powers, there is one thing Yu-Gi-Oh cannot do: remember who he is and where he came from.

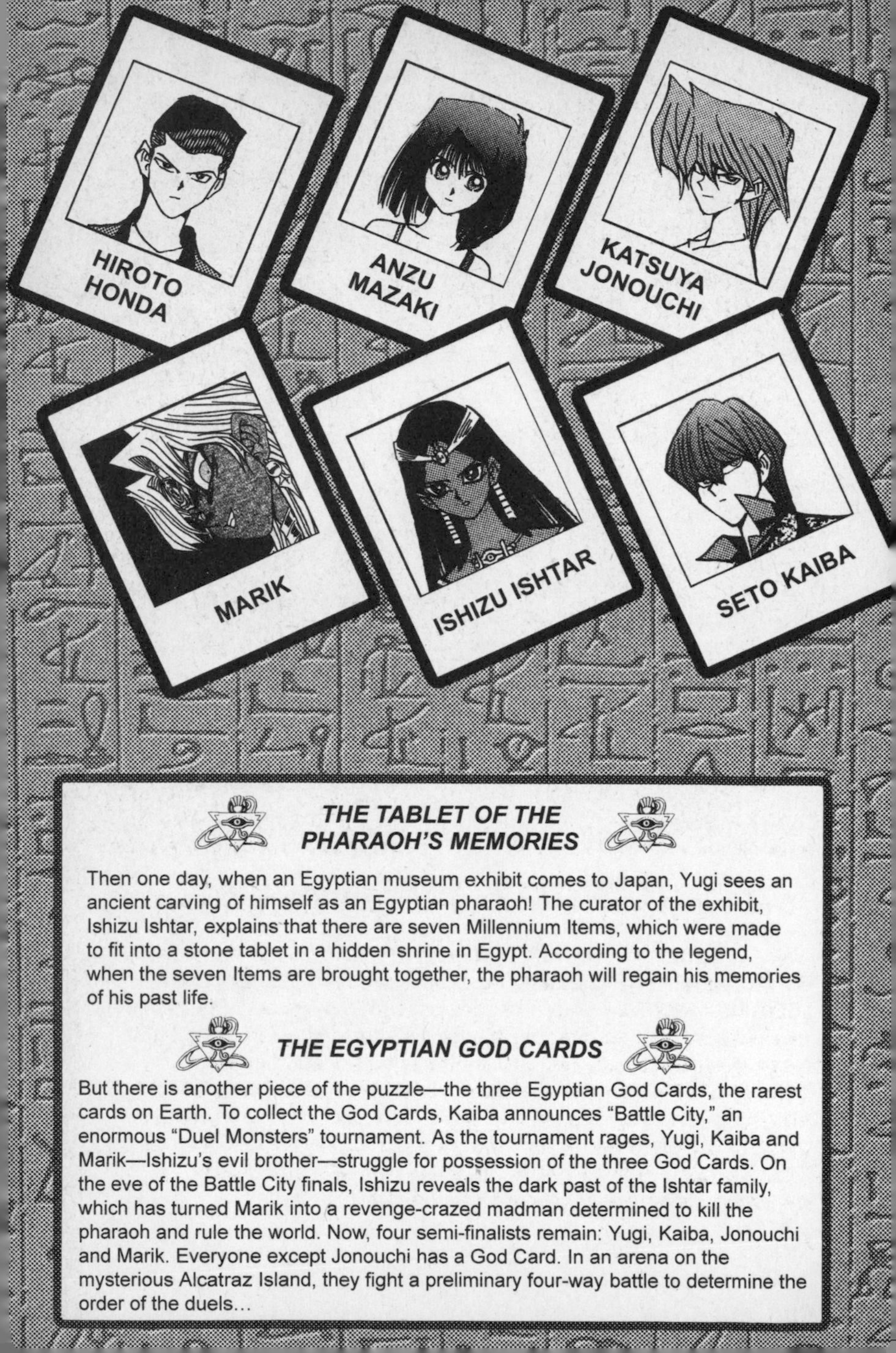
HIROTO HONDA
ANZU MAZAKI
KATSUYA JONOUCHI
MARIK
ISHIZU ISHTAR
SETO KAIBA

THE TABLET OF THE PHARAOH'S MEMORIES

Then one day, when an Egyptian museum exhibit comes to Japan, Yugi sees an ancient carving of himself as an Egyptian pharaoh! The curator of the exhibit, Ishizu Ishtar, explains that there are seven Millennium Items, which were made to fit into a stone tablet in a hidden shrine in Egypt. According to the legend, when the seven Items are brought together, the pharaoh will regain his memories of his past life.

THE EGYPTIAN GOD CARDS

But there is another piece of the puzzle—the three Egyptian God Cards, the rarest cards on Earth. To collect the God Cards, Kaiba announces "Battle City," an enormous "Duel Monsters" tournament. As the tournament rages, Yugi, Kaiba and Marik—Ishizu's evil brother—struggle for possession of the three God Cards. On the eve of the Battle City finals, Ishizu reveals the dark past of the Ishtar family, which has turned Marik into a revenge-crazed madman determined to kill the pharaoh and rule the world. Now, four semi-finalists remain: Yugi, Kaiba, Jonouchi and Marik. Everyone except Jonouchi has a God Card. In an arena on the mysterious Alcatraz Island, they fight a preliminary four-way battle to determine the order of the duels...

Yu-Gi-Oh!
·DUELIST·

Vol. 21

CONTENTS

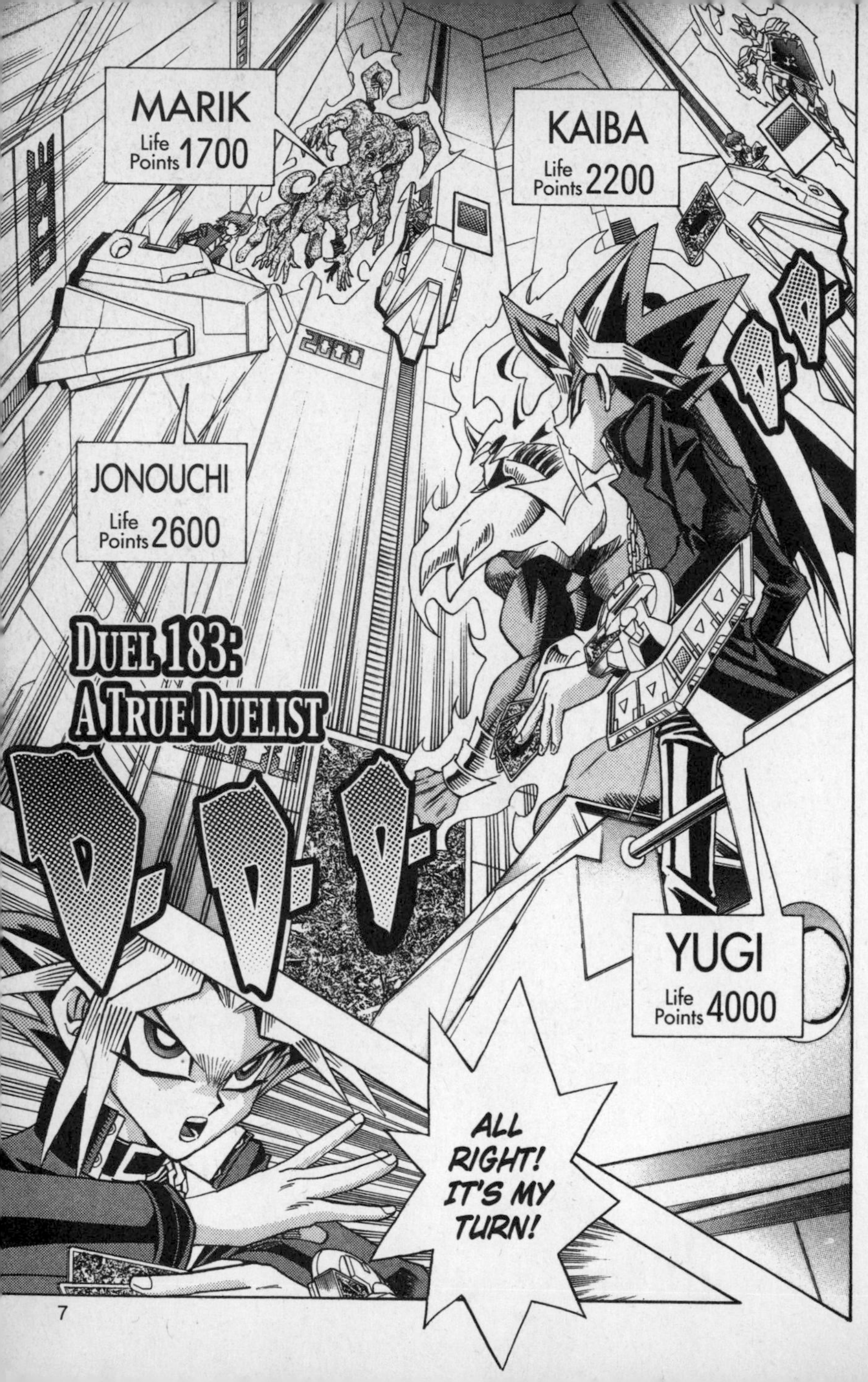
KAIBA Life Points 2200
MARIK Life Points 1700
JONOUCHI Life Points 2600
Duel 183: A True Duelist
YUGI Life Points 4000
ALL RIGHT! IT'S MY TURN!

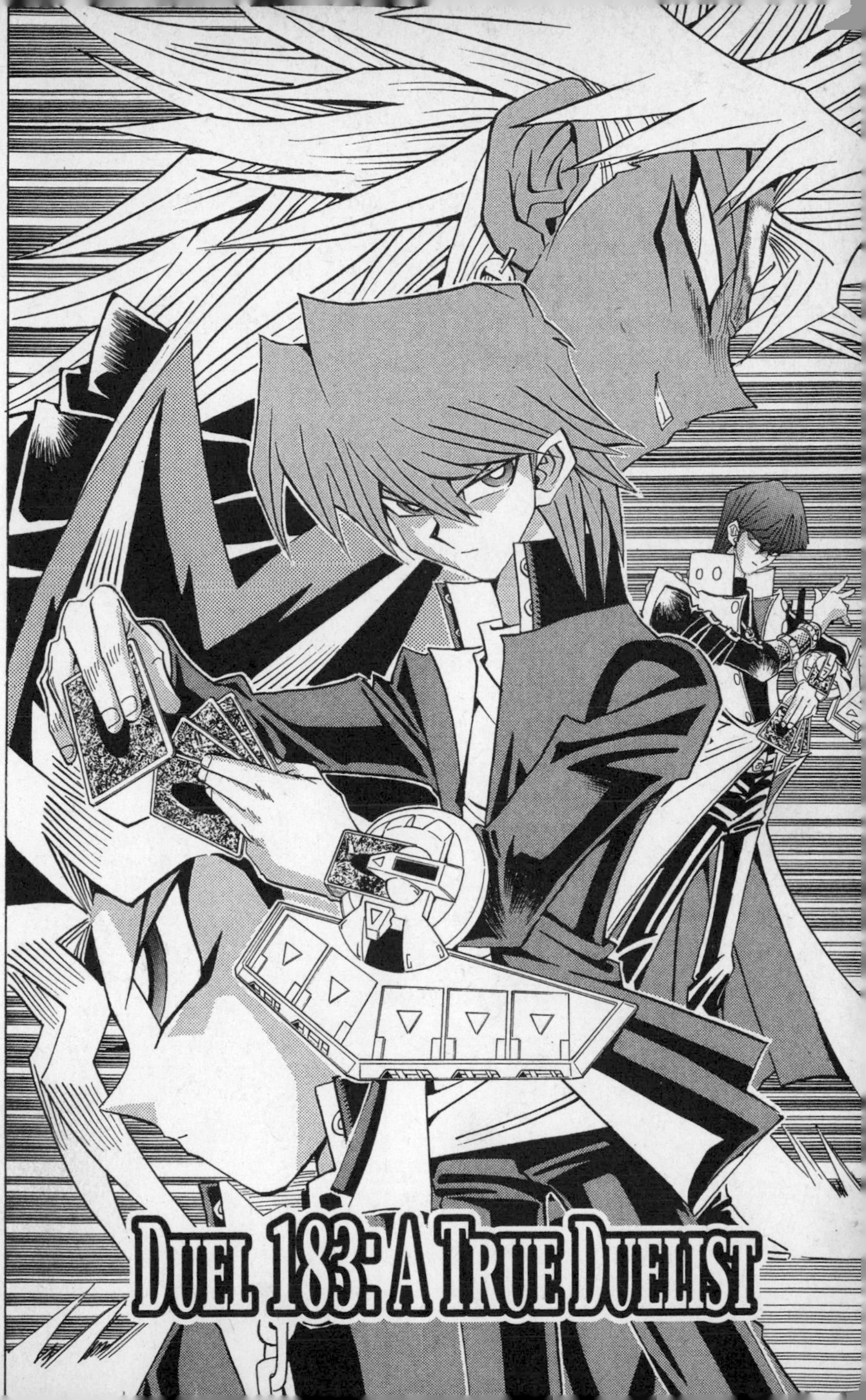
DUEL 183: A TRUE DUELIST

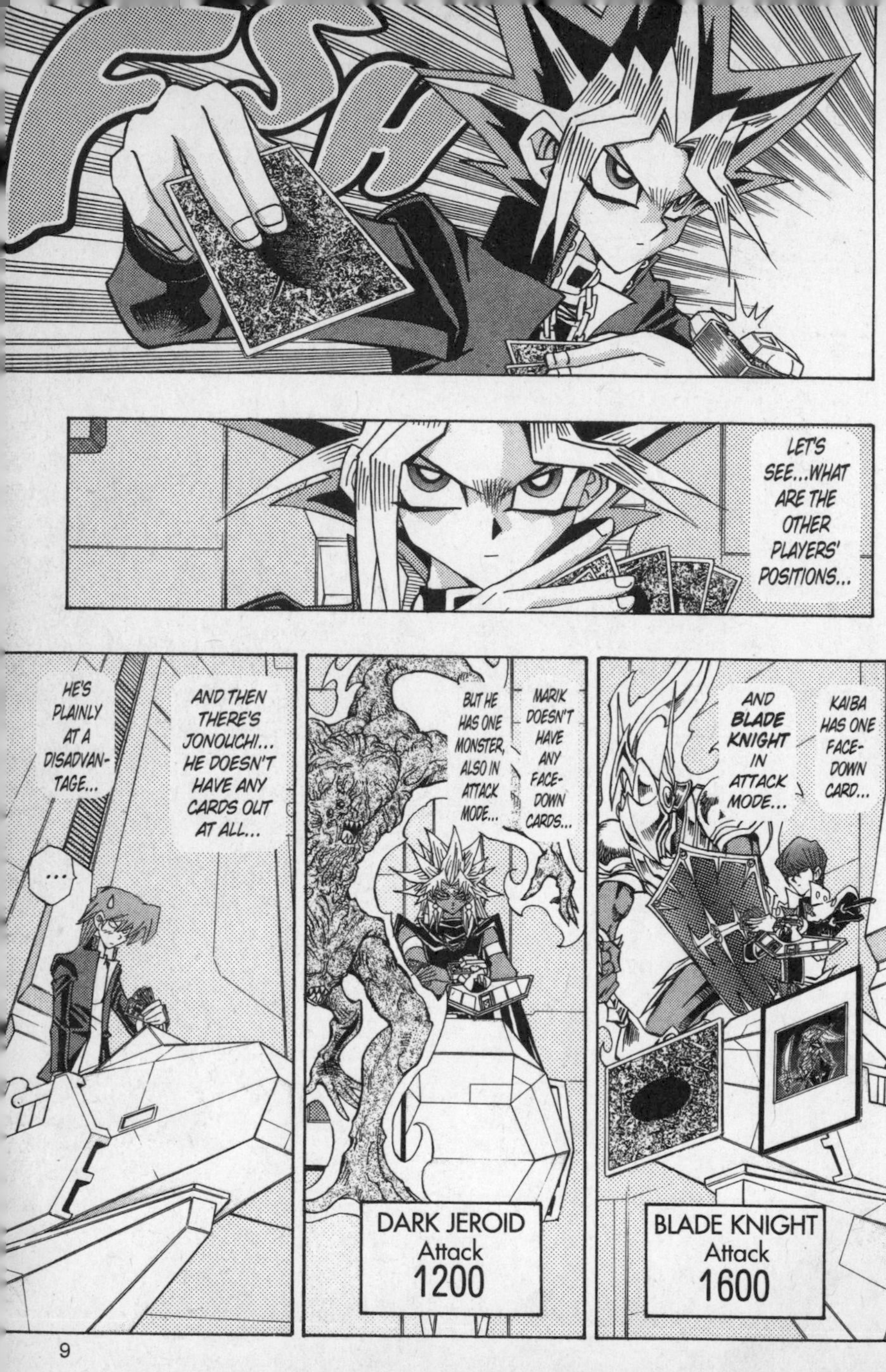

LET'S SEE...WHAT ARE THE OTHER PLAYERS' POSITIONS...
KAIBA HAS ONE FACE-DOWN CARD...
AND BLADE KNIGHT IN ATTACK MODE...
BLADE KNIGHT Attack 1600
MARIK DOESN'T HAVE ANY FACE-DOWN CARDS...
BUT HE HAS ONE MONSTER, ALSO IN ATTACK MODE...
DARK JEROID Attack 1200
AND THEN THERE'S JONOUCHI... HE DOESN'T HAVE ANY CARDS OUT AT ALL...
HE'S PLAINLY AT A DISADVANTAGE...
...

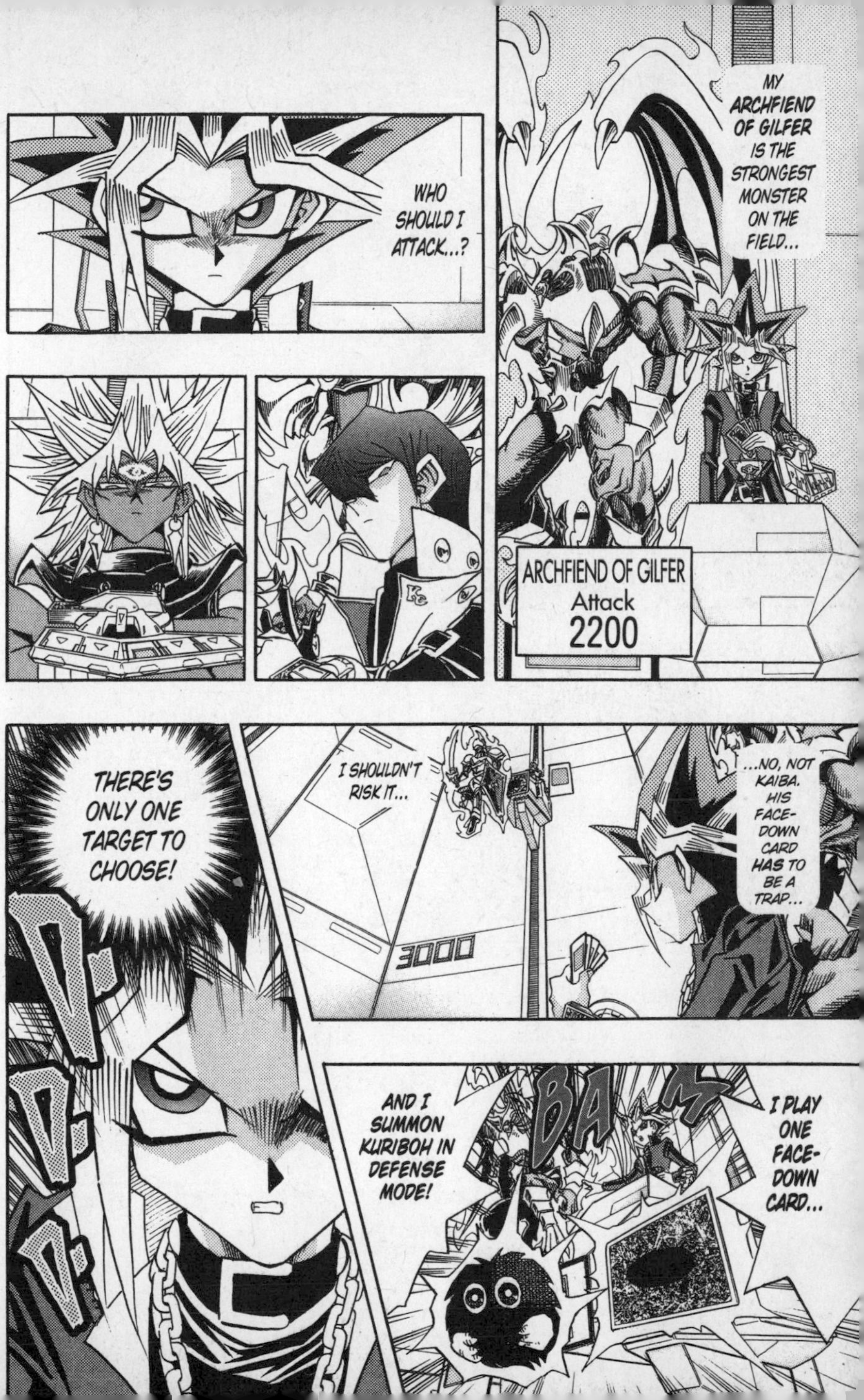
MY ARCHFIEND OF GILFER IS THE STRONGEST MONSTER ON THE FIELD...
ARCHFIEND OF GILFER
Attack
2200
WHO SHOULD I ATTACK...?
...NO, NOT KAIBA. HIS FACE-DOWN CARD HAS TO BE A TRAP...
I SHOULDN'T RISK IT...
3000
I PLAY ONE FACE-DOWN CARD...
BAM
AND I SUMMON KURIBOH IN DEFENSE MODE!
THERE'S ONLY ONE TARGET TO CHOOSE!

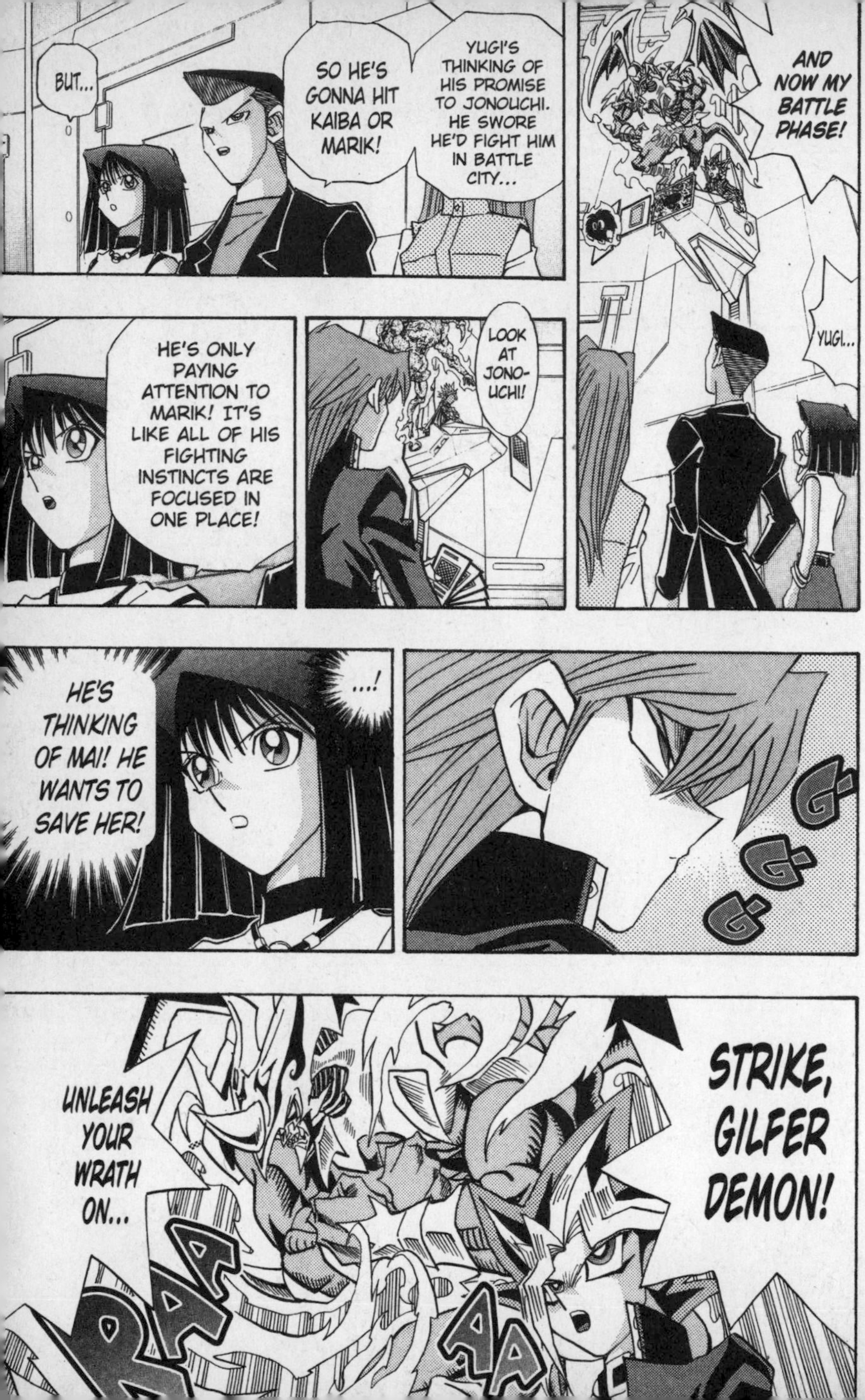
AND NOW MY BATTLE PHASE!
YUGI'S THINKING OF HIS PROMISE TO JONOUCHI. HE SWORE HE'D FIGHT HIM IN BATTLE CITY...
SO HE'S GONNA HIT KAIBA OR MARIK!
BUT...
YUGI...
LOOK AT JONO-UCHI!
HE'S ONLY PAYING ATTENTION TO MARIK! IT'S LIKE ALL OF HIS FIGHTING INSTINCTS ARE FOCUSED IN ONE PLACE!
G G G
...!
HE'S THINKING OF MAI! HE WANTS TO SAVE HER!
STRIKE, GILFER DEMON!
UNLEASH YOUR WRATH ON...
AA
RAA

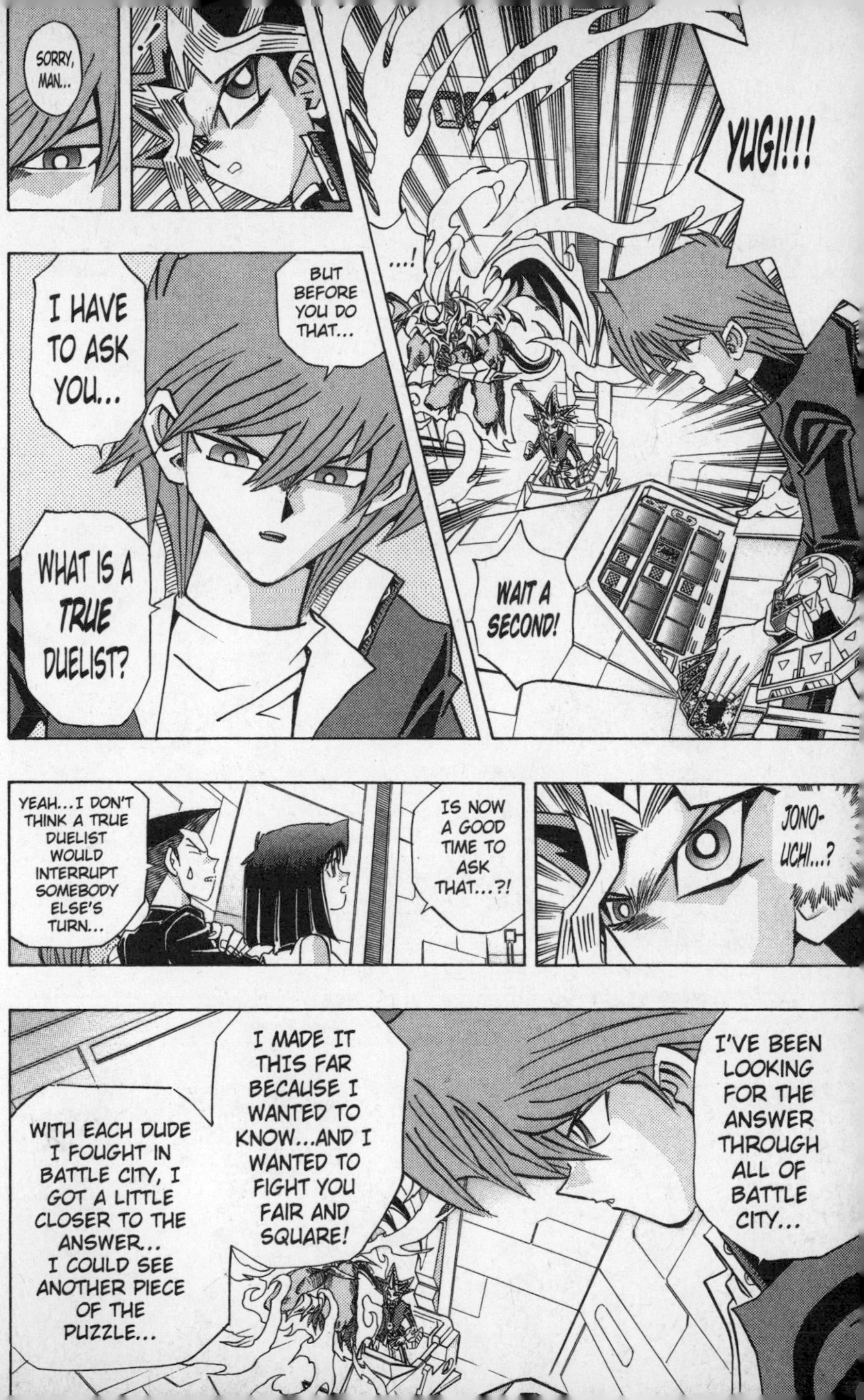
YUGI!!!
...!
WAIT A SECOND!
SORRY, MAN...
BUT BEFORE YOU DO THAT...
I HAVE TO ASK YOU...
WHAT IS A TRUE DUELIST?
JONO-UCHI...?
IS NOW A GOOD TIME TO ASK THAT...?!
YEAH...I DON'T THINK A TRUE DUELIST WOULD INTERRUPT SOMEBODY ELSE'S TURN...
I'VE BEEN LOOKING FOR THE ANSWER THROUGH ALL OF BATTLE CITY...
I MADE IT THIS FAR BECAUSE I WANTED TO KNOW...AND I WANTED TO FIGHT YOU FAIR AND SQUARE!
WITH EACH DUDE I FOUGHT IN BATTLE CITY, I GOT A LITTLE CLOSER TO THE ANSWER... I COULD SEE ANOTHER PIECE OF THE PUZZLE...

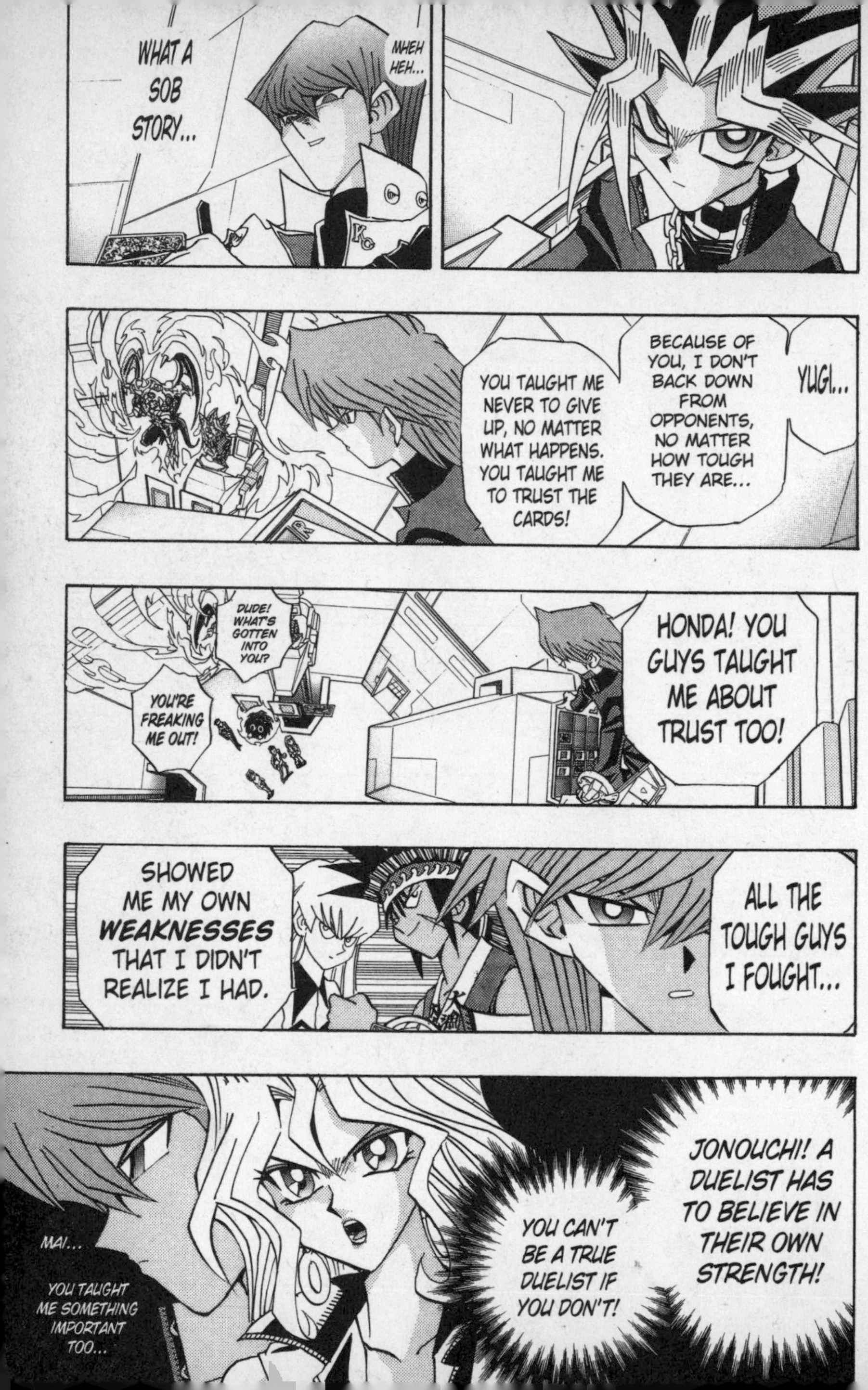
MHEH HEH...
WHAT A SOB STORY...
YUGI...
BECAUSE OF YOU, I DON'T BACK DOWN FROM OPPONENTS, NO MATTER HOW TOUGH THEY ARE...
YOU TAUGHT ME NEVER TO GIVE UP, NO MATTER WHAT HAPPENS. YOU TAUGHT ME TO TRUST THE CARDS!
HONDA! YOU GUYS TAUGHT ME ABOUT TRUST TOO!
DUDE! WHAT'S GOTTEN INTO YOU?
YOU'RE FREAKING ME OUT!
ALL THE TOUGH GUYS I FOUGHT...
SHOWED ME MY OWN WEAKNESSES THAT I DIDN'T REALIZE I HAD.
JONOUCHI! A DUELIST HAS TO BELIEVE IN THEIR OWN STRENGTH!
YOU CAN'T BE A TRUE DUELIST IF YOU DON'T!
MAI...
YOU TAUGHT ME SOMETHING IMPORTANT TOO...

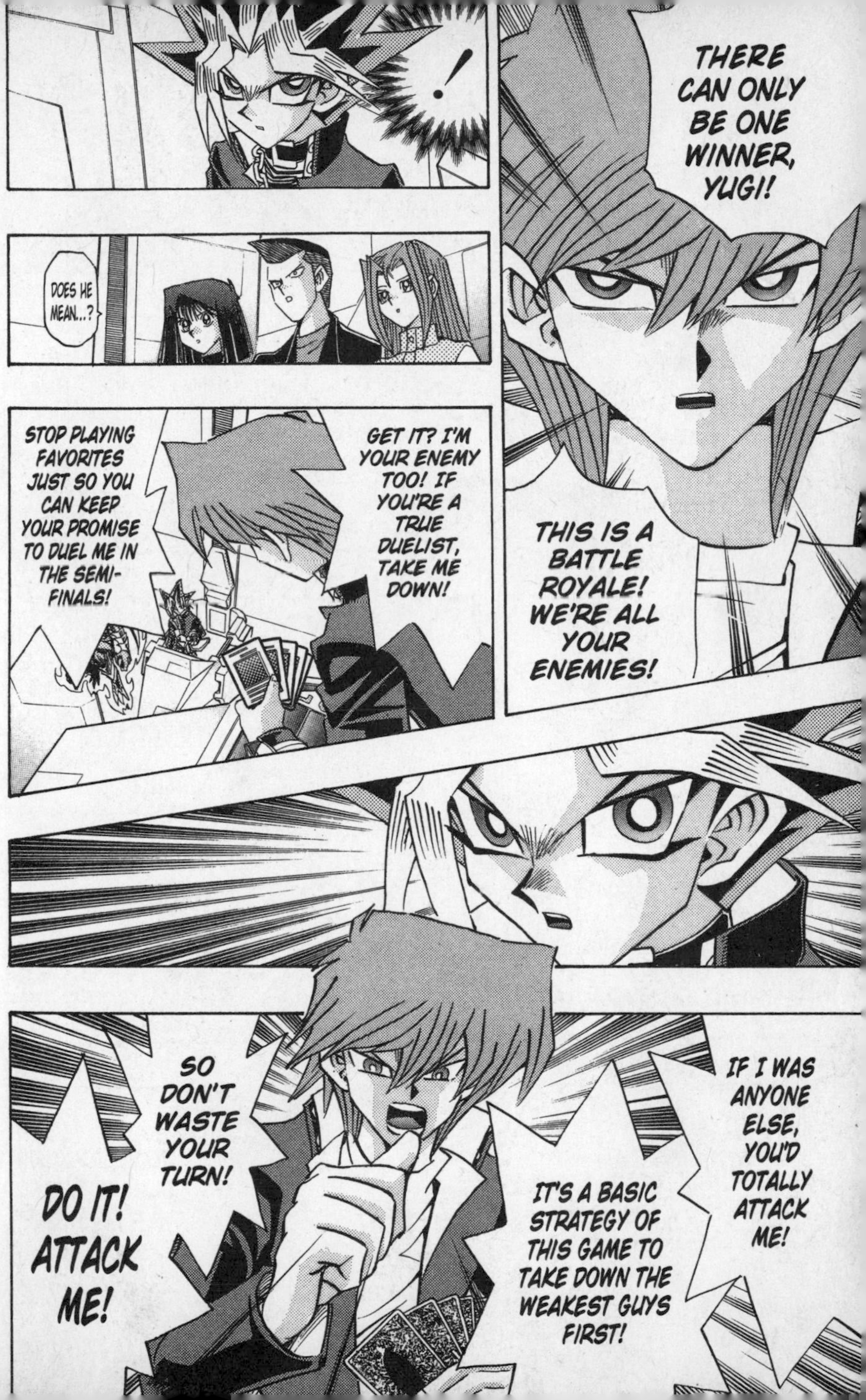
THERE CAN ONLY BE ONE WINNER, YUGI!
THIS IS A BATTLE ROYALE! WE'RE ALL YOUR ENEMIES!
!
DOES HE MEAN...?
STOP PLAYING FAVORITES JUST SO YOU CAN KEEP YOUR PROMISE TO DUEL ME IN THE SEMI-FINALS!
GET IT? I'M YOUR ENEMY TOO! IF YOU'RE A TRUE DUELIST, TAKE ME DOWN!
IF I WAS ANYONE ELSE, YOU'D TOTALLY ATTACK ME!
IT'S A BASIC STRATEGY OF THIS GAME TO TAKE DOWN THE WEAKEST GUYS FIRST!
SO DON'T WASTE YOUR TURN!
DO IT! ATTACK ME!

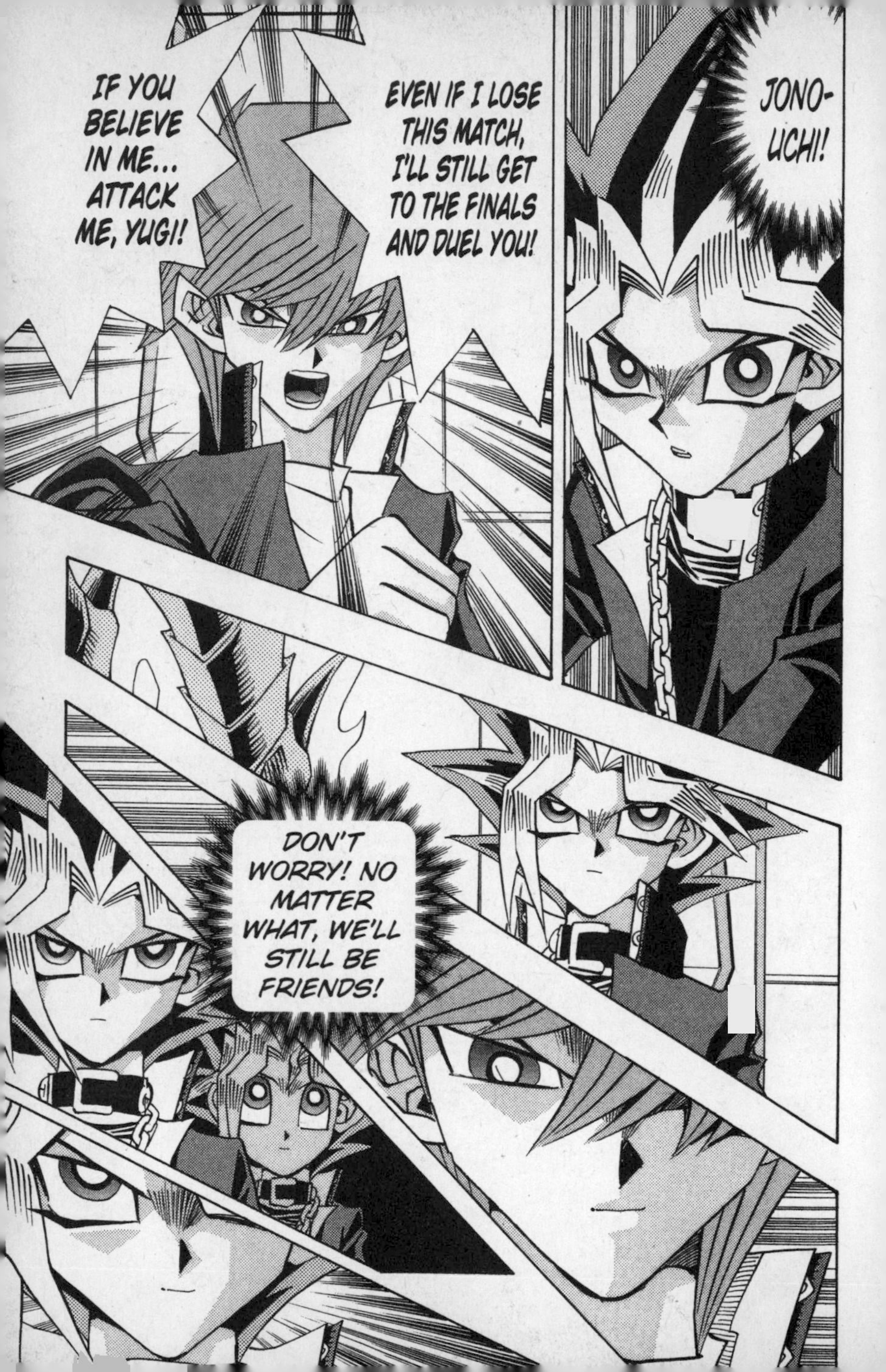
JONO-UCHI!
EVEN IF I LOSE THIS MATCH, I'LL STILL GET TO THE FINALS AND DUEL YOU!
IF YOU BELIEVE IN ME... ATTACK ME, YUGI!
DON'T WORRY! NO MATTER WHAT, WE'LL STILL BE FRIENDS!

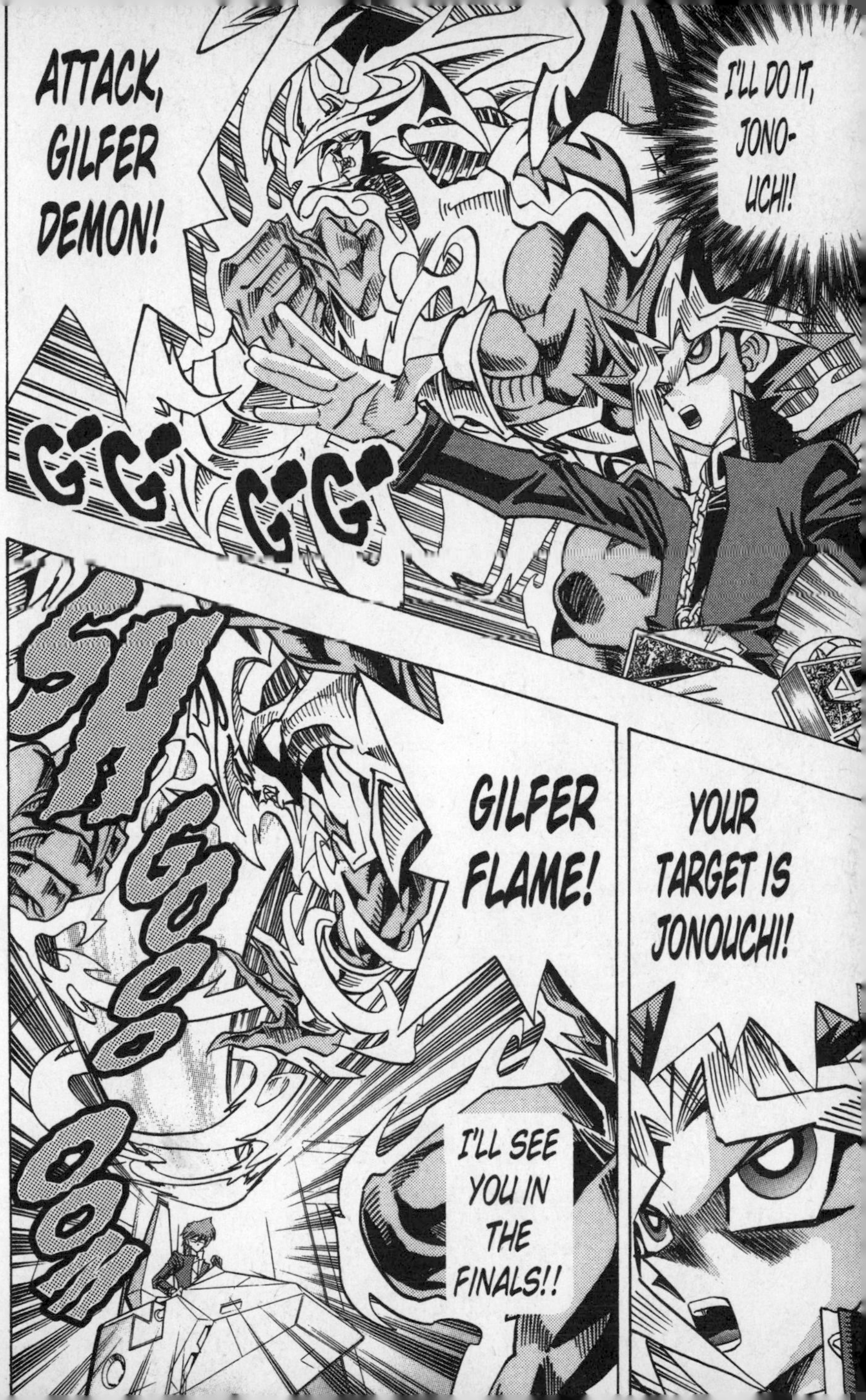
I'LL DO IT, JONOUCHI!
ATTACK, GILFER DEMON!
YOUR TARGET IS JONOUCHI!
GILFER FLAME!
I'LL SEE YOU IN THE FINALS!!

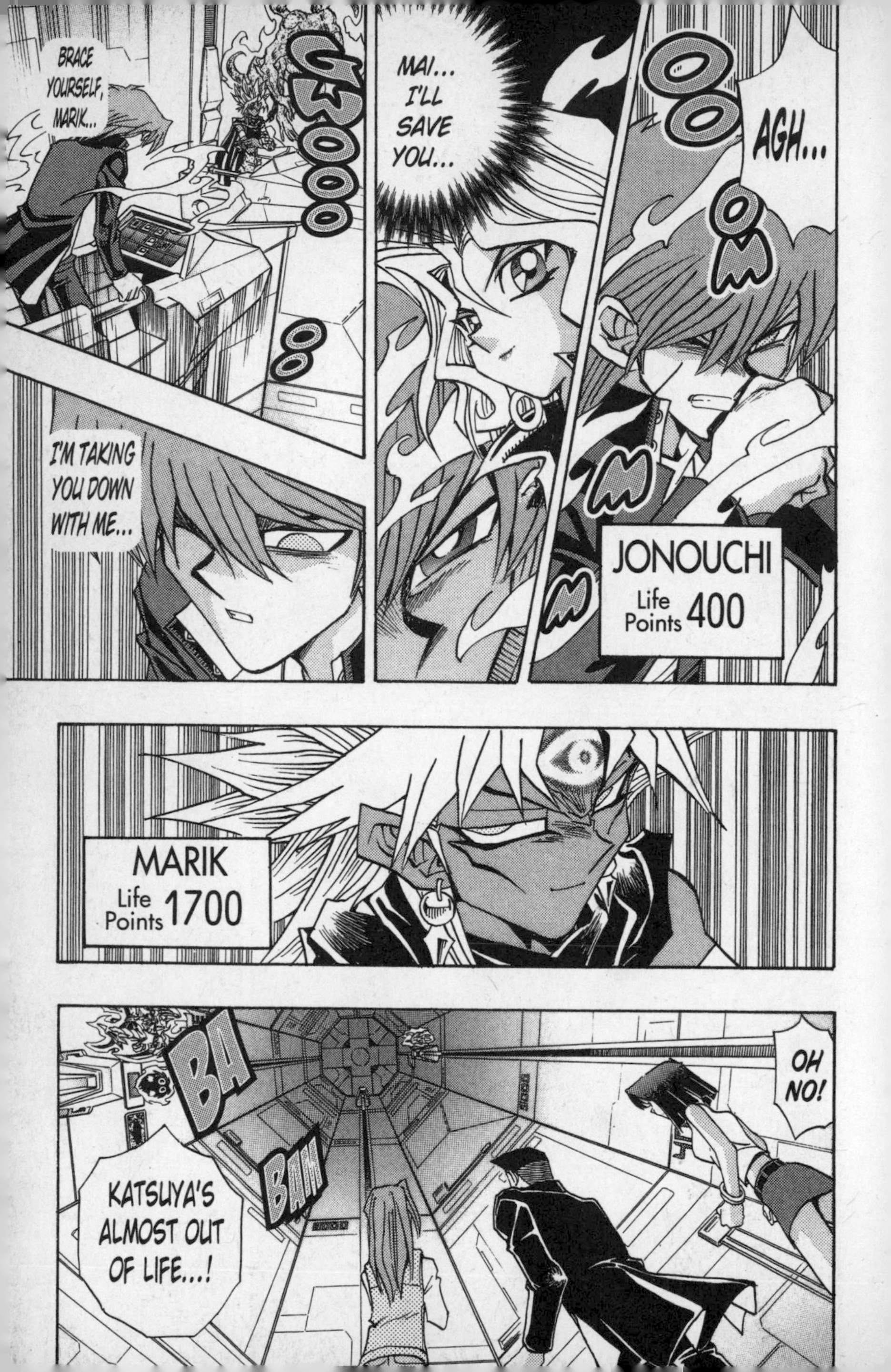
OOOOMMMM
AGH...
JONOUCHI
Life Points 400
MAI... I'LL SAVE YOU...
BRACE YOURSELF, MARIK...
GWOOOOOOO
I'M TAKING YOU DOWN WITH ME...
MARIK
Life Points 1700
OH NO!
BA
BAM
KATSUYA'S ALMOST OUT OF LIFE...!

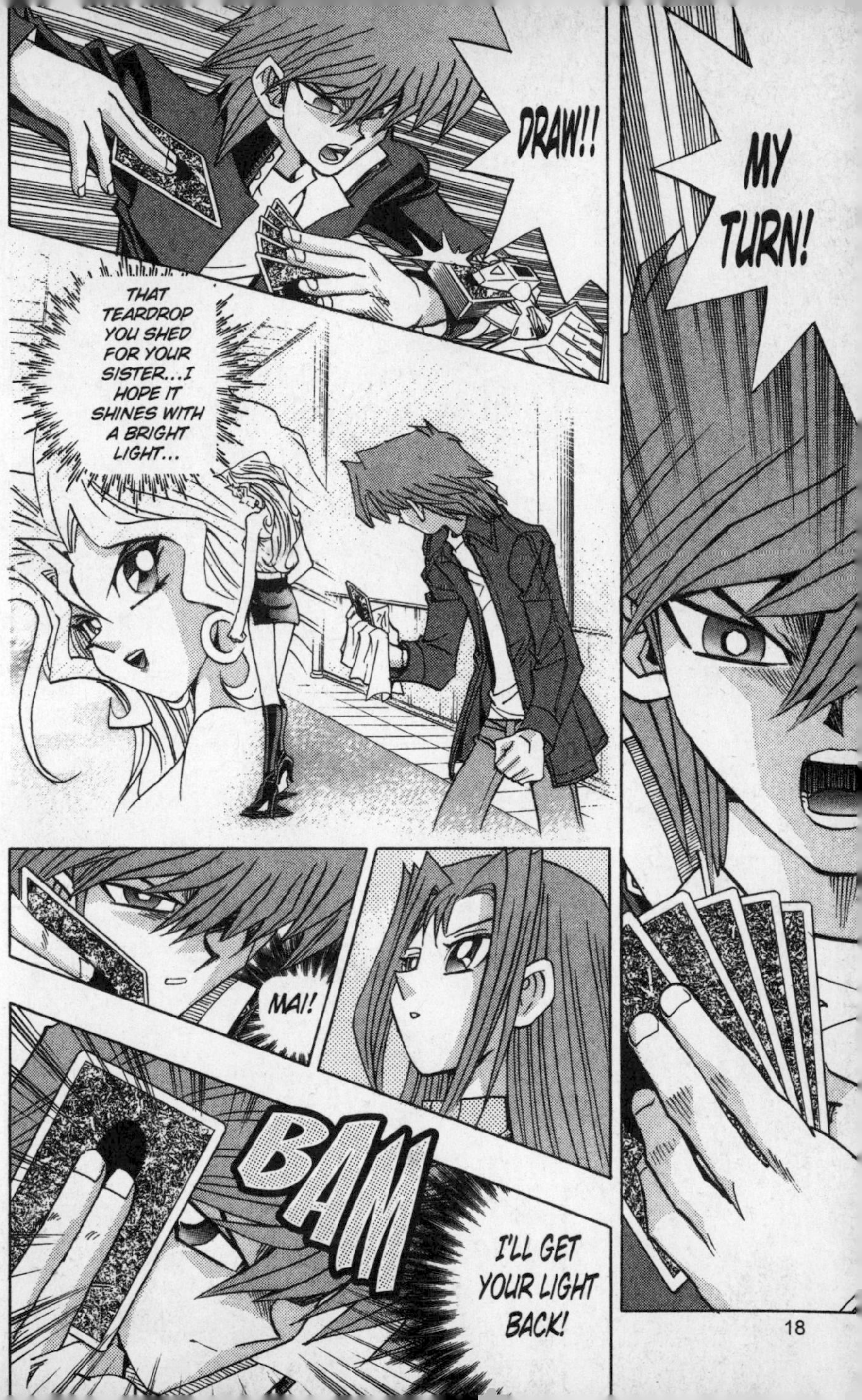
MY TURN!
DRAW!!
THAT TEARDROP YOU SHED FOR YOUR SISTER...I HOPE IT SHINES WITH A BRIGHT LIGHT...
MAI!
BAM
I'LL GET YOUR LIGHT BACK!

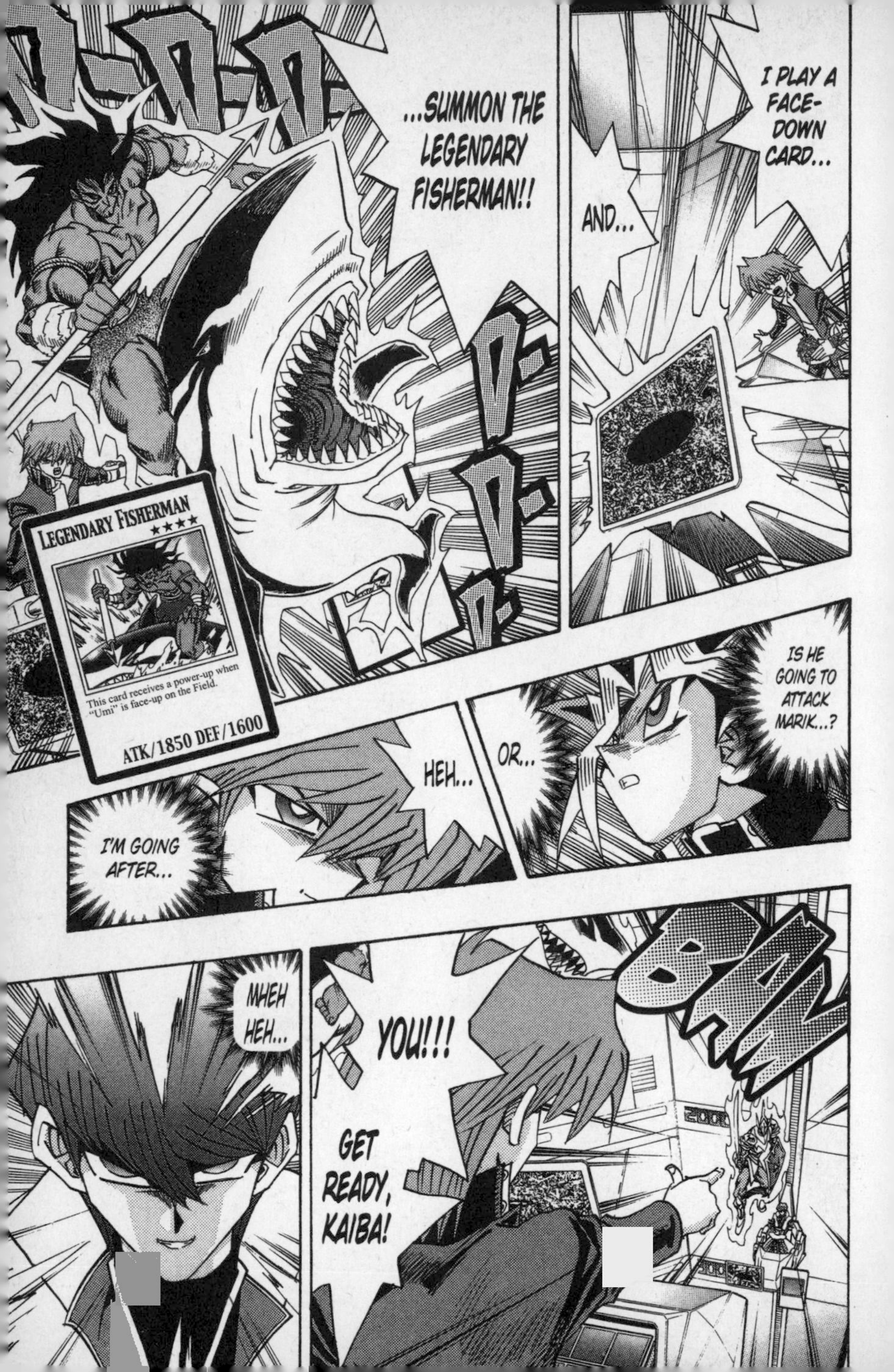
I PLAY A FACE-DOWN CARD...
AND...
...SUMMON THE LEGENDARY FISHERMAN!!
LEGENDARY FISHERMAN
★★★★
This card receives a power-up when "Umi" is face-up on the Field.
ATK/1850 DEF/1600
IS HE GOING TO ATTACK MARIK...?
OR...
HEH...
I'M GOING AFTER...
BAM
YOU!!!
GET READY, KAIBA!
MHEH HEH...

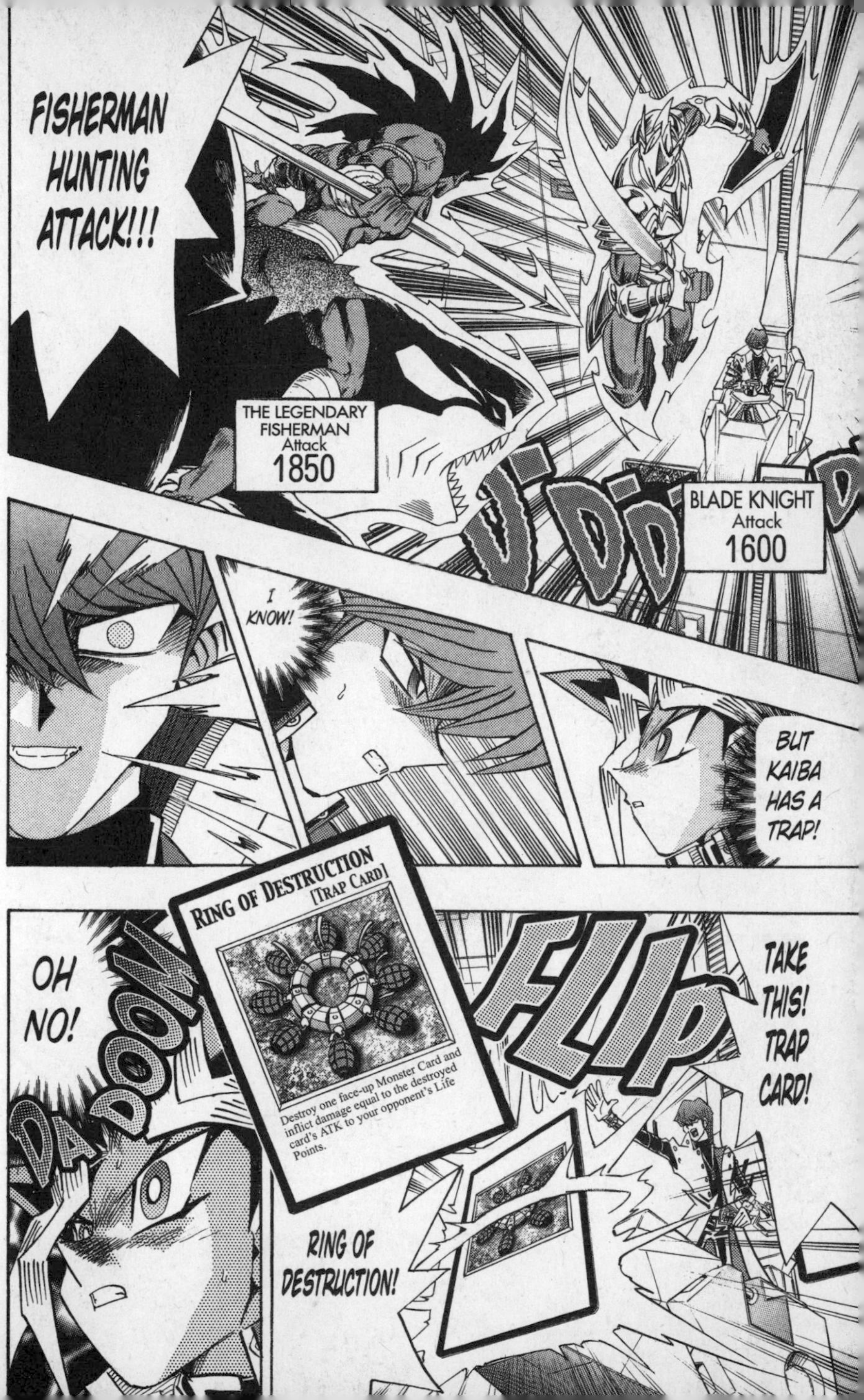
FISHERMAN HUNTING ATTACK!!!
BLADE KNIGHT Attack 1600
THE LEGENDARY FISHERMAN Attack 1850
DDD
BUT KAIBA HAS A TRAP!
I KNOW!
TAKE THIS! TRAP CARD!
FLIP
RING OF DESTRUCTION [TRAP CARD]
Destroy one face-up Monster Card and inflict damage equal to the destroyed card's ATK to your opponent's Life Points.
RING OF DESTRUCTION!
OH NO!
DA DOOOM

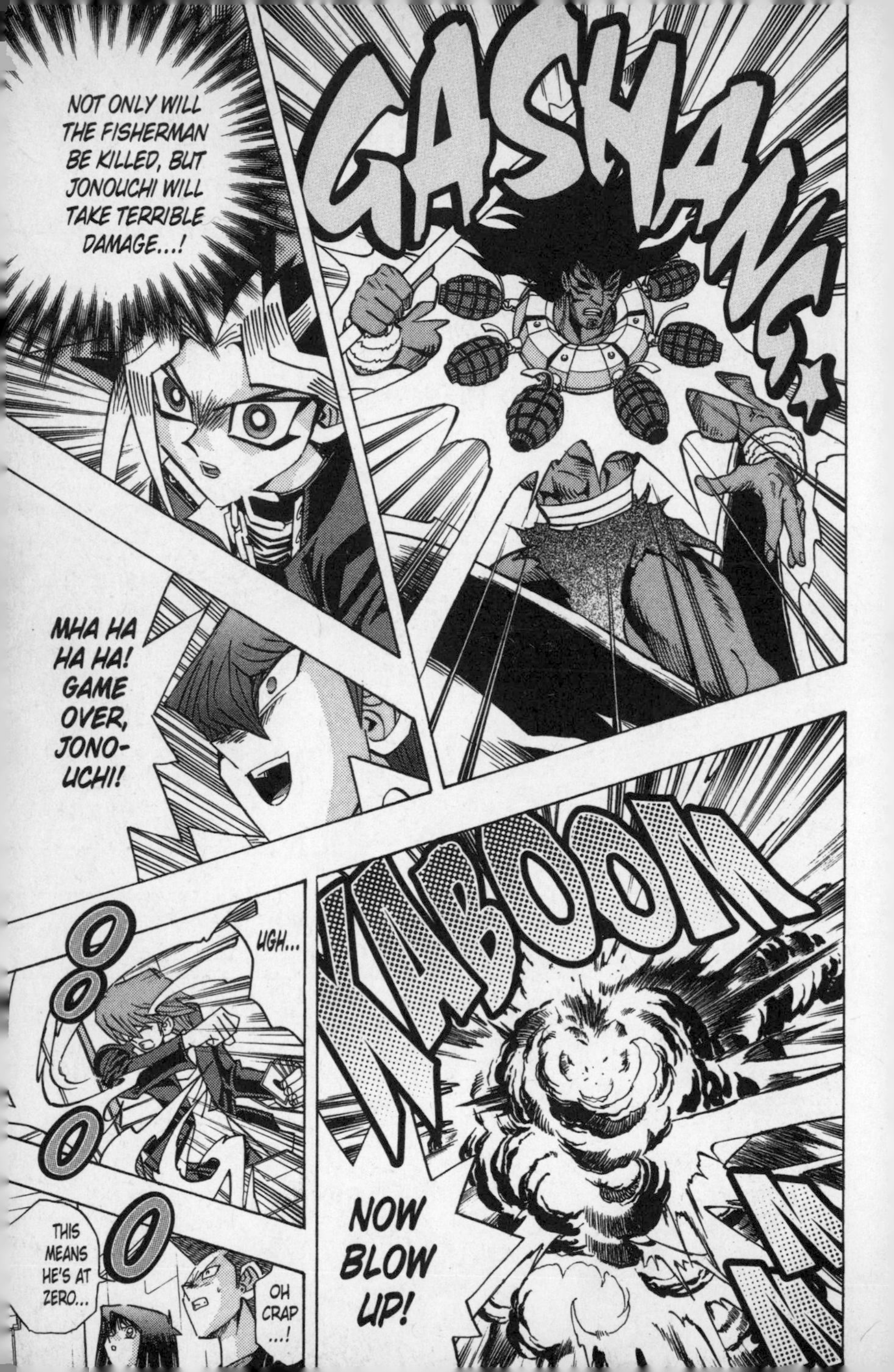
GASHAN
NOT ONLY WILL THE FISHERMAN BE KILLED, BUT JONOUCHI WILL TAKE TERRIBLE DAMAGE...!
MHA HA HA HA! GAME OVER, JONO-UCHI!
NOW BLOW UP!
UGH...
0000
THIS MEANS HE'S AT ZERO...
OH CRAP ...!

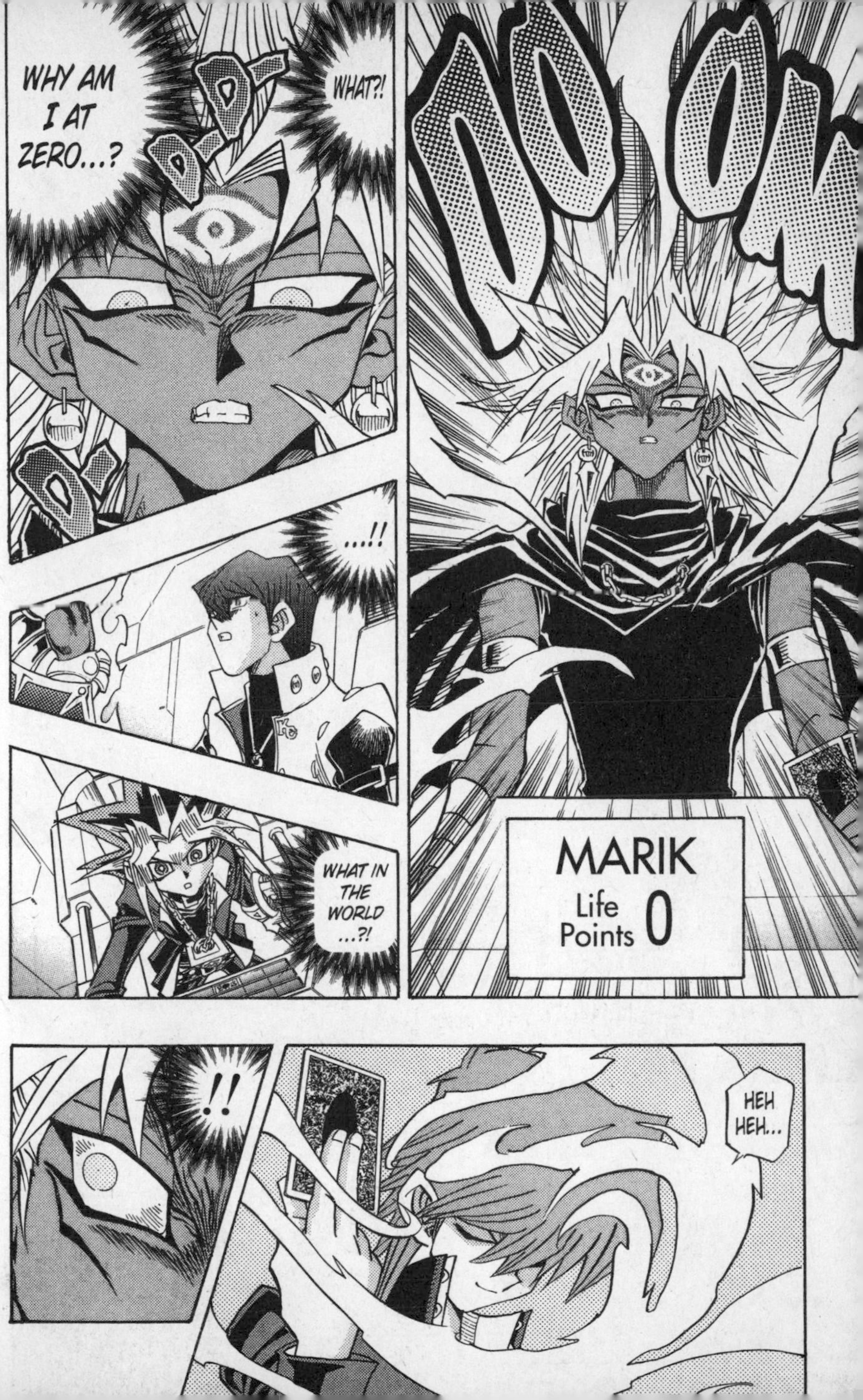
MARIK
Life Points 0
WHAT?!
WHY AM I AT ZERO...?
...!!
WHAT IN THE WORLD ...?!
HEH HEH...
!!

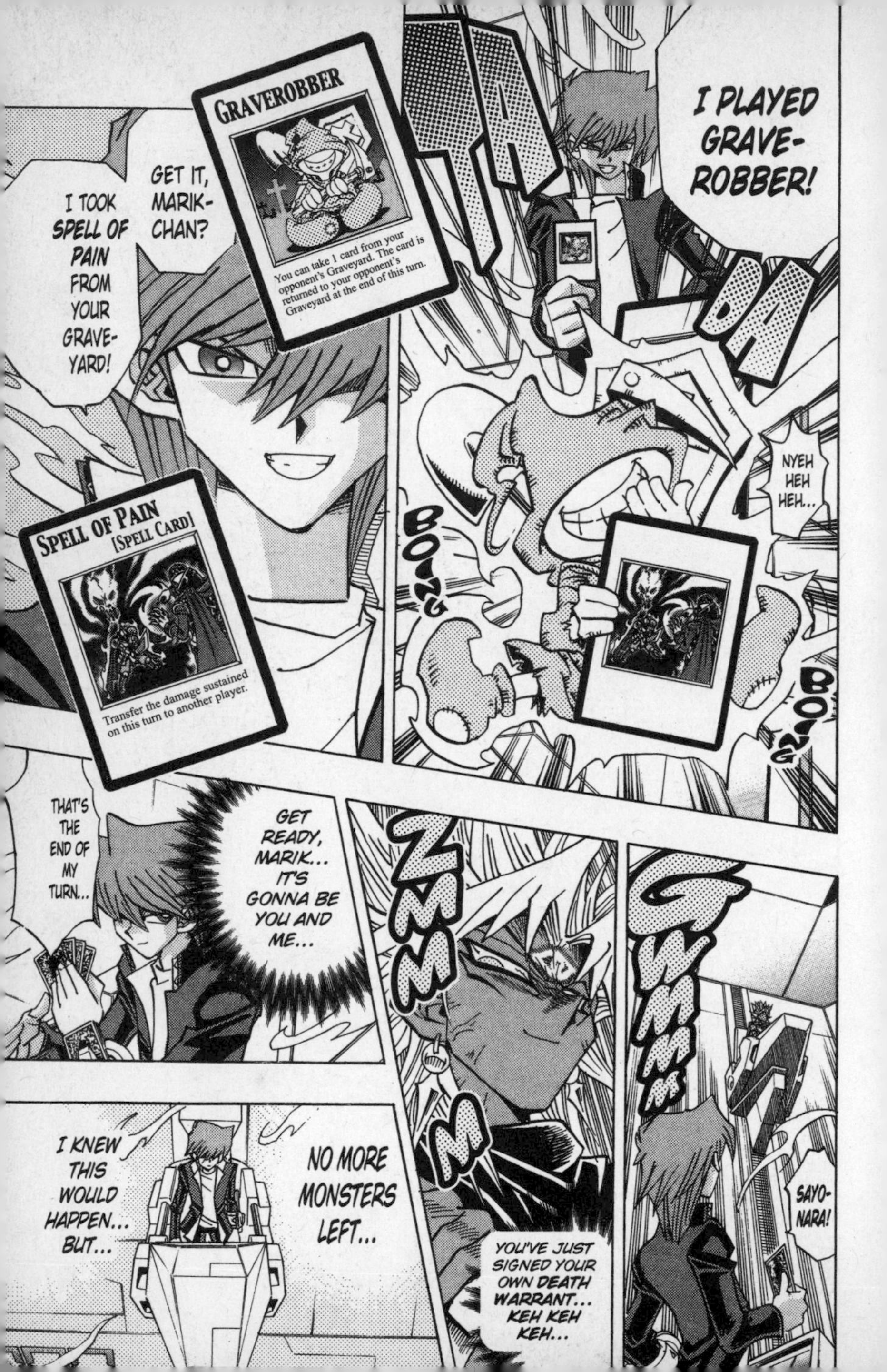
I PLAYED GRAVE-ROBBER!
DA
GRAVEROBBER
You can take 1 card from your opponent's Graveyard. The card is returned to your opponent's Graveyard at the end of this turn.
GET IT, MARIK-CHAN?
I TOOK SPELL OF PAIN FROM YOUR GRAVEYARD!
SPELL OF PAIN [SPELL CARD]
Transfer the damage sustained on this turn to another player.
NYEH HEH HEH...
BOING
BOING
SAYONARA!
YOU'VE JUST SIGNED YOUR OWN DEATH WARRANT... KEH KEH KEH...
THAT'S THE END OF MY TURN...
GET READY, MARIK... IT'S GONNA BE YOU AND ME...
NO MORE MONSTERS LEFT...
I KNEW THIS WOULD HAPPEN... BUT...

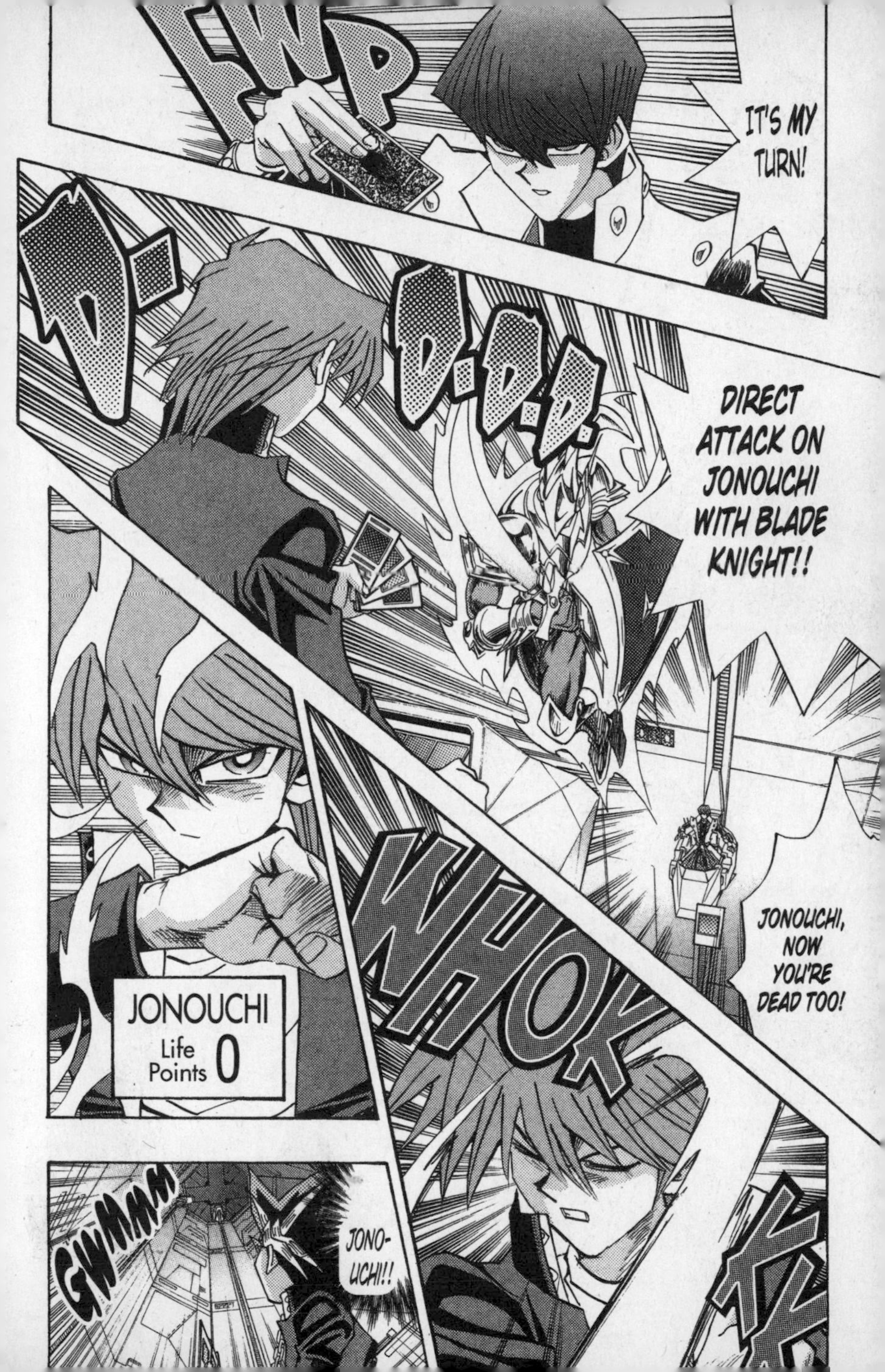
FWP
IT'S MY TURN!
DIRECT ATTACK ON JONOUCHI WITH BLADE KNIGHT!!
WHOK
JONOUCHI, NOW YOU'RE DEAD TOO!
JONOUCHI
Life Points 0
JONO-UCHI!!

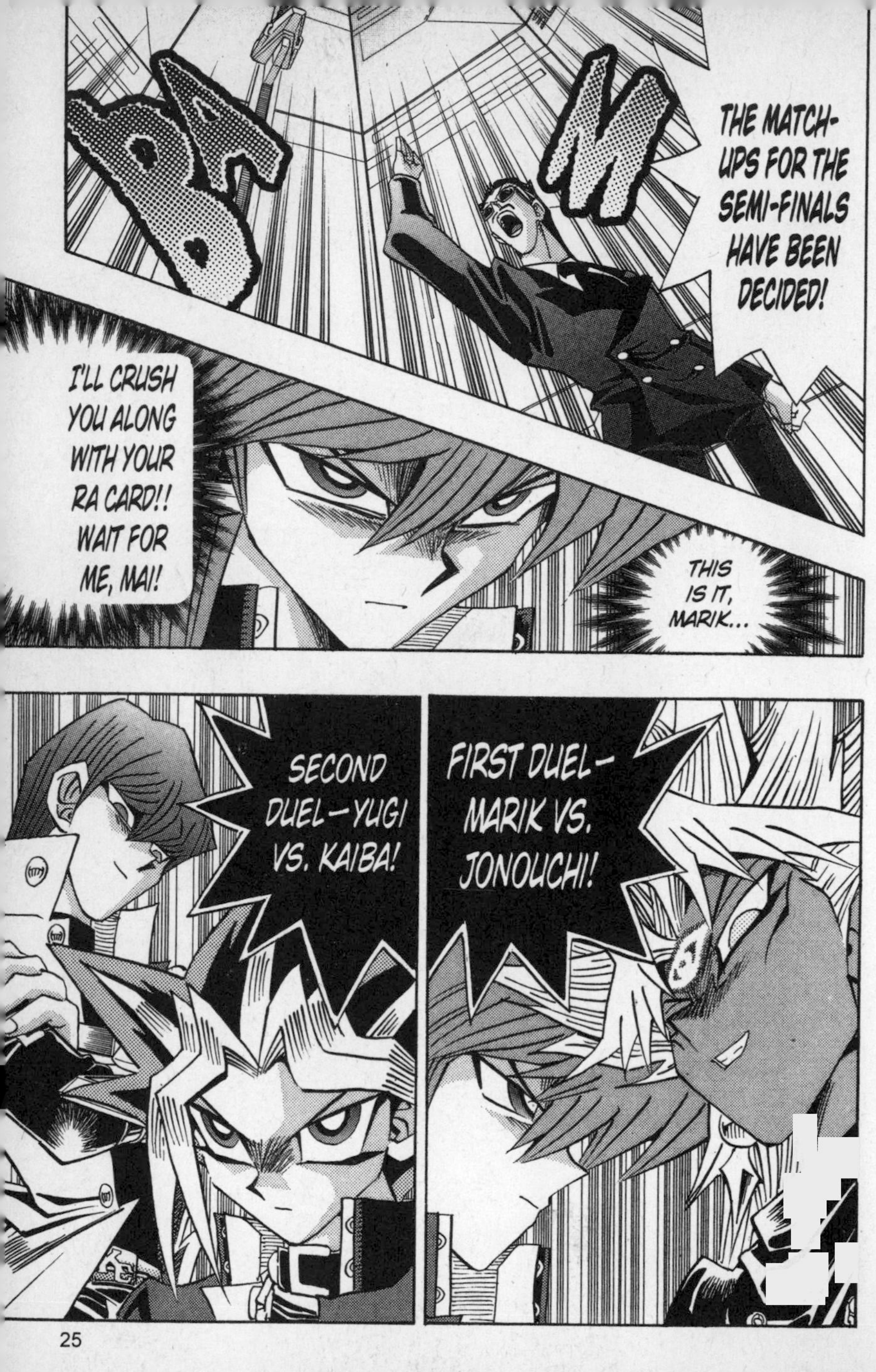
THE MATCH-UPS FOR THE SEMI-FINALS HAVE BEEN DECIDED!
THIS IS IT, MARIK...
I'LL CRUSH YOU ALONG WITH YOUR RA CARD!! WAIT FOR ME, MAI!
FIRST DUEL—MARIK VS. JONOUCHI!
SECOND DUEL—YUGI VS. KAIBA!

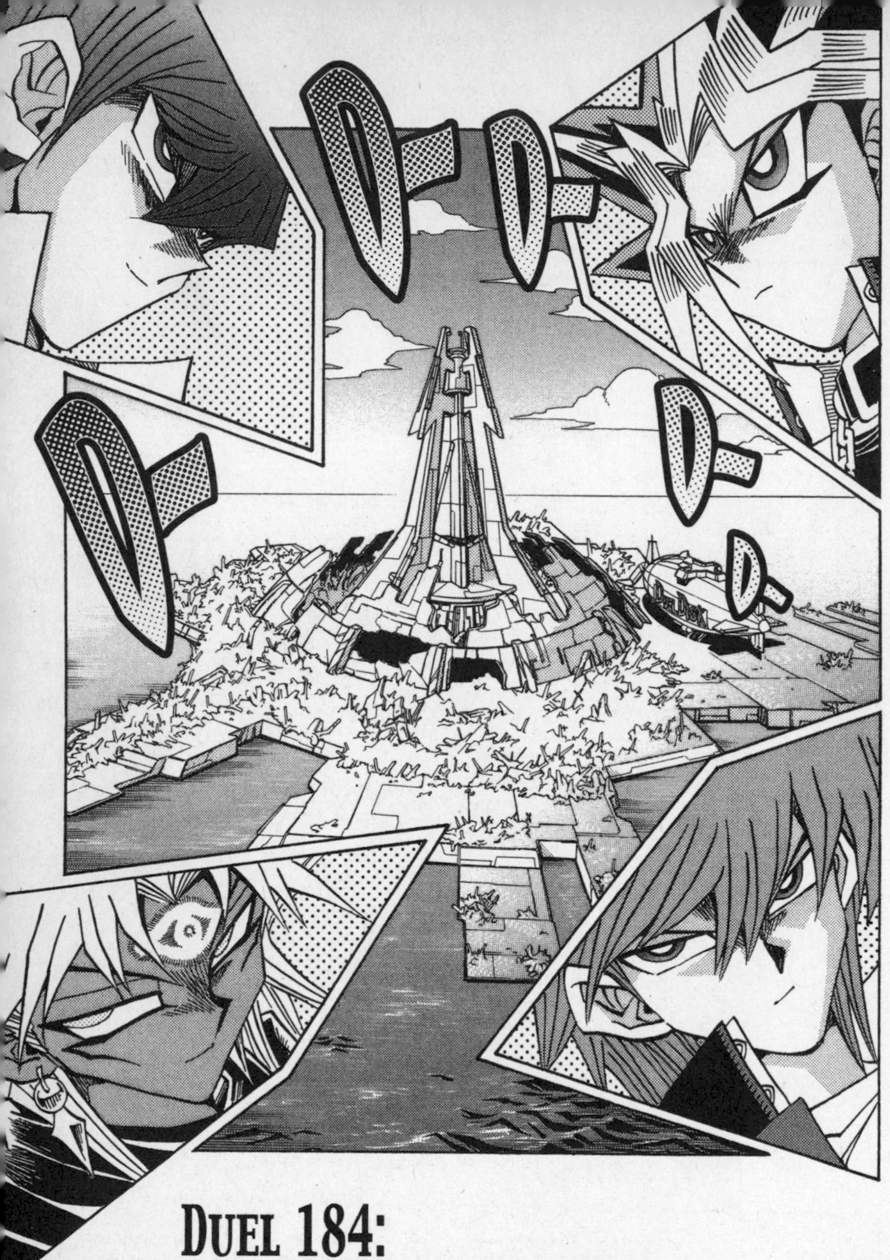
D-D-
D-
D-D-

DUEL 184:
THE FINAL STAGE!

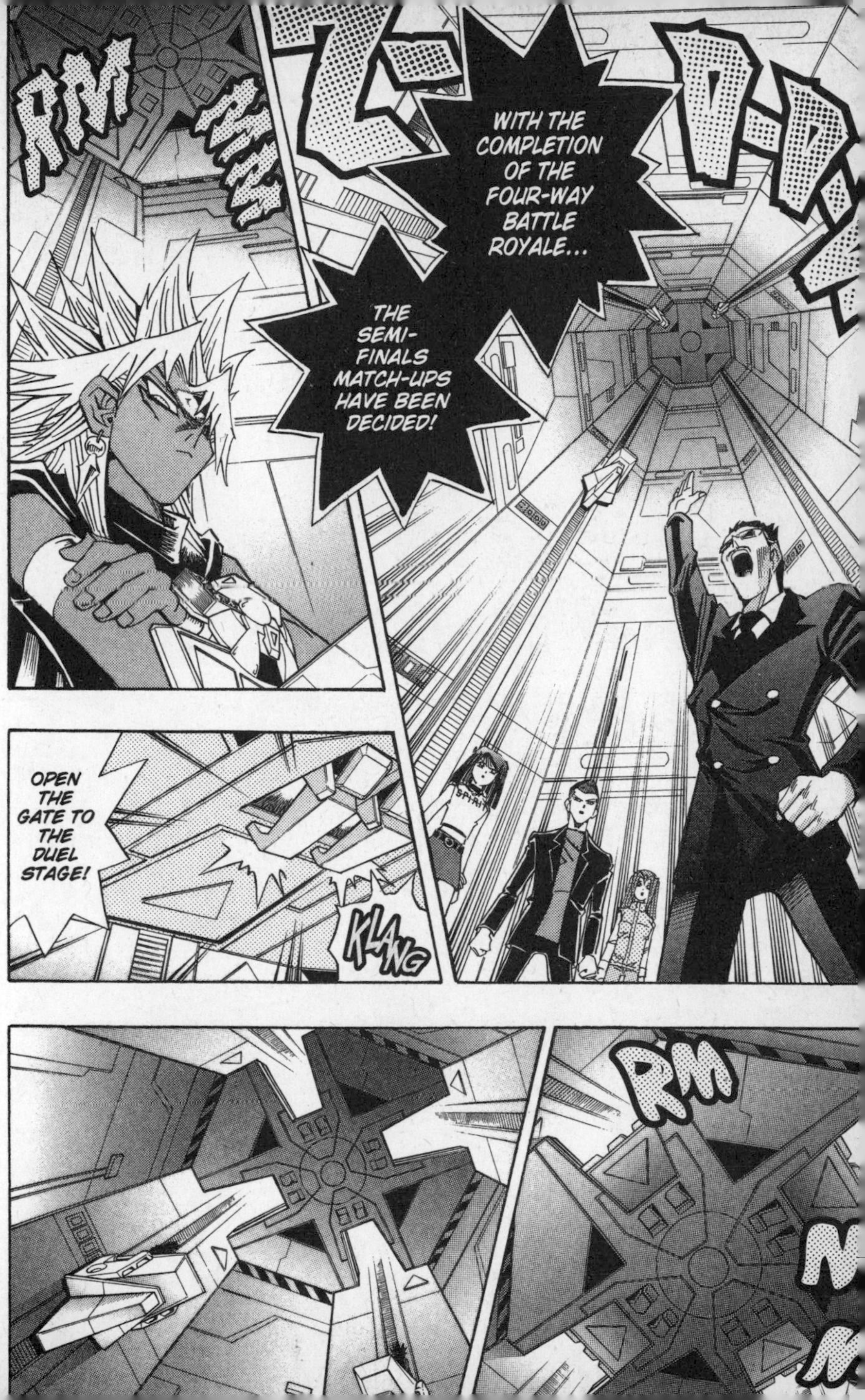
WITH THE COMPLETION OF THE FOUR-WAY BATTLE ROYALE...
THE SEMI-FINALS MATCH-UPS HAVE BEEN DECIDED!
RM
OPEN THE GATE TO THE DUEL STAGE!
KLANG
RM

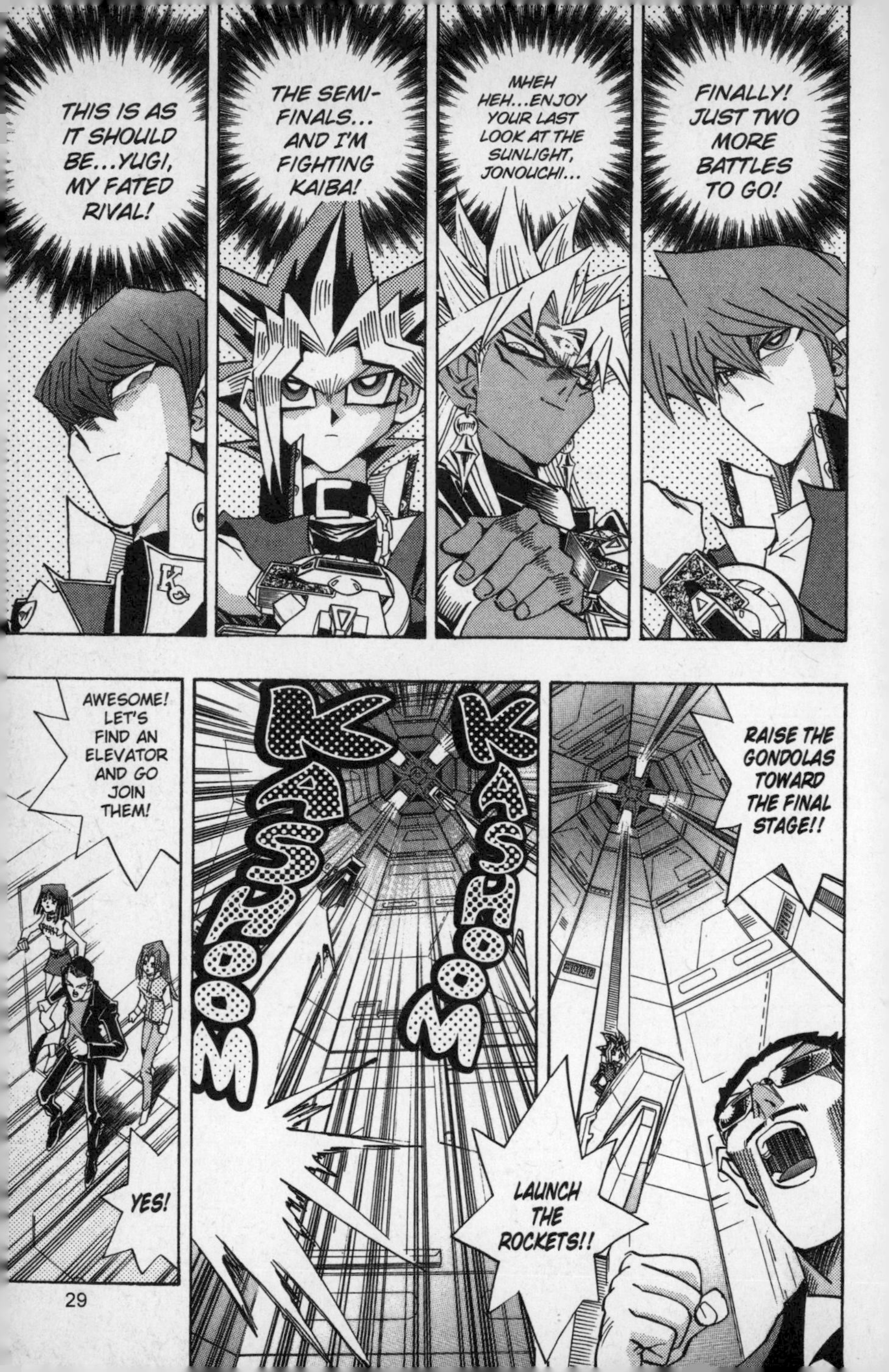
FINALLY! JUST TWO MORE BATTLES TO GO!
MHEH HEH...ENJOY YOUR LAST LOOK AT THE SUNLIGHT, JONOUCHI...
THE SEMI-FINALS... AND I'M FIGHTING KAIBA!
THIS IS AS IT SHOULD BE...YUGI, MY FATED RIVAL!
RAISE THE GONDOLAS TOWARD THE FINAL STAGE!!
LAUNCH THE ROCKETS!!
KASHOOM
KASHOOM
AWESOME! LET'S FIND AN ELEVATOR AND GO JOIN THEM!
YES!

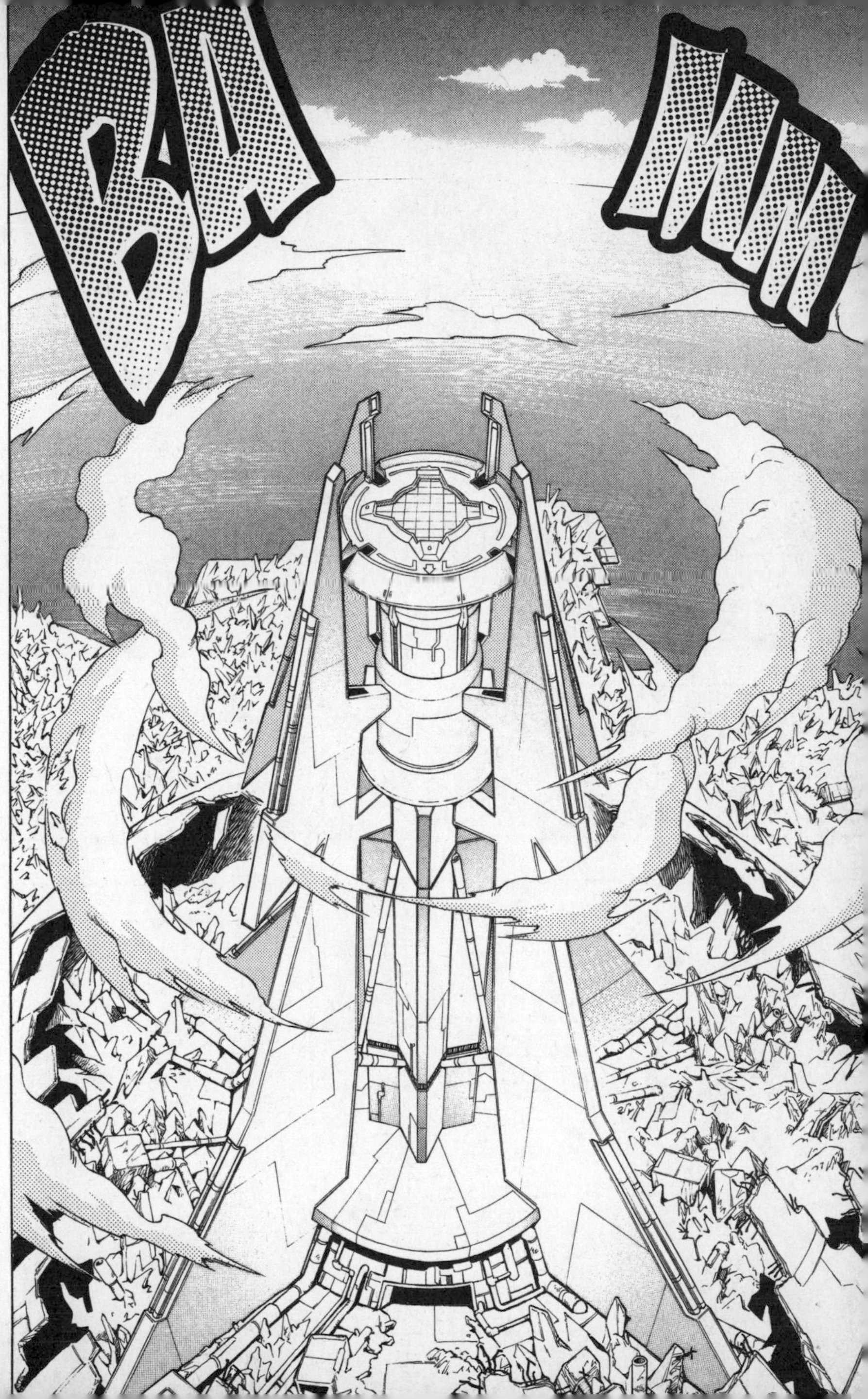
BAMM

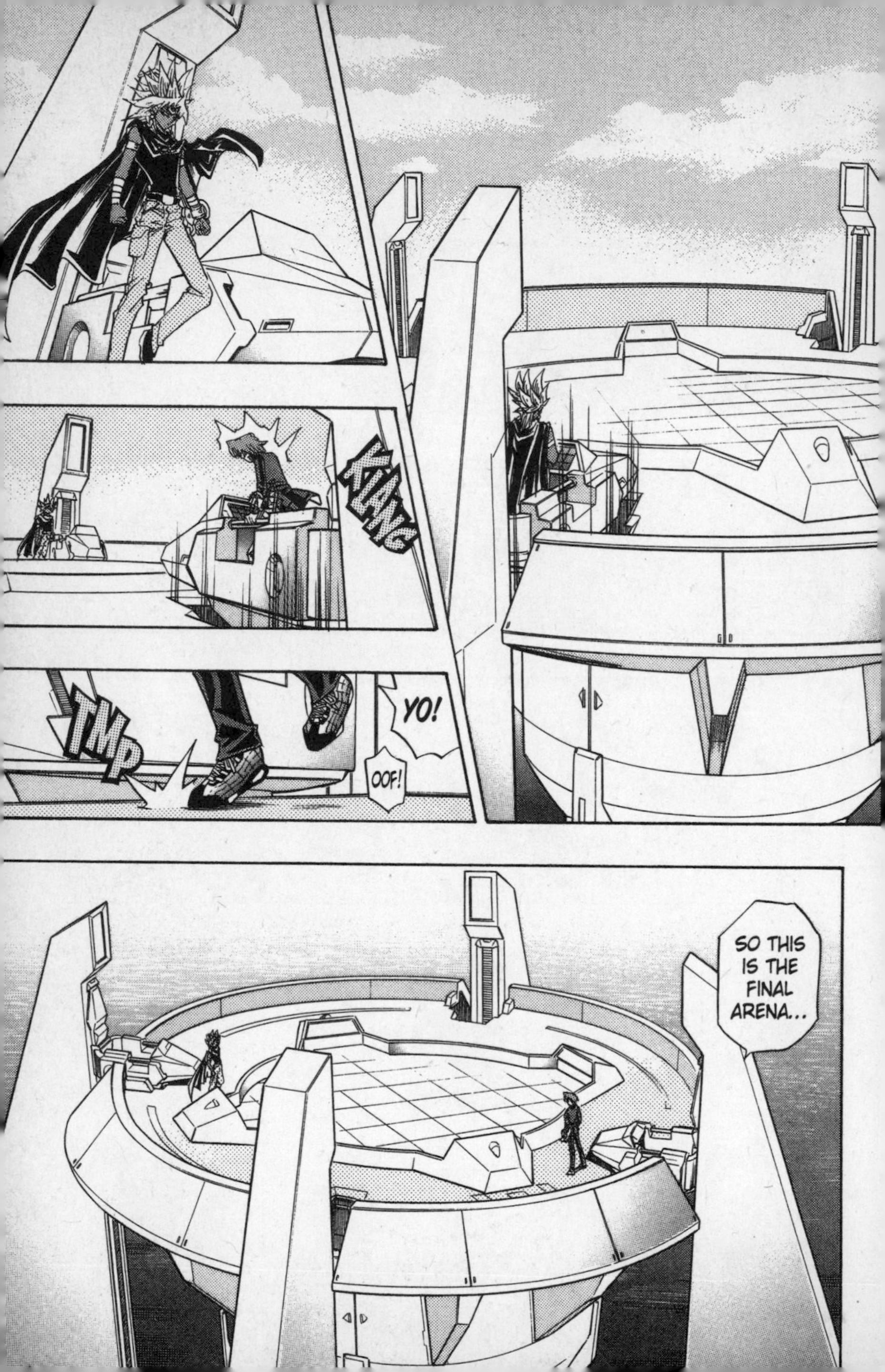
KLANG
YO!
OOF!
TMP
SO THIS IS THE FINAL ARENA...

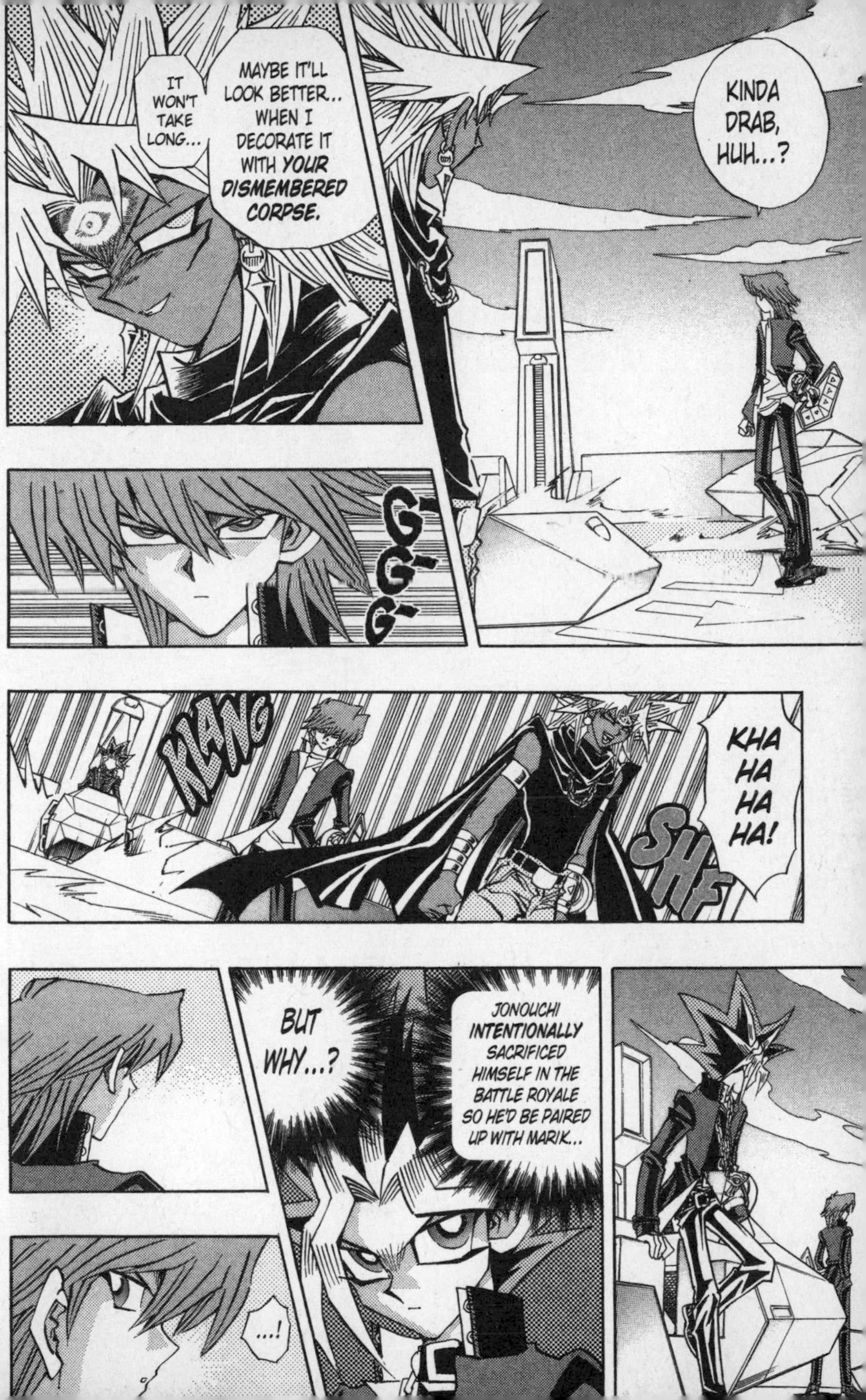
KINDA DRAB, HUH...?
MAYBE IT'LL LOOK BETTER... WHEN I DECORATE IT WITH YOUR DISMEMBERED CORPSE.
IT WON'T TAKE LONG...
G-G-G-
KHA HA HA HA!
SHF
KLANG
JONOUCHI INTENTIONALLY SACRIFICED HIMSELF IN THE BATTLE ROYALE SO HE'D BE PAIRED UP WITH MARIK...
BUT WHY...?
...!

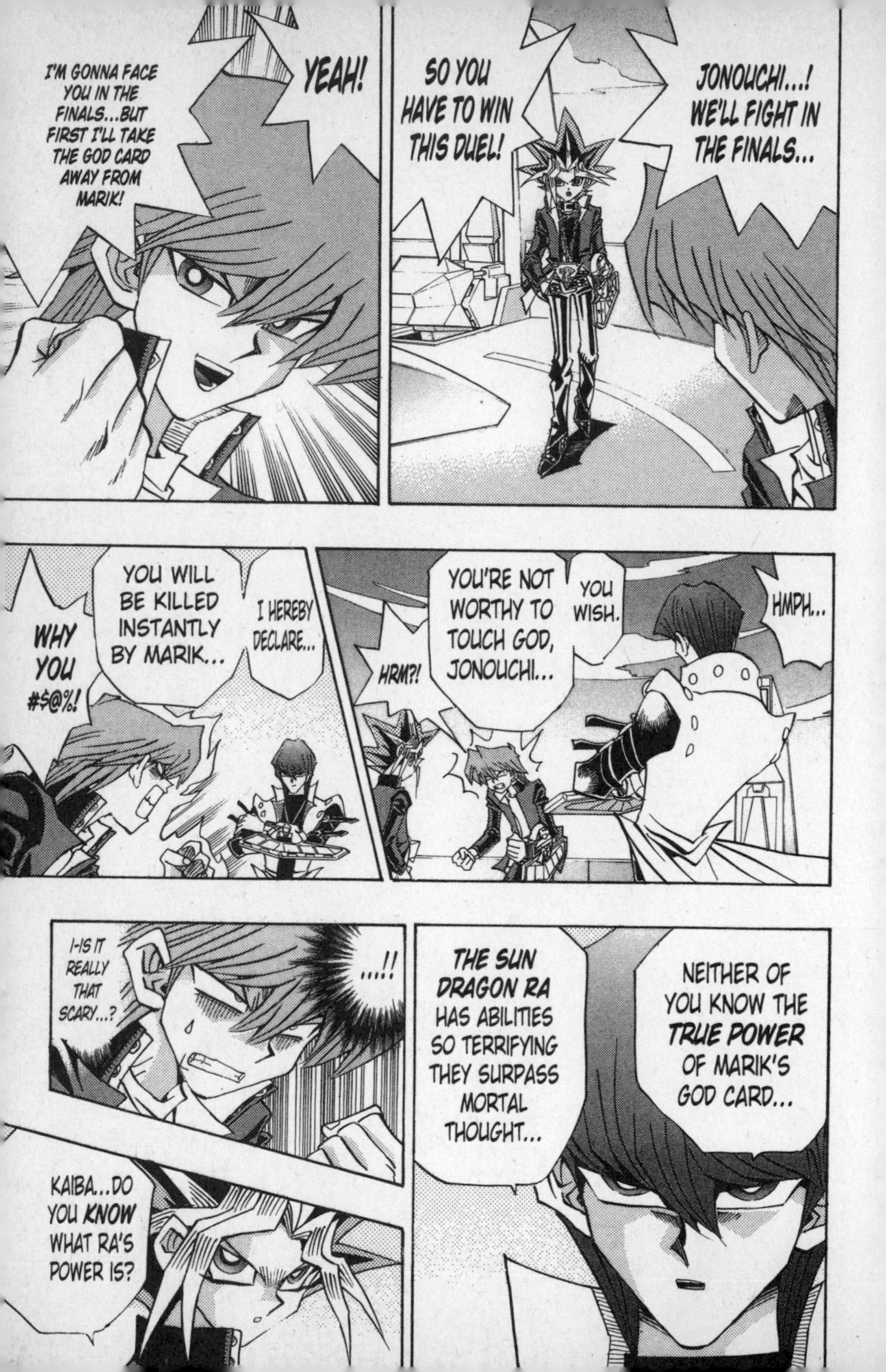
JONOUCHI...! WE'LL FIGHT IN THE FINALS...
SO YOU HAVE TO WIN THIS DUEL!
YEAH!
I'M GONNA FACE YOU IN THE FINALS...BUT FIRST I'LL TAKE THE GOD CARD AWAY FROM MARIK!
HMPH...
YOU WISH.
YOU'RE NOT WORTHY TO TOUCH GOD, JONOUCHI...
HRM?!
I HEREBY DECLARE...
YOU WILL BE KILLED INSTANTLY BY MARIK...
WHY YOU #$@%!
NEITHER OF YOU KNOW THE TRUE POWER OF MARIK'S GOD CARD...
THE SUN DRAGON RA HAS ABILITIES SO TERRIFYING THEY SURPASS MORTAL THOUGHT...
...!!
I-IS IT REALLY THAT SCARY...?
KAIBA...DO YOU KNOW WHAT RA'S POWER IS?

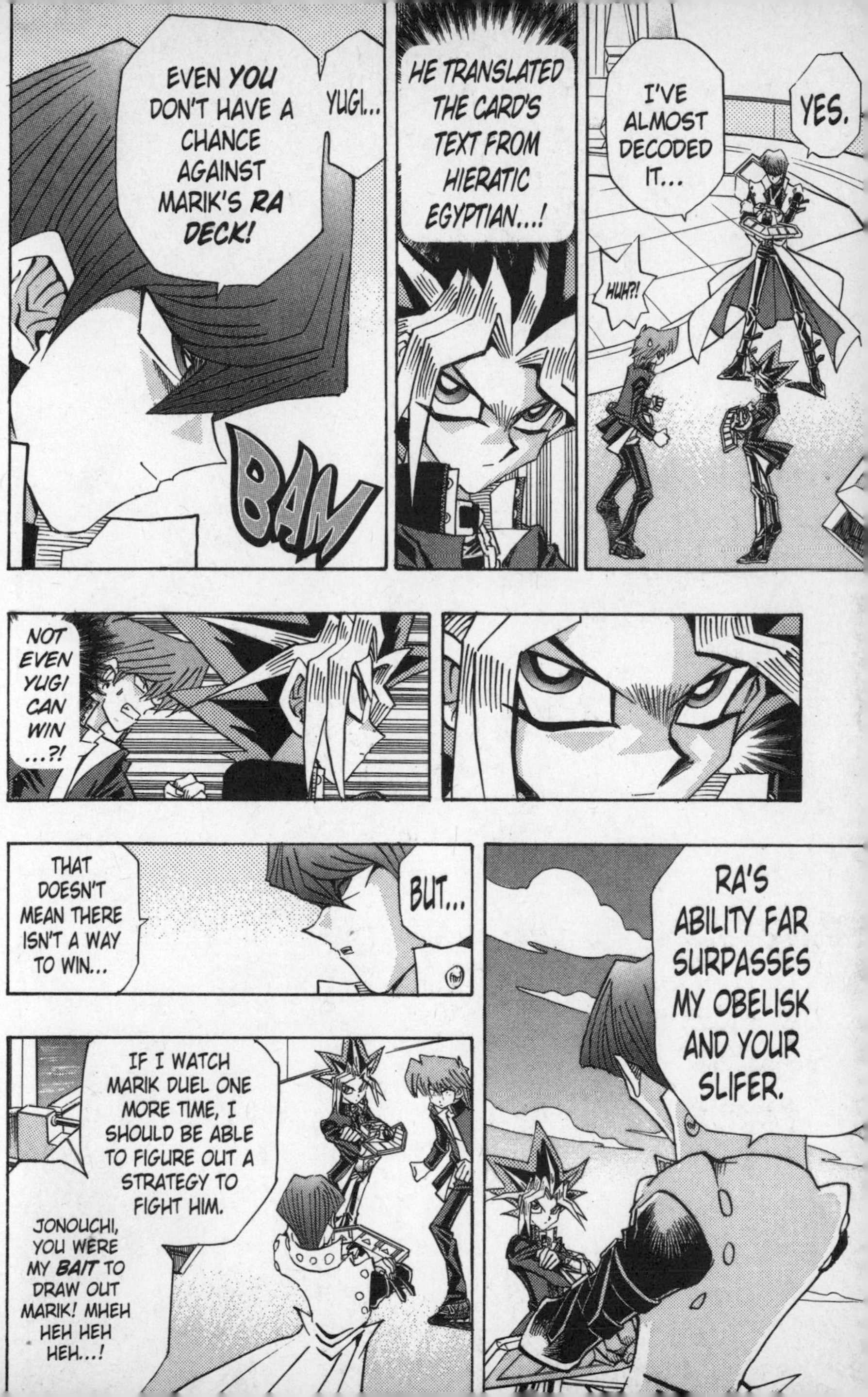
YES.
I'VE ALMOST DECODED IT...
HUH?!
HE TRANSLATED THE CARD'S TEXT FROM HIERATIC EGYPTIAN...!
YUGI...
EVEN YOU DON'T HAVE A CHANCE AGAINST MARIK'S RA DECK!
BAM
NOT EVEN YUGI CAN WIN ...?!
RA'S ABILITY FAR SURPASSES MY OBELISK AND YOUR SLIFER.
BUT...
THAT DOESN'T MEAN THERE ISN'T A WAY TO WIN...
IF I WATCH MARIK DUEL ONE MORE TIME, I SHOULD BE ABLE TO FIGURE OUT A STRATEGY TO FIGHT HIM.
JONOUCHI, YOU WERE MY BAIT TO DRAW OUT MARIK! MHEH HEH HEH HEH...!

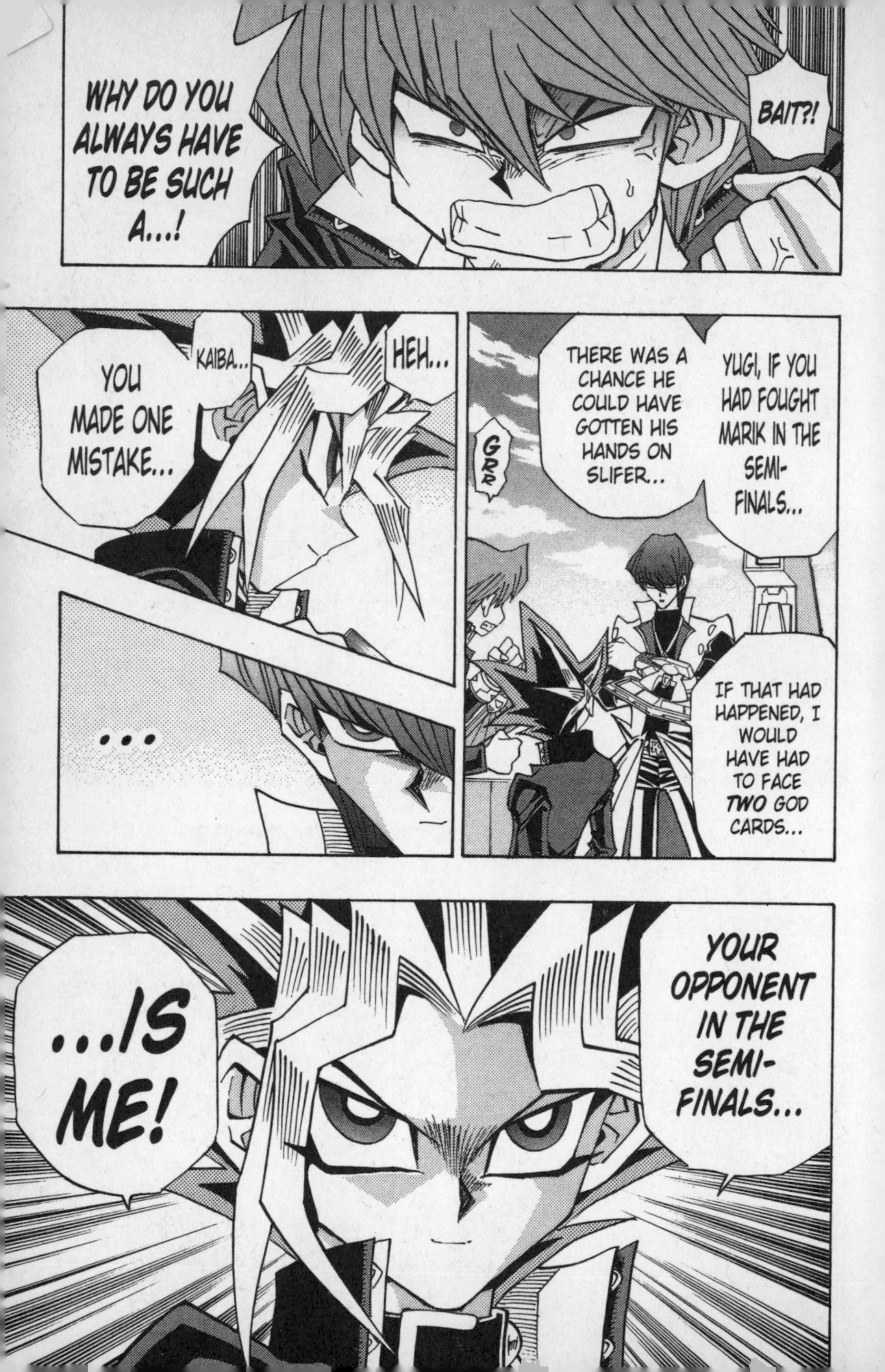
BAIT?!
WHY DO YOU ALWAYS HAVE TO BE SUCH A...!
YUGI, IF YOU HAD FOUGHT MARIK IN THE SEMI-FINALS...
THERE WAS A CHANCE HE COULD HAVE GOTTEN HIS HANDS ON SLIFER...
GRR
IF THAT HAD HAPPENED, I WOULD HAVE HAD TO FACE TWO GOD CARDS...
HEH...
KAIBA...
YOU MADE ONE MISTAKE...
...
YOUR OPPONENT IN THE SEMI-FINALS...
...IS ME!

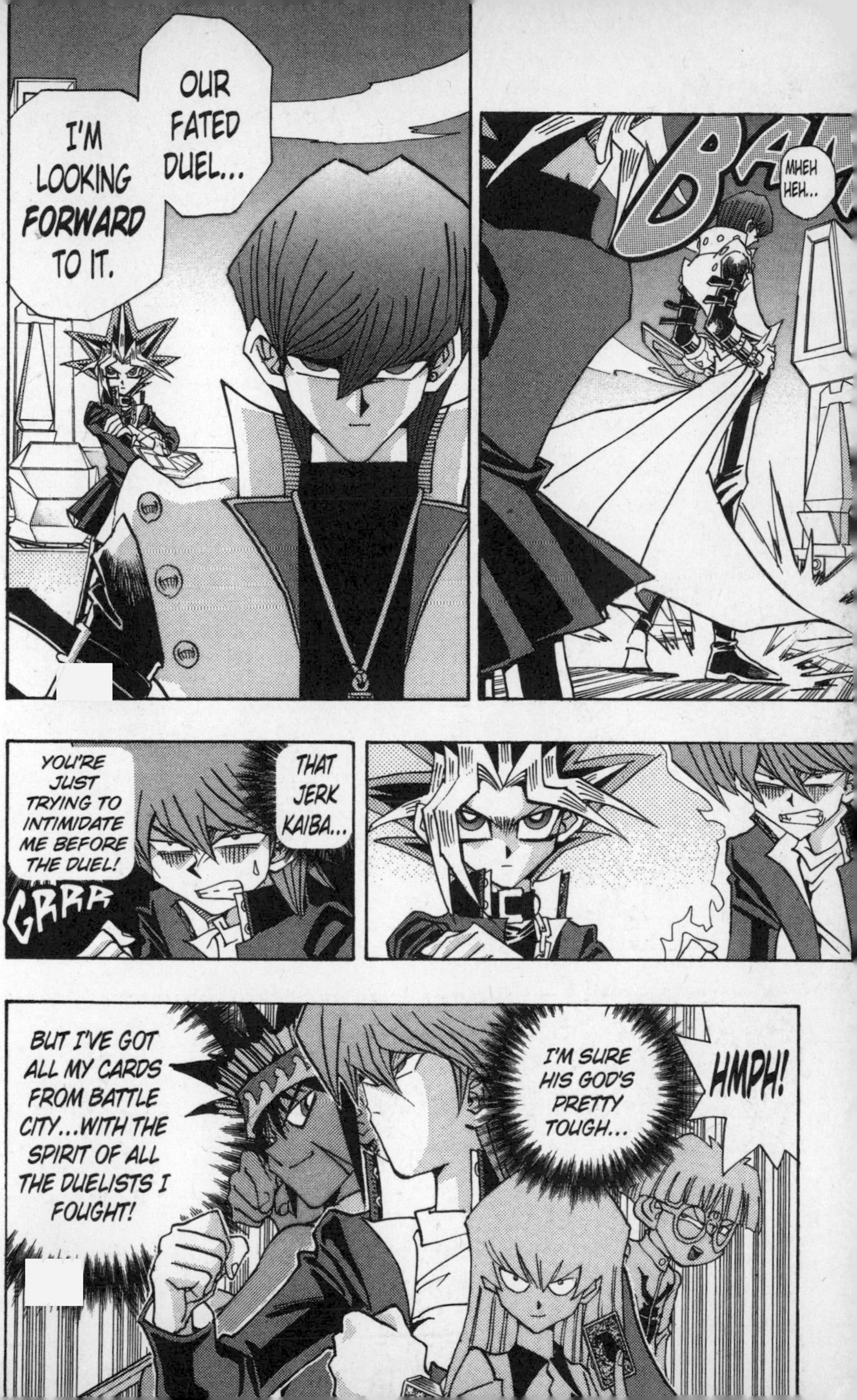
MHEH HEH...
OUR FATED DUEL...
I'M LOOKING FORWARD TO IT.
THAT JERK KAIBA...
YOU'RE JUST TRYING TO INTIMIDATE ME BEFORE THE DUEL!
GRRR
HMPH!
I'M SURE HIS GOD'S PRETTY TOUGH...
BUT I'VE GOT ALL MY CARDS FROM BATTLE CITY...WITH THE SPIRIT OF ALL THE DUELISTS I FOUGHT!

READ THIS WAY

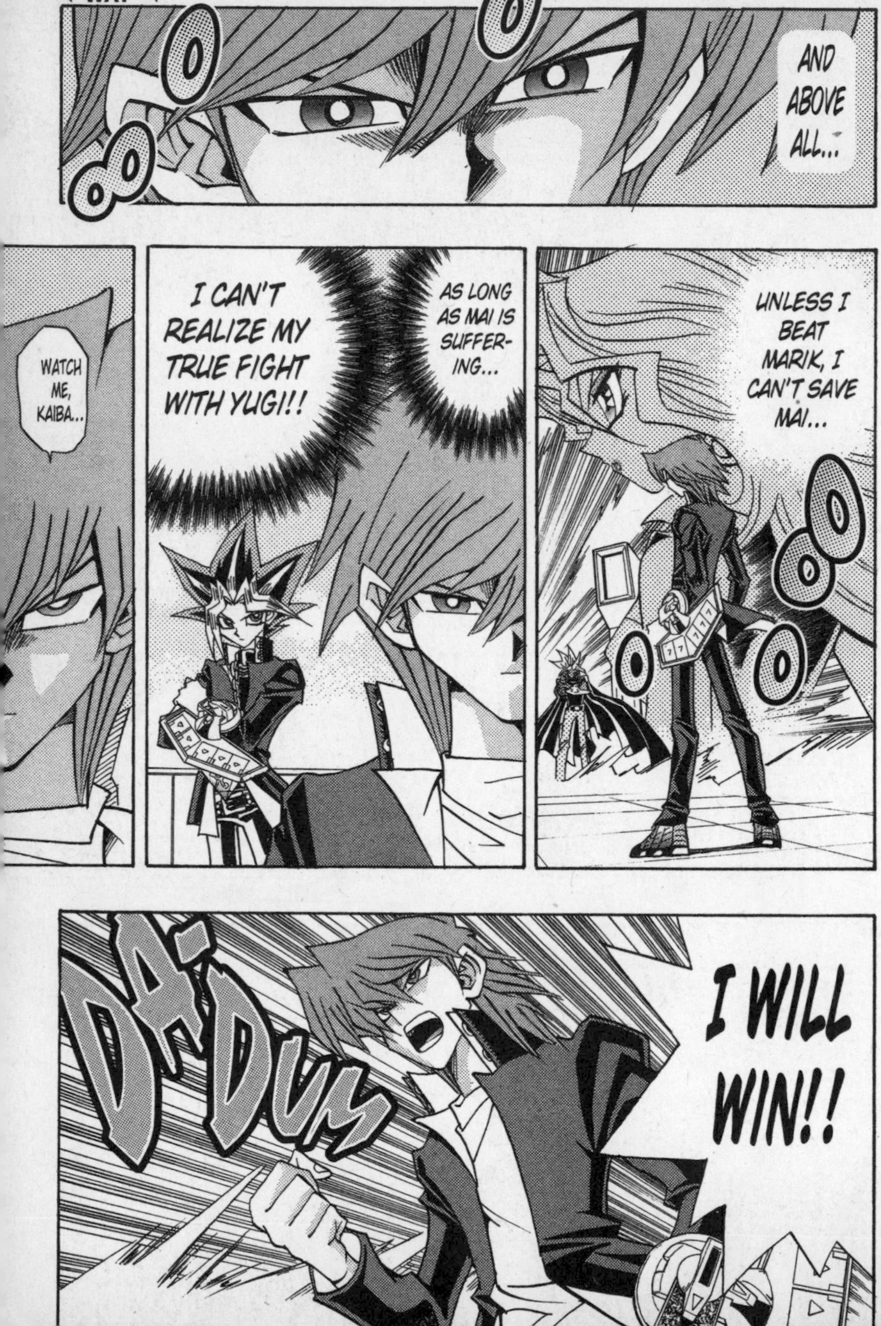

AND ABOVE ALL...
UNLESS I BEAT MARIK, I CAN'T SAVE MAI...
AS LONG AS MAI IS SUFFER-ING...
I CAN'T REALIZE MY TRUE FIGHT WITH YUGI!!
WATCH ME, KAIBA...
I WILL WIN!!
DA-DUM

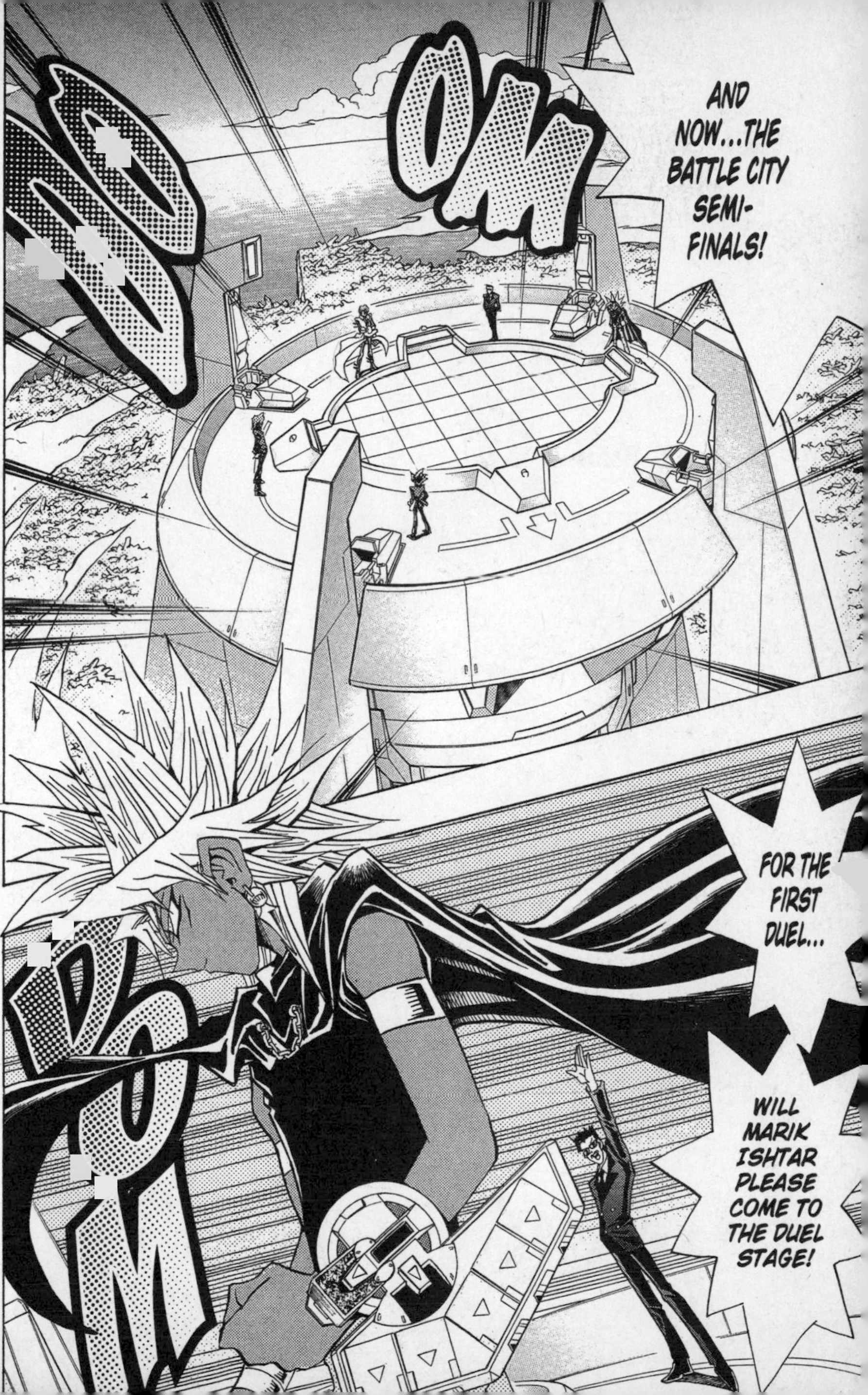
AND NOW...THE BATTLE CITY SEMI-FINALS!
FOR THE FIRST DUEL...
WILL MARIK ISHTAR PLEASE COME TO THE DUEL STAGE!

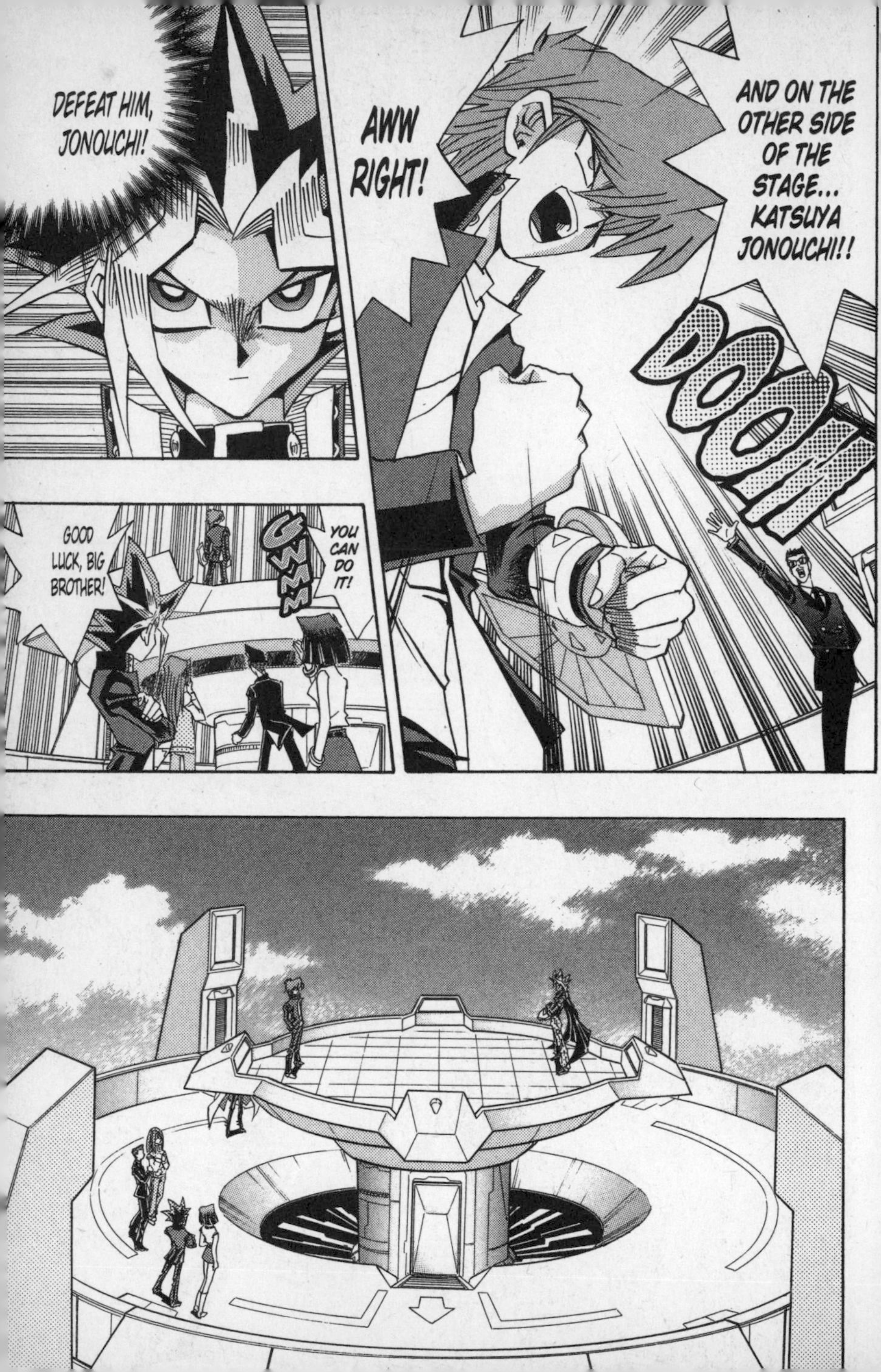
AND ON THE OTHER SIDE OF THE STAGE... KATSUYA JONOUCHI!!
AWW RIGHT!
DOOM
DEFEAT HIM, JONOUCHI!
YOU CAN DO IT!
GOOD LUCK, BIG BROTHER!

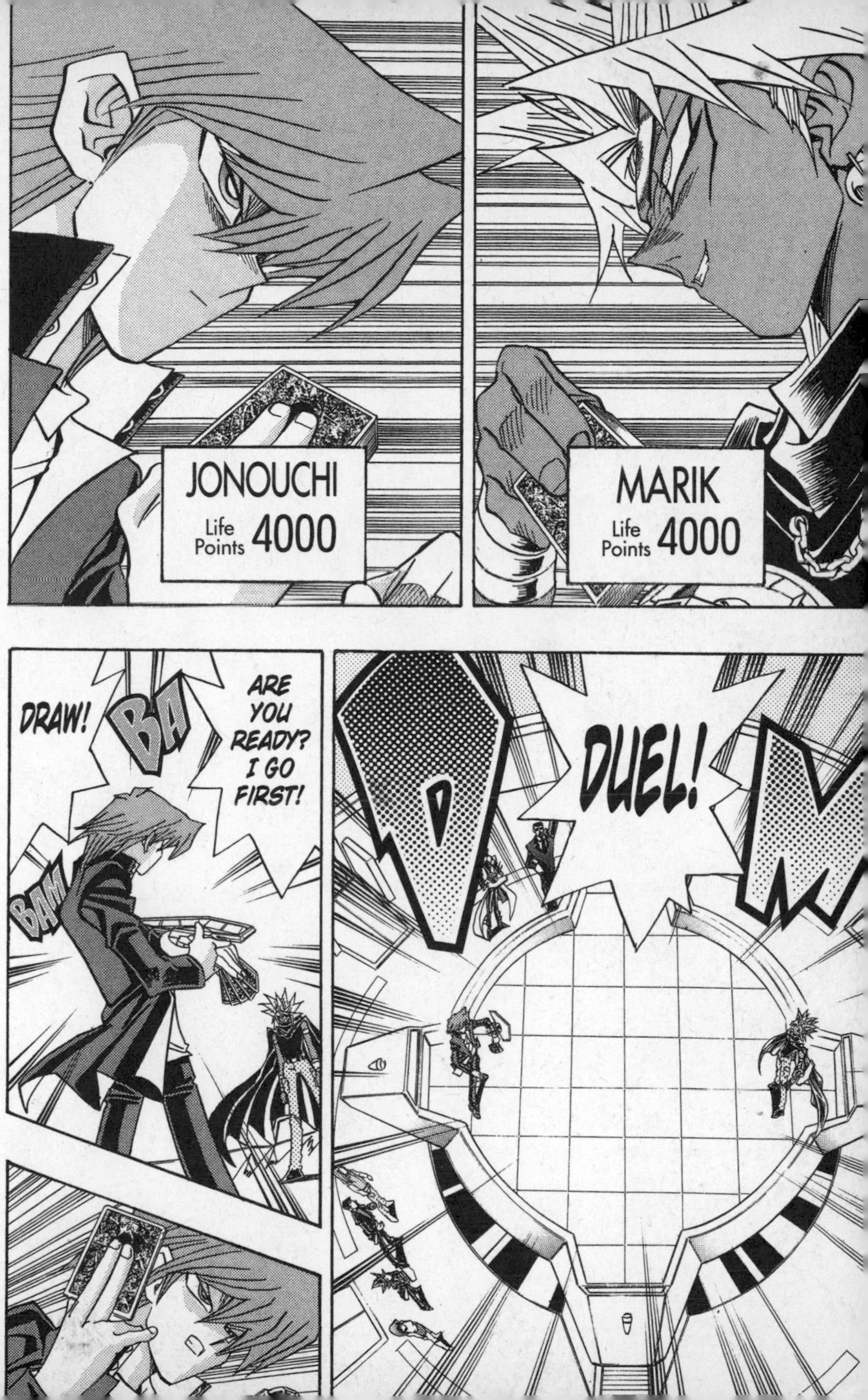
MARIK
Life Points 4000
JONOUCHI
Life Points 4000
DUEL!
ARE YOU READY? I GO FIRST!
BA
DRAW!
BAM

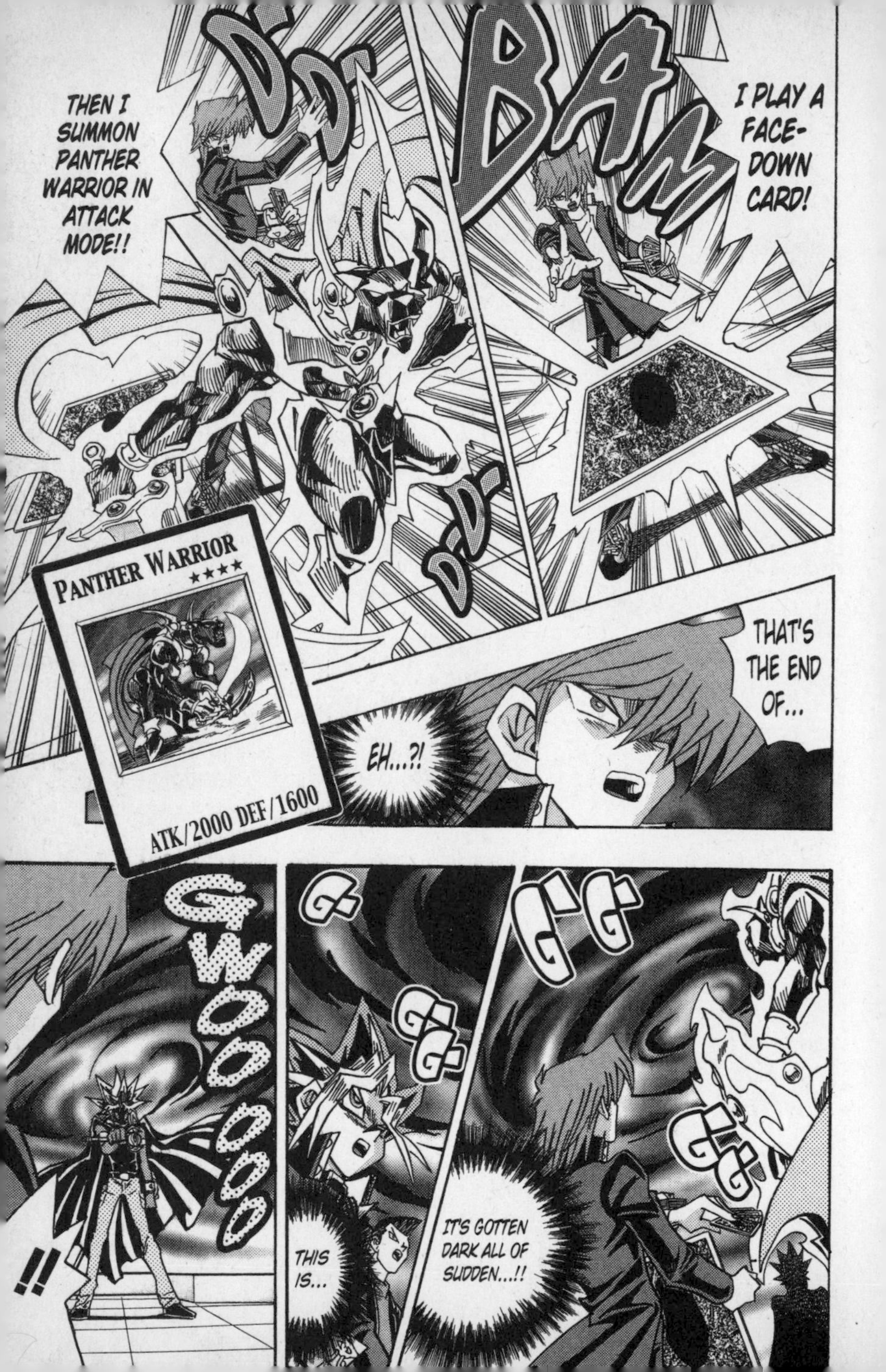
BAM
I PLAY A FACE-DOWN CARD!
THEN I SUMMON PANTHER WARRIOR IN ATTACK MODE!!
PANTHER WARRIOR
★★★★
ATK/2000 DEF/1600
THAT'S THE END OF...
EH...?!
IT'S GOTTEN DARK ALL OF SUDDEN...!!
THIS IS...
GWOOOOOO!!

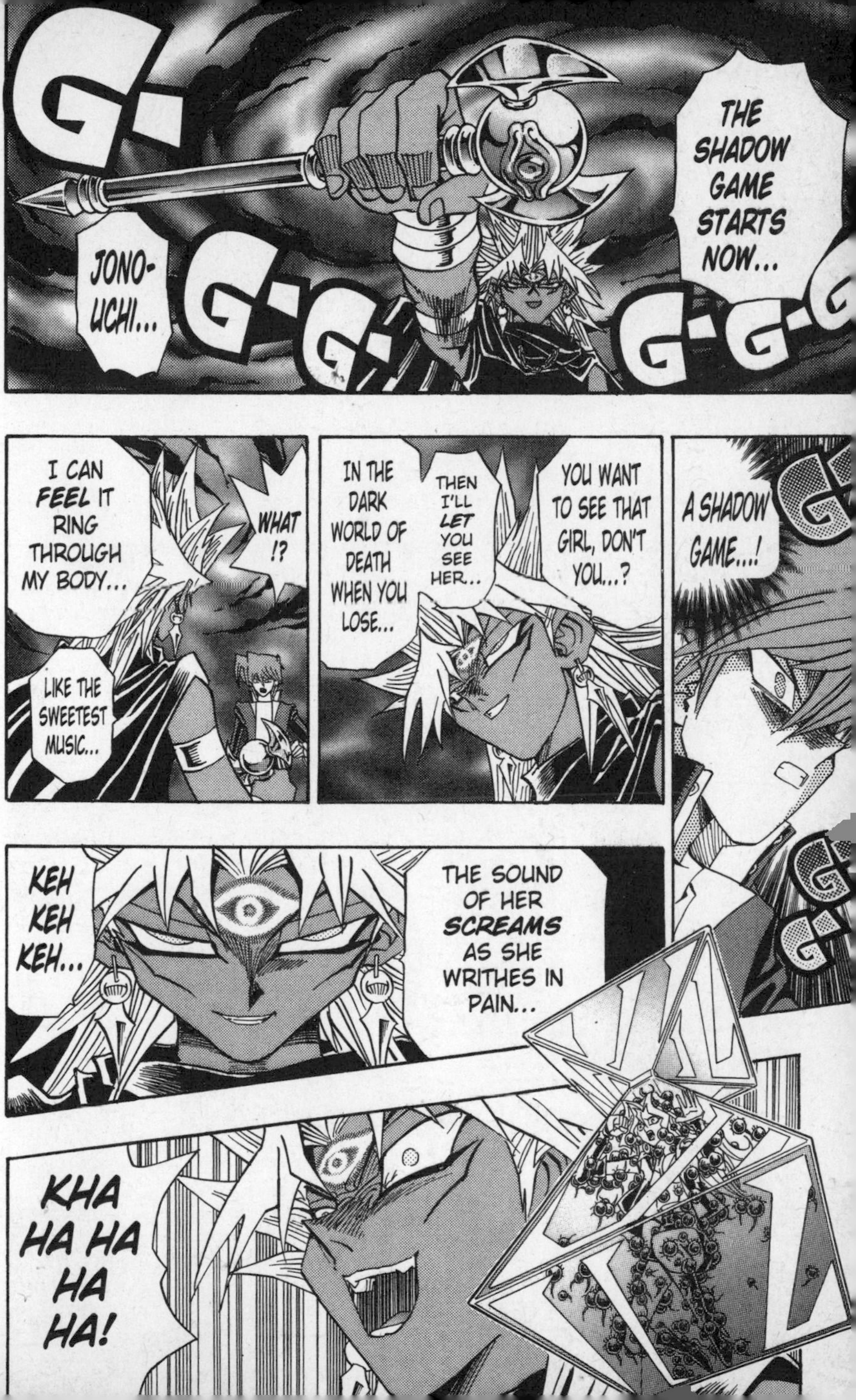
THE SHADOW GAME STARTS NOW...
G-G-G
G-G-G
JONO-UCHI...
G-
A SHADOW GAME...!
G
G
G
YOU WANT TO SEE THAT GIRL, DON'T YOU...?
THEN I'LL *LET* YOU SEE HER...
IN THE DARK WORLD OF DEATH WHEN YOU LOSE...
WHAT!?
I CAN *FEEL* IT RING THROUGH MY BODY...
LIKE THE SWEETEST MUSIC...
THE SOUND OF HER *SCREAMS* AS SHE WRITHES IN PAIN...
KEH KEH KEH...
KHA HA HA HA HA!

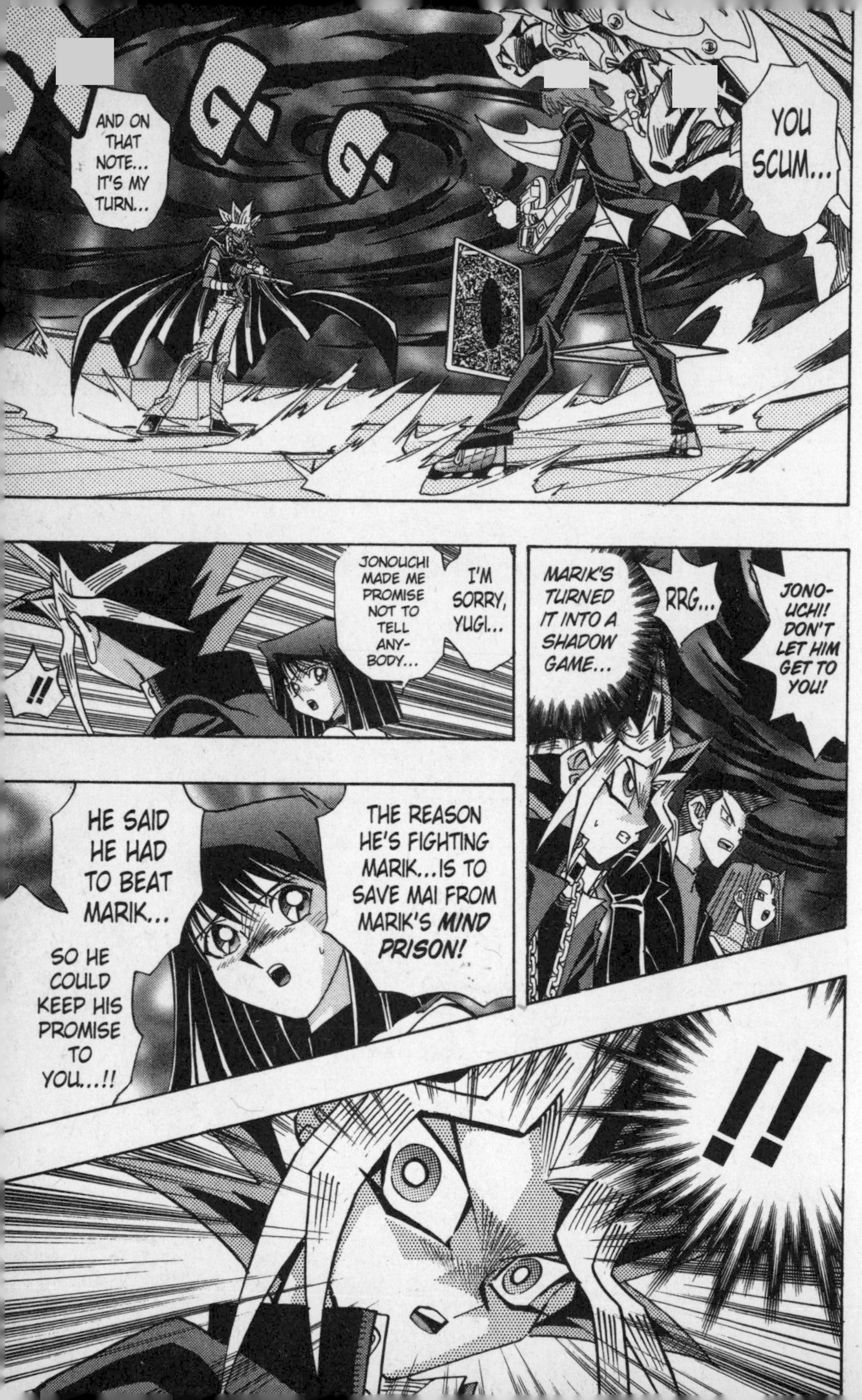
YOU SCUM...
AND ON THAT NOTE... IT'S MY TURN...
JONO-UCHI! DON'T LET HIM GET TO YOU!
RRG...
MARIK'S TURNED IT INTO A SHADOW GAME...
I'M SORRY, YUGI...
JONOUCHI MADE ME PROMISE NOT TO TELL ANY-BODY...
!!
THE REASON HE'S FIGHTING MARIK...IS TO SAVE MAI FROM MARIK'S *MIND PRISON!*
HE SAID HE HAD TO BEAT MARIK...
SO HE COULD KEEP HIS PROMISE TO YOU...!!
!!

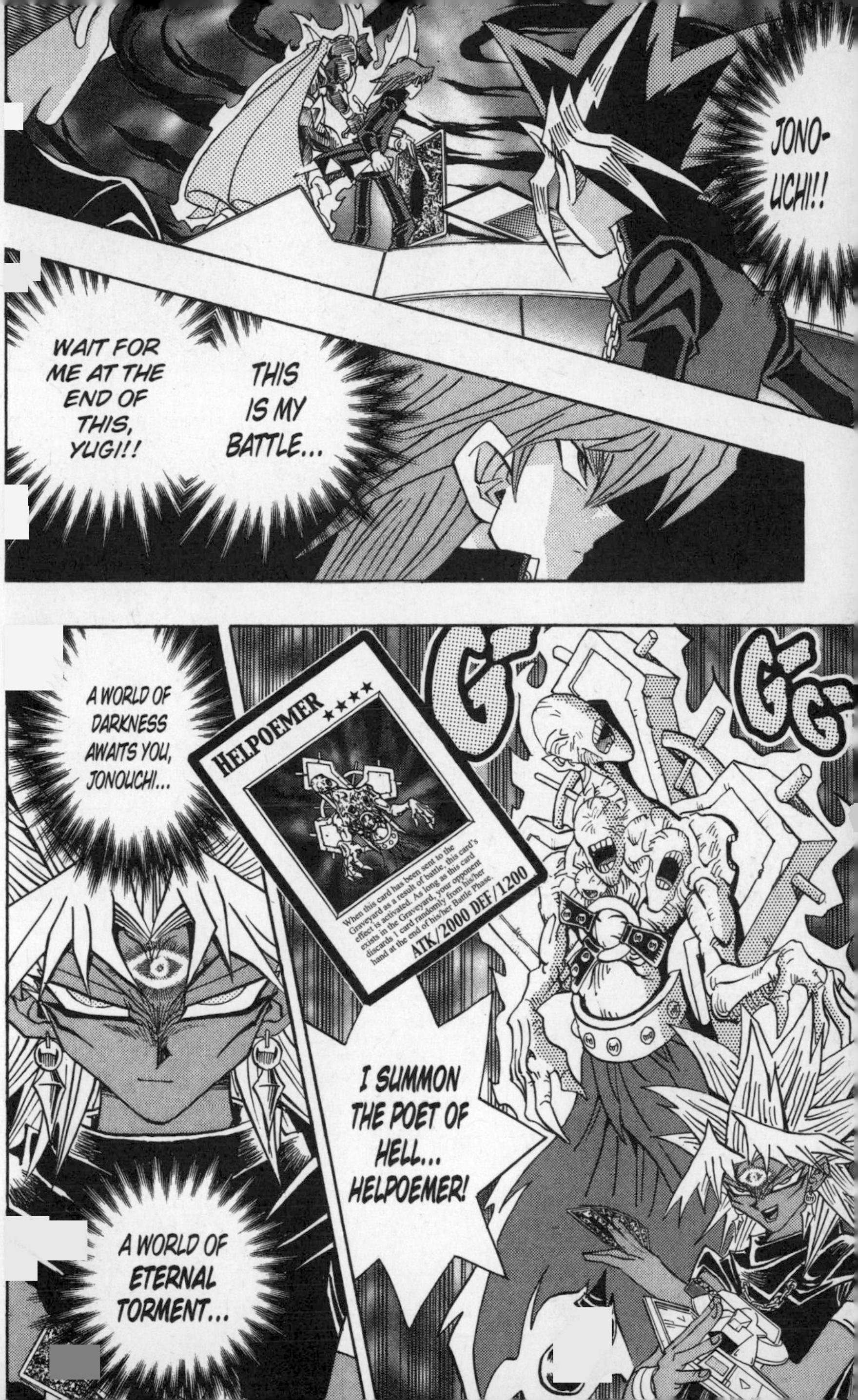
JONO-UCHI!!
THIS IS MY BATTLE...
WAIT FOR ME AT THE END OF THIS, YUGI!!
GG
HELPOEMER
When this card has been sent to the Graveyard as a result of battle, this card's effect is activated. As long as this card exists in the Graveyard, your opponent discards 1 card randomly from his/her hand at the end of his/her Battle Phase.
ATK/2000 DEF/1200
I SUMMON THE POET OF HELL... HELPOEMER!
A WORLD OF DARKNESS AWAITS YOU, JONOUCHI...
A WORLD OF ETERNAL TORMENT...

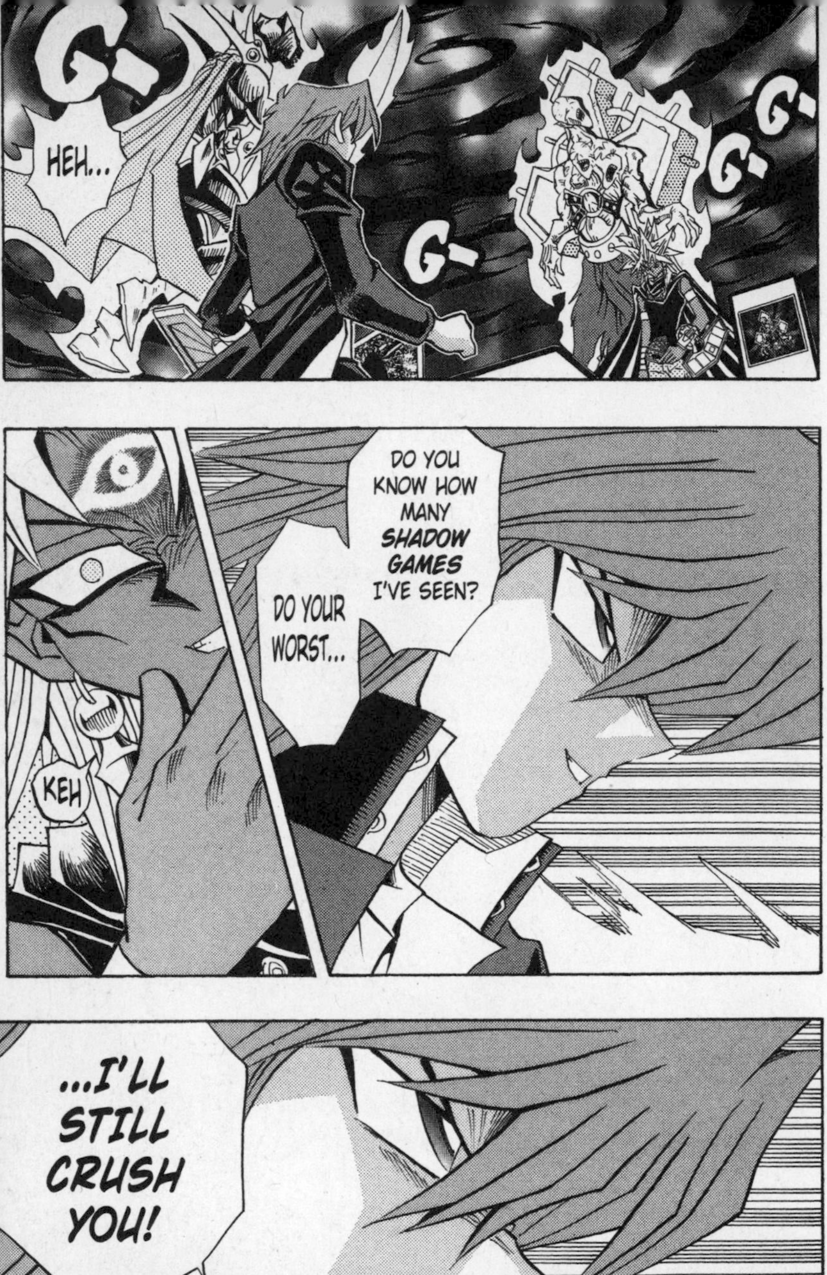
G-
G-
G-
G-
HEH...
DO YOU KNOW HOW MANY SHADOW GAMES I'VE SEEN?
DO YOUR WORST...
KEH
...I'LL STILL CRUSH YOU!

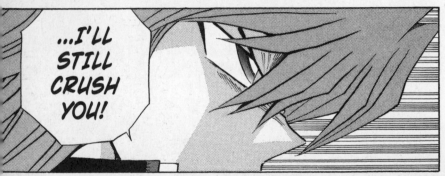

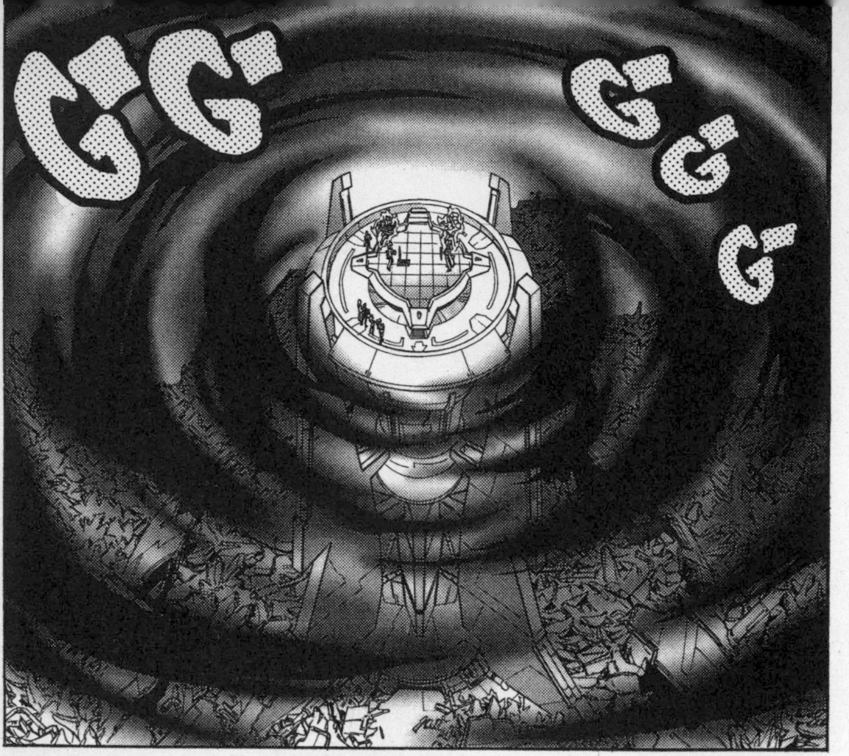

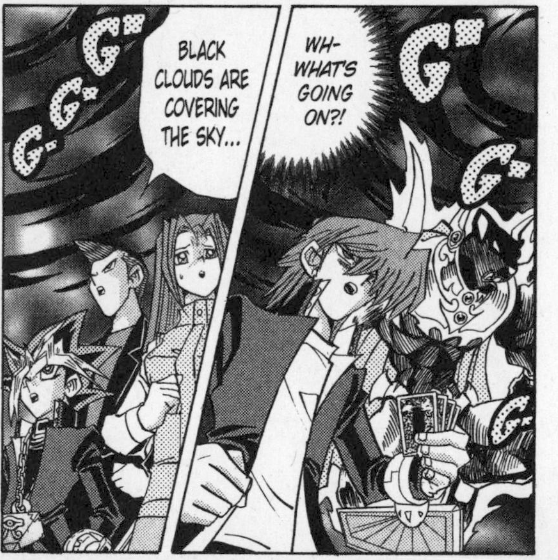
WH-WHAT'S GOING ON?!
BLACK CLOUDS ARE COVERING THE SKY...

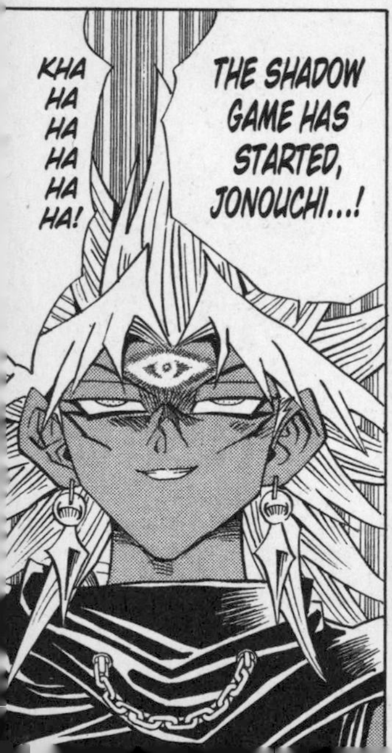
THE SHADOW GAME HAS STARTED, JONOUCHI...!
KHA HA HA HA HA HA!

Duel 185: The Hymn of Hell

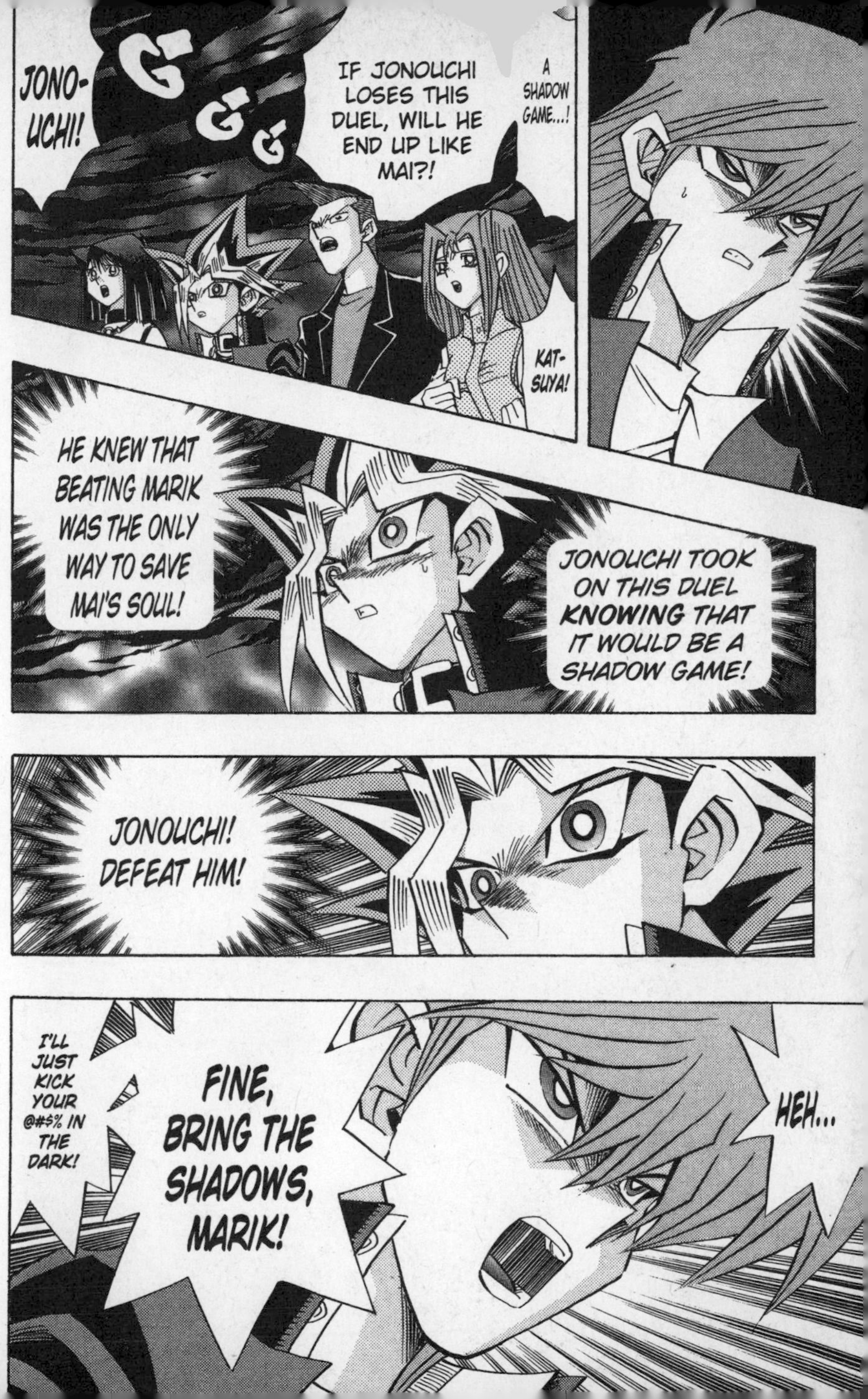
A SHADOW GAME...!
IF JONOUCHI LOSES THIS DUEL, WILL HE END UP LIKE MAI?!
JONO-UCHI!
KAT-SUYA!
JONOUCHI TOOK ON THIS DUEL KNOWING THAT IT WOULD BE A SHADOW GAME!
HE KNEW THAT BEATING MARIK WAS THE ONLY WAY TO SAVE MAI'S SOUL!
JONOUCHI! DEFEAT HIM!
HEH...
FINE, BRING THE SHADOWS, MARIK!
I'LL JUST KICK YOUR @#$% IN THE DARK!

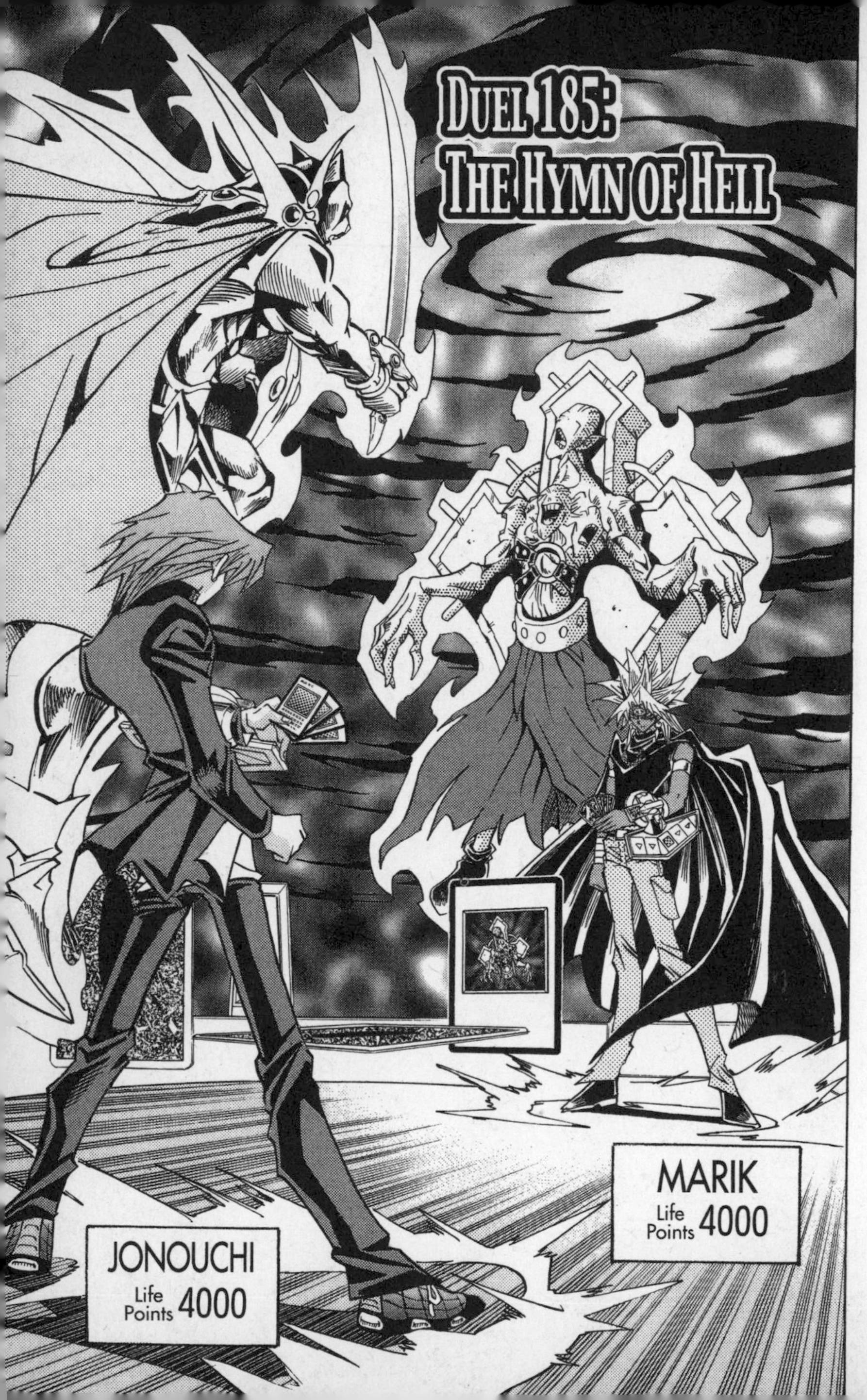
Duel 185:
The Hymn of Hell
MARIK
Life Points 4000
JONOUCHI
Life Points 4000

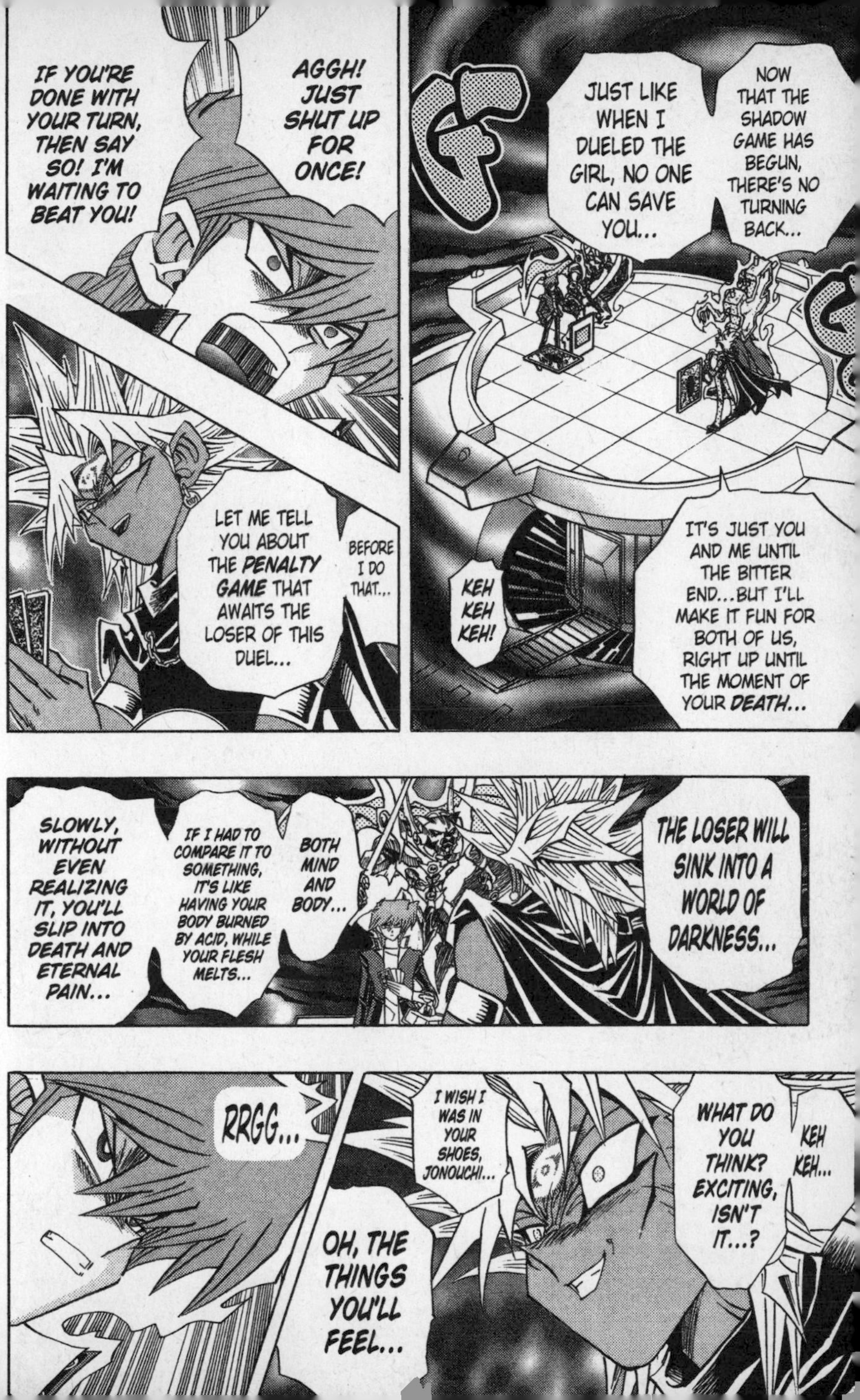
NOW THAT THE SHADOW GAME HAS BEGUN, THERE'S NO TURNING BACK...
JUST LIKE WHEN I DUELED THE GIRL, NO ONE CAN SAVE YOU...
IT'S JUST YOU AND ME UNTIL THE BITTER END...BUT I'LL MAKE IT FUN FOR BOTH OF US, RIGHT UP UNTIL THE MOMENT OF YOUR *DEATH*...
KEH KEH KEH!
AGGH! JUST SHUT UP FOR ONCE!
IF YOU'RE DONE WITH YOUR TURN, THEN SAY SO! I'M WAITING TO BEAT YOU!
BEFORE I DO THAT...
LET ME TELL YOU ABOUT THE *PENALTY GAME* THAT AWAITS THE LOSER OF THIS DUEL...
THE LOSER WILL SINK INTO A WORLD OF DARKNESS...
BOTH MIND AND BODY...
IF I HAD TO COMPARE IT TO SOMETHING, IT'S LIKE HAVING YOUR BODY BURNED BY ACID, WHILE YOUR FLESH MELTS...
SLOWLY, WITHOUT EVEN REALIZING IT, YOU'LL SLIP INTO DEATH AND ETERNAL PAIN...
KEH KEH...
WHAT DO YOU THINK? EXCITING, ISN'T IT...?
I WISH I WAS IN YOUR SHOES, JONOUCHI...
OH, THE THINGS YOU'LL FEEL...
RRGG...

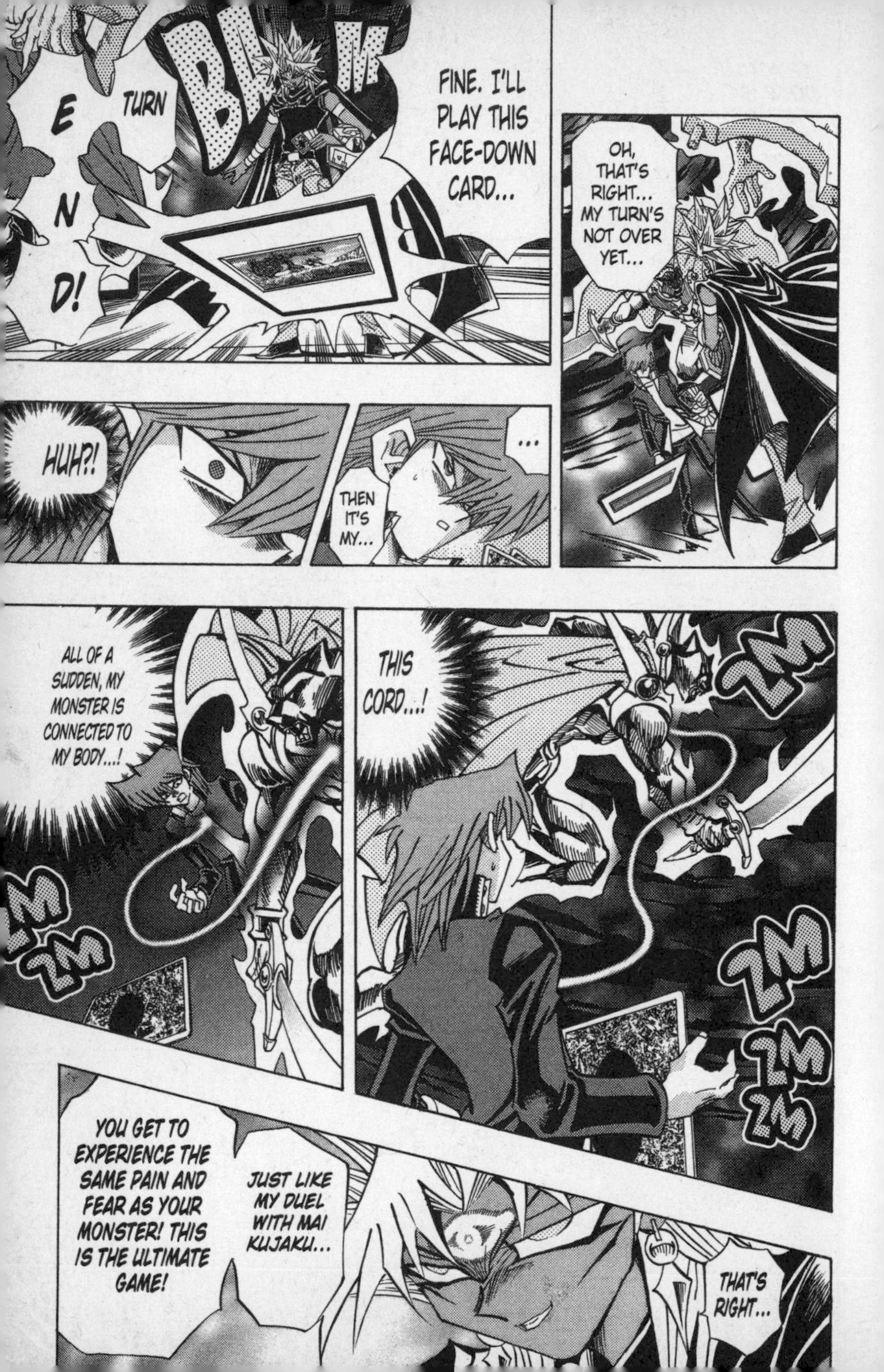
BLAM
FINE. I'LL PLAY THIS FACE-DOWN CARD...
TURN END!
...
THEN IT'S MY...
OH, THAT'S RIGHT... MY TURN'S NOT OVER YET...
HUH?!
THIS CORD...!
ZM
ZM
ZM
ALL OF A SUDDEN, MY MONSTER IS CONNECTED TO MY BODY...!
ZM
ZM
THAT'S RIGHT...
JUST LIKE MY DUEL WITH MAI KUJAKU...
YOU GET TO EXPERIENCE THE SAME PAIN AND FEAR AS YOUR MONSTER! THIS IS THE ULTIMATE GAME!

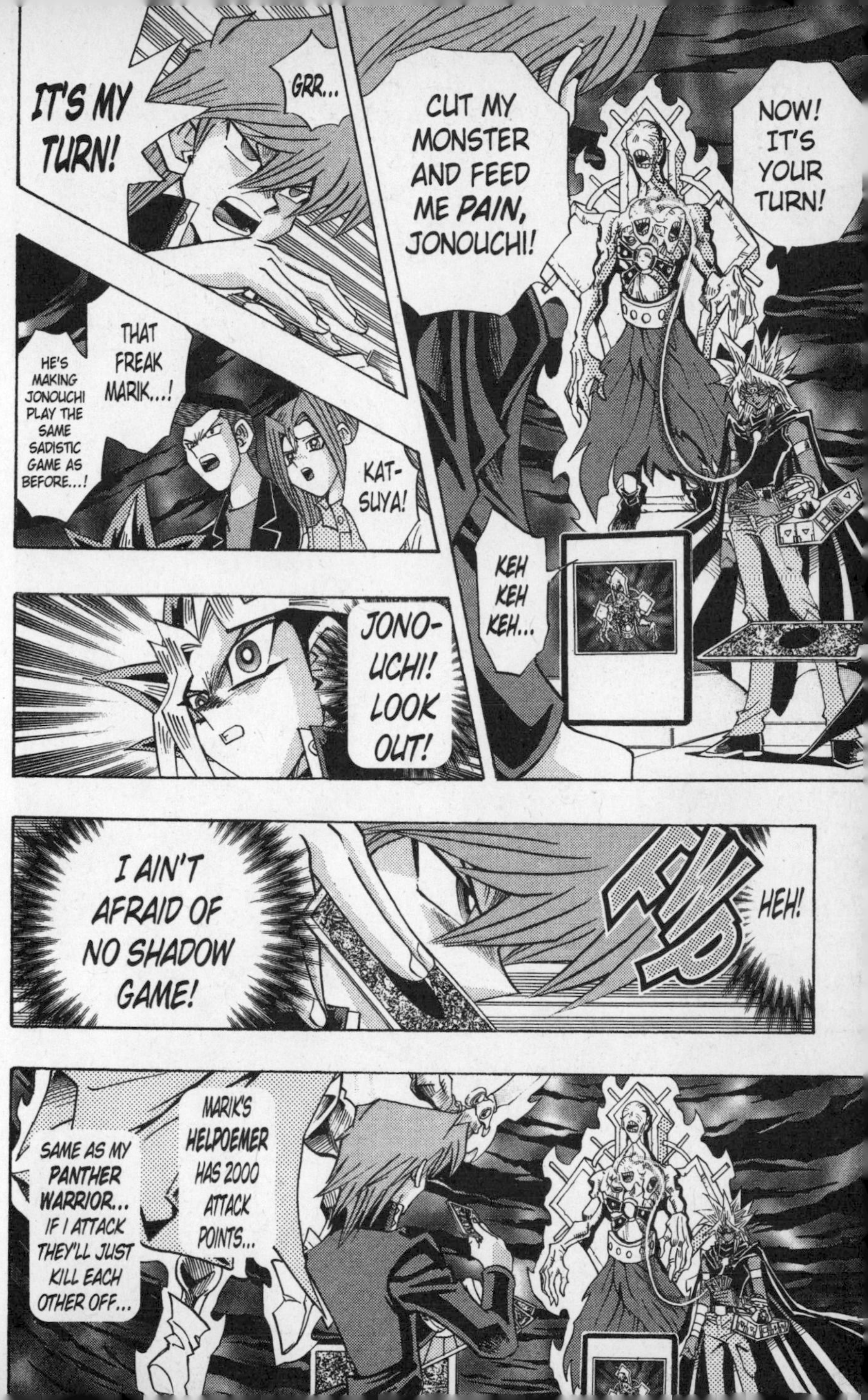
NOW! IT'S YOUR TURN!
CUT MY MONSTER AND FEED ME PAIN, JONOUCHI!
KEH KEH KEH...
GRR...
IT'S MY TURN!
KAT-SUYA!
THAT FREAK MARIK...!
HE'S MAKING JONOUCHI PLAY THE SAME SADISTIC GAME AS BEFORE...!
JONO-UCHI! LOOK OUT!
HEH!
I AIN'T AFRAID OF NO SHADOW GAME!
MARIK'S HELPOEMER HAS 2000 ATTACK POINTS...
SAME AS MY PANTHER WARRIOR... IF I ATTACK THEY'LL JUST KILL EACH OTHER OFF...

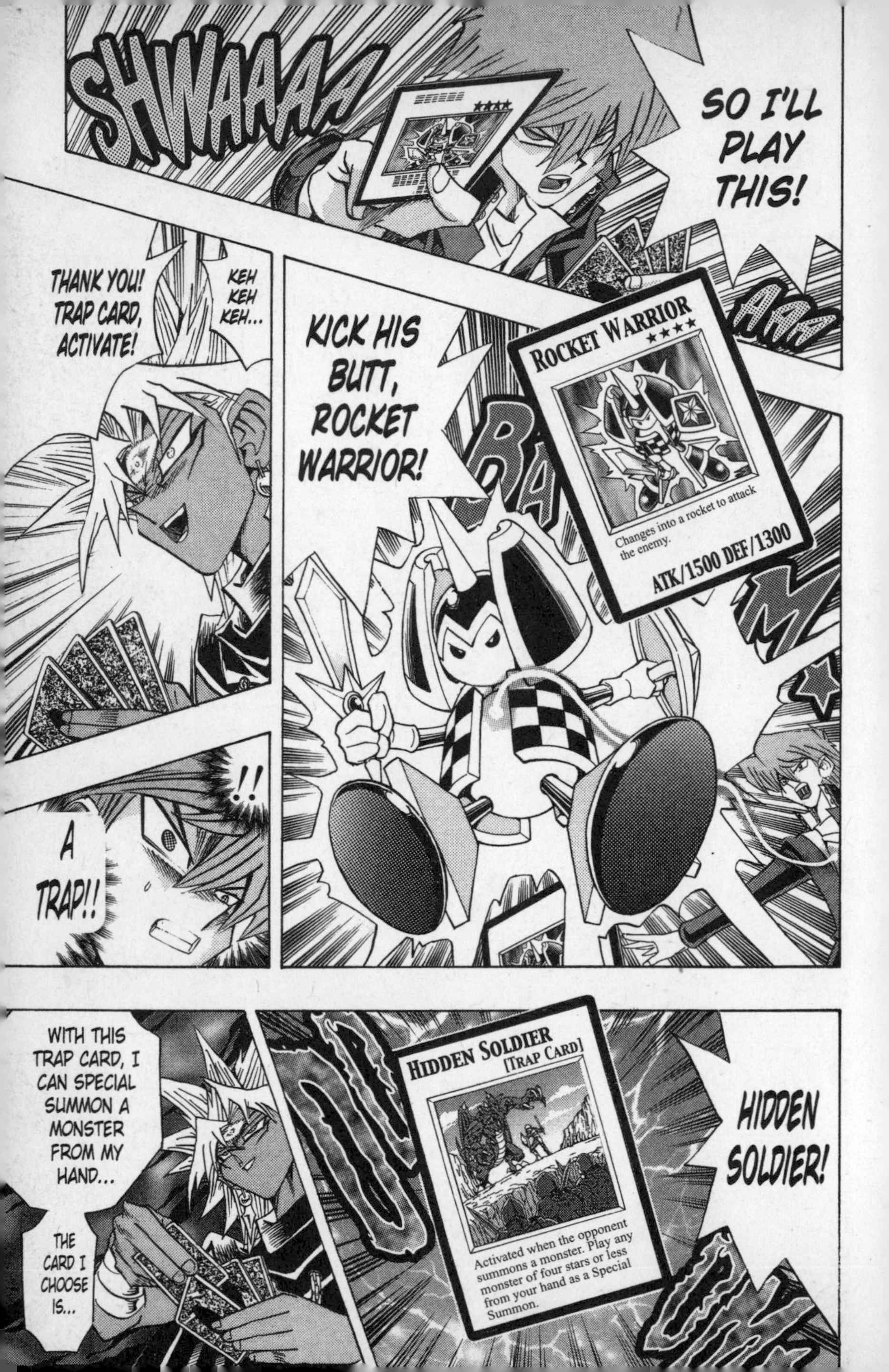
SO I'LL PLAY THIS!
SHWAAAA
KICK HIS BUTT, ROCKET WARRIOR!
ROCKET WARRIOR ★★★★
Changes into a rocket to attack the enemy.
ATK/1500 DEF/1300
KEH KEH KEH...
THANK YOU! TRAP CARD, ACTIVATE!
!!
A TRAP!!
HIDDEN SOLDIER!
HIDDEN SOLDIER [TRAP CARD]
Activated when the opponent summons a monster. Play any monster of four stars or less from your hand as a Special Summon.
WITH THIS TRAP CARD, I CAN SPECIAL SUMMON A MONSTER FROM MY HAND...
THE CARD I CHOOSE IS...

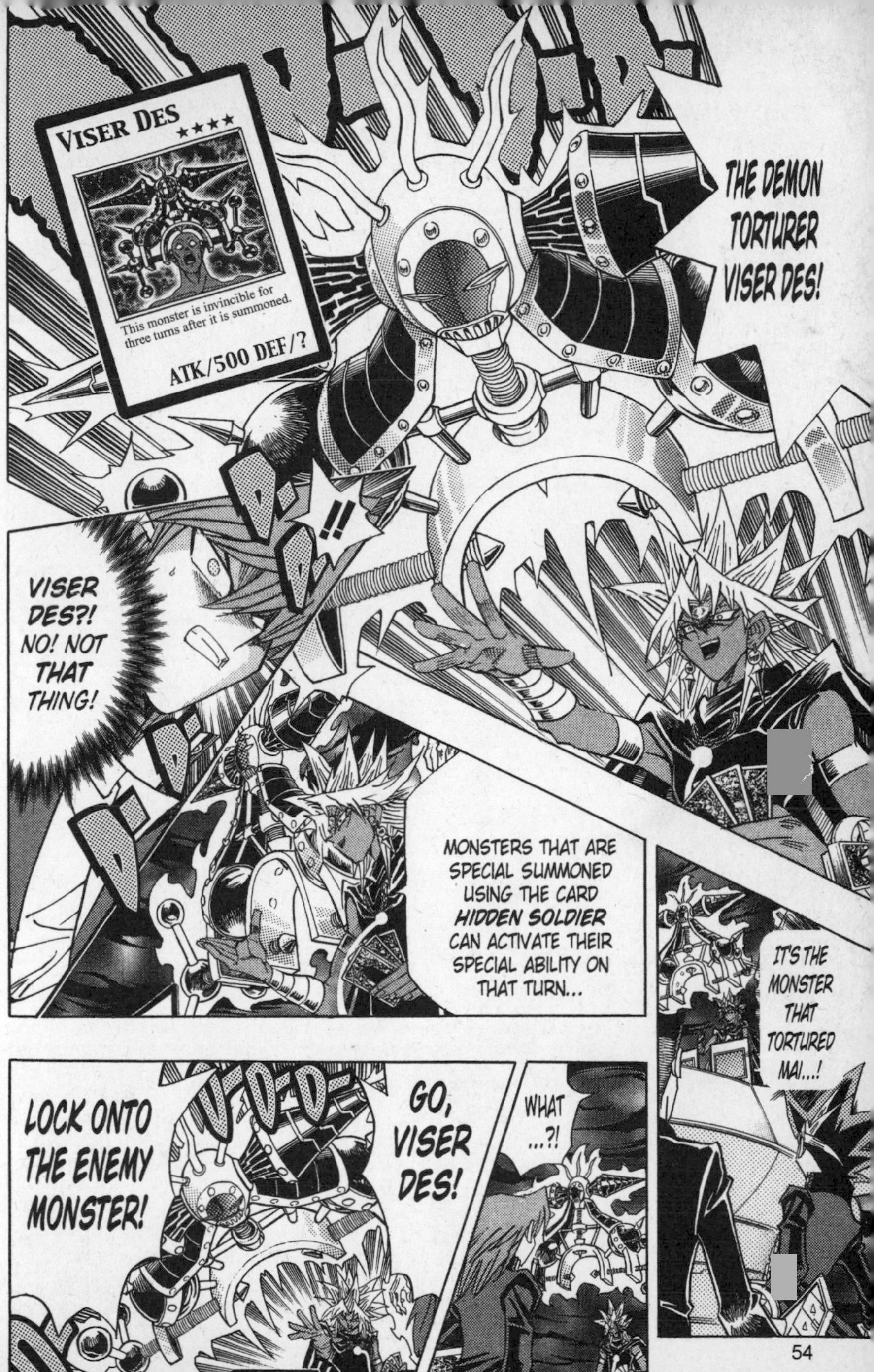
VISER DES ★★★★
This monster is invincible for three turns after it is summoned.
ATK/500 DEF/?
THE DEMON TORTURER VISER DES!
VISER DES?! NO! NOT THAT THING!
MONSTERS THAT ARE SPECIAL SUMMONED USING THE CARD HIDDEN SOLDIER CAN ACTIVATE THEIR SPECIAL ABILITY ON THAT TURN...
IT'S THE MONSTER THAT TORTURED MAI...!
WHAT ...?!
GO, VISER DES!
LOCK ONTO THE ENEMY MONSTER!

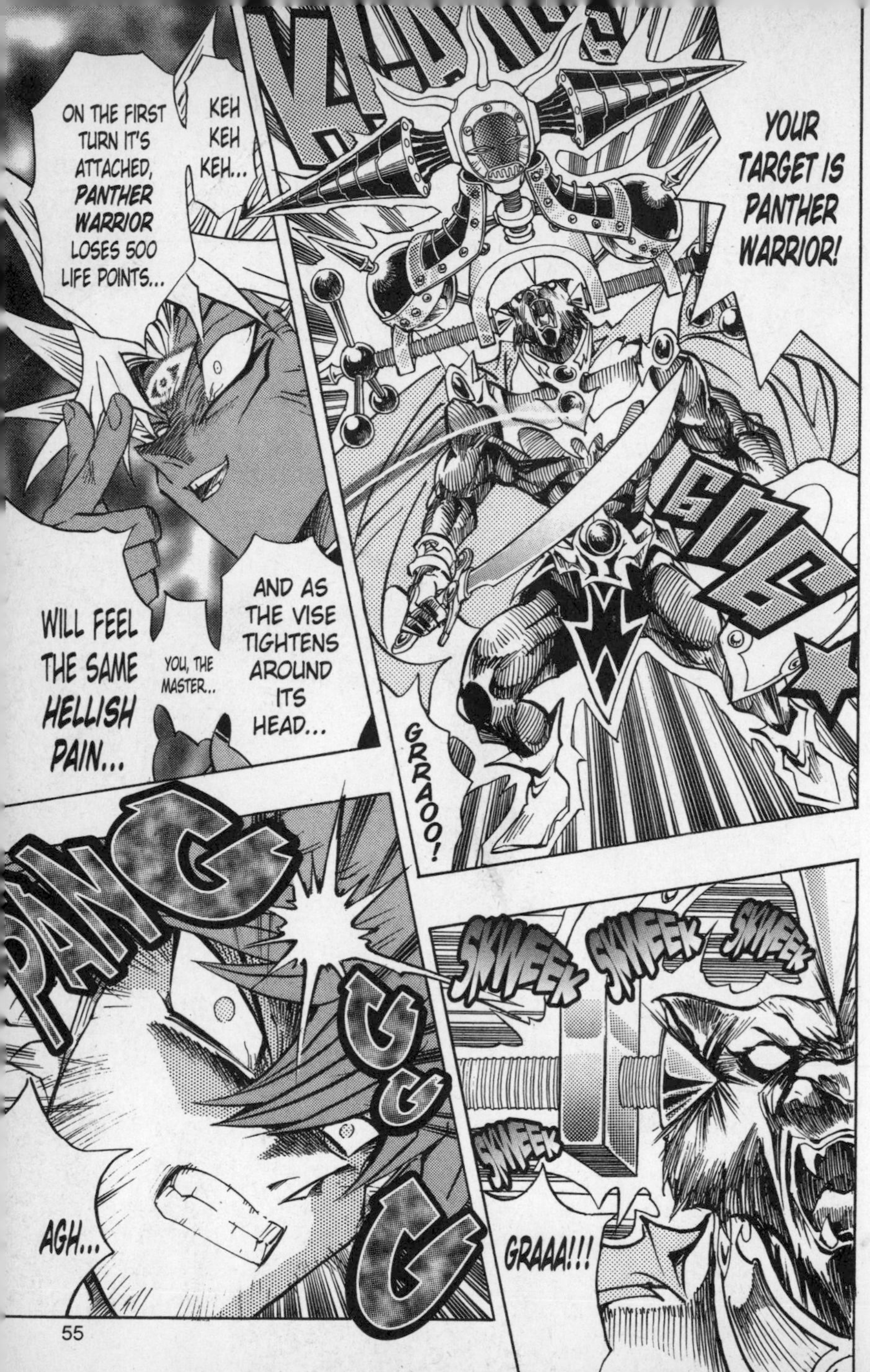
YOUR TARGET IS PANTHER WARRIOR!
GRRAOO!
KEH KEH KEH...
ON THE FIRST TURN IT'S ATTACHED, PANTHER WARRIOR LOSES 500 LIFE POINTS...
AND AS THE VISE TIGHTENS AROUND ITS HEAD...
YOU, THE MASTER...
WILL FEEL THE SAME HELLISH PAIN...
SKWEEK SKWEEK SKWEEK
SKWEEK
GRAAA!!!
PANG
AGH...

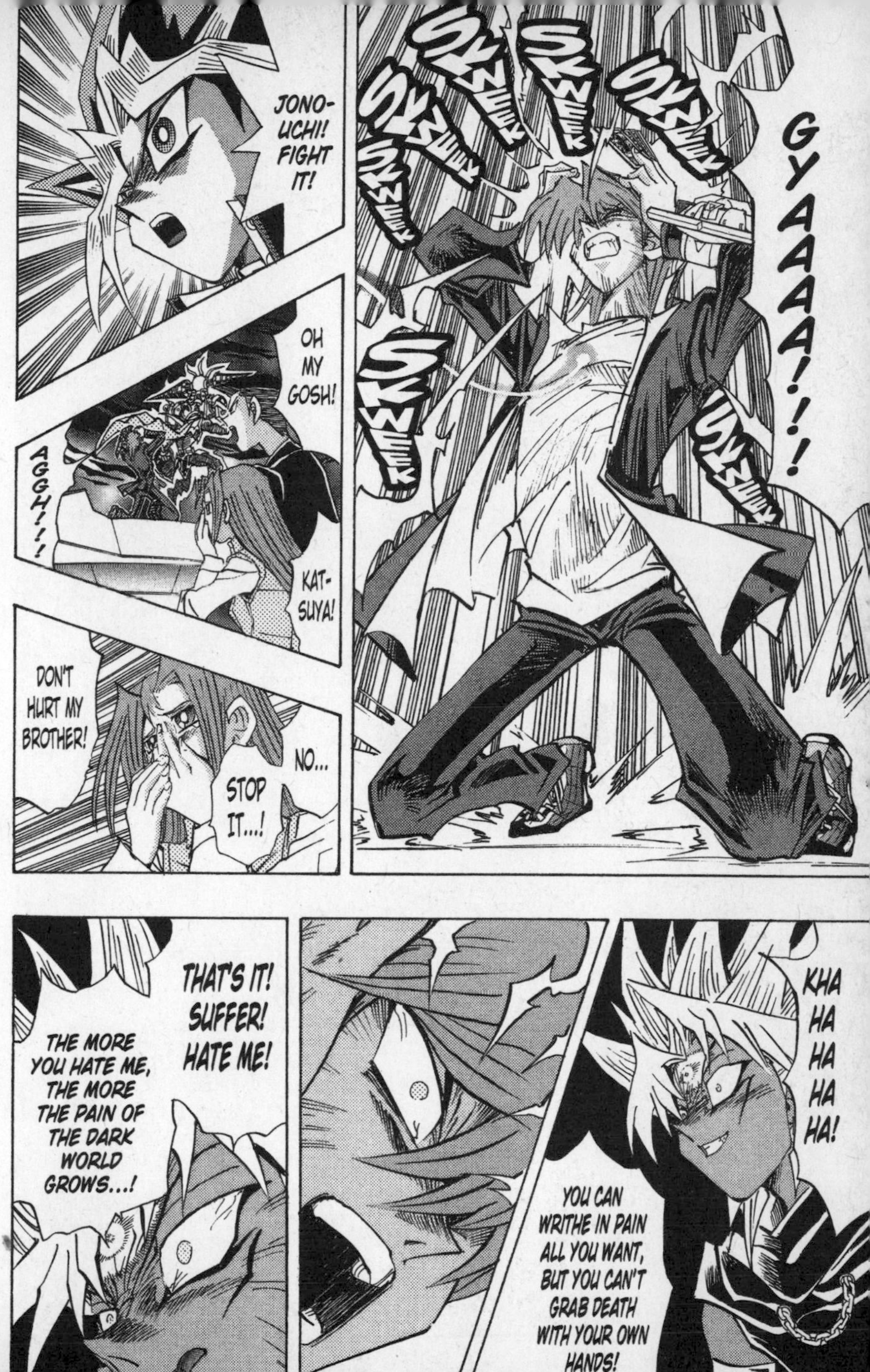
SKWEEK
SKWEEK
SKWEEK
SKWEEK
SKWEEK
SKWEEK
GYAAAA!!!
SKWEEK
SKWEEK
JONO-UCHI! FIGHT IT!
OH MY GOSH!
AGGH!!!
KAT-SUYA!
DON'T HURT MY BROTHER!
NO...
STOP IT...!
KHA HA HA HA HA HA!
YOU CAN WRITHE IN PAIN ALL YOU WANT, BUT YOU CAN'T GRAB DEATH WITH YOUR OWN HANDS!
THAT'S IT! SUFFER! HATE ME!
THE MORE YOU HATE ME, THE MORE THE PAIN OF THE DARK WORLD GROWS...!

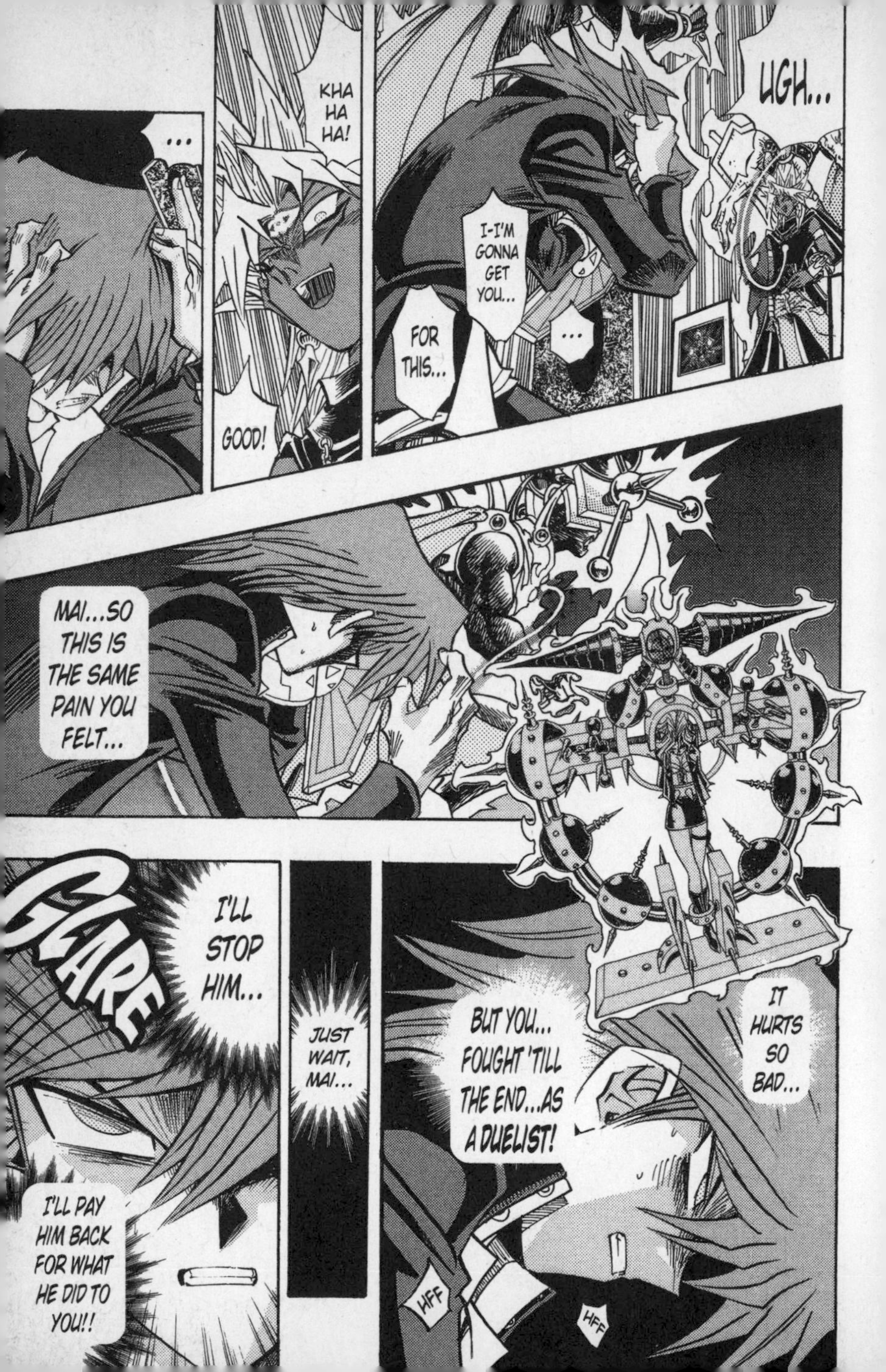
UGH...
I-I'M GONNA GET YOU...
FOR THIS...
...
KHA HA HA!
GOOD!
...
MAI...SO THIS IS THE SAME PAIN YOU FELT...
IT HURTS SO BAD...
BUT YOU... FOUGHT 'TILL THE END...AS A DUELIST!
HFF
HFF
JUST WAIT, MAI...
I'LL STOP HIM...
GLARE
I'LL PAY HIM BACK FOR WHAT HE DID TO YOU!!

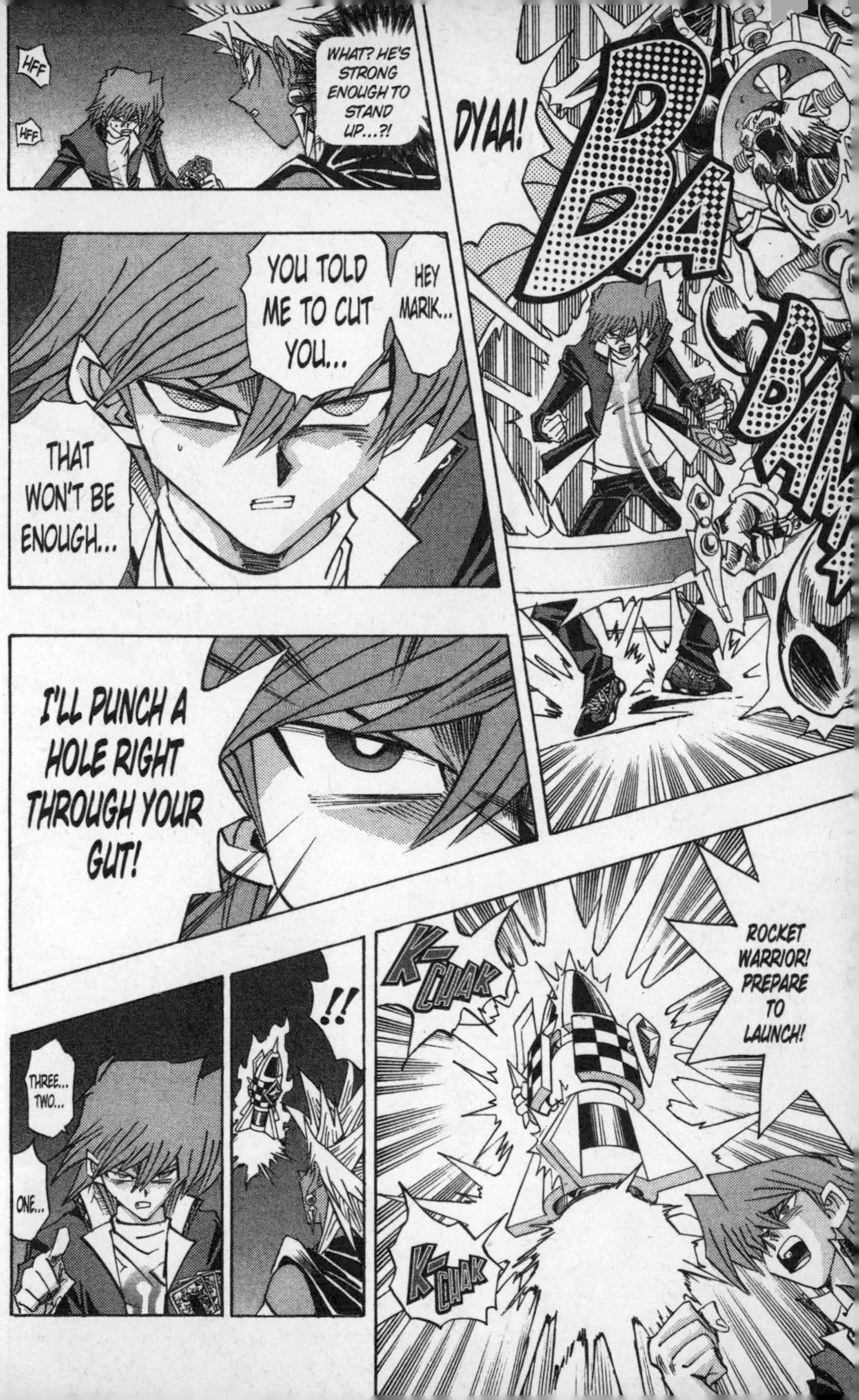
DYAA!
WHAT? HE'S STRONG ENOUGH TO STAND UP...?!
HFF
HFF
HEY MARIK...
YOU TOLD ME TO CUT YOU...
THAT WON'T BE ENOUGH...
I'LL PUNCH A HOLE RIGHT THROUGH YOUR GUT!
ROCKET WARRIOR! PREPARE TO LAUNCH!
K-CHAK
K-CHAK
!!
THREE... TWO...
ONE...

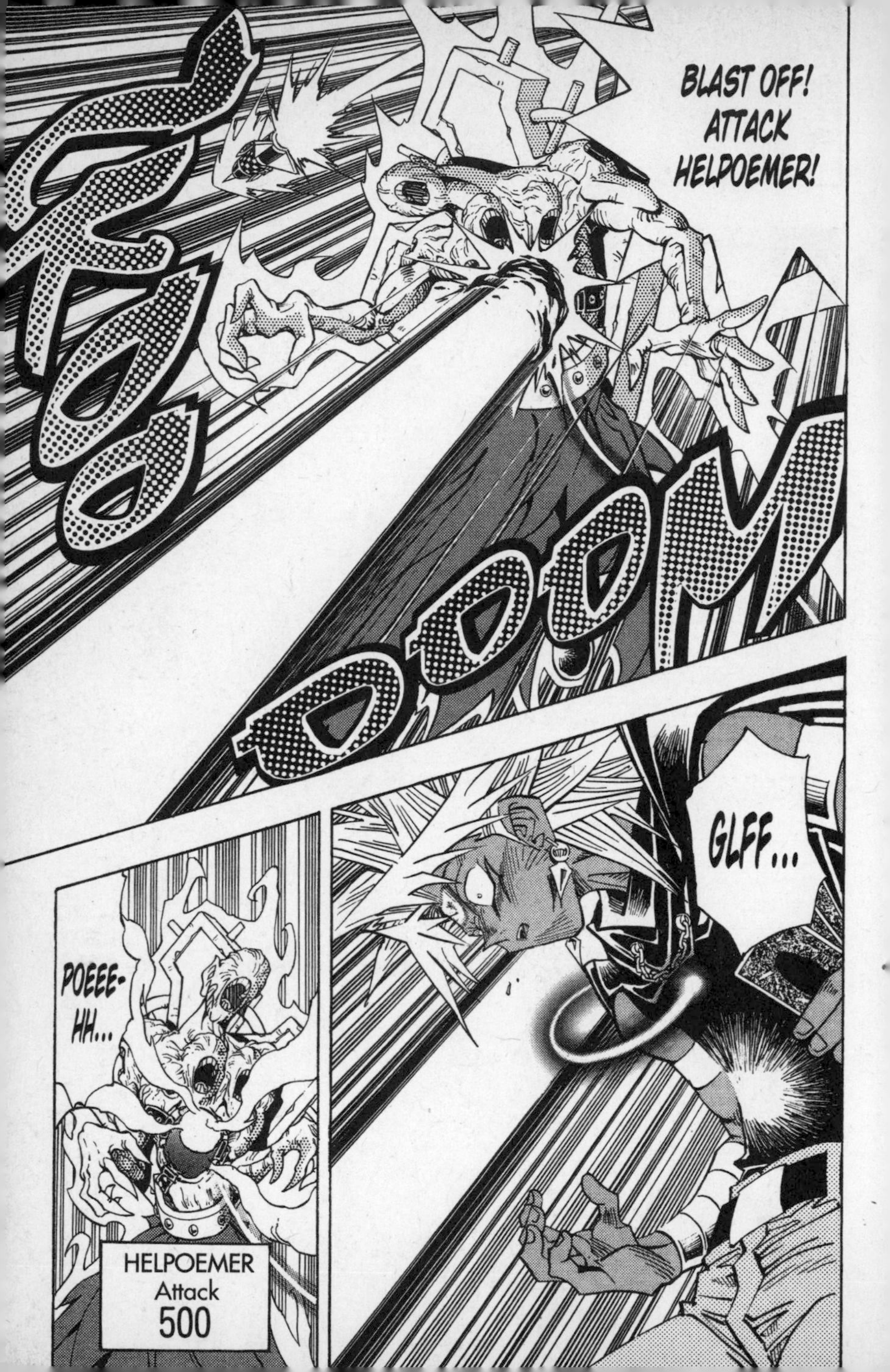
BLAST OFF! ATTACK HELPOEMER!
GLFF...
POEEE-HH...
HELPOEMER
Attack
500

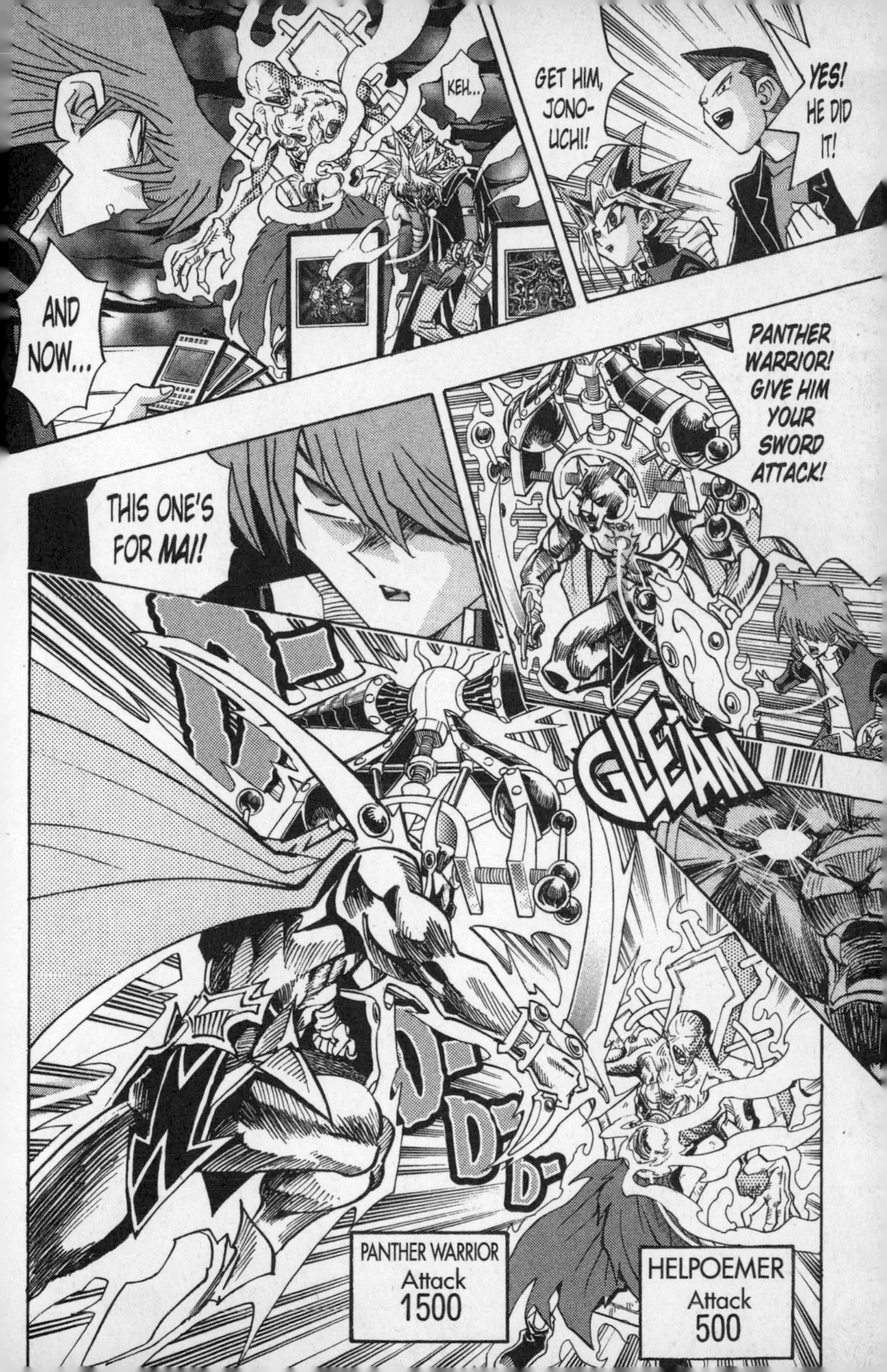
YES! HE DID IT!
GET HIM, JONO-UCHI!
KEH...
AND NOW...
PANTHER WARRIOR! GIVE HIM YOUR SWORD ATTACK!
THIS ONE'S FOR MAI!
GLEAM
D-D-D-
HELPOEMER Attack 500
PANTHER WARRIOR Attack 1500

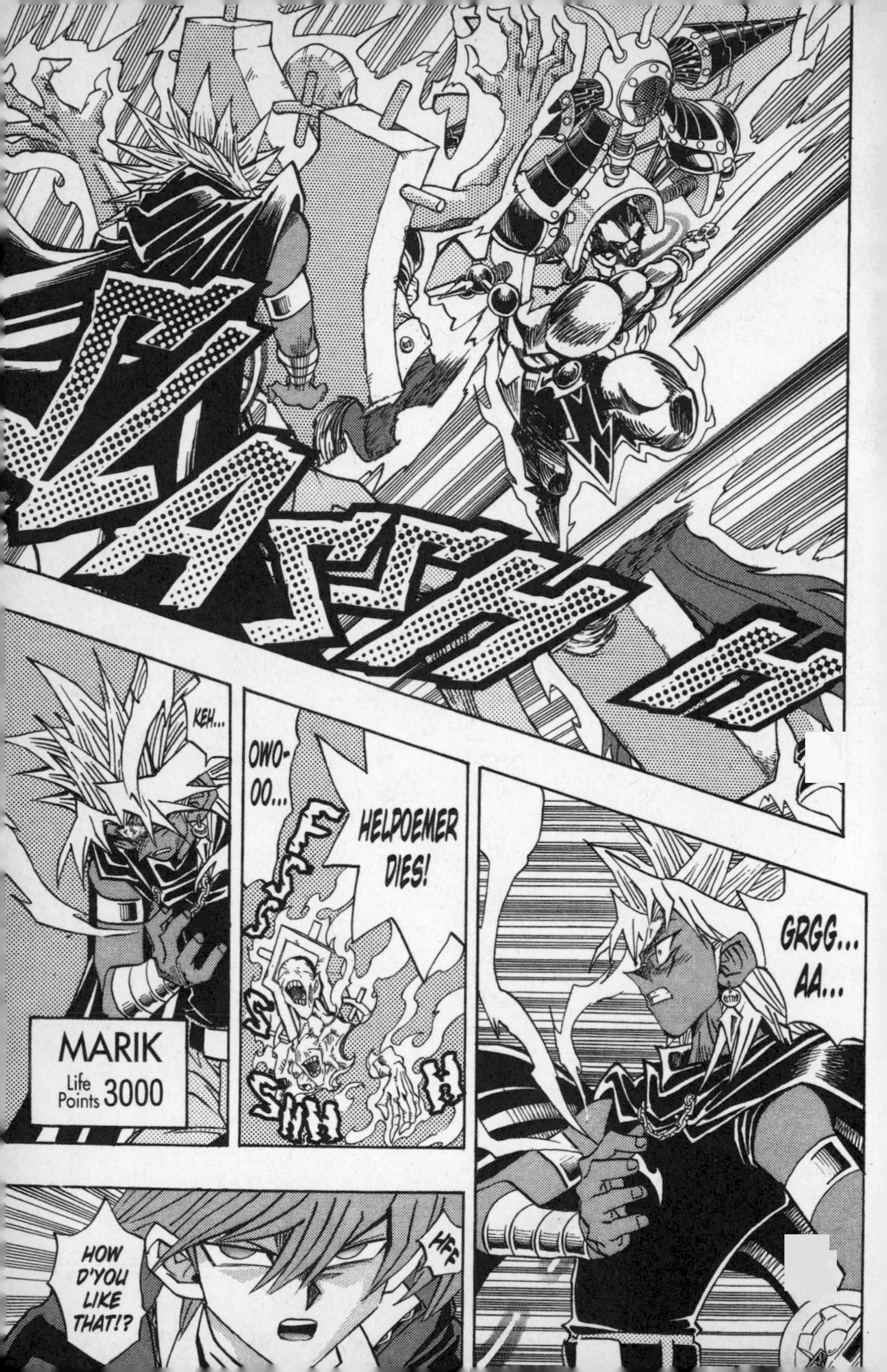
GRGG... AA...
OWO-OO...
HELPOEMER DIES!
KEH...
MARIK
Life Points 3000
HFF
HOW D'YOU LIKE THAT!?

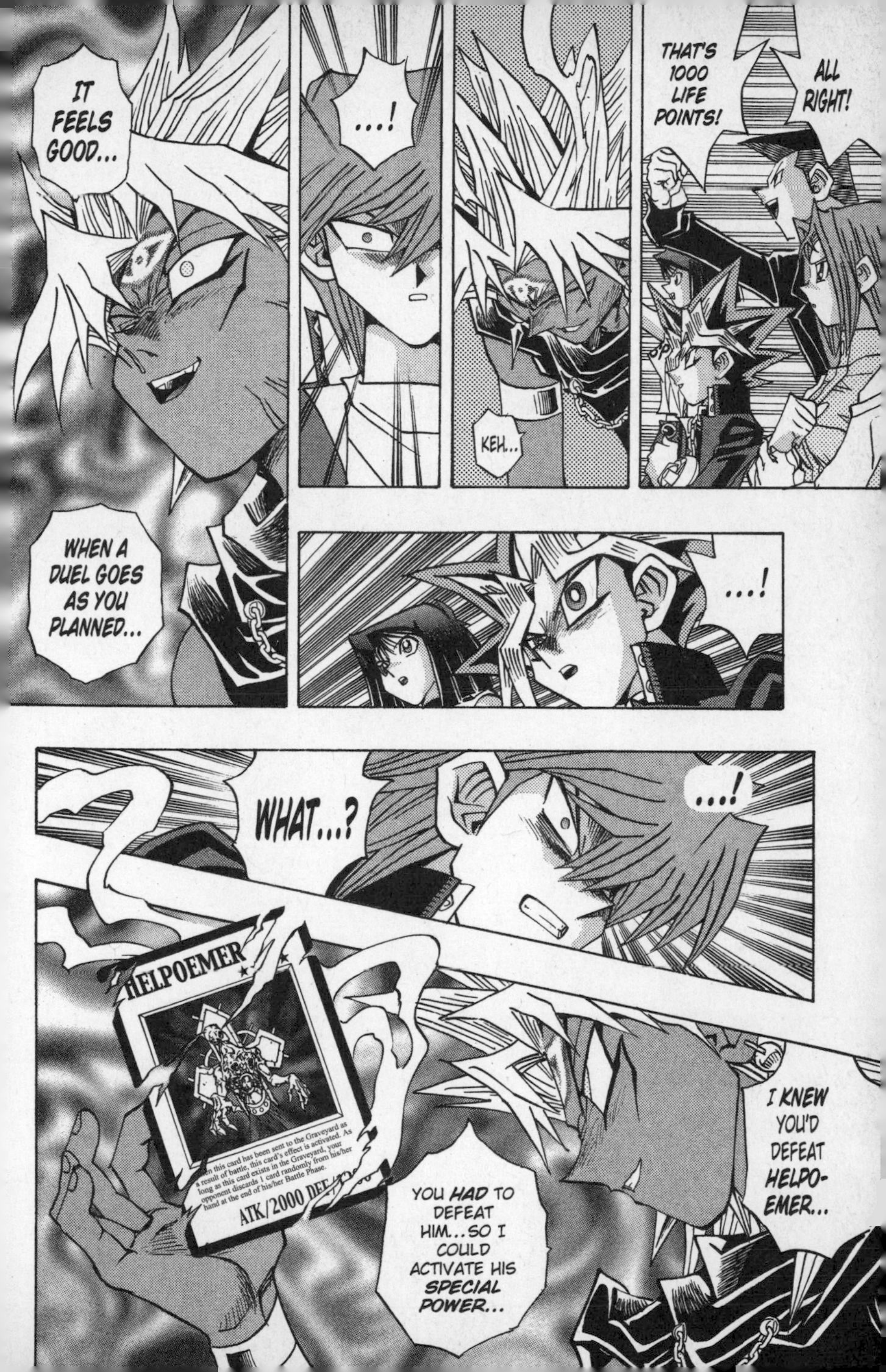

ALL RIGHT!
THAT'S 1000 LIFE POINTS!
KEH...
...!
...!
IT FEELS GOOD...
WHEN A DUEL GOES AS YOU PLANNED...
...!
WHAT...?
HELPOEMER
en this card has been sent to the Graveyard as a result of battle, this card's effect is activated. As long as this card exists in the Graveyard, your opponent discards 1 card randomly from his/her hand at the end of his/her Battle Phase.
ATK/2000 DEF
I KNEW YOU'D DEFEAT HELPOEMER...
YOU *HAD* TO DEFEAT HIM...SO I COULD ACTIVATE HIS *SPECIAL POWER*...

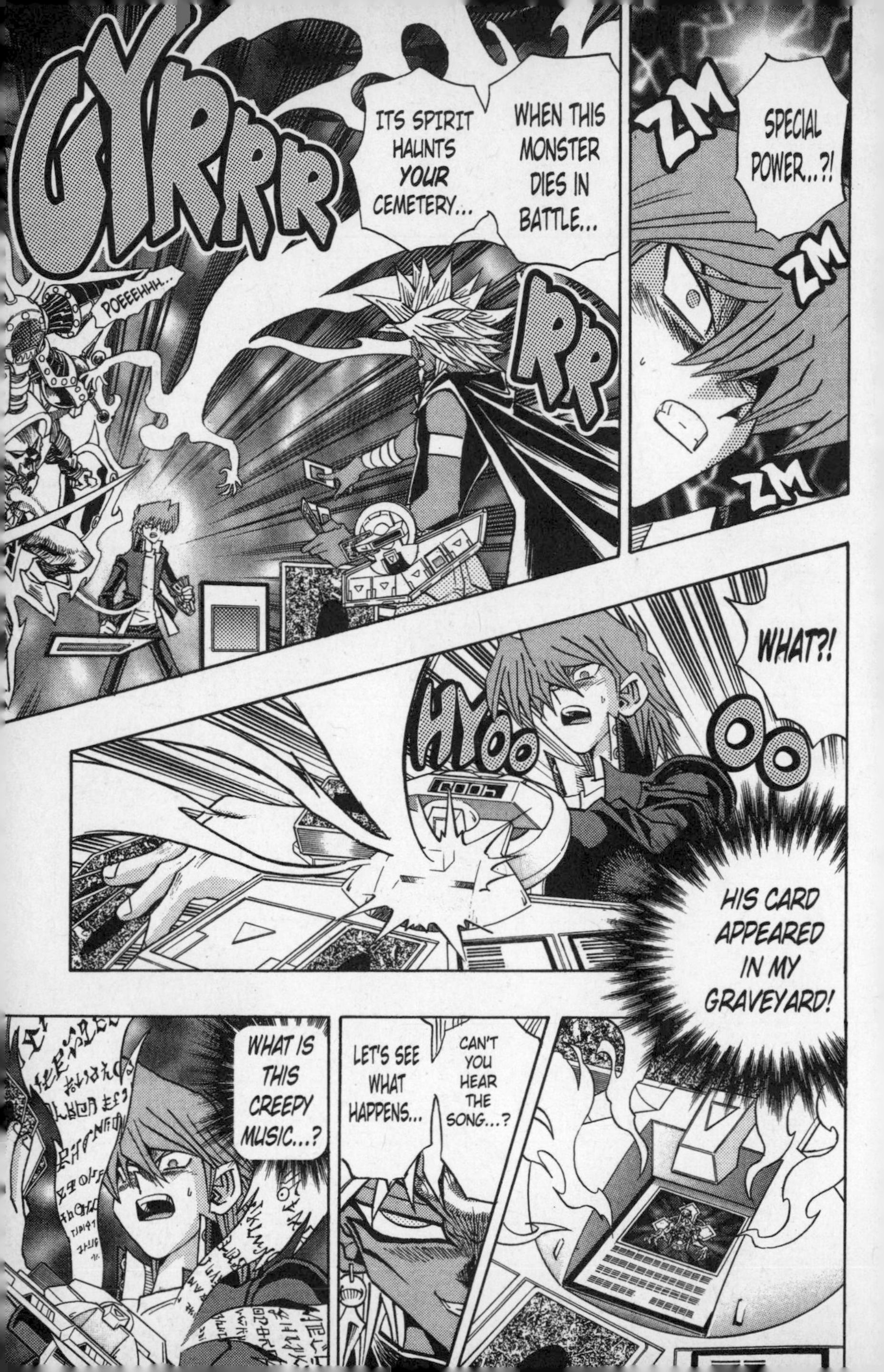
ZM
SPECIAL POWER...?!
ZM
ZM
GYRRRR
WHEN THIS MONSTER DIES IN BATTLE...
ITS SPIRIT HAUNTS *YOUR* CEMETERY...
RR
POEEEHHH...
WHAT?!
HYOOOO
HIS CARD APPEARED IN MY GRAVEYARD!
CAN'T YOU HEAR THE SONG...?
LET'S SEE WHAT HAPPENS...
WHAT IS THIS CREEPY MUSIC...?

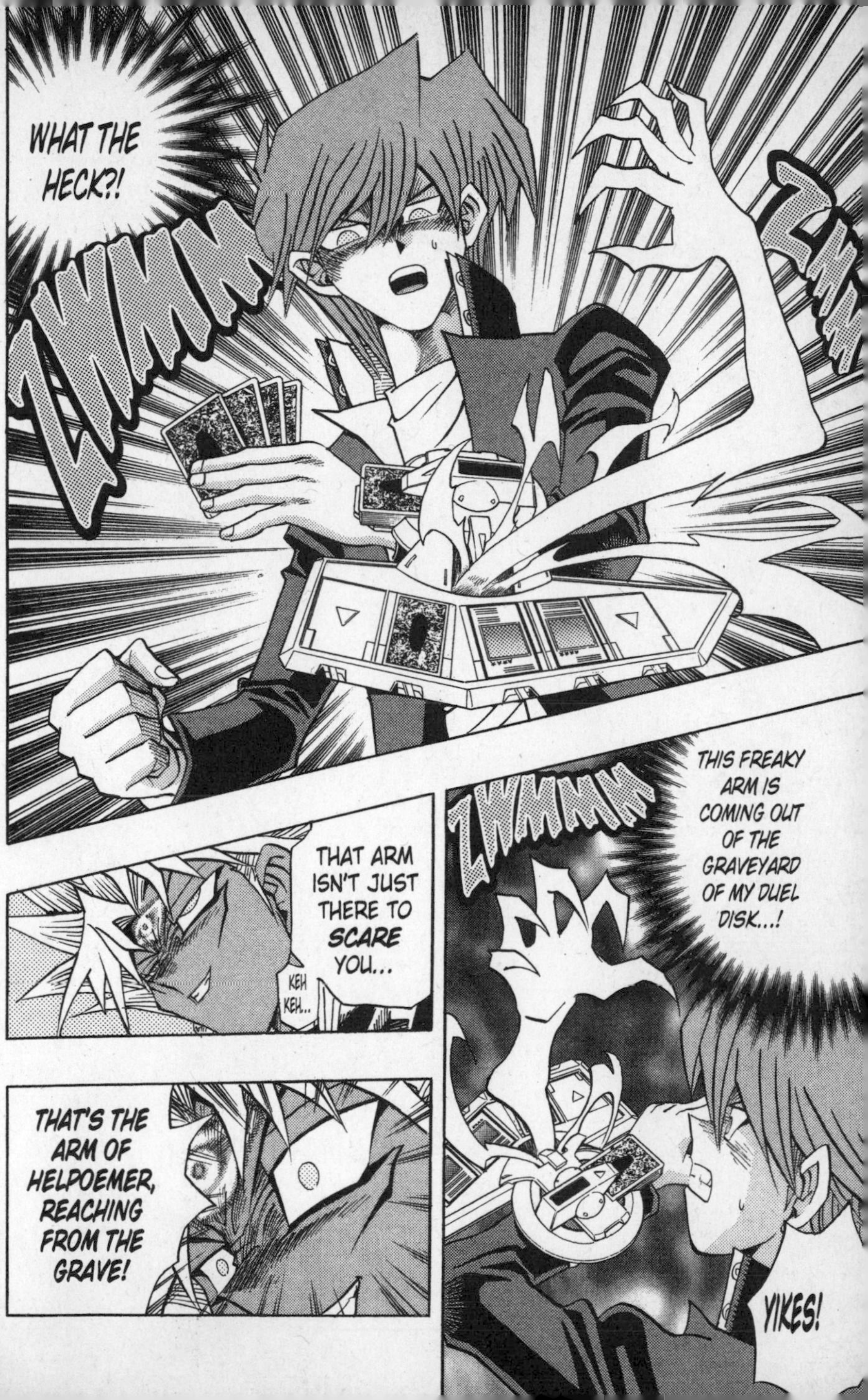
WHAT THE HECK?!
ZWMMM
ZWM
ZWMMM
THIS FREAKY ARM IS COMING OUT OF THE GRAVEYARD OF MY DUEL DISK...!
YIKES!
THAT ARM ISN'T JUST THERE TO **SCARE** YOU...
KEH KEH...
THAT'S THE ARM OF HELPOEMER, REACHING FROM THE GRAVE!

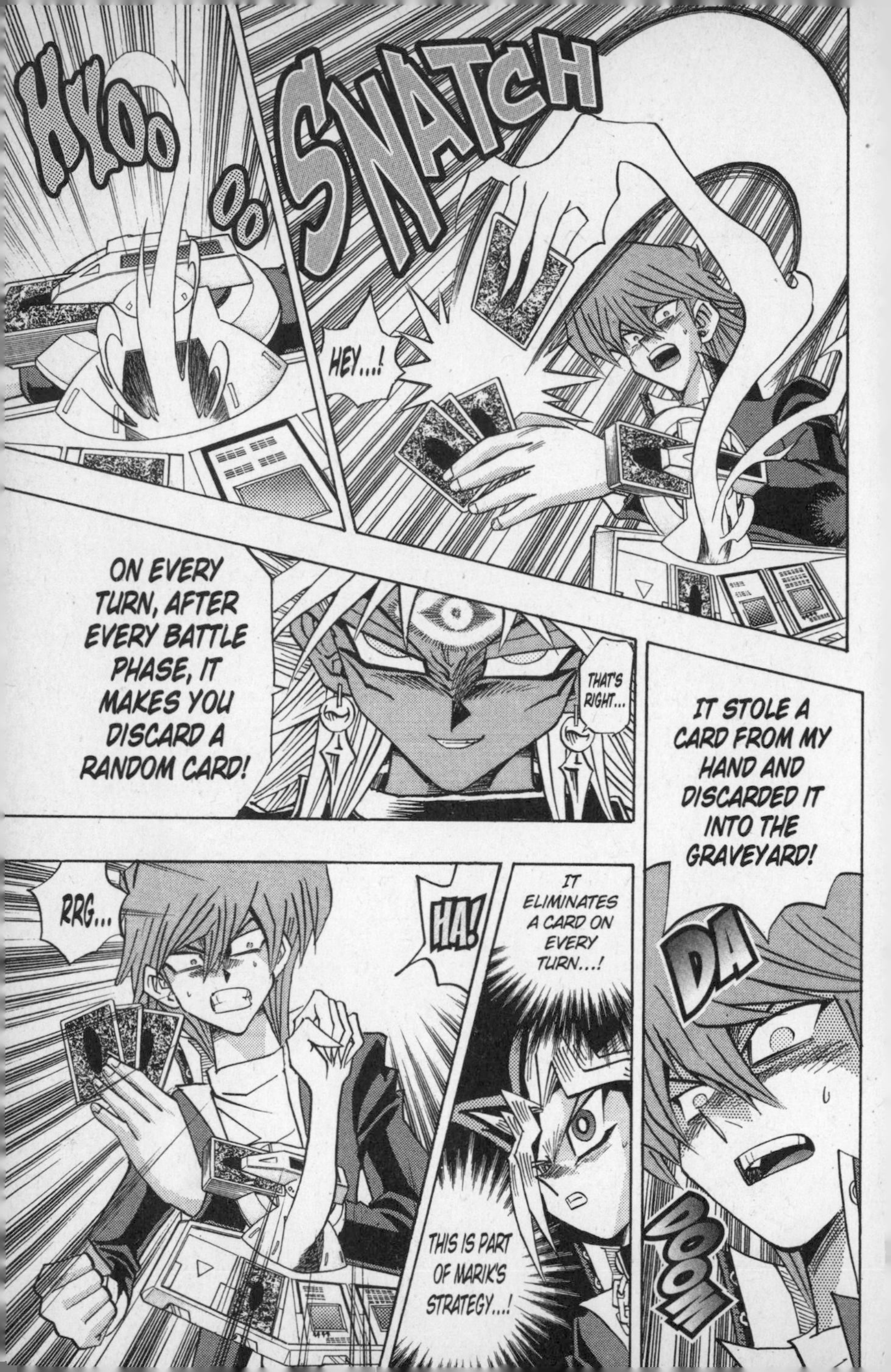
SNATCH
HEY...!
HYOO..
IT STOLE A CARD FROM MY HAND AND DISCARDED IT INTO THE GRAVEYARD!
DA
DOOM
THAT'S RIGHT...
ON EVERY TURN, AFTER EVERY BATTLE PHASE, IT MAKES YOU DISCARD A RANDOM CARD!
IT ELIMINATES A CARD ON EVERY TURN...!
THIS IS PART OF MARIK'S STRATEGY...!
HA!
RRG...

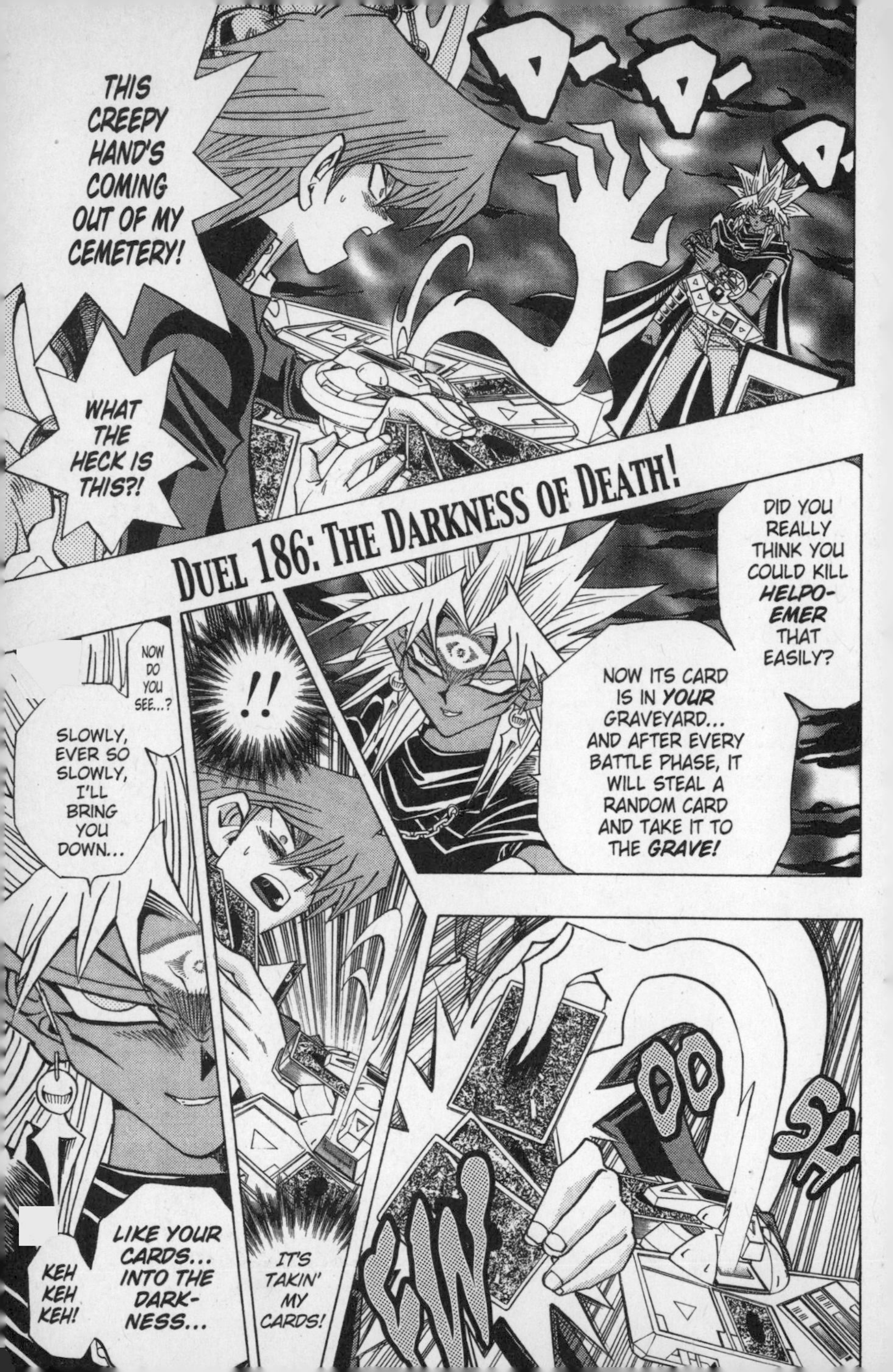
D-D-D-D
THIS CREEPY HAND'S COMING OUT OF MY CEMETERY!
WHAT THE HECK IS THIS?!
DUEL 186: THE DARKNESS OF DEATH!
DID YOU REALLY THINK YOU COULD KILL HELPOEMER THAT EASILY?
NOW ITS CARD IS IN YOUR GRAVEYARD... AND AFTER EVERY BATTLE PHASE, IT WILL STEAL A RANDOM CARD AND TAKE IT TO THE GRAVE!
!!
NOW DO YOU SEE...?
SLOWLY, EVER SO SLOWLY, I'LL BRING YOU DOWN...
IT'S TAKIN' MY CARDS!
LIKE YOUR CARDS... INTO THE DARKNESS...
KEH KEH KEH!

DUEL 186: THE DARKNESS OF DEATH!

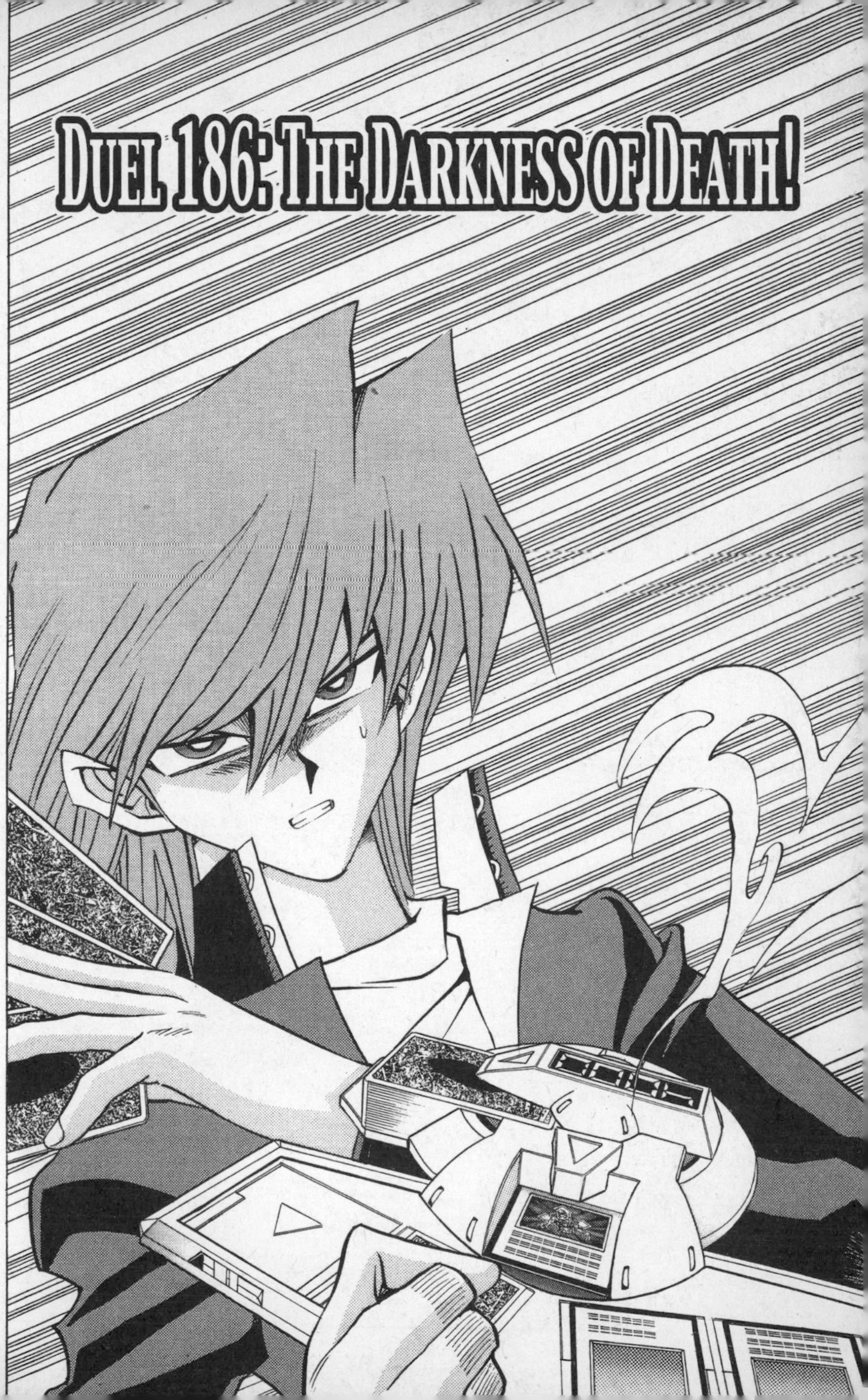

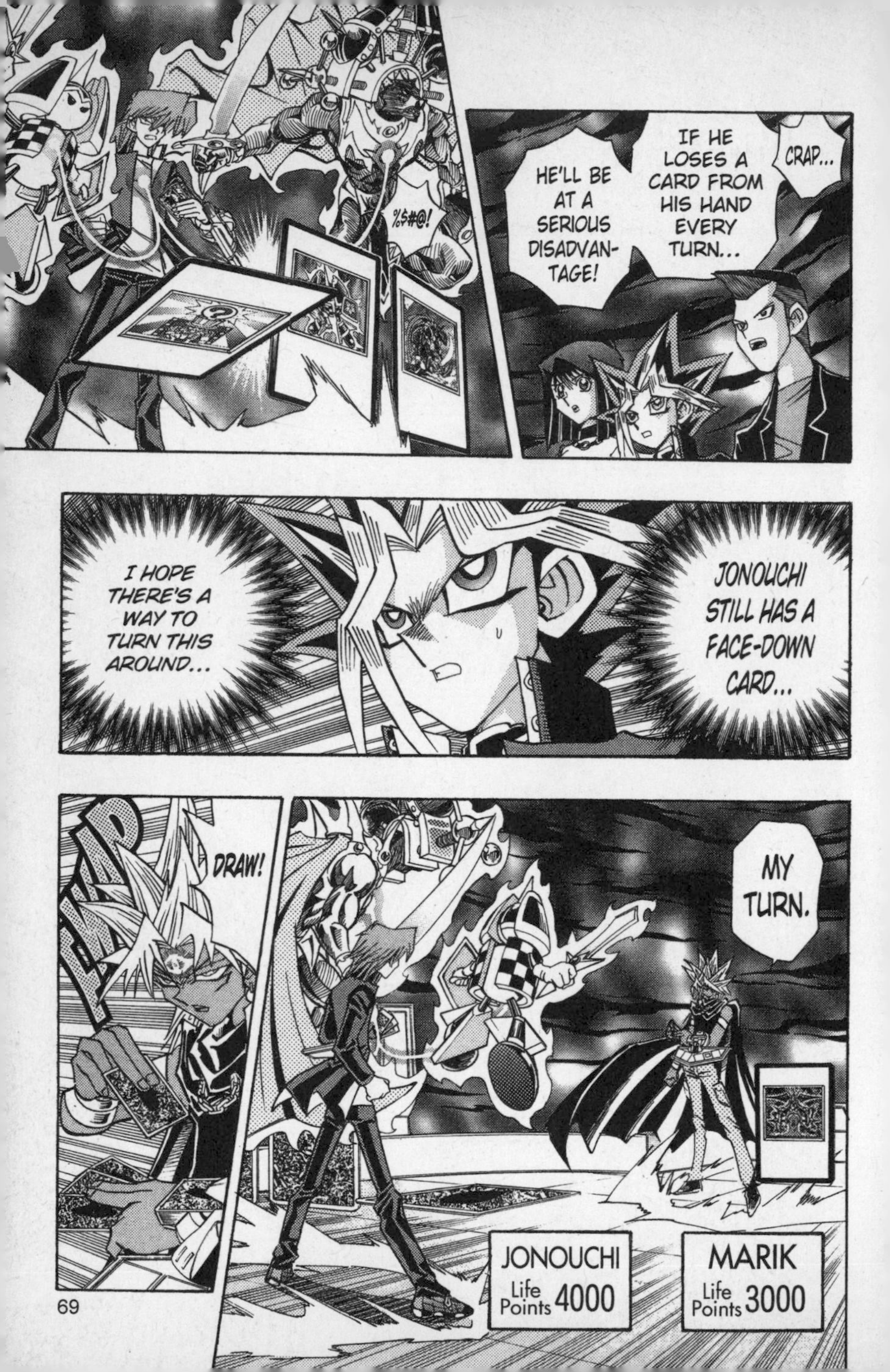
CRAP...
IF HE LOSES A CARD FROM HIS HAND EVERY TURN...
HE'LL BE AT A SERIOUS DISADVANTAGE!
%$#@!
JONOUCHI STILL HAS A FACE-DOWN CARD...
I HOPE THERE'S A WAY TO TURN THIS AROUND...
MY TURN.
MARIK
Life Points 3000
JONOUCHI
Life Points 4000
DRAW!

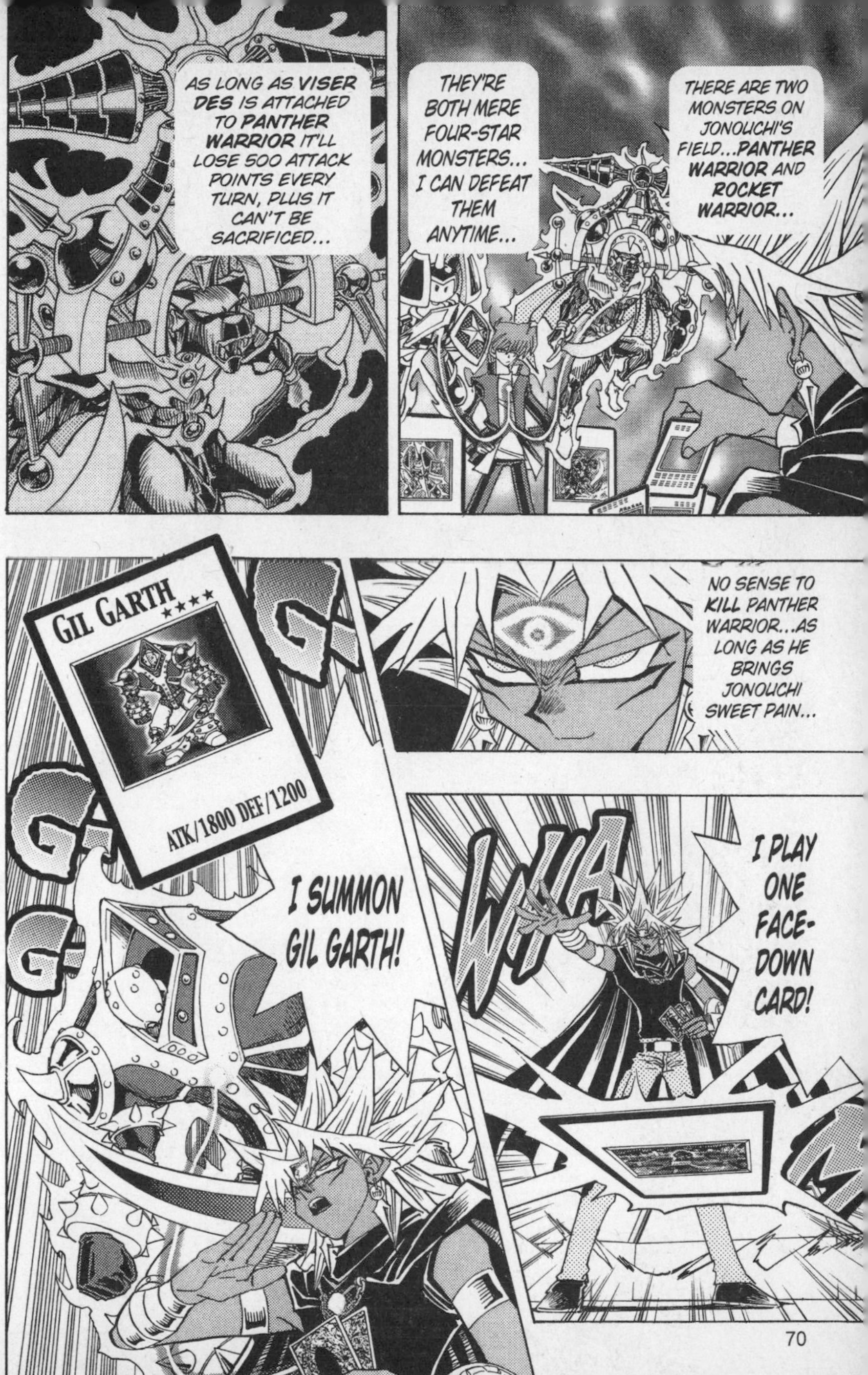
THERE ARE TWO MONSTERS ON JONOUCHI'S FIELD...PANTHER WARRIOR AND ROCKET WARRIOR...
THEY'RE BOTH MERE FOUR-STAR MONSTERS... I CAN DEFEAT THEM ANYTIME...
AS LONG AS VISER DES IS ATTACHED TO PANTHER WARRIOR IT'LL LOSE 500 ATTACK POINTS EVERY TURN, PLUS IT CAN'T BE SACRIFICED...
NO SENSE TO KILL PANTHER WARRIOR...AS LONG AS HE BRINGS JONOUCHI SWEET PAIN...
WHA
I PLAY ONE FACE-DOWN CARD!
GIL GARTH
ATK/1800 DEF/1200
I SUMMON GIL GARTH!

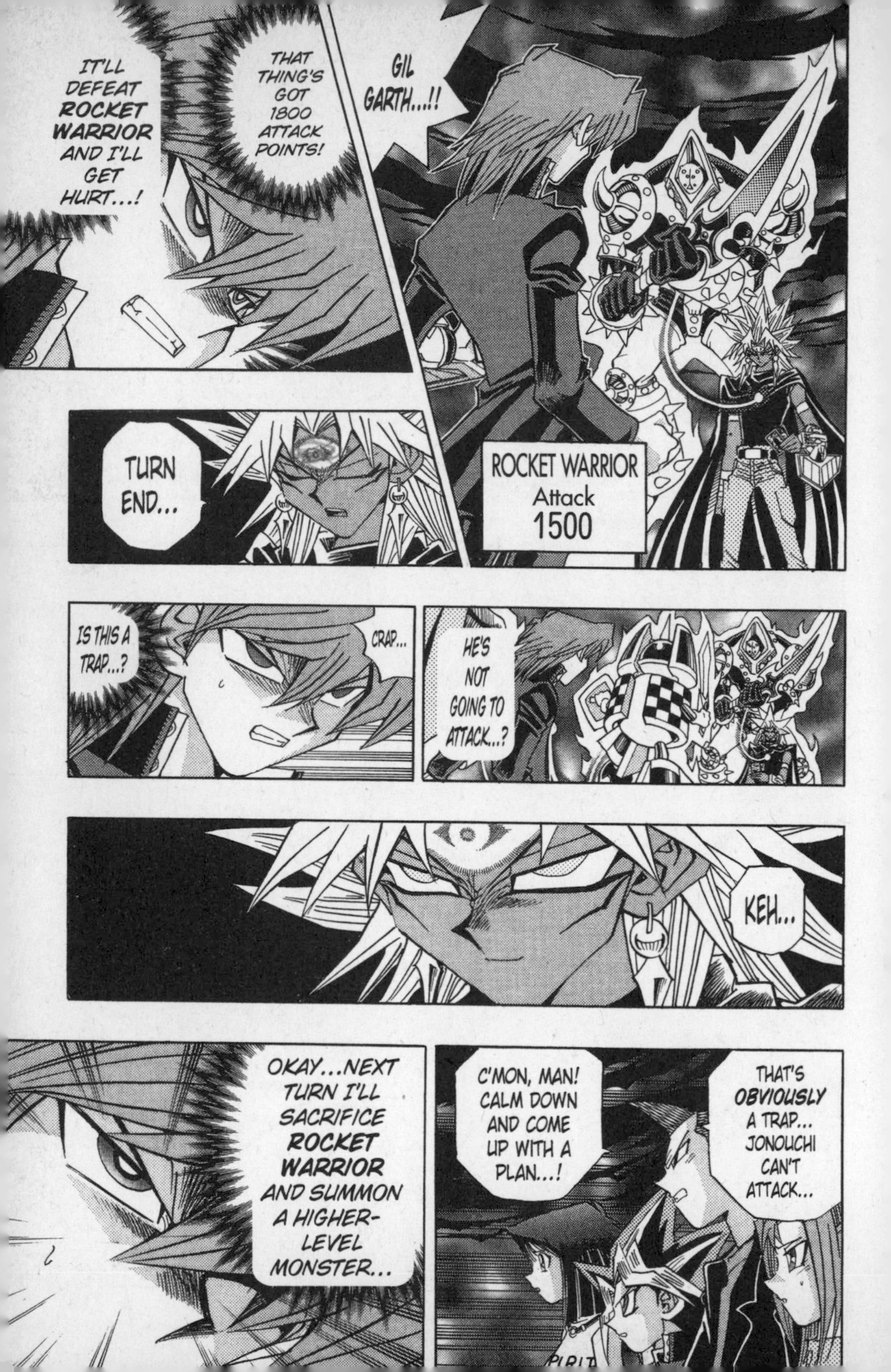
GIL GARTH...!!
ROCKET WARRIOR
Attack
1500
THAT THING'S GOT 1800 ATTACK POINTS!
IT'LL DEFEAT ROCKET WARRIOR AND I'LL GET HURT...!
TURN END...
HE'S NOT GOING TO ATTACK...?
CRAP...
IS THIS A TRAP...?
KEH...
THAT'S OBVIOUSLY A TRAP... JONOUCHI CAN'T ATTACK...
C'MON, MAN! CALM DOWN AND COME UP WITH A PLAN...!
OKAY...NEXT TURN I'LL SACRIFICE ROCKET WARRIOR AND SUMMON A HIGHER-LEVEL MONSTER...

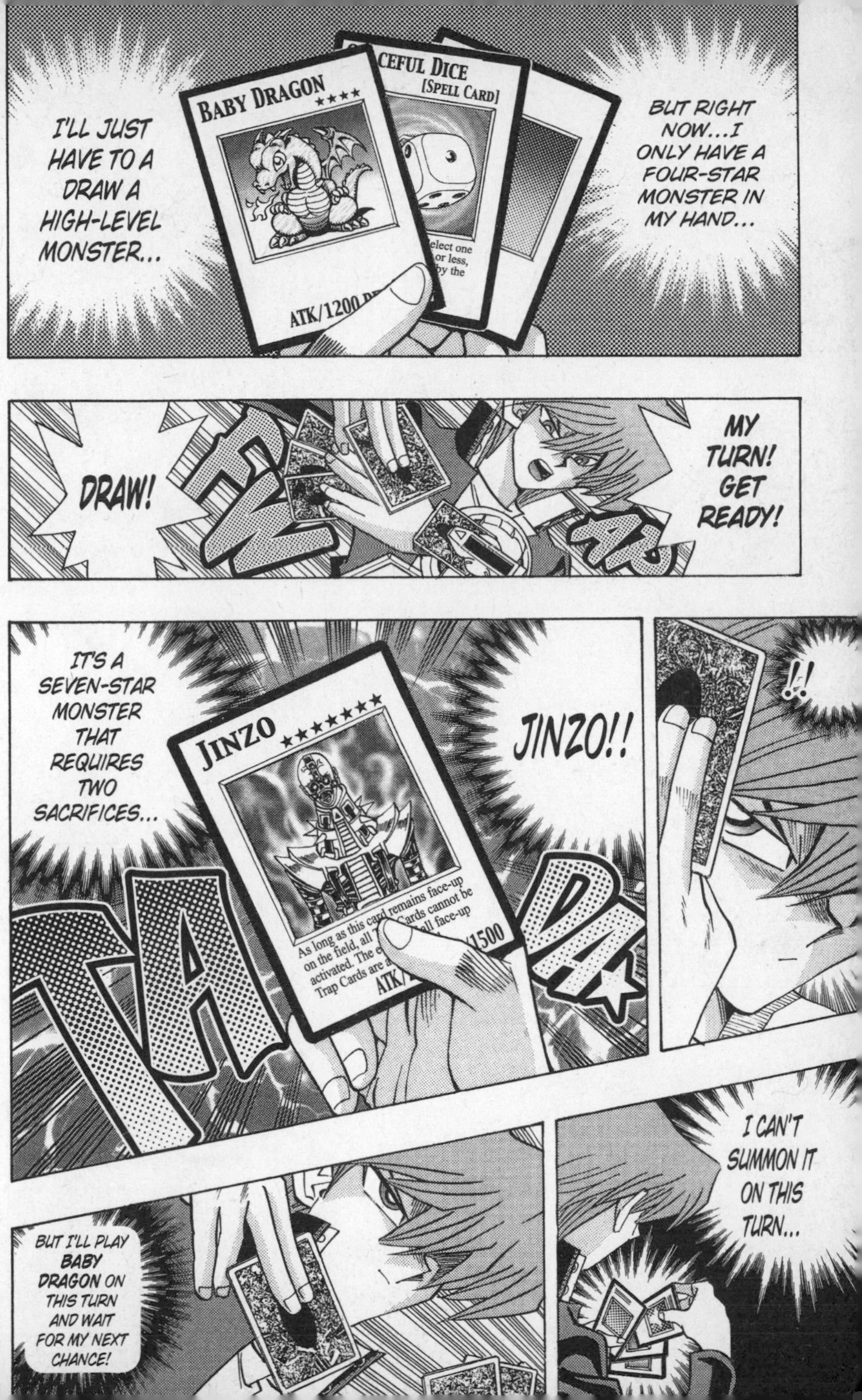
BUT RIGHT NOW...I ONLY HAVE A FOUR-STAR MONSTER IN MY HAND...
BABY DRAGON
[SPELL CARD]
ATK/1200
I'LL JUST HAVE TO A DRAW A HIGH-LEVEL MONSTER...
MY TURN! GET READY!
DRAW!
!!
JINZO!!
JINZO
IT'S A SEVEN-STAR MONSTER THAT REQUIRES TWO SACRIFICES...
TA DA★
I CAN'T SUMMON IT ON THIS TURN...
BUT I'LL PLAY BABY DRAGON ON THIS TURN AND WAIT FOR MY NEXT CHANCE!

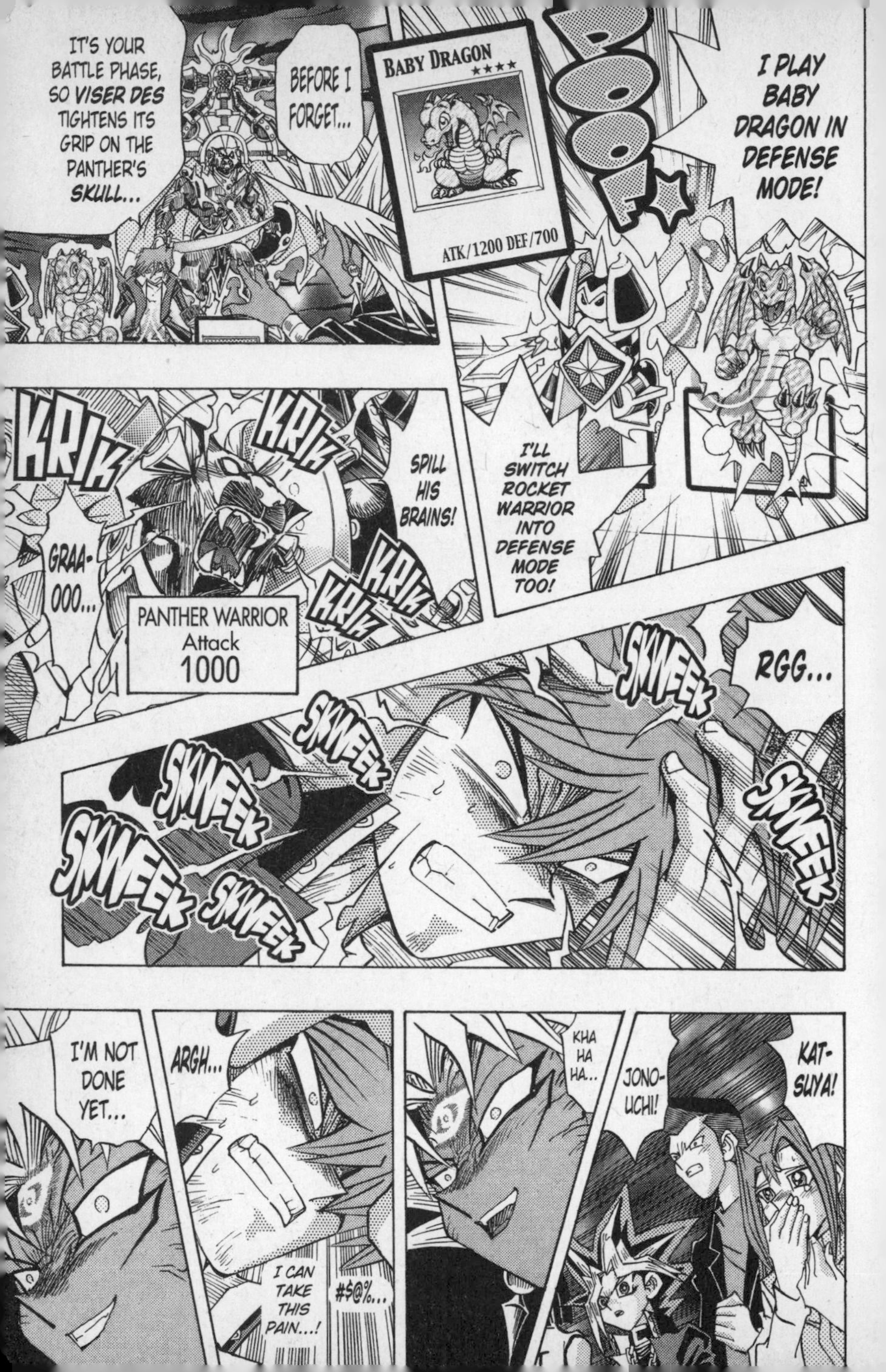
BOOOF
I PLAY BABY DRAGON IN DEFENSE MODE!
BABY DRAGON ★★★★
ATK/1200 DEF/700
BEFORE I FORGET...
IT'S YOUR BATTLE PHASE, SO VISER DES TIGHTENS ITS GRIP ON THE PANTHER'S SKULL...
I'LL SWITCH ROCKET WARRIOR INTO DEFENSE MODE TOO!
SPILL HIS BRAINS!
KRIK
KRIK
KRIK
KRIK
GRAA-OOO...
PANTHER WARRIOR
Attack
1000
RGG...
SKWEEK
SKWEEK
SKWEEK
SKWEEK
SKWEEK
SKWEEK
KAT-SUYA!
JONO-UCHI!
KHA HA HA...
#$%...
I CAN TAKE THIS PAIN...!
ARGH...
I'M NOT DONE YET...

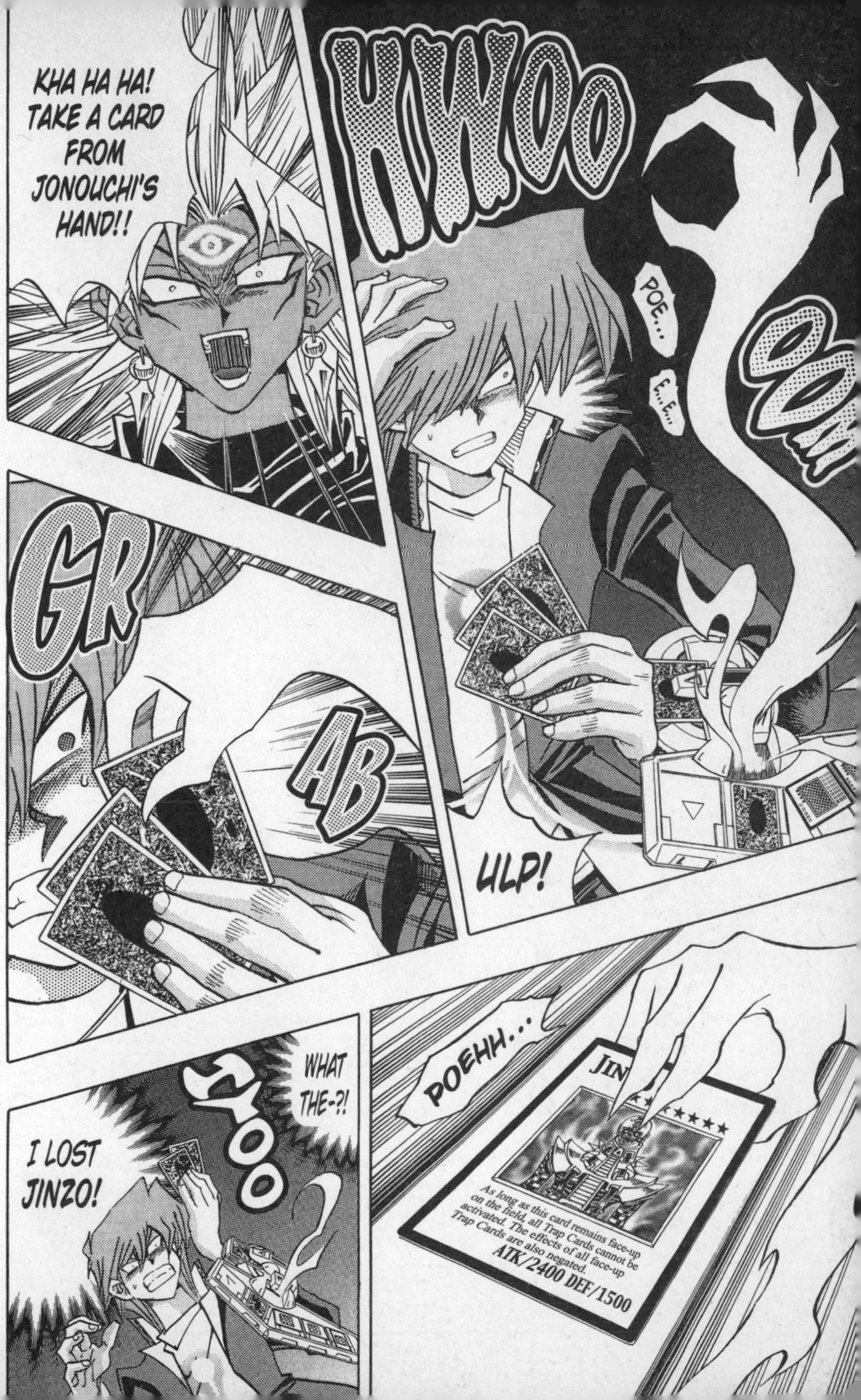
POE...
E...E...
ULP!
KHA HA HA! TAKE A CARD FROM JONOUCHI'S HAND!!
GR
AB
POEHH...
As long as this card remains face-up on the field, all Trap Cards cannot be activated. The effects of all face-up Trap Cards are also negated.
ATK/2400 DEF/1500
WHAT THE-?!
I LOST JINZO!

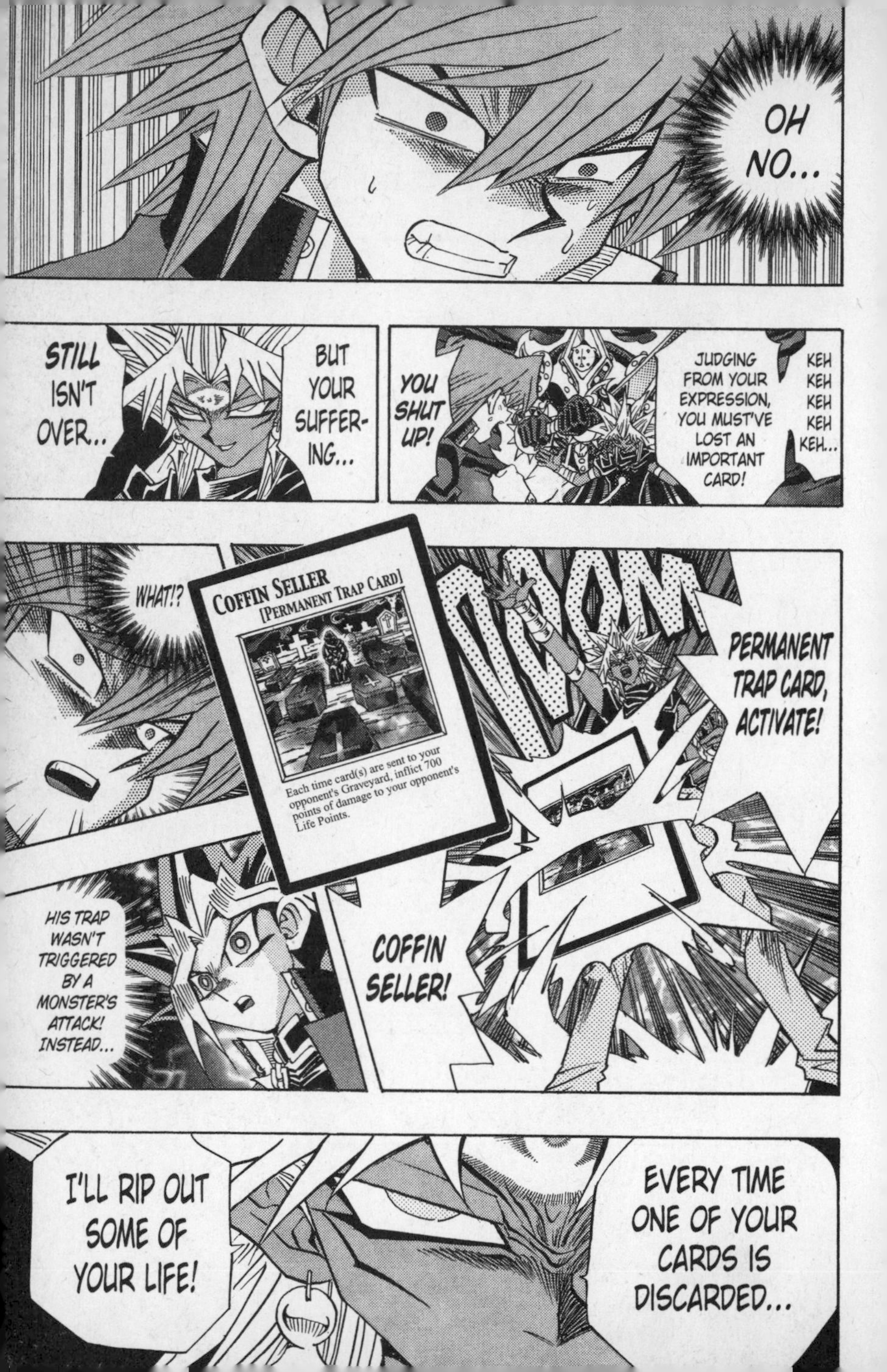
OH NO...
KEH KEH KEH KEH KEH...
JUDGING FROM YOUR EXPRESSION, YOU MUST'VE LOST AN IMPORTANT CARD!
YOU SHUT UP!
BUT YOUR SUFFER-ING...
STILL ISN'T OVER...
DOOM
PERMANENT TRAP CARD, ACTIVATE!
WHAT!?
COFFIN SELLER
[PERMANENT TRAP CARD]
Each time card(s) are sent to your opponent's Graveyard, inflict 700 points of damage to your opponent's Life Points.
COFFIN SELLER!
HIS TRAP WASN'T TRIGGERED BY A MONSTER'S ATTACK! INSTEAD...
EVERY TIME ONE OF YOUR CARDS IS DISCARDED...
I'LL RIP OUT SOME OF YOUR LIFE!

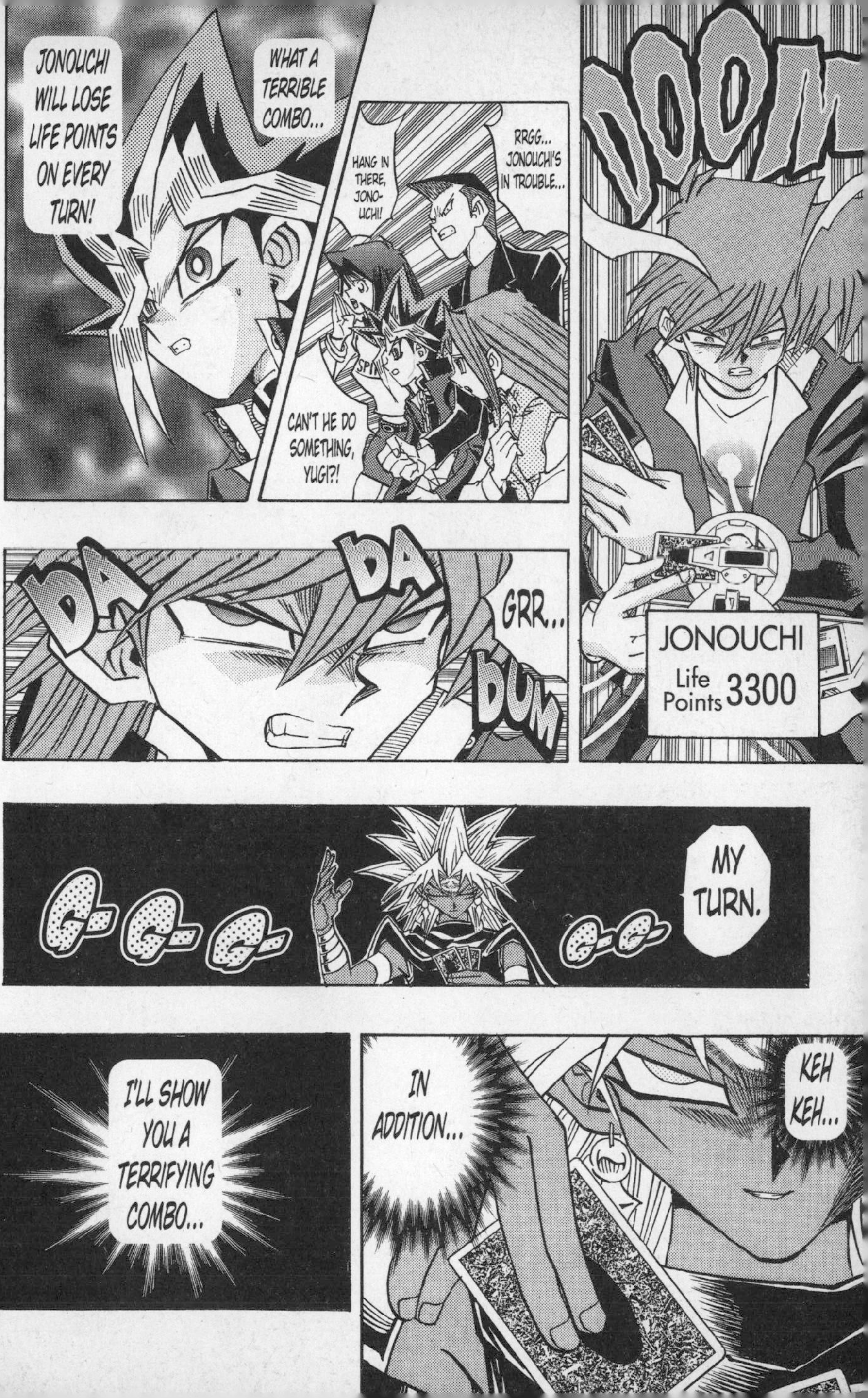
DOOM
JONOUCHI
Life Points 3300
RRGG... JONOUCHI'S IN TROUBLE...
HANG IN THERE, JONO-UCHI!
SPIN
CAN'T HE DO SOMETHING, YUGI?!
WHAT A TERRIBLE COMBO...
JONOUCHI WILL LOSE LIFE POINTS ON EVERY TURN!
GRR...
DA
DA
DUM
MY TURN.
G-G-G-
G-G-
KEH KEH...
IN ADDITION...
I'LL SHOW YOU A TERRIFYING COMBO...

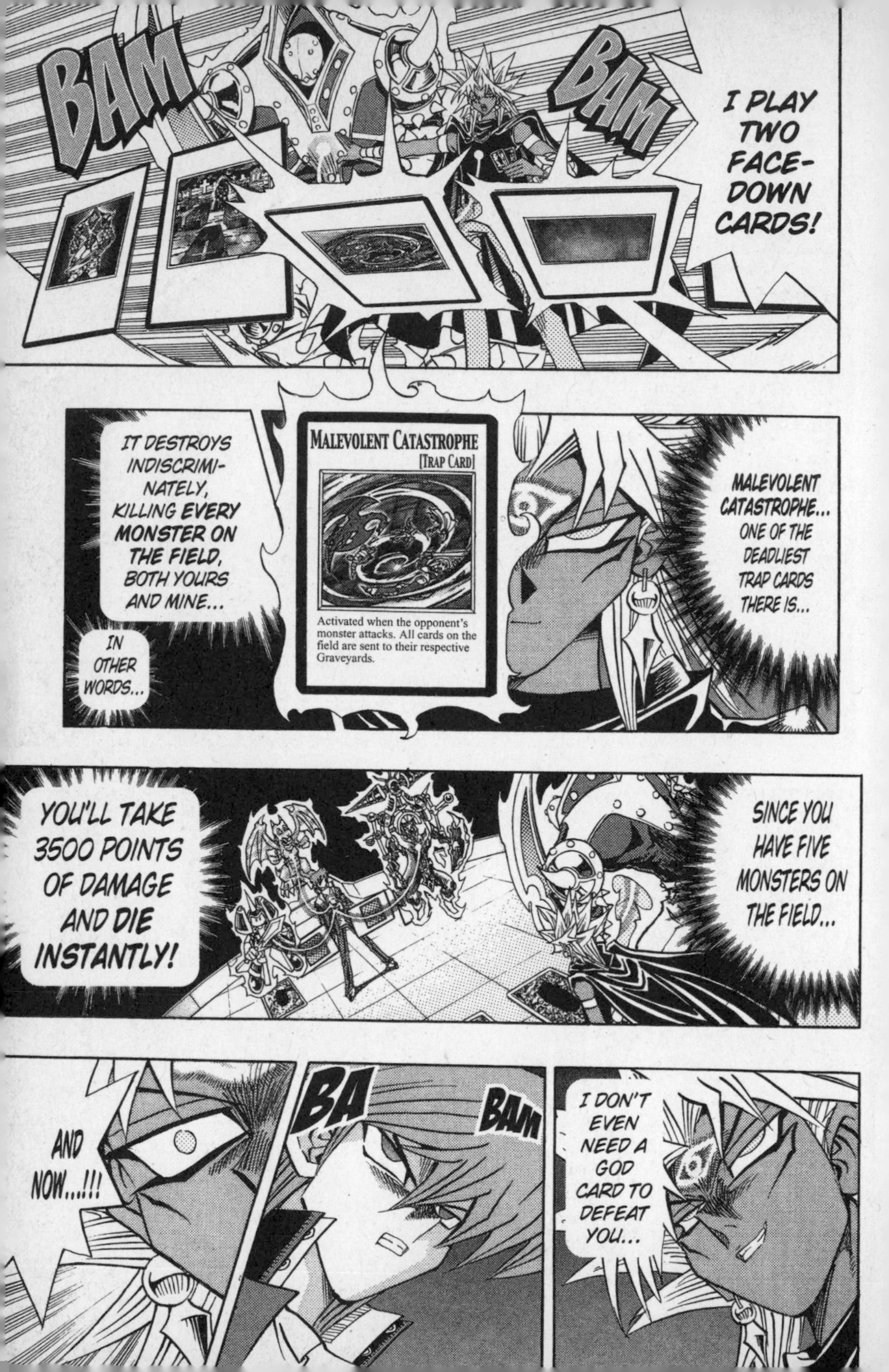
I PLAY TWO FACE-DOWN CARDS!
BAM
BAM
MALEVOLENT CATASTROPHE... ONE OF THE DEADLIEST TRAP CARDS THERE IS...
MALEVOLENT CATASTROPHE
[TRAP CARD]
Activated when the opponent's monster attacks. All cards on the field are sent to their respective Graveyards.
IT DESTROYS INDISCRIMINATELY, KILLING EVERY MONSTER ON THE FIELD, BOTH YOURS AND MINE...
IN OTHER WORDS...
SINCE YOU HAVE FIVE MONSTERS ON THE FIELD...
YOU'LL TAKE 3500 POINTS OF DAMAGE AND DIE INSTANTLY!
I DON'T EVEN NEED A GOD CARD TO DEFEAT YOU...
BA
BAM
AND NOW...!!!

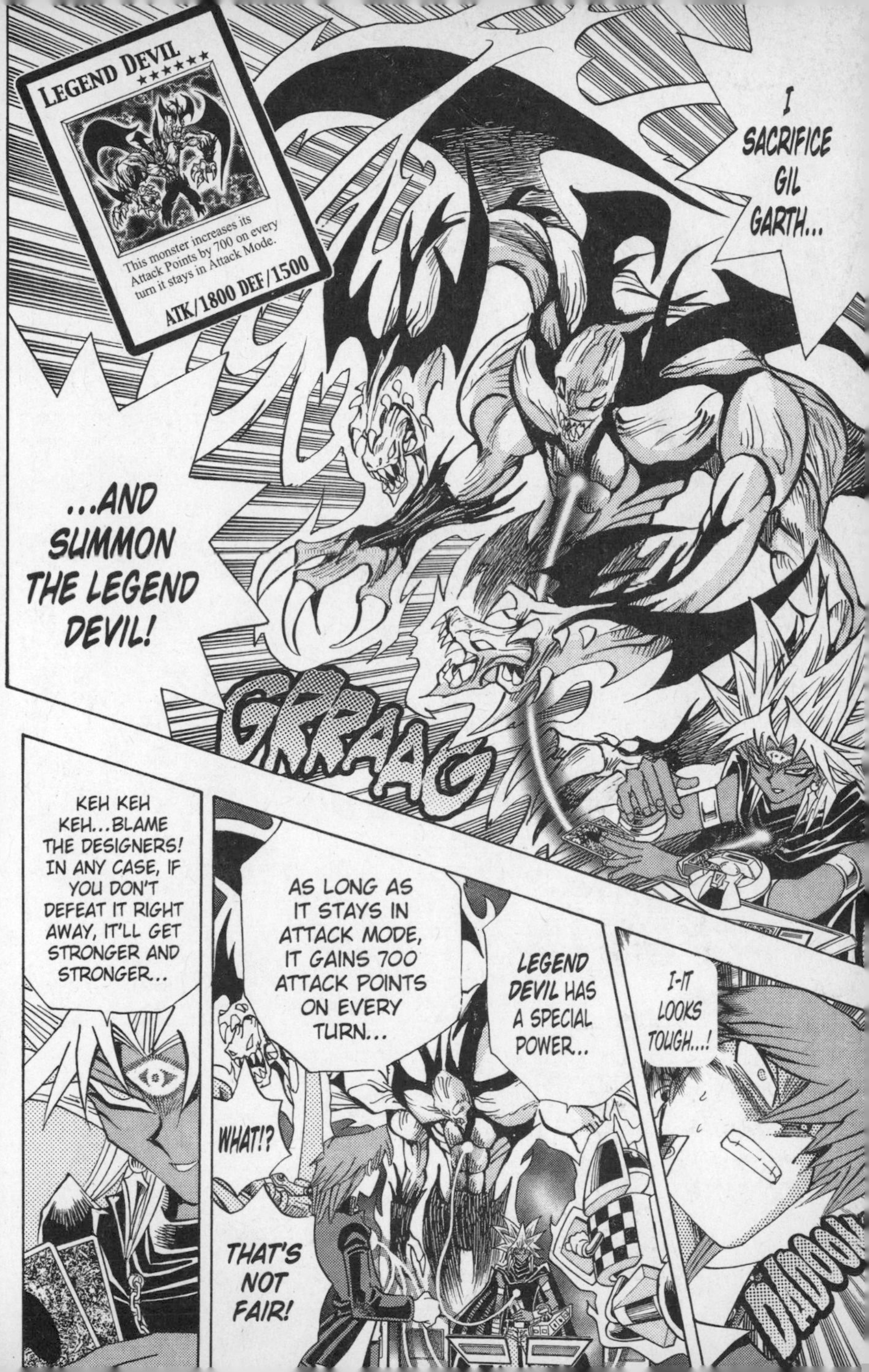
I SACRIFICE GIL GARTH...
LEGEND DEVIL
This monster increases its Attack Points by 700 on every turn it stays in Attack Mode.
ATK/1800 DEF/1500
...AND SUMMON THE LEGEND DEVIL!
GRRAAG
I-IT LOOKS TOUGH...!
LEGEND DEVIL HAS A SPECIAL POWER...
AS LONG AS IT STAYS IN ATTACK MODE, IT GAINS 700 ATTACK POINTS ON EVERY TURN...
WHAT!?
THAT'S NOT FAIR!
KEH KEH KEH...BLAME THE DESIGNERS! IN ANY CASE, IF YOU DON'T DEFEAT IT RIGHT AWAY, IT'LL GET STRONGER AND STRONGER...

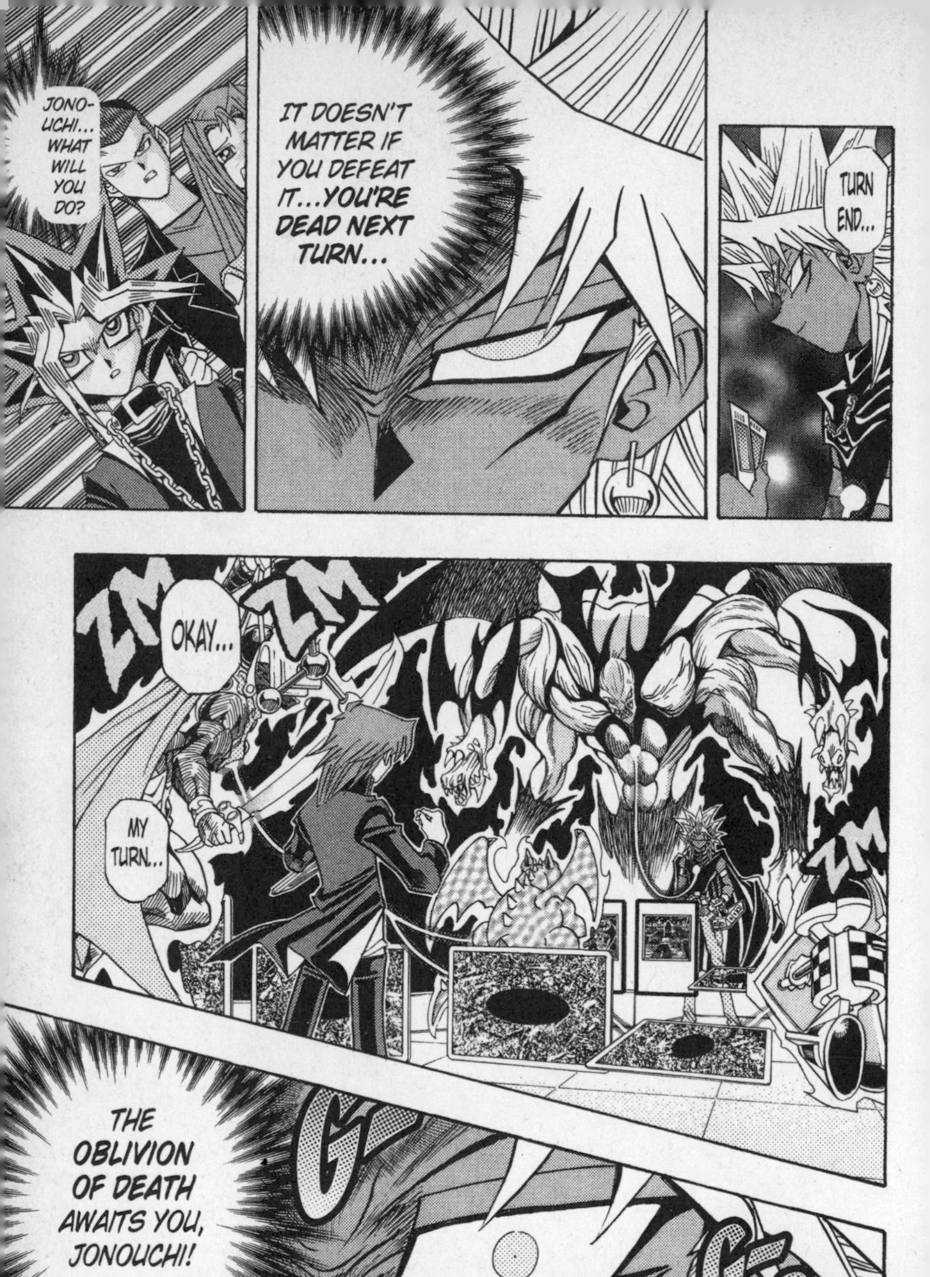
TURN END...
IT DOESN'T MATTER IF YOU DEFEAT IT...YOU'RE DEAD NEXT TURN...
JONOUCHI... WHAT WILL YOU DO?
ZM ZM
OKAY...
MY TURN...
ZM
THE OBLIVION OF DEATH AWAITS YOU, JONOUCHI!
G
G-G-

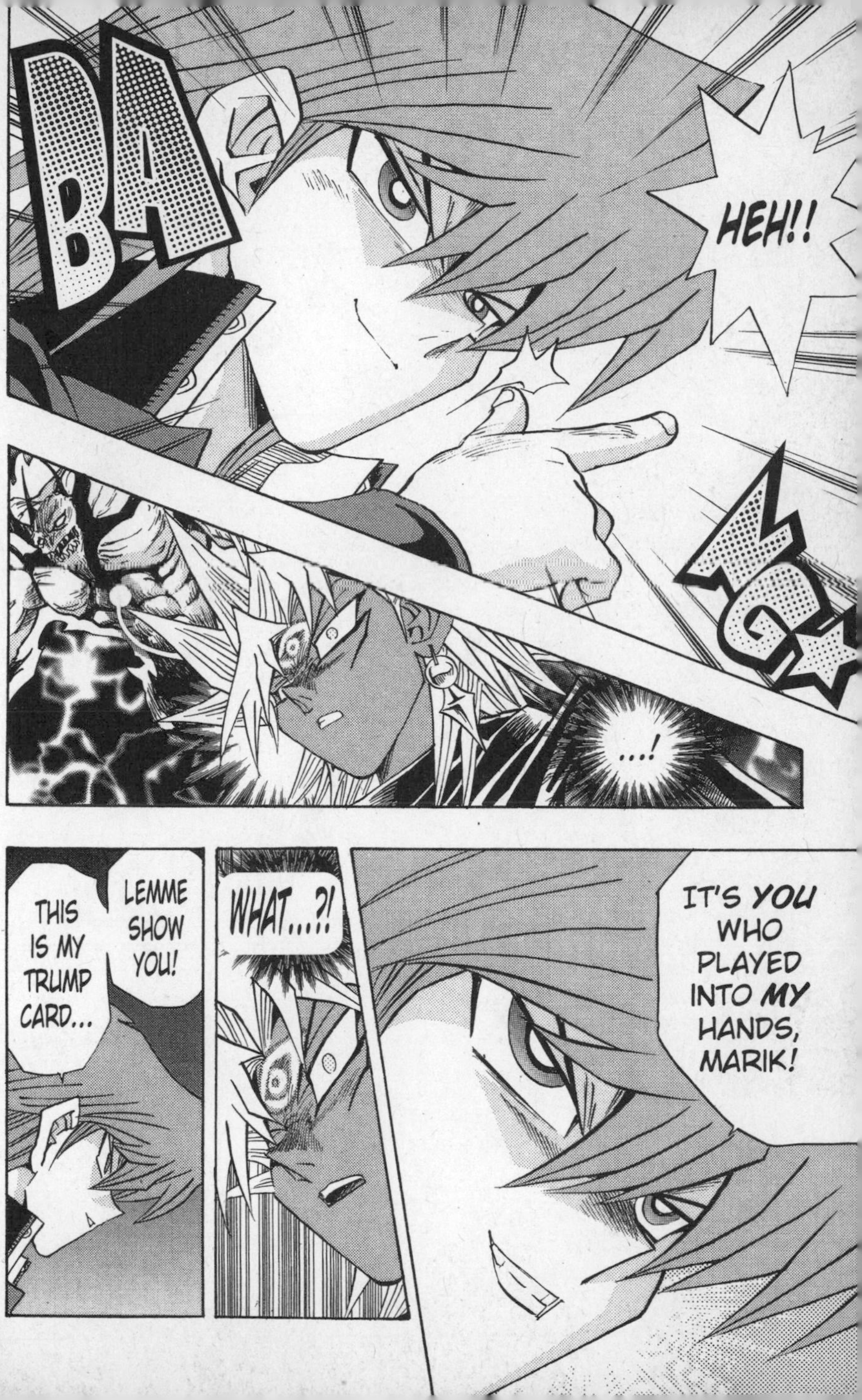
HEH!!
BA
G
...!
IT'S YOU WHO PLAYED INTO MY HANDS, MARIK!
WHAT...?!
LEMME SHOW YOU!
THIS IS MY TRUMP CARD...

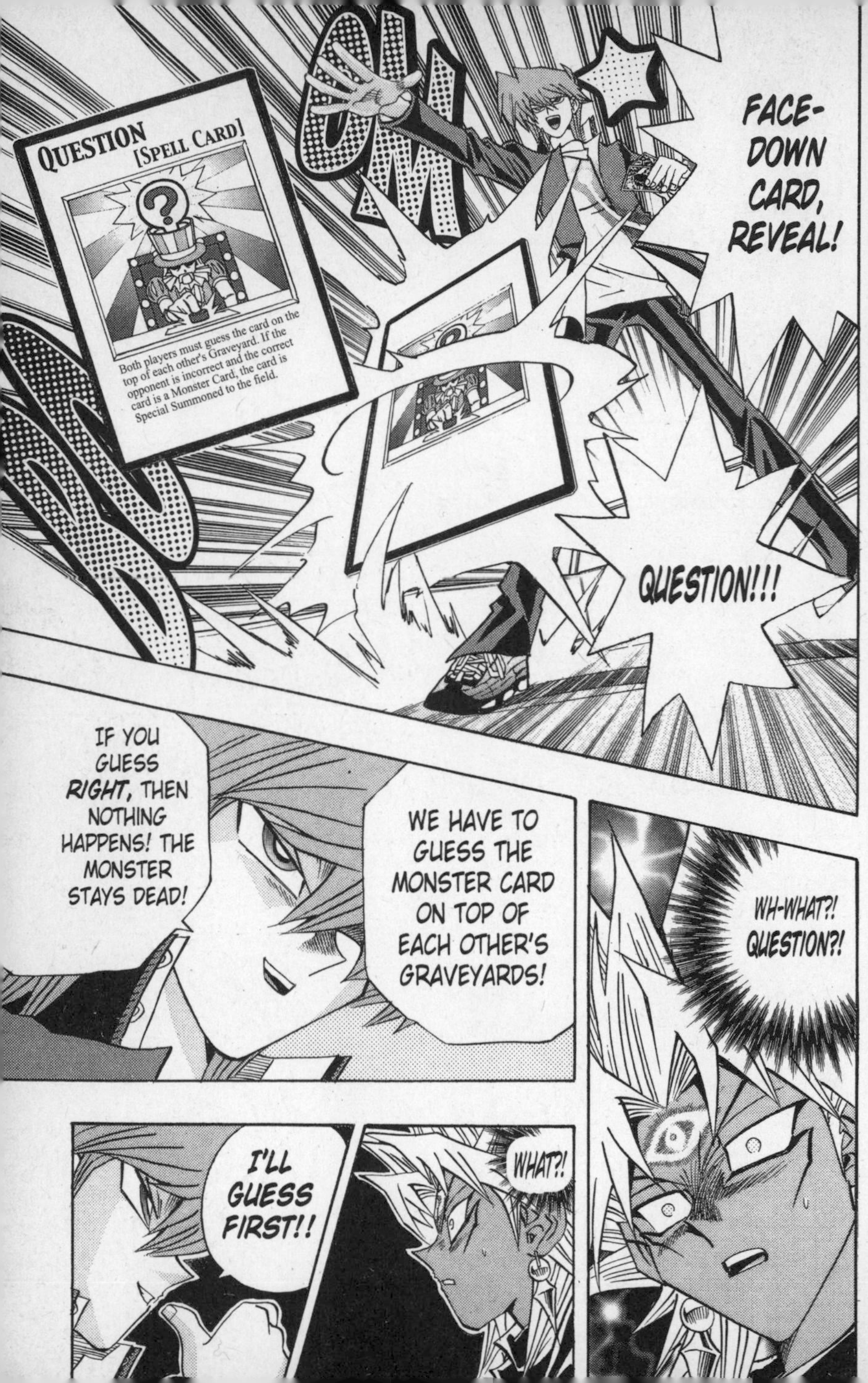
FACE-DOWN CARD, REVEAL!
QUESTION [SPELL CARD]
Both players must guess the card on the top of each other's Graveyard. If the opponent is incorrect and the correct card is a Monster Card, the card is Special Summoned to the field.
QUESTION!!!
WH-WHAT?! QUESTION?!
WE HAVE TO GUESS THE MONSTER CARD ON TOP OF EACH OTHER'S GRAVEYARDS!
IF YOU GUESS RIGHT, THEN NOTHING HAPPENS! THE MONSTER STAYS DEAD!
WHAT?!
I'LL GUESS FIRST!!

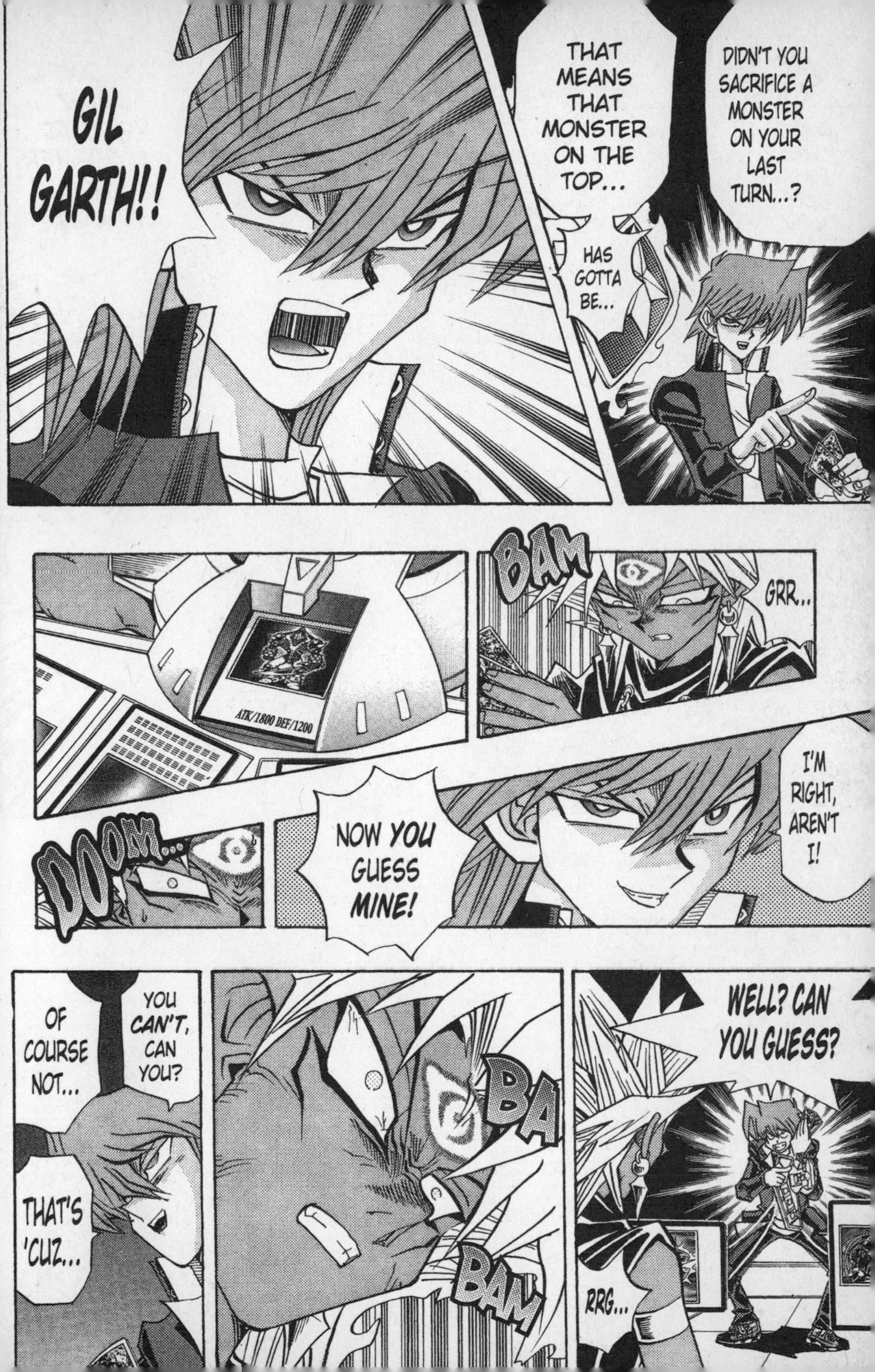
DIDN'T YOU SACRIFICE A MONSTER ON YOUR LAST TURN...?
THAT MEANS THAT MONSTER ON THE TOP...
HAS GOTTA BE...
GIL GARTH!!
BAM
GRR...
ATK/1800 DEF/1200
I'M RIGHT, AREN'T I!
NOW YOU GUESS MINE!
DOOM...
WELL? CAN YOU GUESS?
RRG...
BA
BAM
YOU CAN'T, CAN YOU?
OF COURSE NOT...
THAT'S 'CUZ...

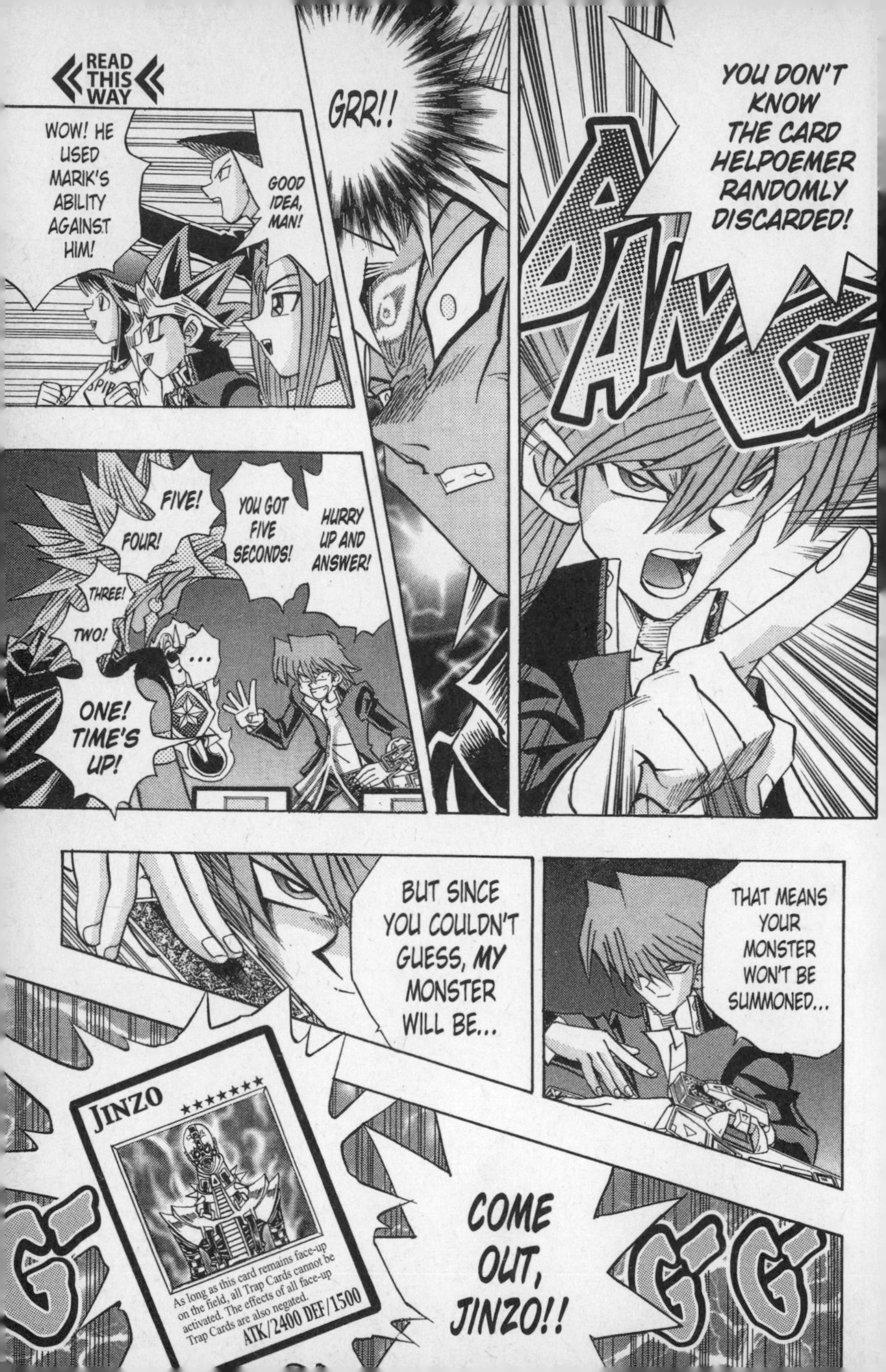
READ THIS WAY
YOU DON'T KNOW THE CARD HELPOEMER RANDOMLY DISCARDED!
GRR!!
WOW! HE USED MARIK'S ABILITY AGAINST HIM!
GOOD IDEA, MAN!
HURRY UP AND ANSWER!
YOU GOT FIVE SECONDS!
FIVE!
FOUR!
THREE!
TWO!
...
ONE! TIME'S UP!
THAT MEANS YOUR MONSTER WON'T BE SUMMONED...
BUT SINCE YOU COULDN'T GUESS, MY MONSTER WILL BE...
COME OUT, JINZO!!
JINZO
As long as this card remains face-up on the field, all Trap Cards cannot be activated. The effects of all face-up Trap Cards are also negated.
ATK/2400 DEF/1500

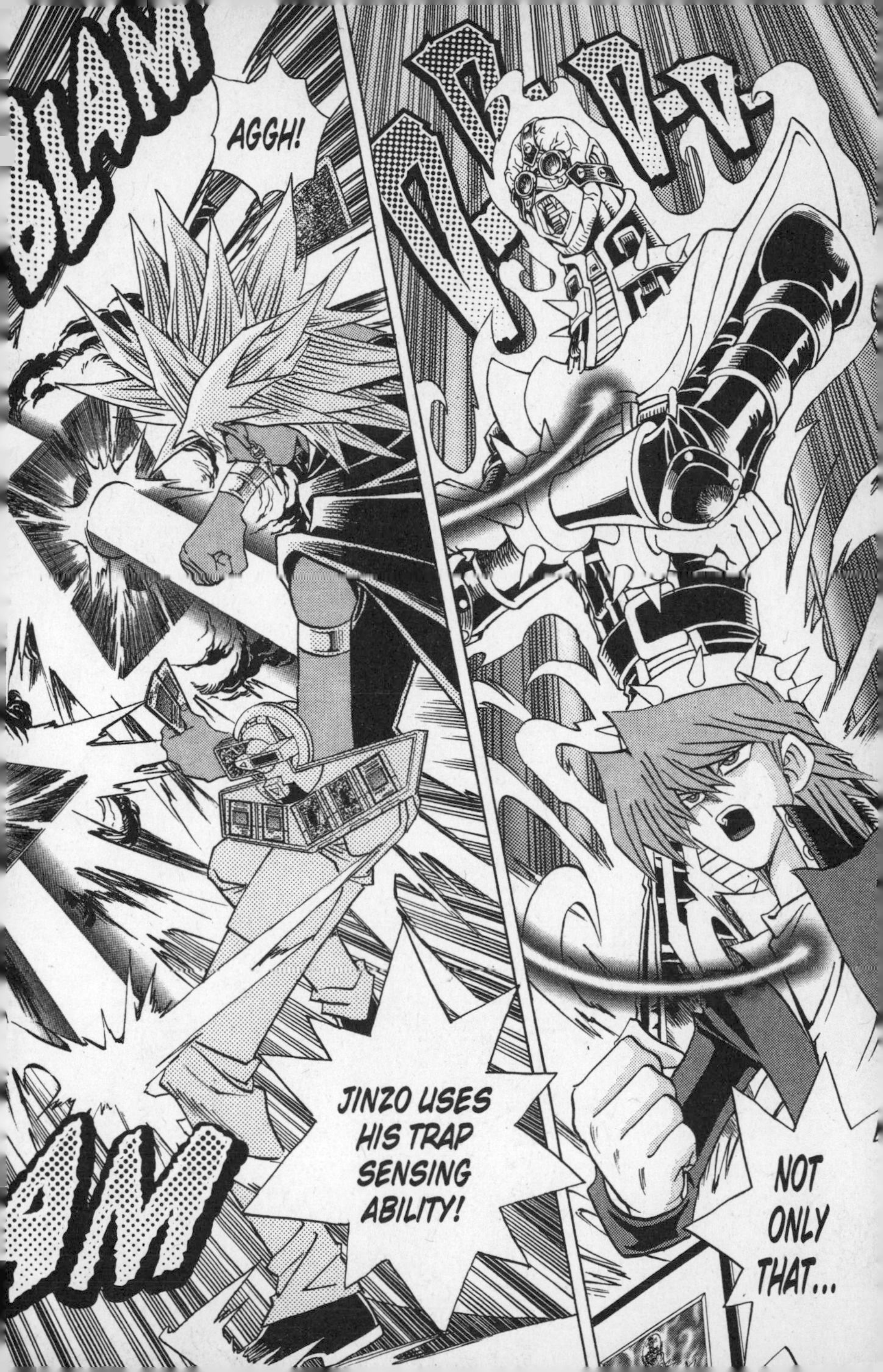
SLAM
AGGH!
JINZO USES HIS TRAP SENSING ABILITY!
SLAM
NOT ONLY THAT...

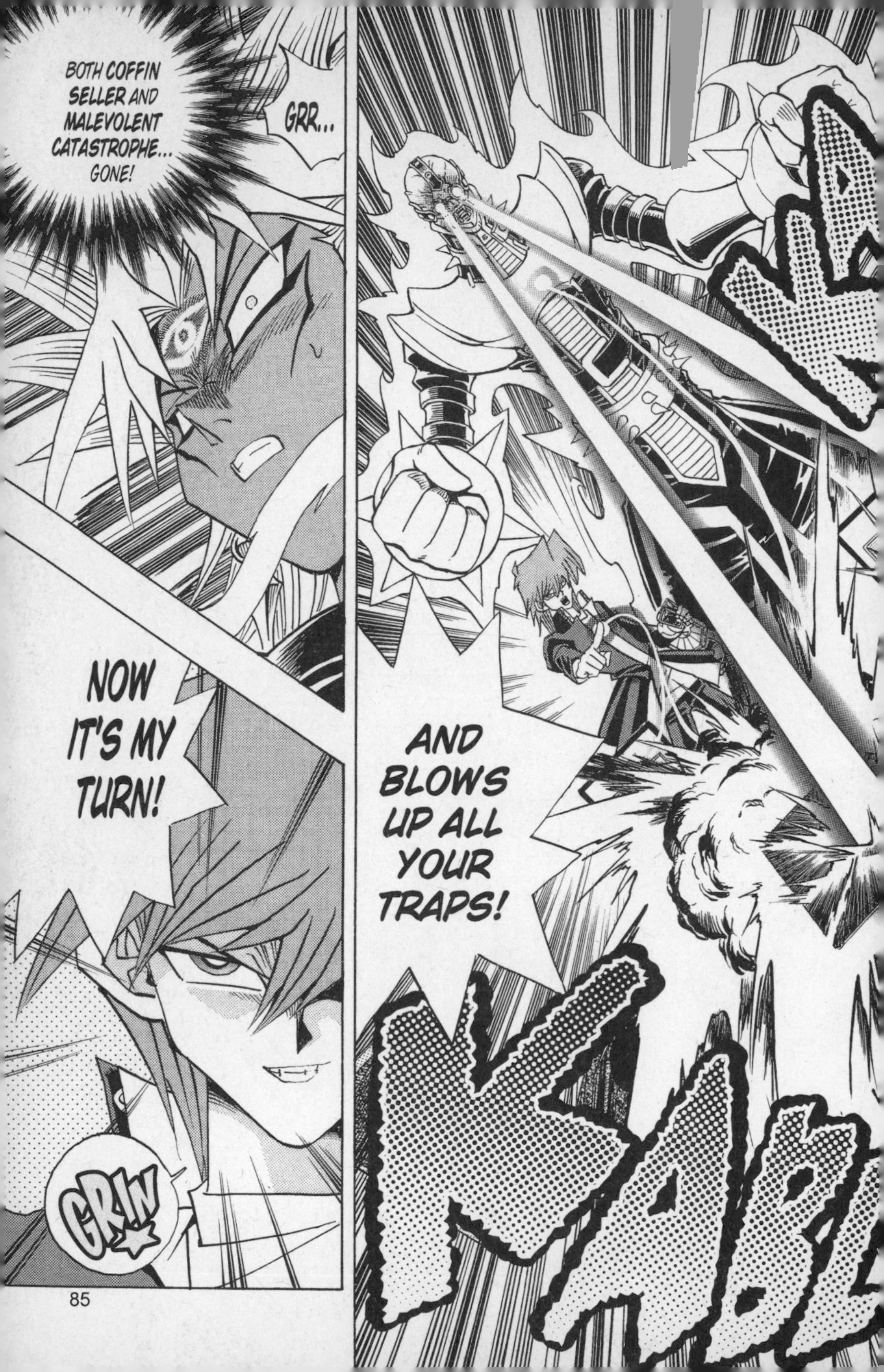
AND BLOWS UP ALL YOUR TRAPS!
BOTH COFFIN SELLER AND MALEVOLENT CATASTROPHE... GONE!
GRR...
NOW IT'S MY TURN!
GRIN

DUEL 187: CAGE OF FIRE!

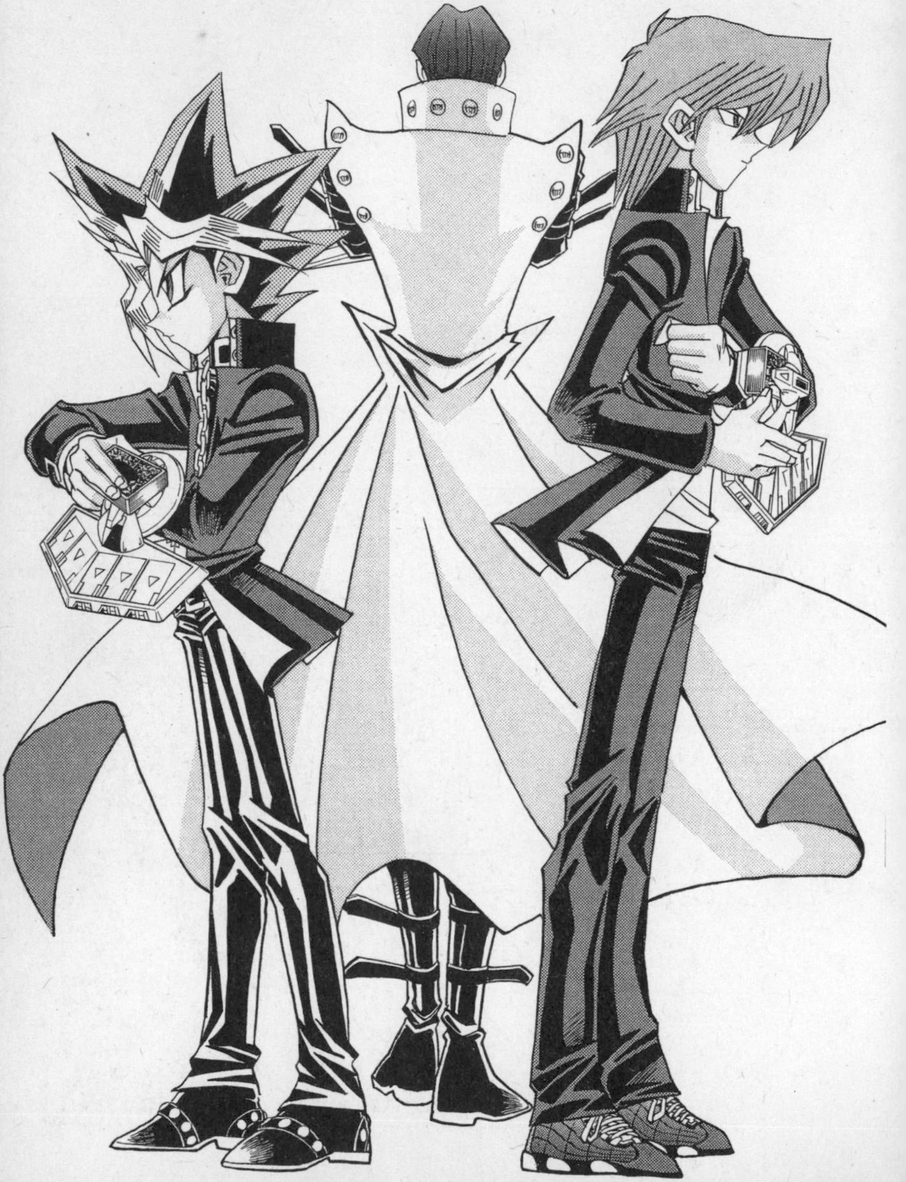

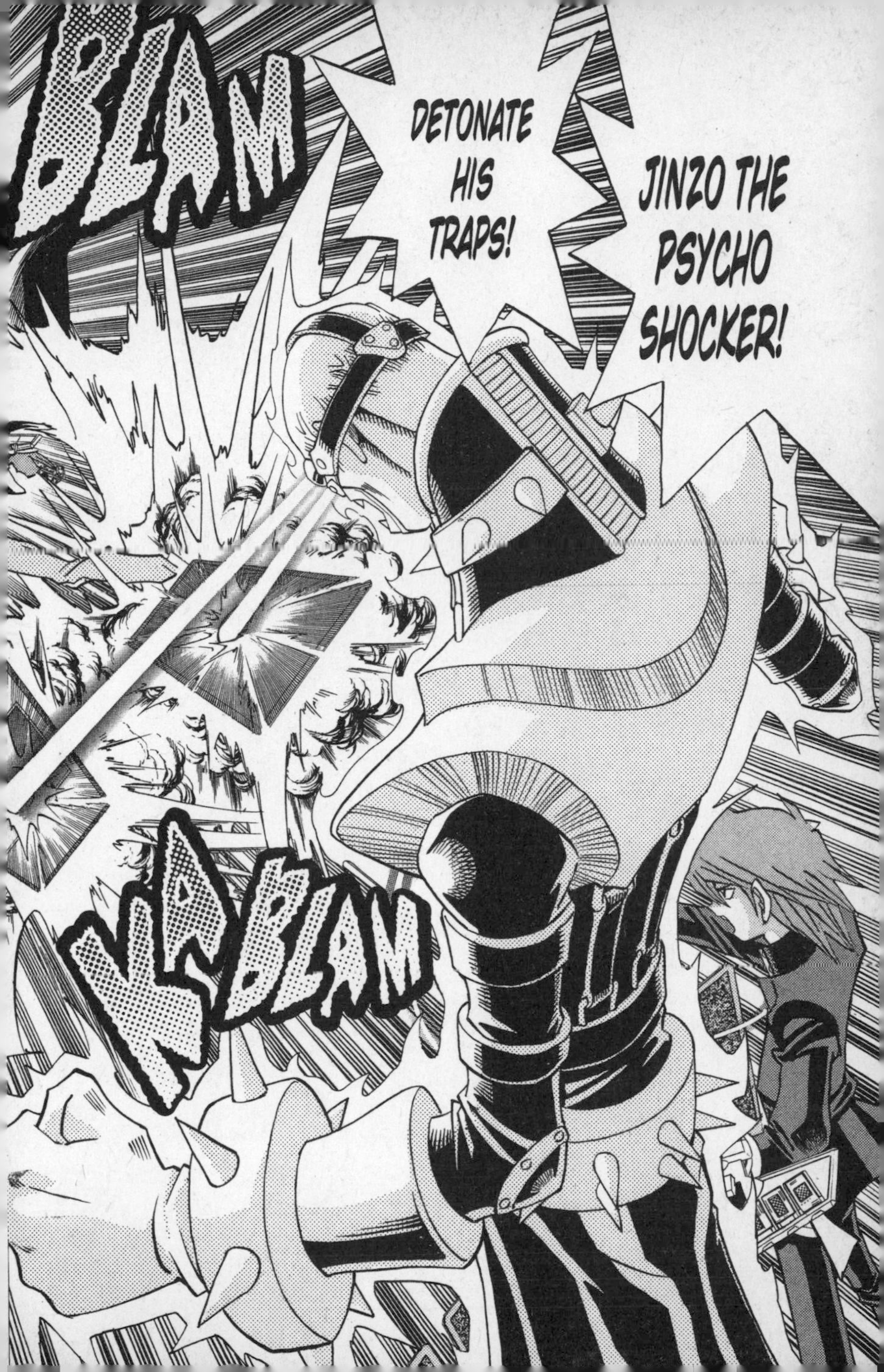
JINZO THE PSYCHO SHOCKER!
DETONATE HIS TRAPS!
BLAM
KABLAM

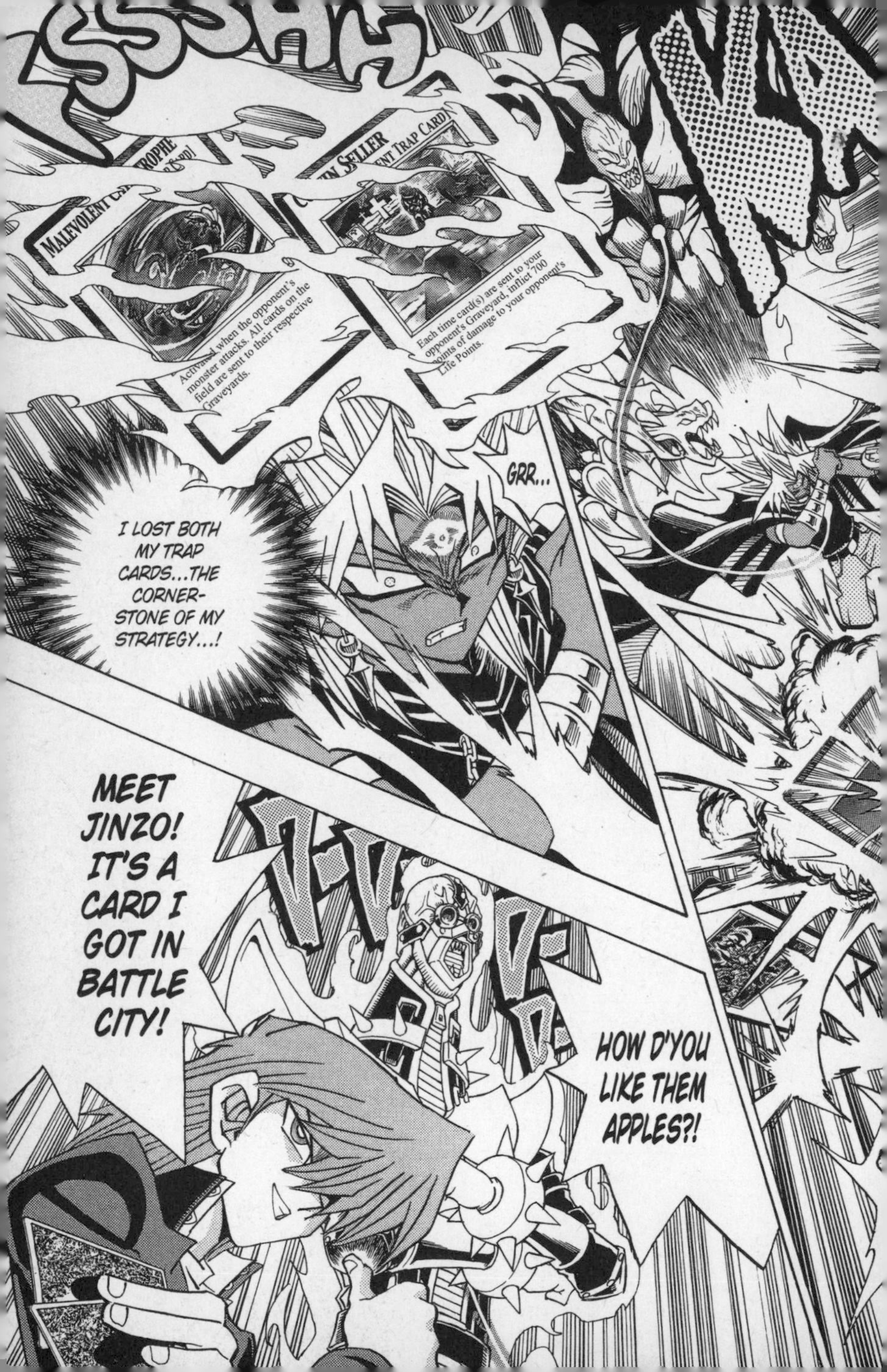
Activated when the opponent's monster attacks. All cards on the field are sent to their respective Graveyards.
Each time card(s) are sent to your opponent's Graveyard, inflict 700 points of damage to your opponent's Life Points.
GRR...
I LOST BOTH MY TRAP CARDS...THE CORNER-STONE OF MY STRATEGY...!
HOW D'YOU LIKE THEM APPLES?!
MEET JINZO! IT'S A CARD I GOT IN BATTLE CITY!

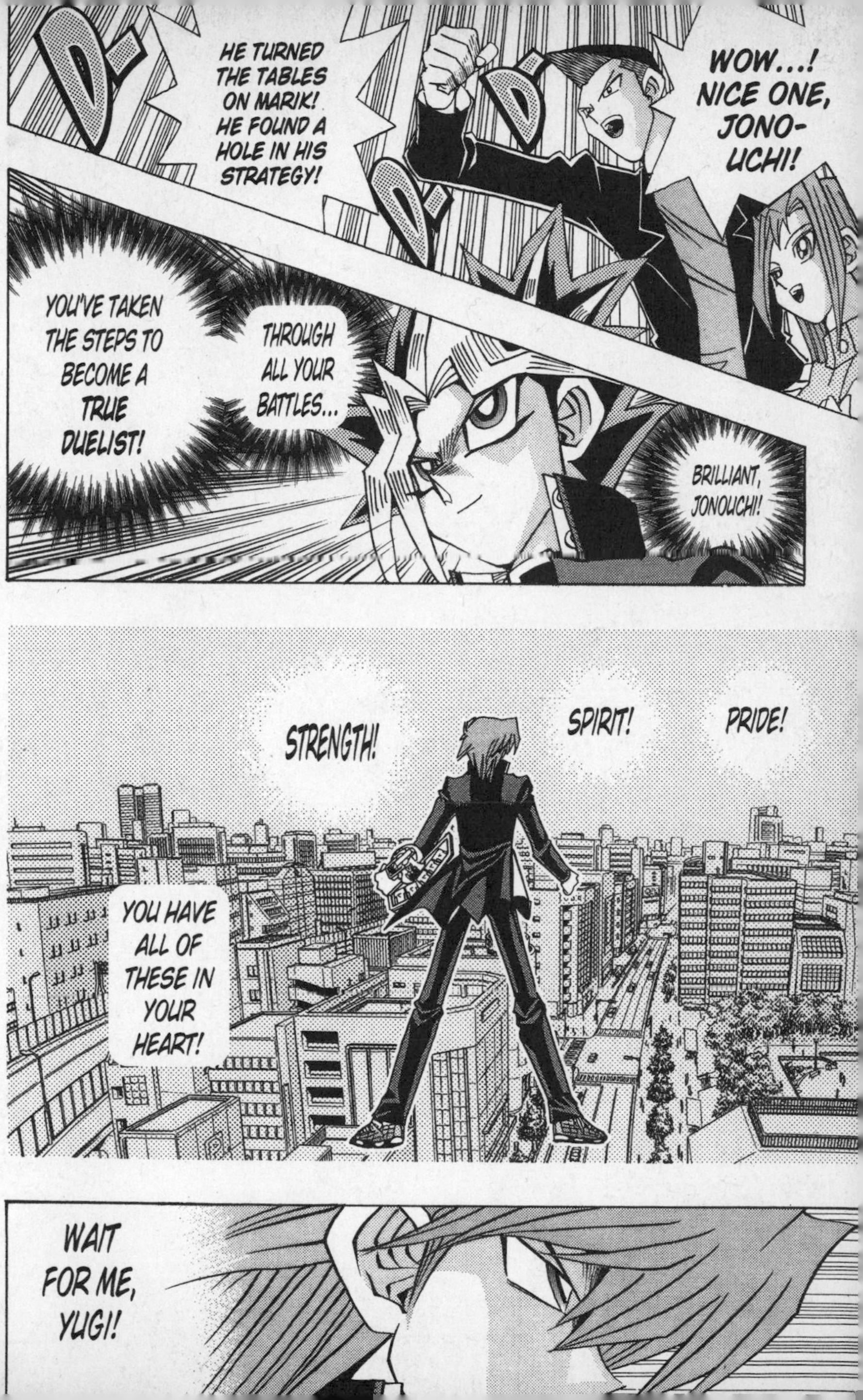
WOW...! NICE ONE, JONO-UCHI!
HE TURNED THE TABLES ON MARIK! HE FOUND A HOLE IN HIS STRATEGY!
D
BRILLIANT, JONOUCHI!
THROUGH ALL YOUR BATTLES...
YOU'VE TAKEN THE STEPS TO BECOME A TRUE DUELIST!
PRIDE!
SPIRIT!
STRENGTH!
YOU HAVE ALL OF THESE IN YOUR HEART!
WAIT FOR ME, YUGI!

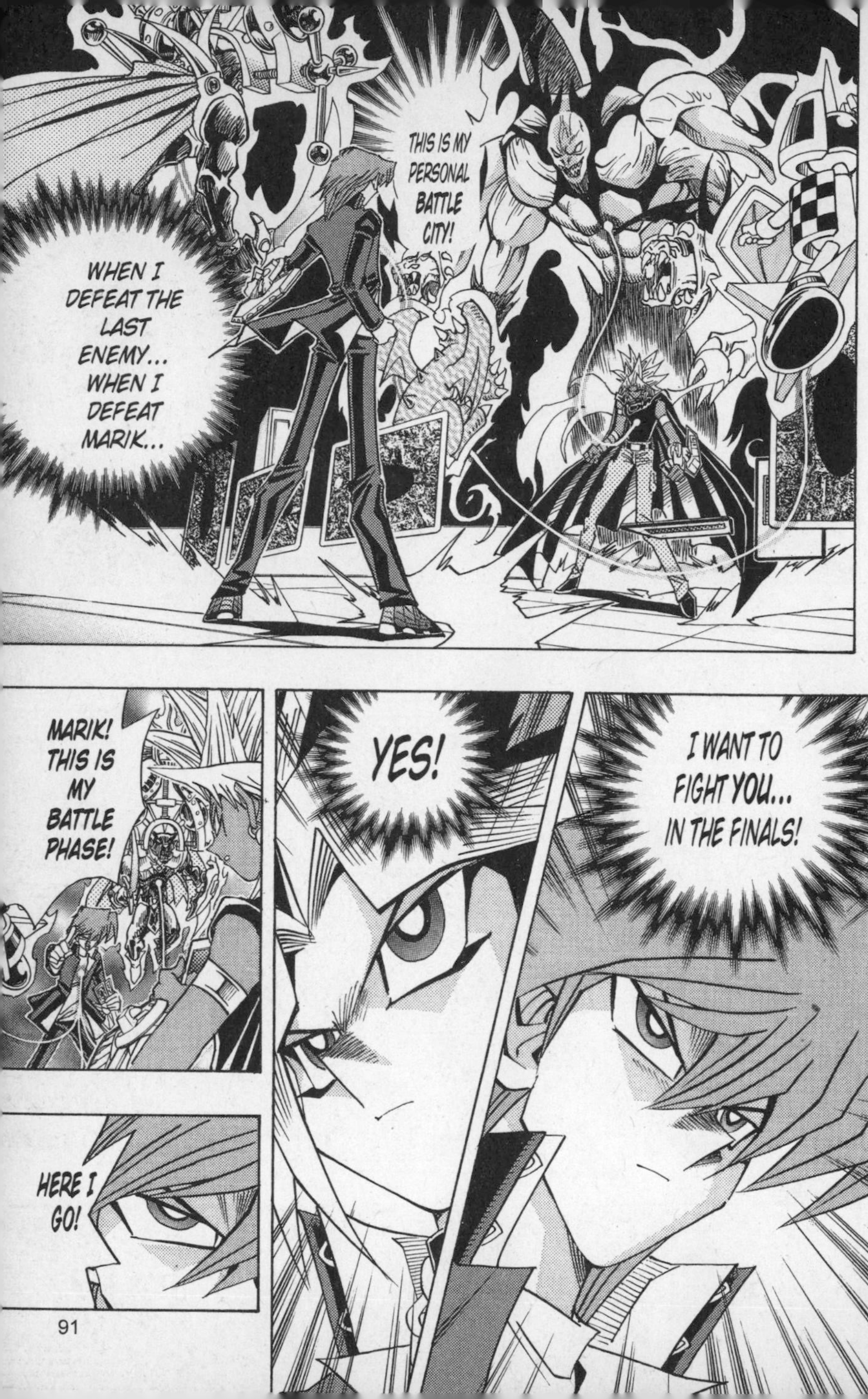
THIS IS MY PERSONAL BATTLE CITY!
WHEN I DEFEAT THE LAST ENEMY... WHEN I DEFEAT MARIK...
I WANT TO FIGHT YOU... IN THE FINALS!
YES!
MARIK! THIS IS MY BATTLE PHASE!
HERE I GO!

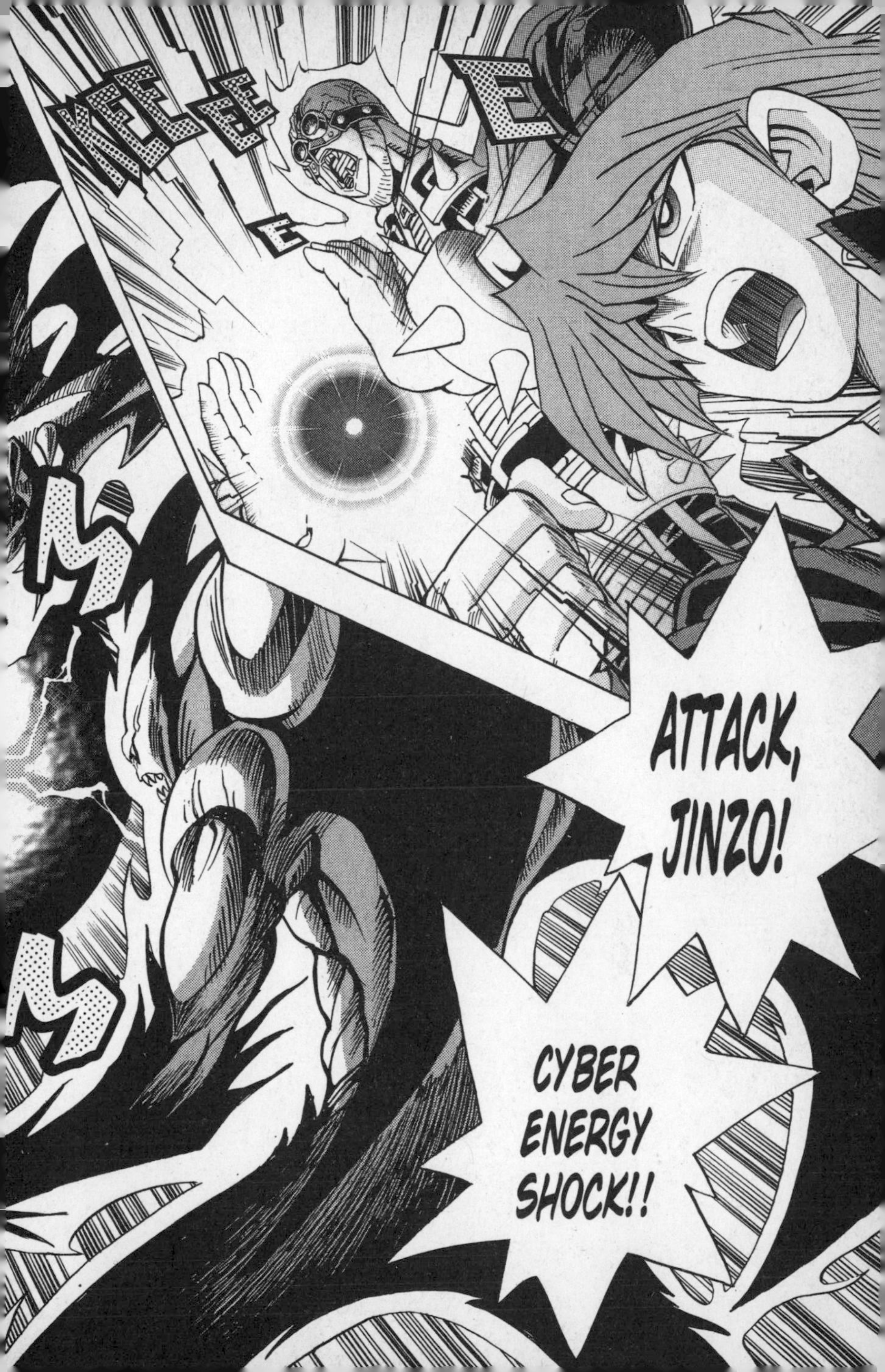
ATTACK, JINZO!
CYBER ENERGY SHOCK!!

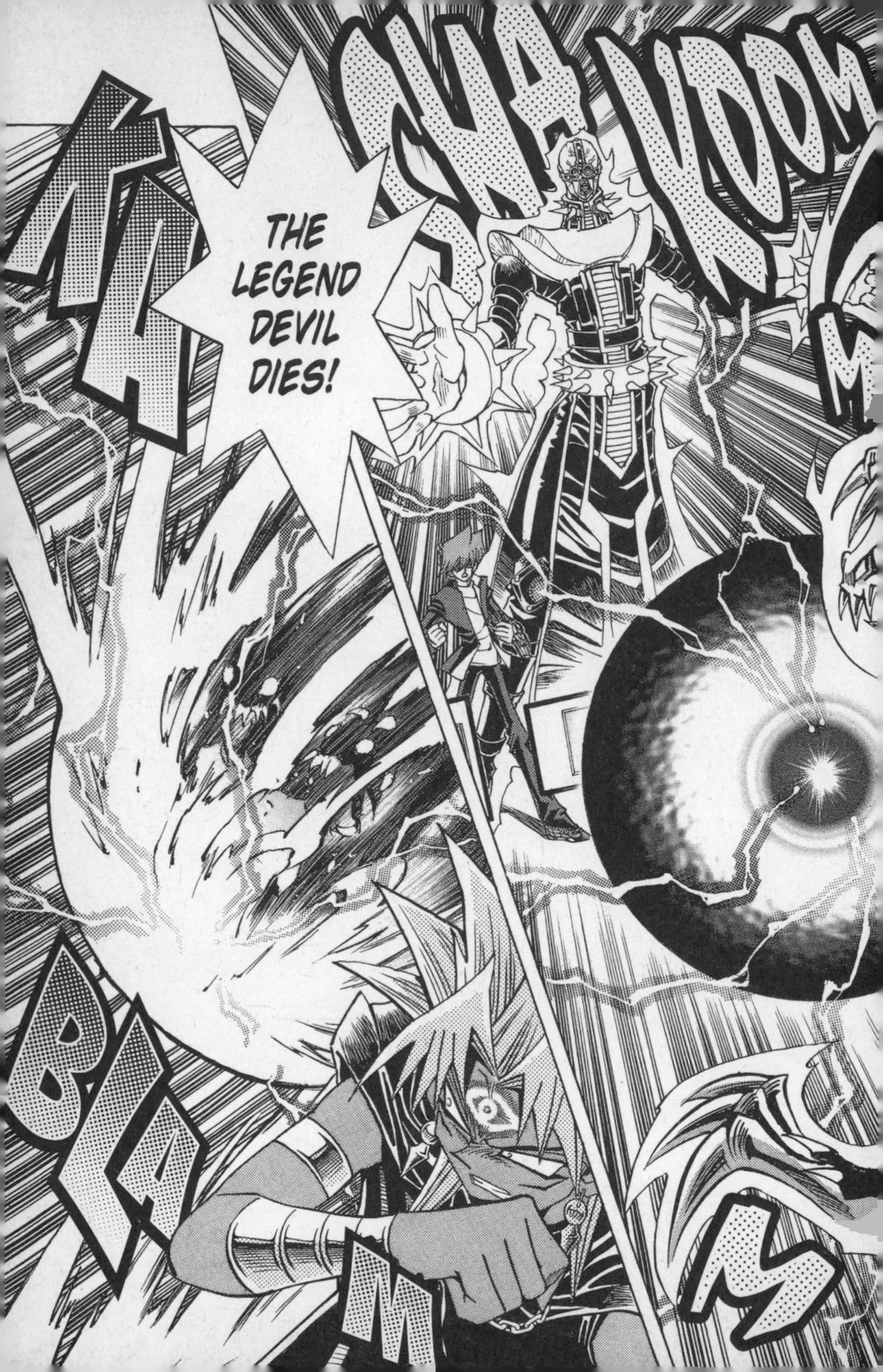
THE LEGEND DEVIL DIES!
BLAM

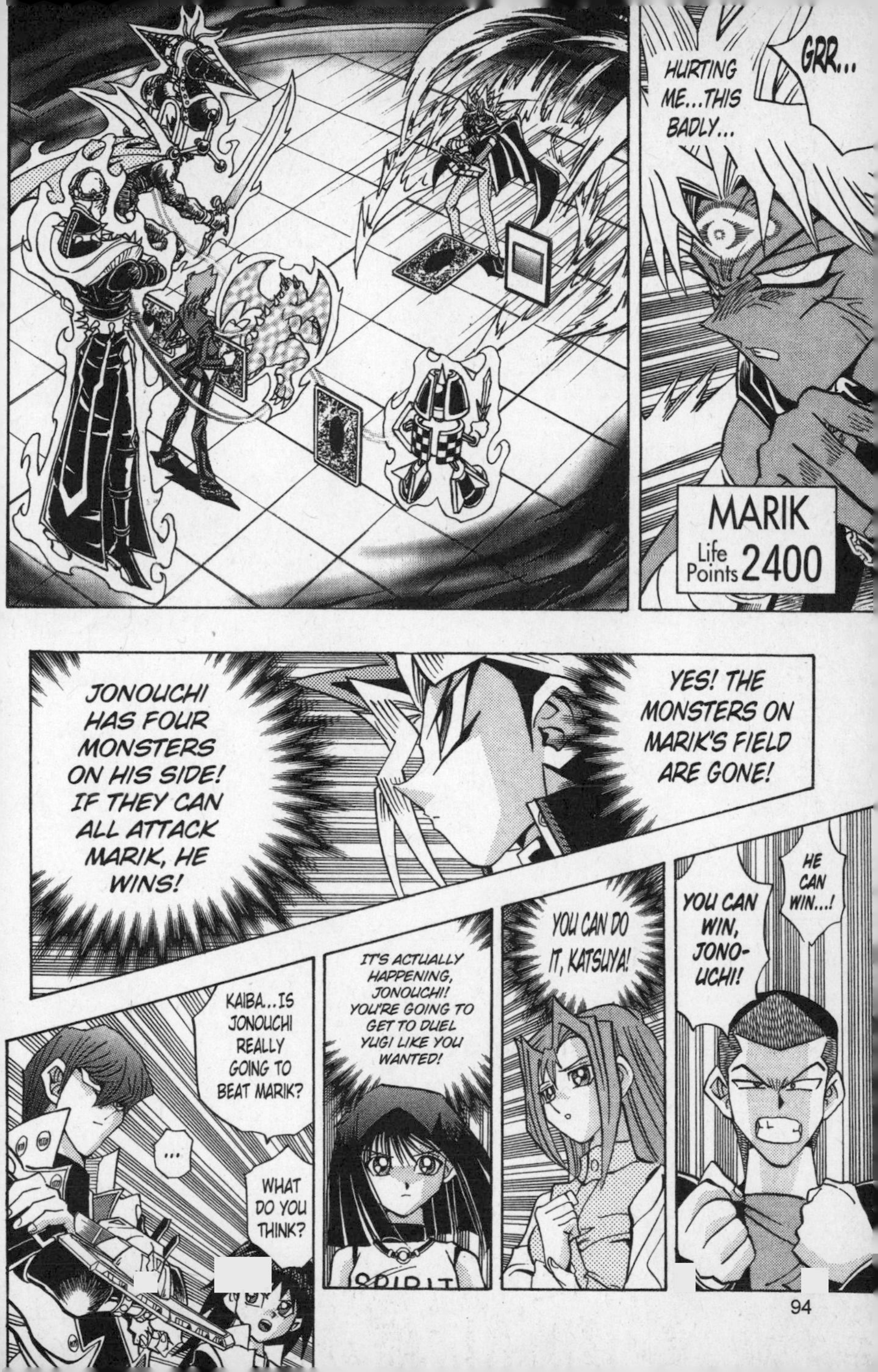
GRR...
HURTING ME...THIS BADLY...
MARIK
Life Points 2400
YES! THE MONSTERS ON MARIK'S FIELD ARE GONE!
JONOUCHI HAS FOUR MONSTERS ON HIS SIDE! IF THEY CAN ALL ATTACK MARIK, HE WINS!
HE CAN WIN...!
YOU CAN WIN, JONO-UCHI!
YOU CAN DO IT, KATSUYA!
IT'S ACTUALLY HAPPENING, JONOUCHI! YOU'RE GOING TO GET TO DUEL YUGI LIKE YOU WANTED!
KAIBA...IS JONOUCHI REALLY GOING TO BEAT MARIK?
...
WHAT DO YOU THINK?

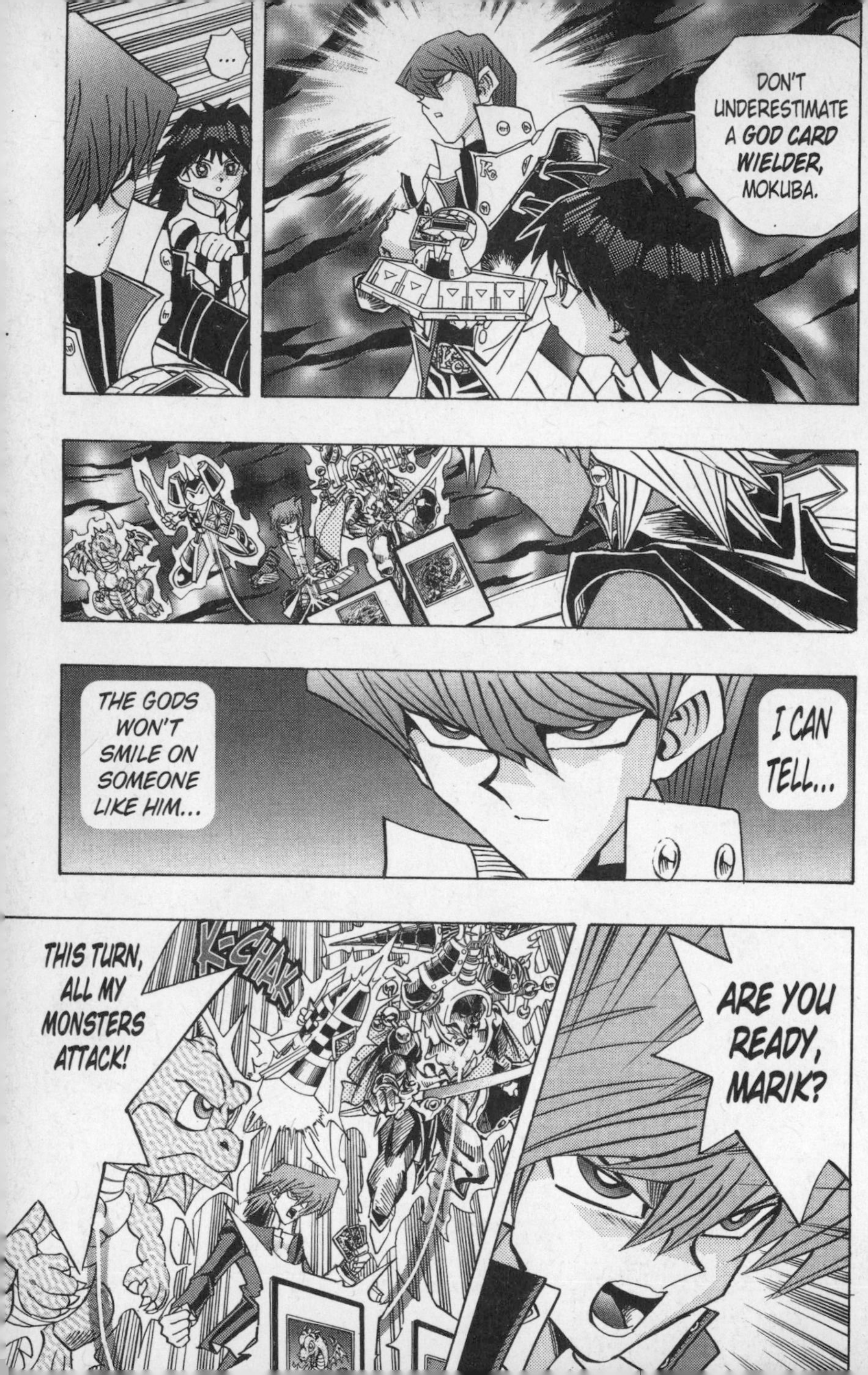
DON'T UNDERESTIMATE A GOD CARD WIELDER, MOKUBA.
...
I CAN TELL...
THE GODS WON'T SMILE ON SOMEONE LIKE HIM...
ARE YOU READY, MARIK?
THIS TURN, ALL MY MONSTERS ATTACK!
K-CHAK

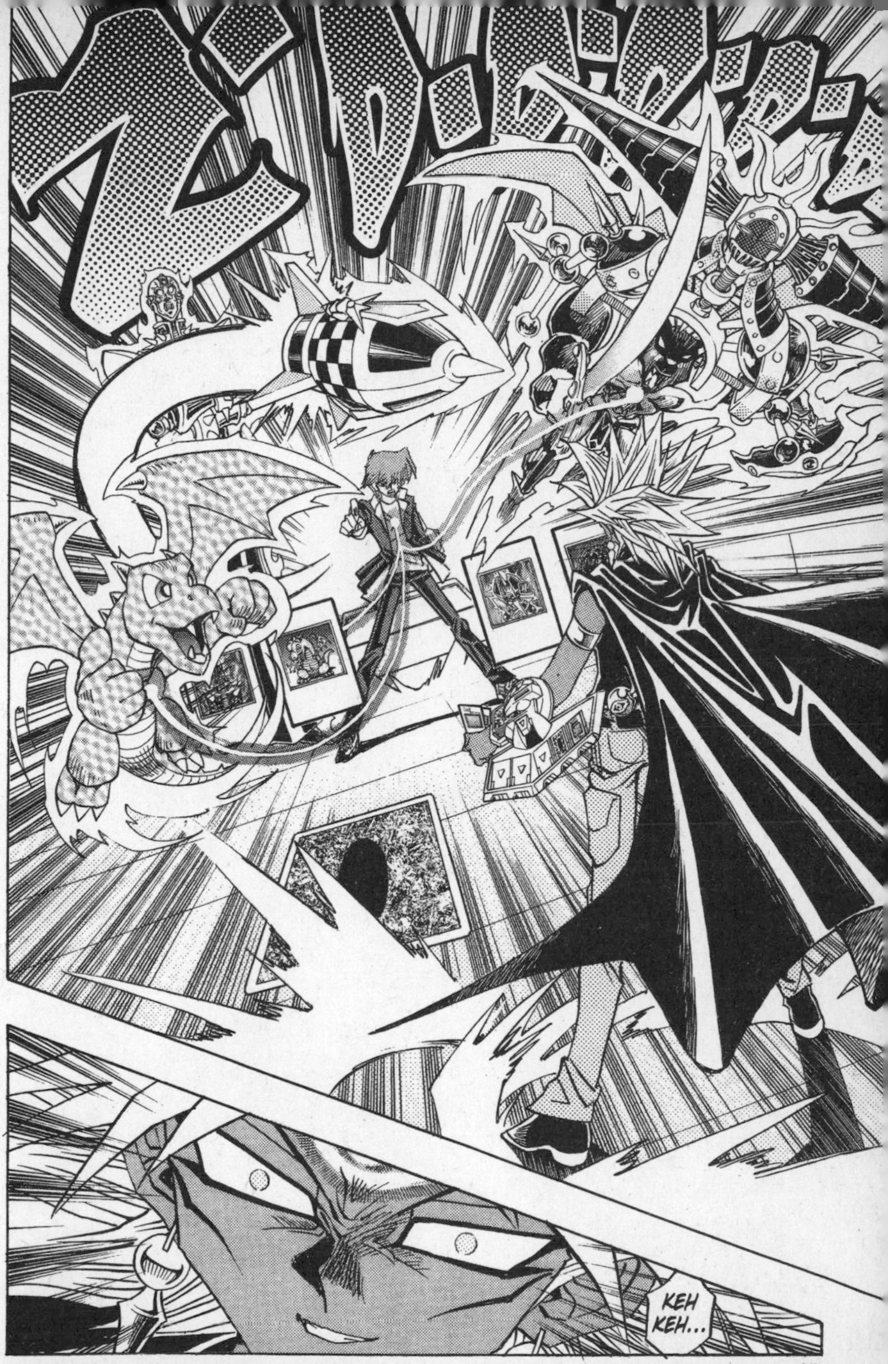
KEH KEH...

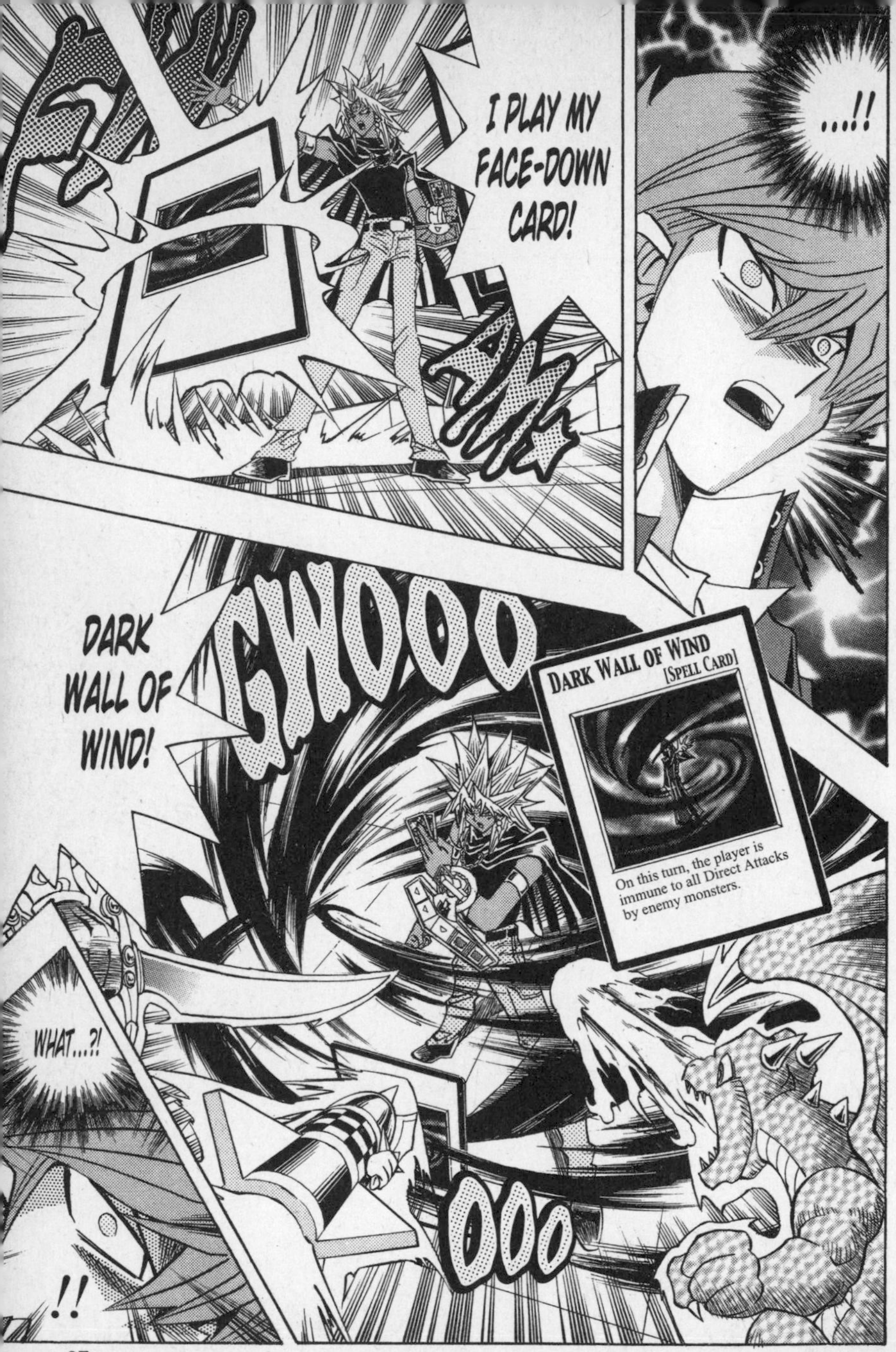
...!!
I PLAY MY FACE-DOWN CARD!
DARK WALL OF WIND!
GWOOOO
OOO
DARK WALL OF WIND
[SPELL CARD]
On this turn, the player is immune to all Direct Attacks by enemy monsters.
WHAT...?!
!!

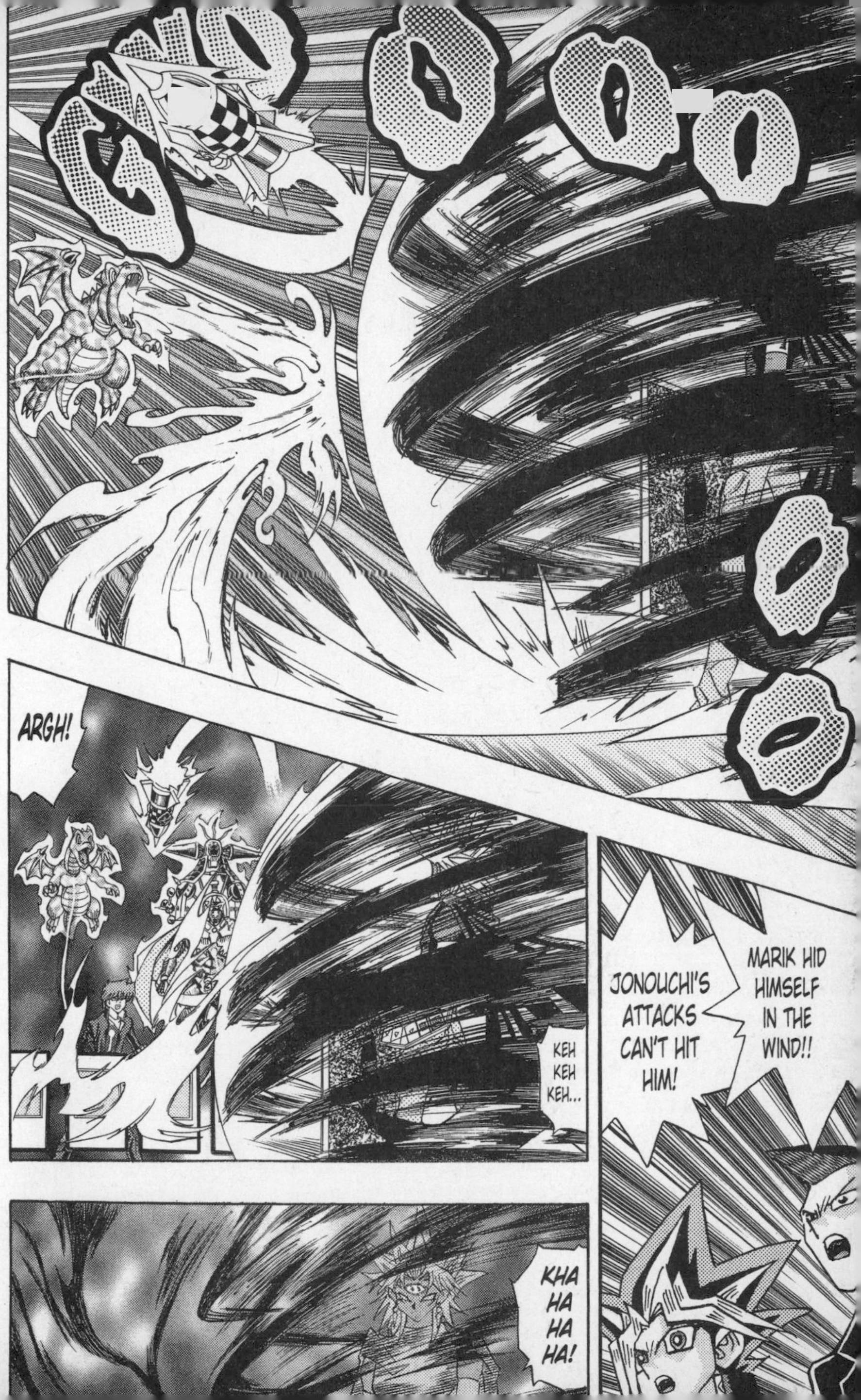
MARIK HID HIMSELF IN THE WIND!!
JONOUCHI'S ATTACKS CAN'T HIT HIM!
ARGH!
KEH KEH KEH...
KHA HA HA HA!

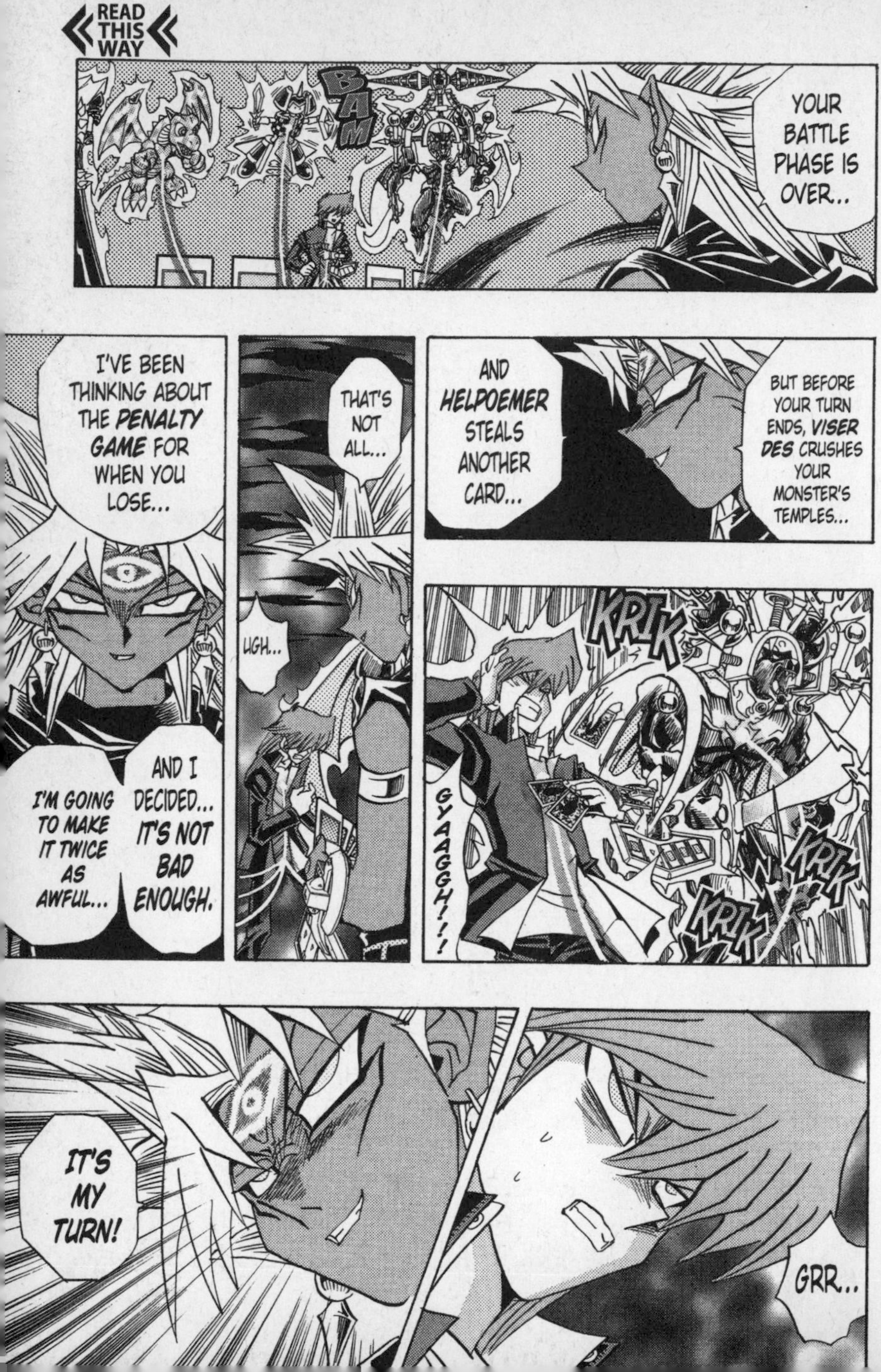
READ THIS WAY
YOUR BATTLE PHASE IS OVER...
BAM
BUT BEFORE YOUR TURN ENDS, VISER DES CRUSHES YOUR MONSTER'S TEMPLES...
AND HELPOEMER STEALS ANOTHER CARD...
KRIK
GYAAGGH!!!
KRIK
KRIK
THAT'S NOT ALL...
UGH...
I'VE BEEN THINKING ABOUT THE PENALTY GAME FOR WHEN YOU LOSE...
AND I DECIDED... IT'S NOT BAD ENOUGH.
I'M GOING TO MAKE IT TWICE AS AWFUL...
GRR...
IT'S MY TURN!

DRAW!

LAVA GOLEM

This card can only be Special Summoned by Tributing 2 monsters on your opponent's side of the field, and is S... Summoned to your opponent's side ... This card inflicts 700 points of dama... Points of this card's controller durin... Standby Phases.

ATK/ /2500

HERE'S A NEW PENALTY GAME FOR YOU...

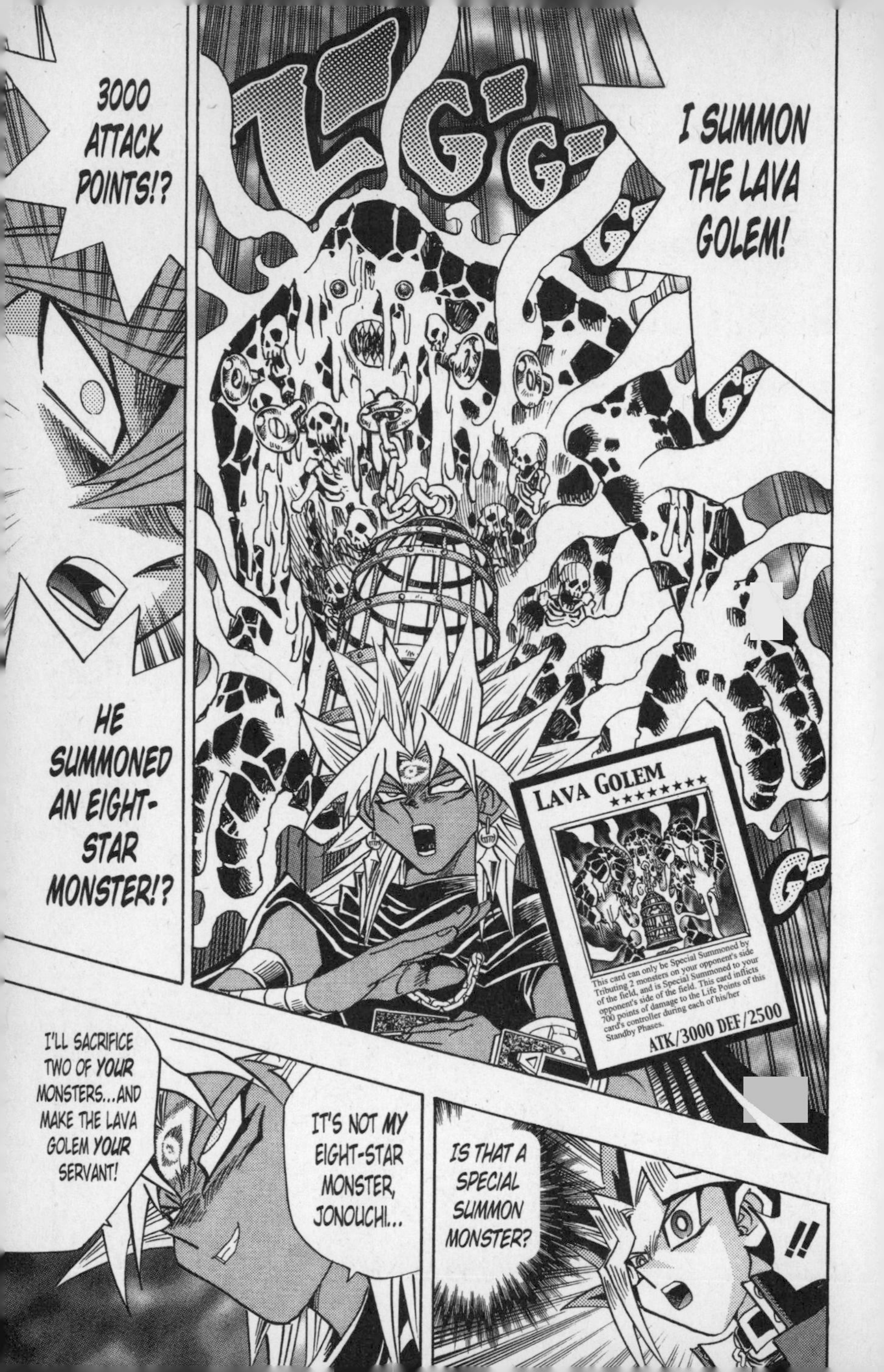
I SUMMON THE LAVA GOLEM!
LAVA GOLEM
This card can only be Special Summoned by Tributing 2 monsters on your opponent's side of the field, and is Special Summoned to your opponent's side of the field. This card inflicts 700 points of damage to the Life Points of this card's controller during each of his/her Standby Phases.
ATK/3000 DEF/2500
3000 ATTACK POINTS!?
HE SUMMONED AN EIGHT-STAR MONSTER!?
!!
IS THAT A SPECIAL SUMMON MONSTER?
IT'S NOT MY EIGHT-STAR MONSTER, JONOUCHI...
I'LL SACRIFICE TWO OF YOUR MONSTERS...AND MAKE THE LAVA GOLEM YOUR SERVANT!

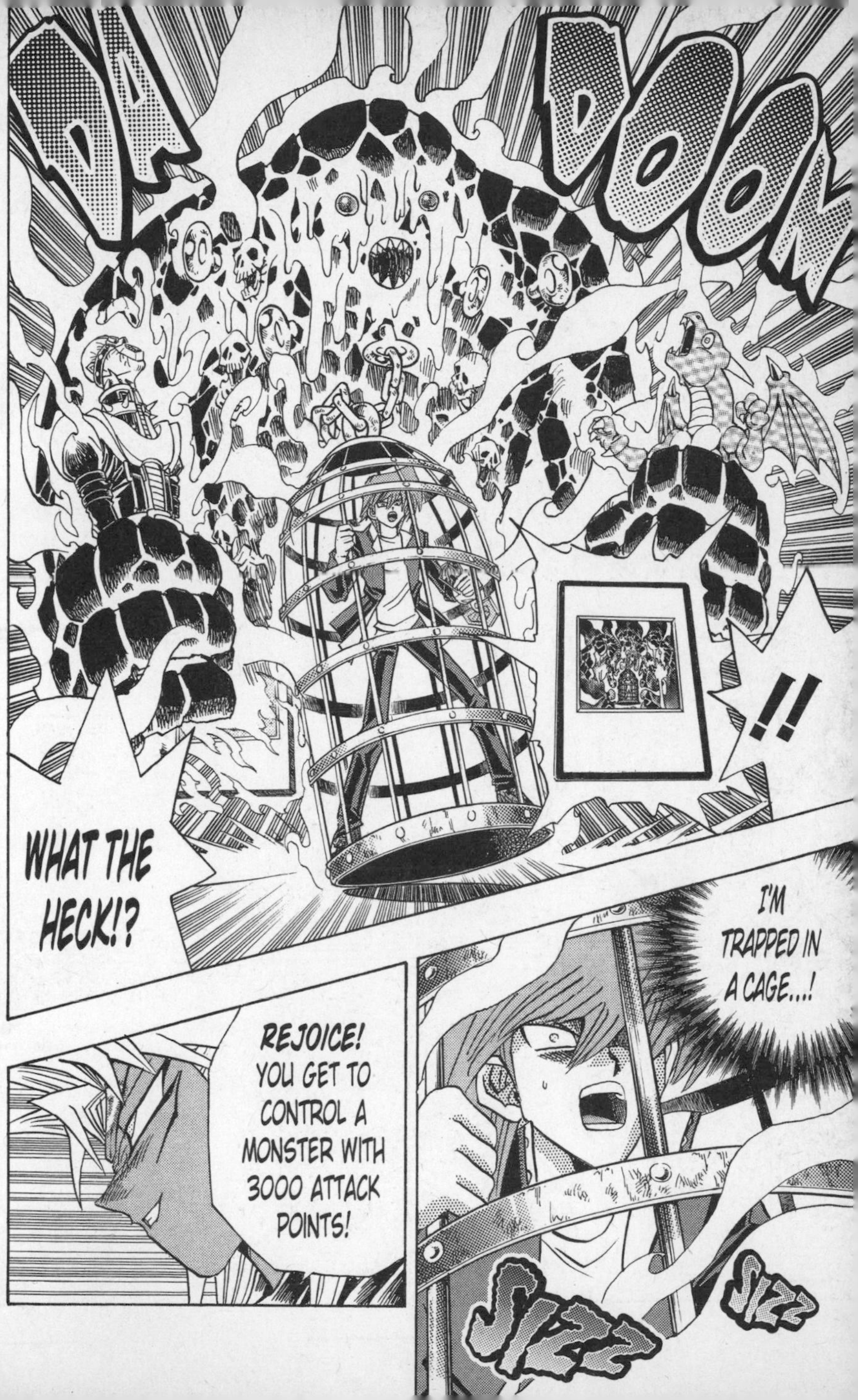
DA DOOOM
!!
WHAT THE HECK!?
I'M TRAPPED IN A CAGE...!
SIZZ
SIZZ
REJOICE! YOU GET TO CONTROL A MONSTER WITH 3000 ATTACK POINTS!

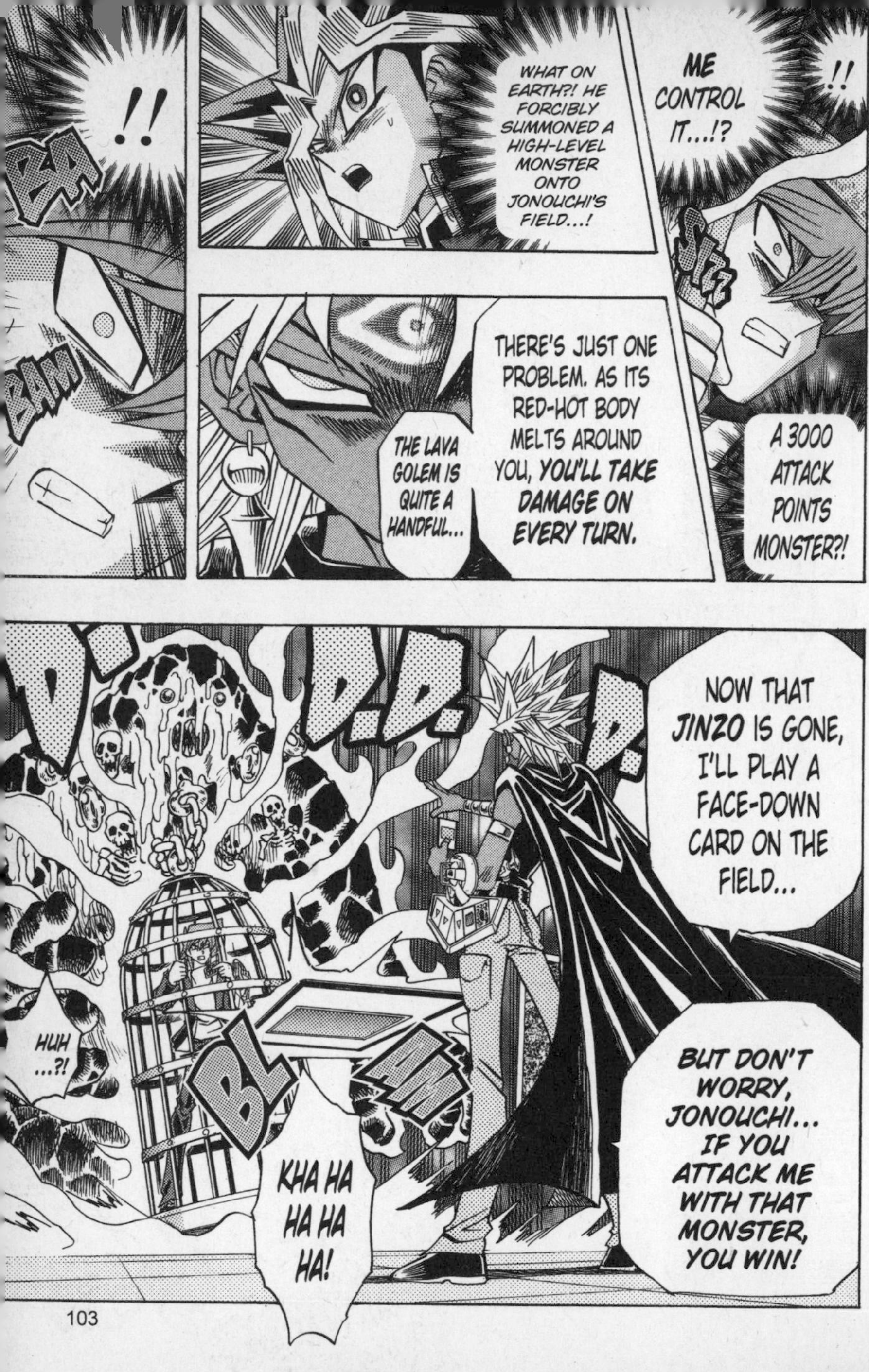
ME CONTROL IT...!?
!!
A 3000 ATTACK POINTS MONSTER?!
WHAT ON EARTH?! HE FORCIBLY SUMMONED A HIGH-LEVEL MONSTER ONTO JONOUCHI'S FIELD...!
THERE'S JUST ONE PROBLEM. AS ITS RED-HOT BODY MELTS AROUND YOU, YOU'LL TAKE DAMAGE ON EVERY TURN.
THE LAVA GOLEM IS QUITE A HANDFUL...
!!
BAM
NOW THAT JINZO IS GONE, I'LL PLAY A FACE-DOWN CARD ON THE FIELD...
BUT DON'T WORRY, JONOUCHI... IF YOU ATTACK ME WITH THAT MONSTER, YOU WIN!
KHA HA HA HA HA!
HUH ...?!

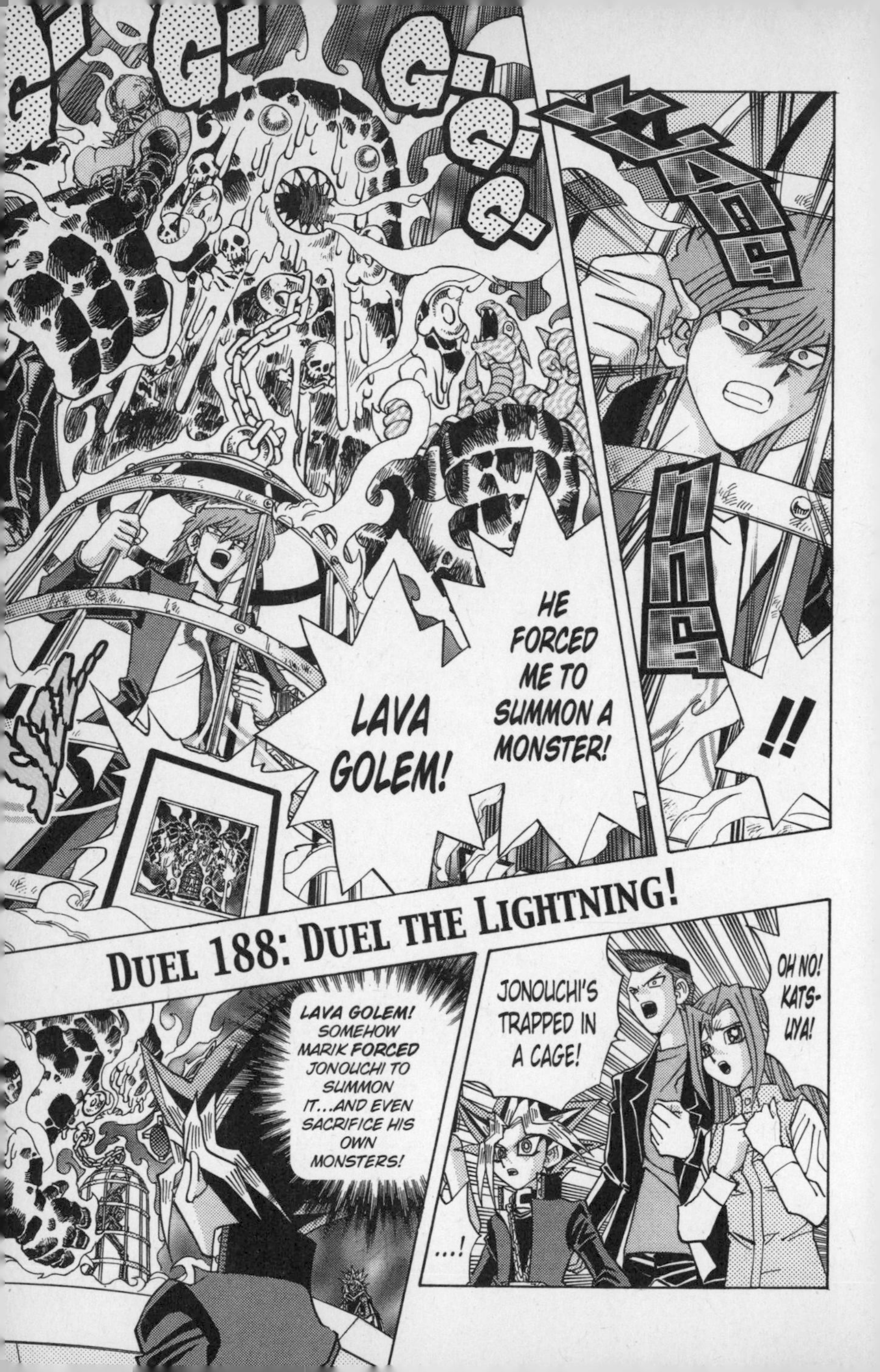
!!
HE FORCED ME TO SUMMON A MONSTER!
LAVA GOLEM!
DUEL 188: DUEL THE LIGHTNING!
OH NO! KATS-UYA!
JONOUCHI'S TRAPPED IN A CAGE!
...!
LAVA GOLEM! SOMEHOW MARIK FORCED JONOUCHI TO SUMMON IT...AND EVEN SACRIFICE HIS OWN MONSTERS!

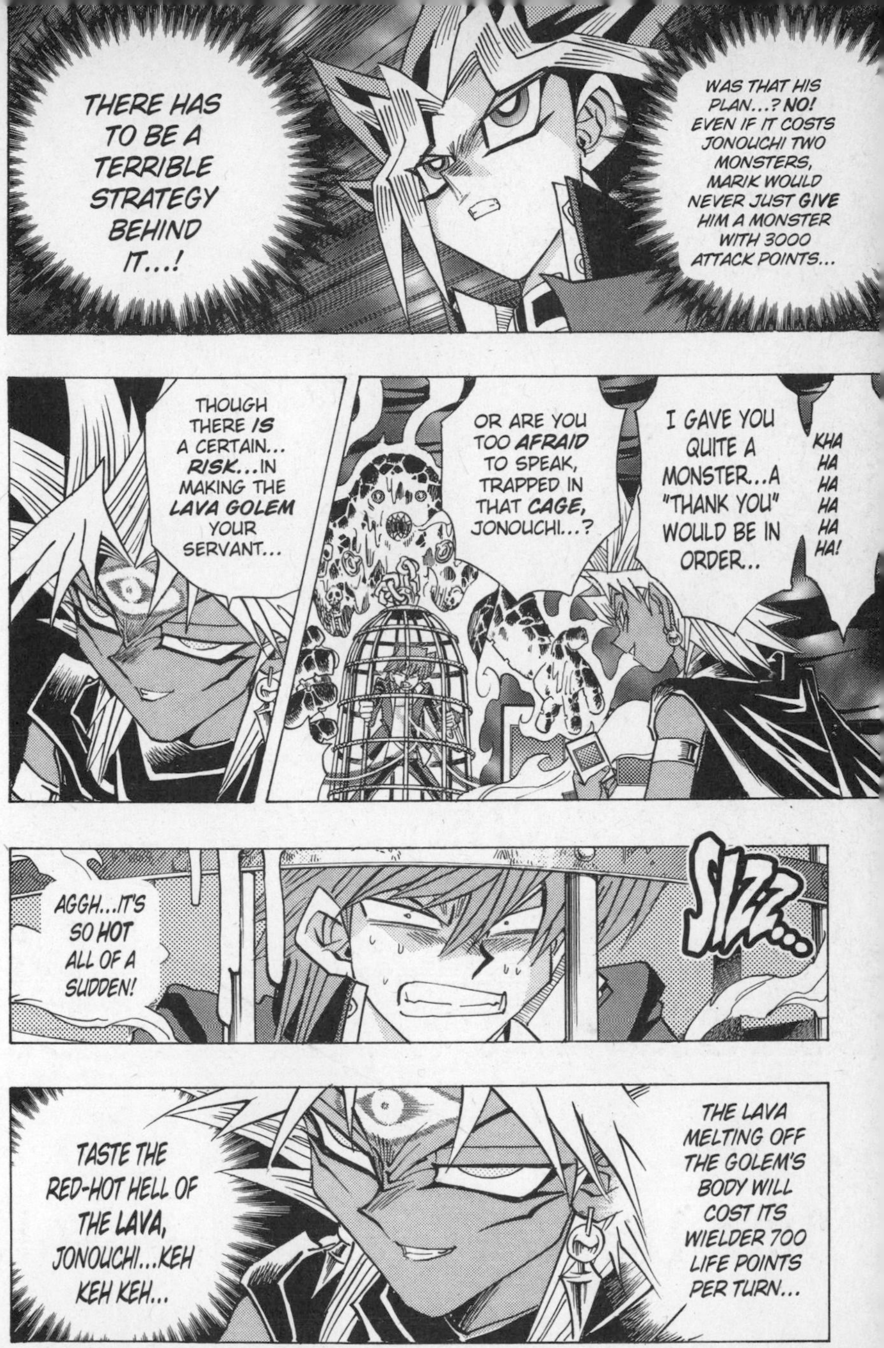
WAS THAT HIS PLAN...? NO! EVEN IF IT COSTS JONOUCHI TWO MONSTERS, MARIK WOULD NEVER JUST GIVE HIM A MONSTER WITH 3000 ATTACK POINTS...
THERE HAS TO BE A TERRIBLE STRATEGY BEHIND IT...!
KHA HA HA HA HA HA!
I GAVE YOU QUITE A MONSTER...A "THANK YOU" WOULD BE IN ORDER...
OR ARE YOU TOO AFRAID TO SPEAK, TRAPPED IN THAT CAGE, JONOUCHI...?
THOUGH THERE IS A CERTAIN... RISK...IN MAKING THE LAVA GOLEM YOUR SERVANT...
SIZZZ...
AGGH...IT'S SO HOT ALL OF A SUDDEN!
THE LAVA MELTING OFF THE GOLEM'S BODY WILL COST ITS WIELDER 700 LIFE POINTS PER TURN...
TASTE THE RED-HOT HELL OF THE LAVA, JONOUCHI...KEH KEH KEH...

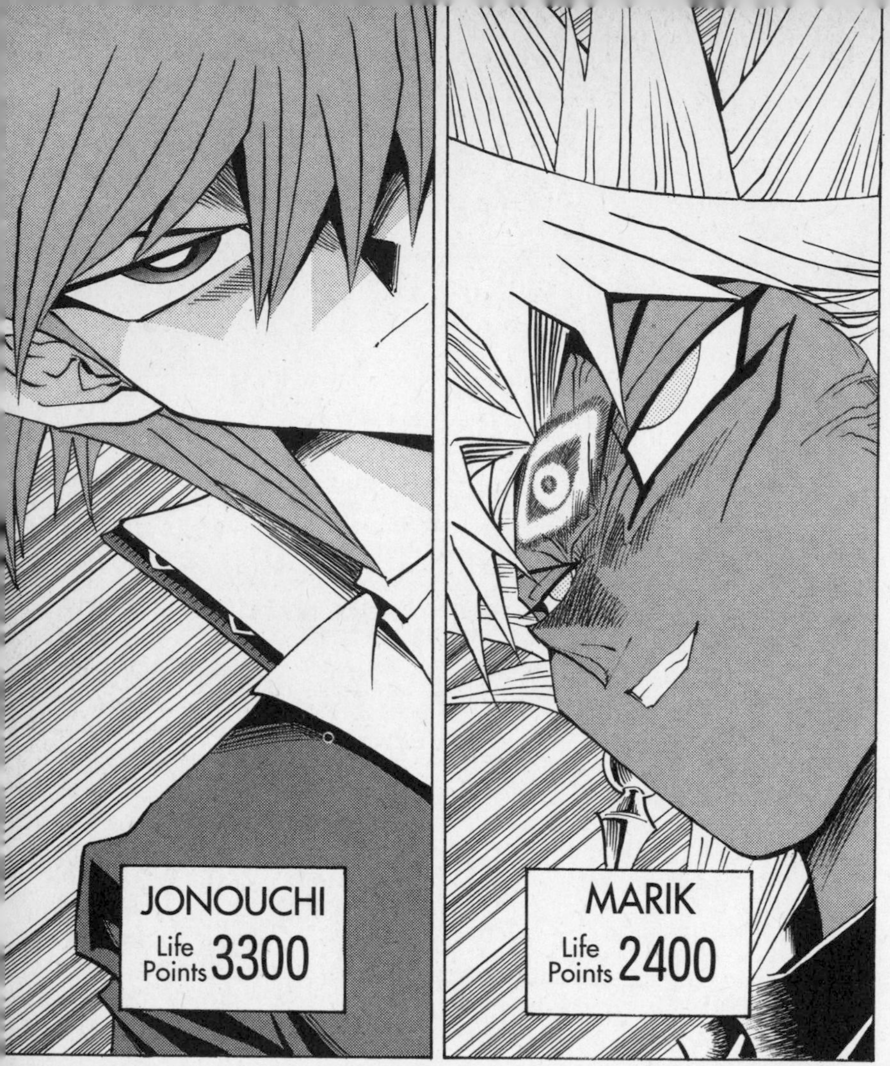
MARIK
Life Points 2400
JONOUCHI
Life Points 3300

Duel 188: Duel the Lightning!

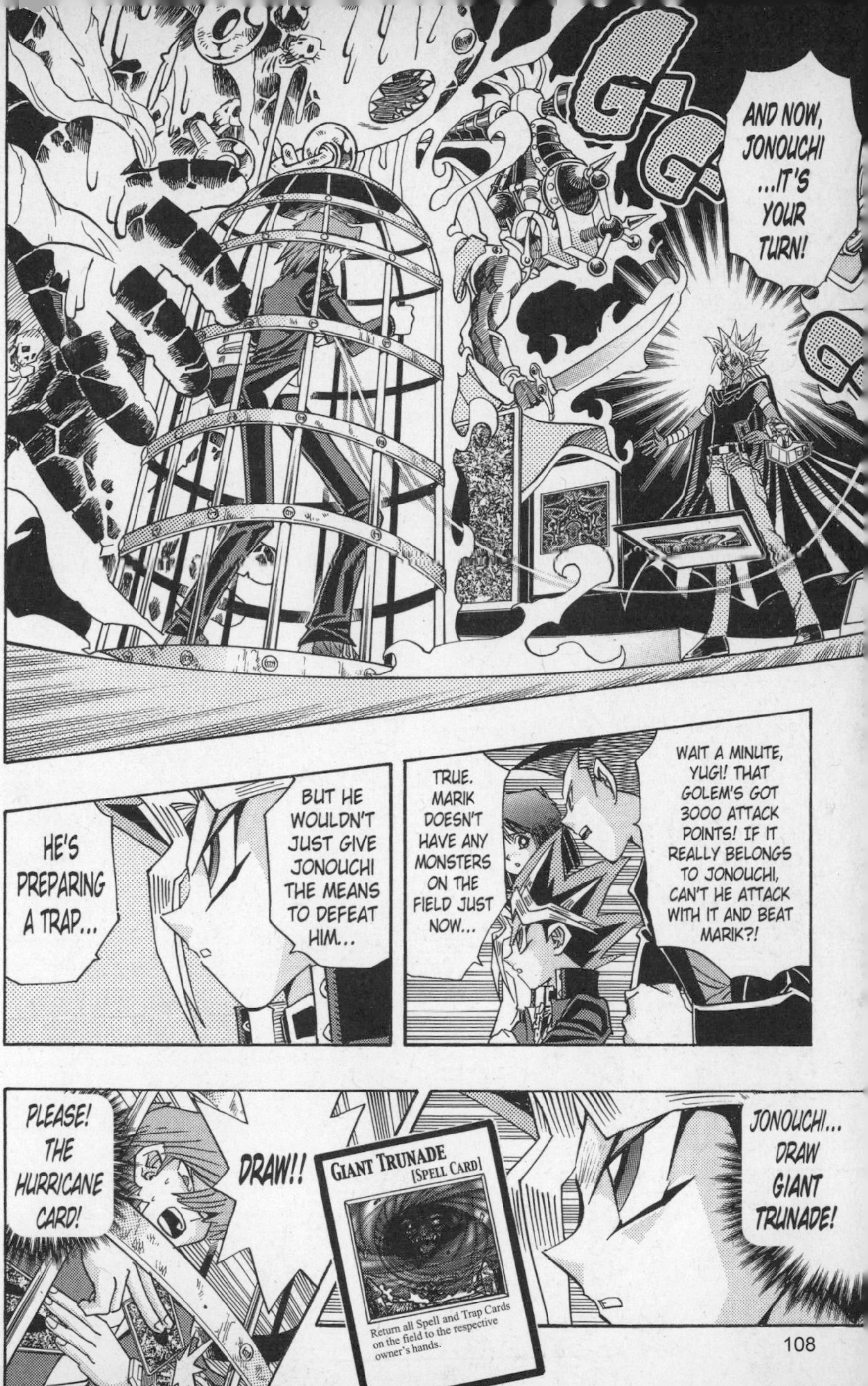
AND NOW, JONOUCHI ...IT'S YOUR TURN!
WAIT A MINUTE, YUGI! THAT GOLEM'S GOT 3000 ATTACK POINTS! IF IT REALLY BELONGS TO JONOUCHI, CAN'T HE ATTACK WITH IT AND BEAT MARIK?!
TRUE. MARIK DOESN'T HAVE ANY MONSTERS ON THE FIELD JUST NOW...
BUT HE WOULDN'T JUST GIVE JONOUCHI THE MEANS TO DEFEAT HIM...
HE'S PREPARING A TRAP...
JONOUCHI... DRAW GIANT TRUNADE!
GIANT TRUNADE
[SPELL CARD]
Return all Spell and Trap Cards on the field to the respective owner's hands.
DRAW!!
PLEASE! THE HURRICANE CARD!

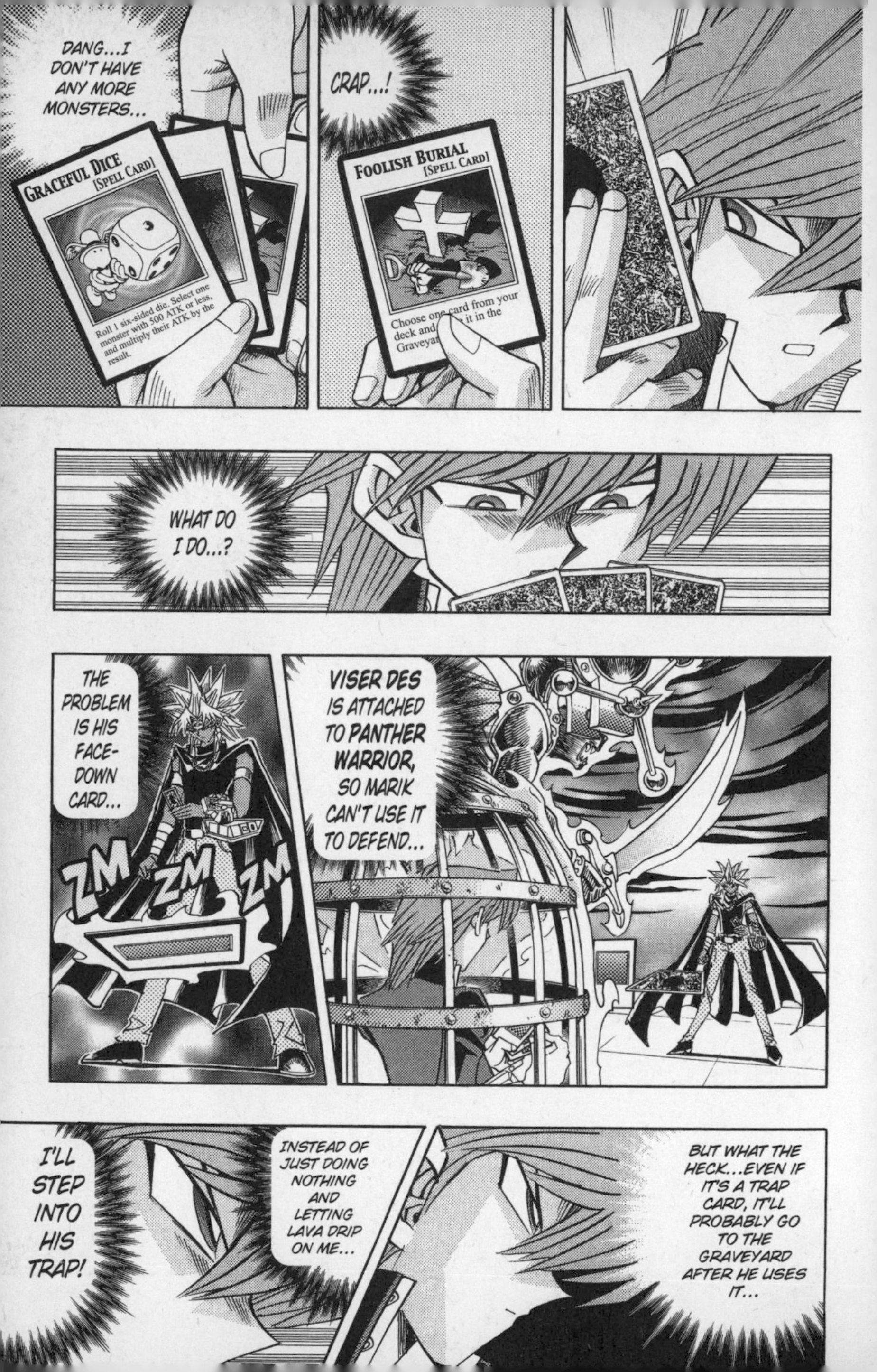
CRAP...!
FOOLISH BURIAL
[SPELL CARD]
Choose one card from your
deck and
it in the
Graveyar
DANG...I DON'T HAVE ANY MORE MONSTERS...
GRACEFUL DICE
[SPELL CARD]
Roll 1 six-sided die. Select one monster with 500 ATK or less, and multiply their ATK by the result.
WHAT DO I DO...?
VISER DES IS ATTACHED TO PANTHER WARRIOR, SO MARIK CAN'T USE IT TO DEFEND...
THE PROBLEM IS HIS FACE-DOWN CARD...
ZM ZM ZM
BUT WHAT THE HECK...EVEN IF IT'S A TRAP CARD, IT'LL PROBABLY GO TO THE GRAVEYARD AFTER HE USES IT...
INSTEAD OF JUST DOING NOTHING AND LETTING LAVA DRIP ON ME...
I'LL STEP INTO HIS TRAP!

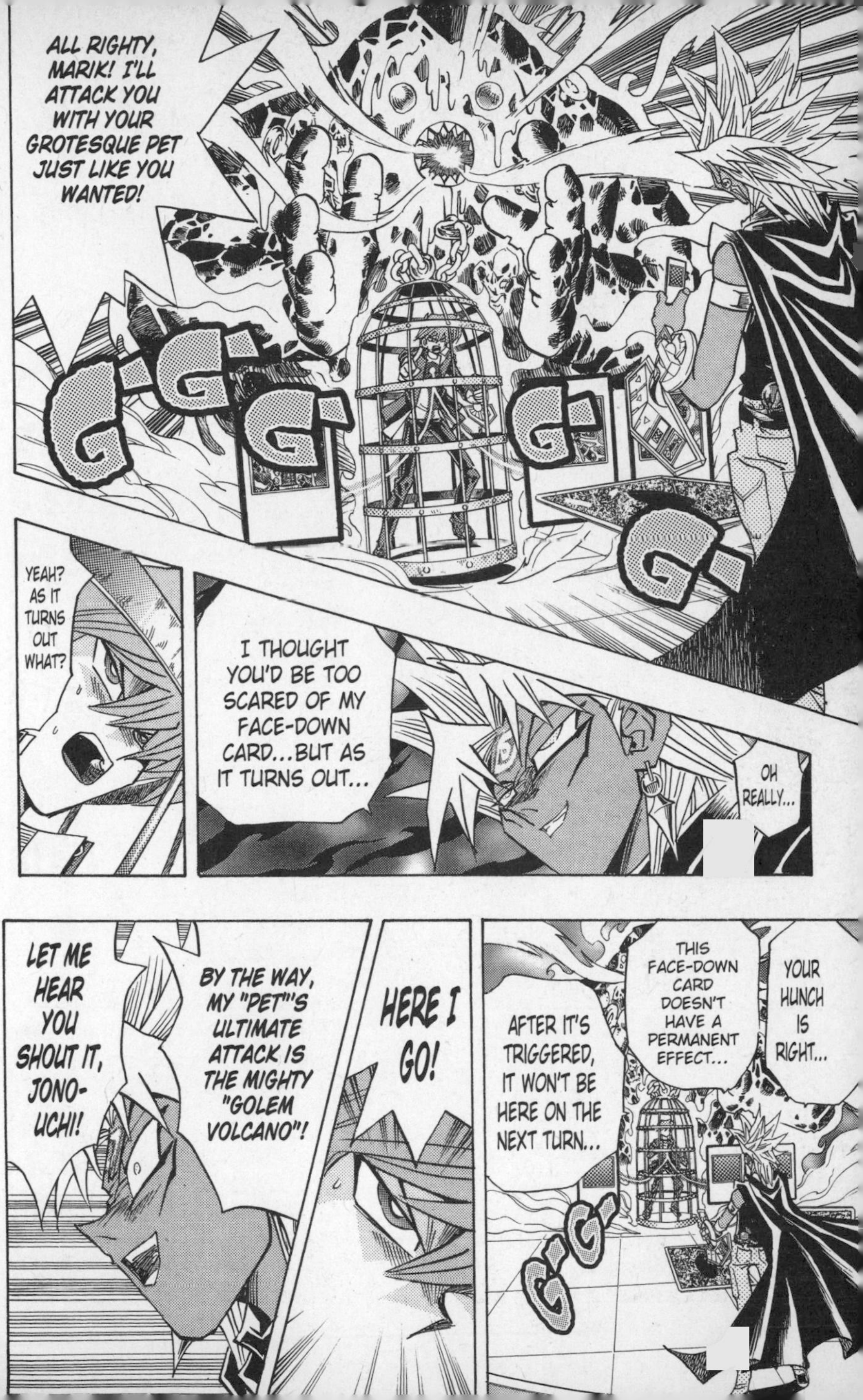
ALL RIGHTY, MARIK! I'LL ATTACK YOU WITH YOUR GROTESQUE PET JUST LIKE YOU WANTED!
G G G G G
OH REALLY...
I THOUGHT YOU'D BE TOO SCARED OF MY FACE-DOWN CARD...BUT AS IT TURNS OUT...
YEAH? AS IT TURNS OUT WHAT?
YOUR HUNCH IS RIGHT...
THIS FACE-DOWN CARD DOESN'T HAVE A PERMANENT EFFECT...
AFTER IT'S TRIGGERED, IT WON'T BE HERE ON THE NEXT TURN...
G G G
HERE I GO!
BY THE WAY, MY "PET"'S ULTIMATE ATTACK IS THE MIGHTY "GOLEM VOLCANO"!
LET ME HEAR YOU SHOUT IT, JONO-UCHI!

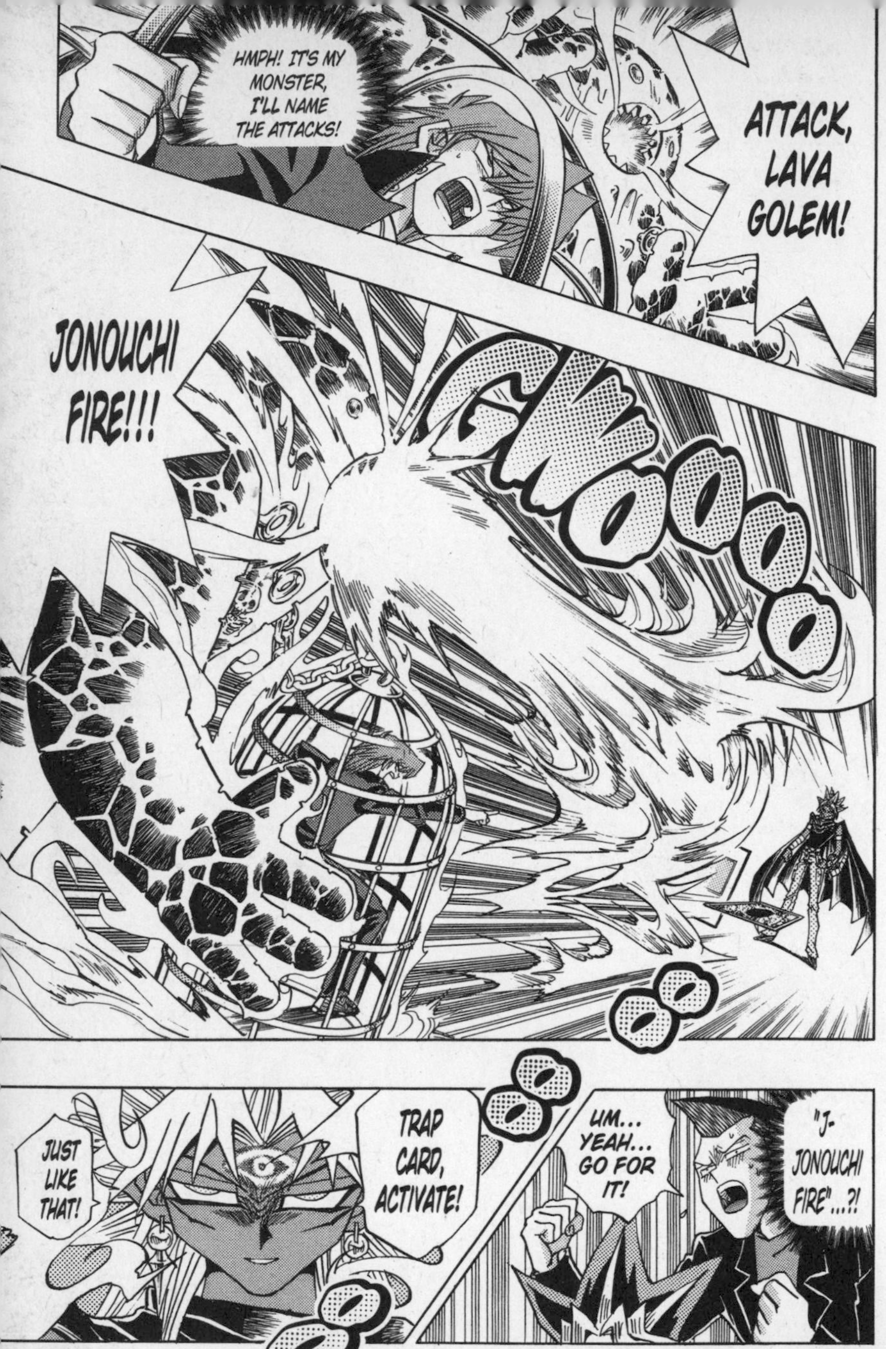
ATTACK, LAVA GOLEM!
HMPH! IT'S MY MONSTER, I'LL NAME THE ATTACKS!
JONOUCHI FIRE!!!
GWOOOOO
"J-JONOUCHI FIRE"...?!
UM... YEAH... GO FOR IT!
TRAP CARD, ACTIVATE!
JUST LIKE THAT!

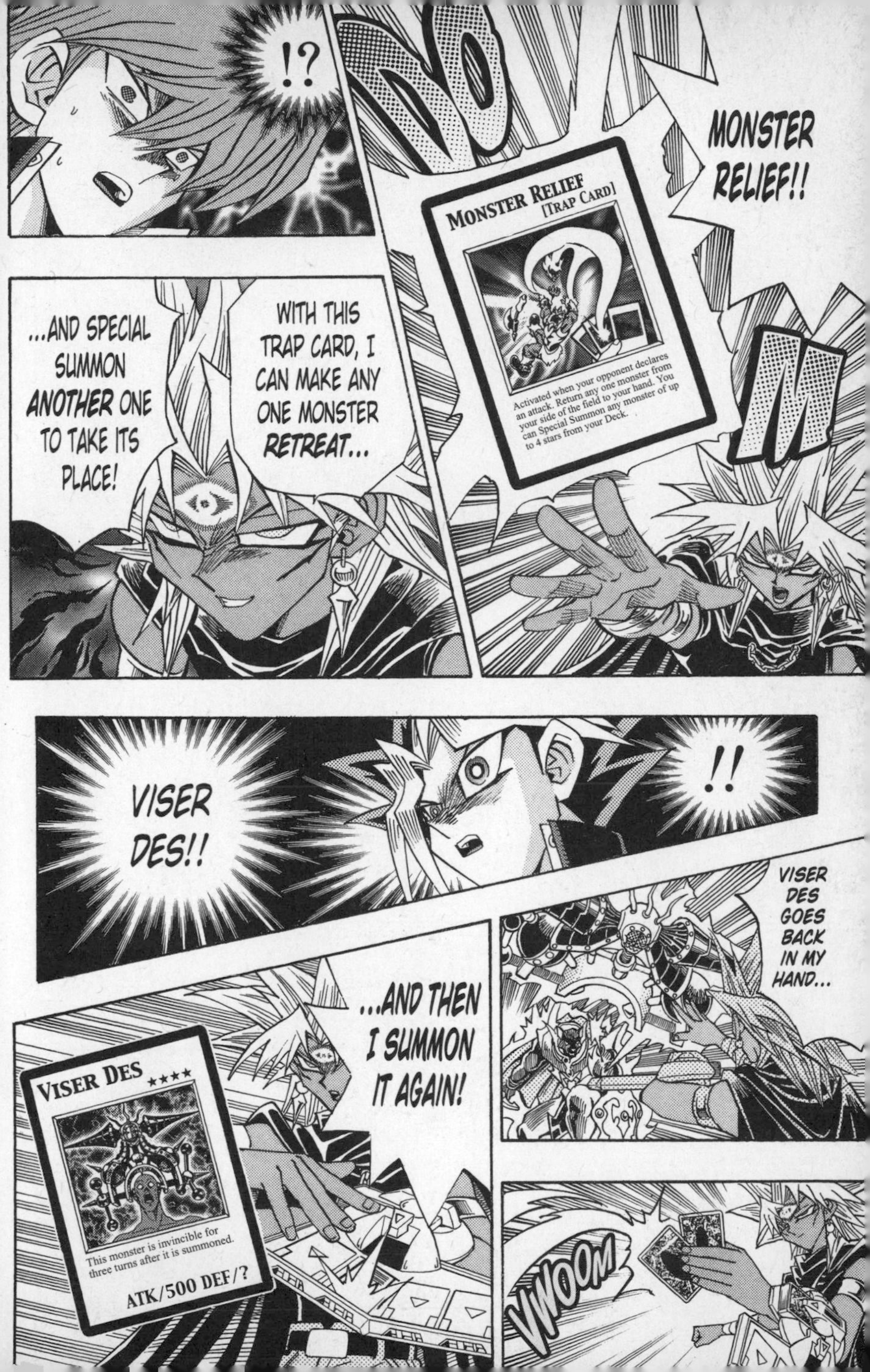
NO
MONSTER RELIEF!!
MONSTER RELIEF [TRAP CARD]
Activated when your opponent declares an attack. Return any one monster from your side of the field to your hand. You can Special Summon any monster of up to 4 stars from your Deck.
M
!?
WITH THIS TRAP CARD, I CAN MAKE ANY ONE MONSTER RETREAT...
...AND SPECIAL SUMMON ANOTHER ONE TO TAKE ITS PLACE!
!!
VISER DES!!
VISER DES GOES BACK IN MY HAND...
VWOOM
...AND THEN I SUMMON IT AGAIN!
VISER DES ★★★★
This monster is invincible for three turns after it is summoned.
ATK/500 DEF/?

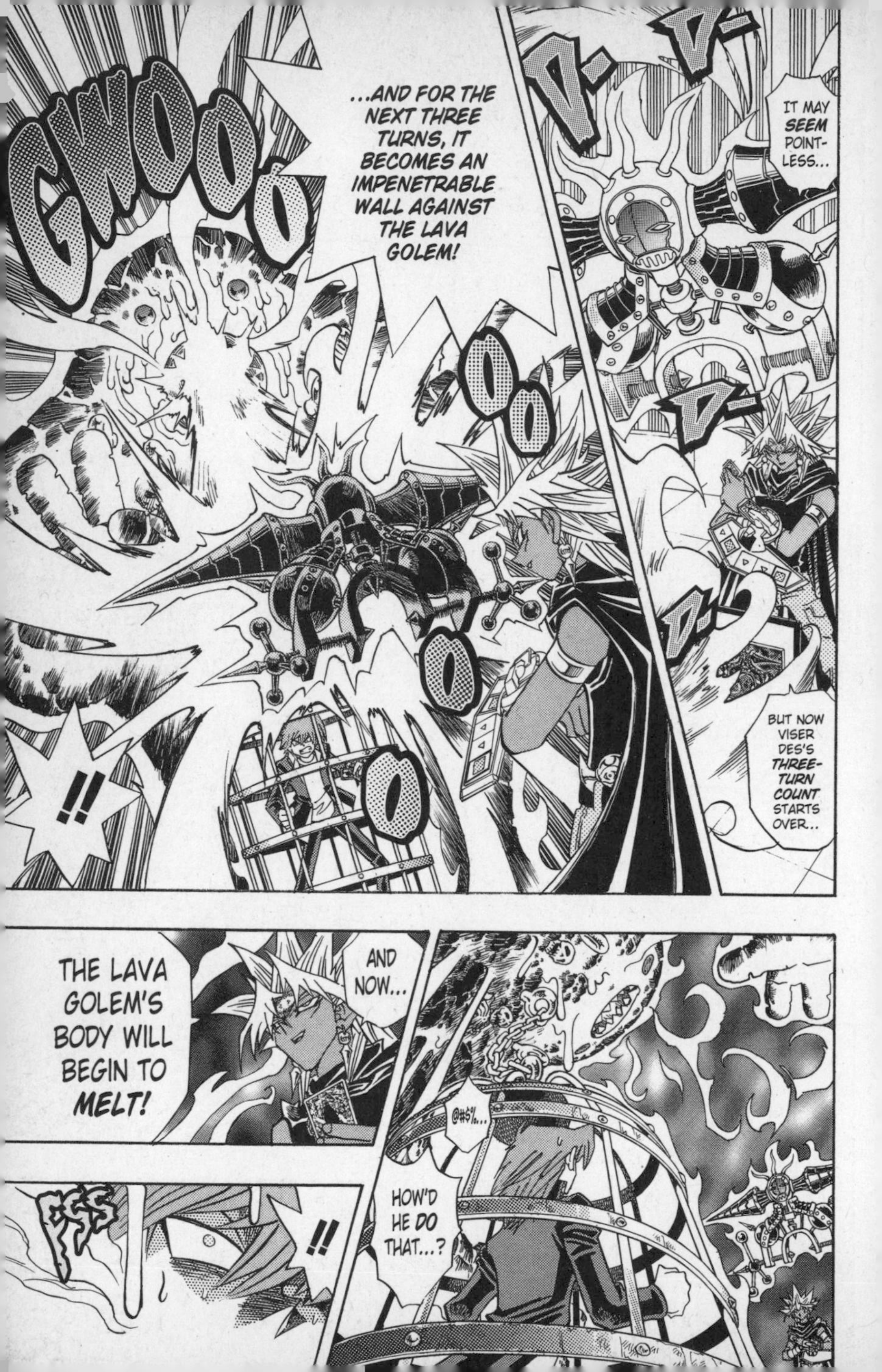
D- D-
IT MAY SEEM POINT-LESS...
D-
D-
BUT NOW VISER DES'S THREE-TURN COUNT STARTS OVER...
GWOOO
...AND FOR THE NEXT THREE TURNS, IT BECOMES AN IMPENETRABLE WALL AGAINST THE LAVA GOLEM!
OOOO
!!
@#$%...
HOW'D HE DO THAT...?
AND NOW...
THE LAVA GOLEM'S BODY WILL BEGIN TO MELT!
FSS
!!

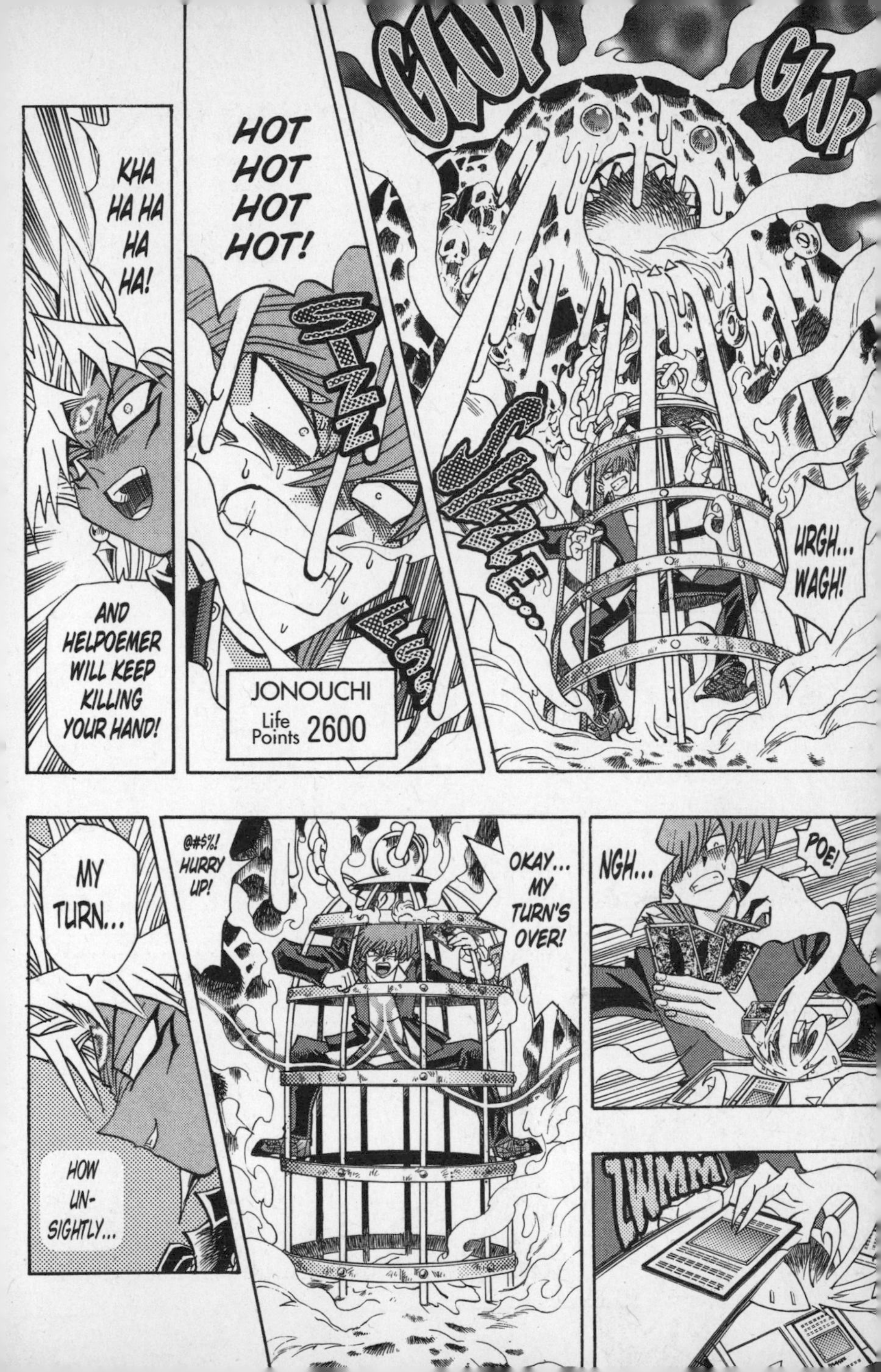
GLUP
GLUP
URGH... WAGH!
HOT HOT HOT HOT!
JONOUCHI Life Points 2600
KHA HA HA HA HA!
AND HELPOEMER WILL KEEP KILLING YOUR HAND!
NGH...
POE!
OKAY... MY TURN'S OVER!
@#$%! HURRY UP!
MY TURN...
HOW UN-SIGHTLY...

READ THIS WAY

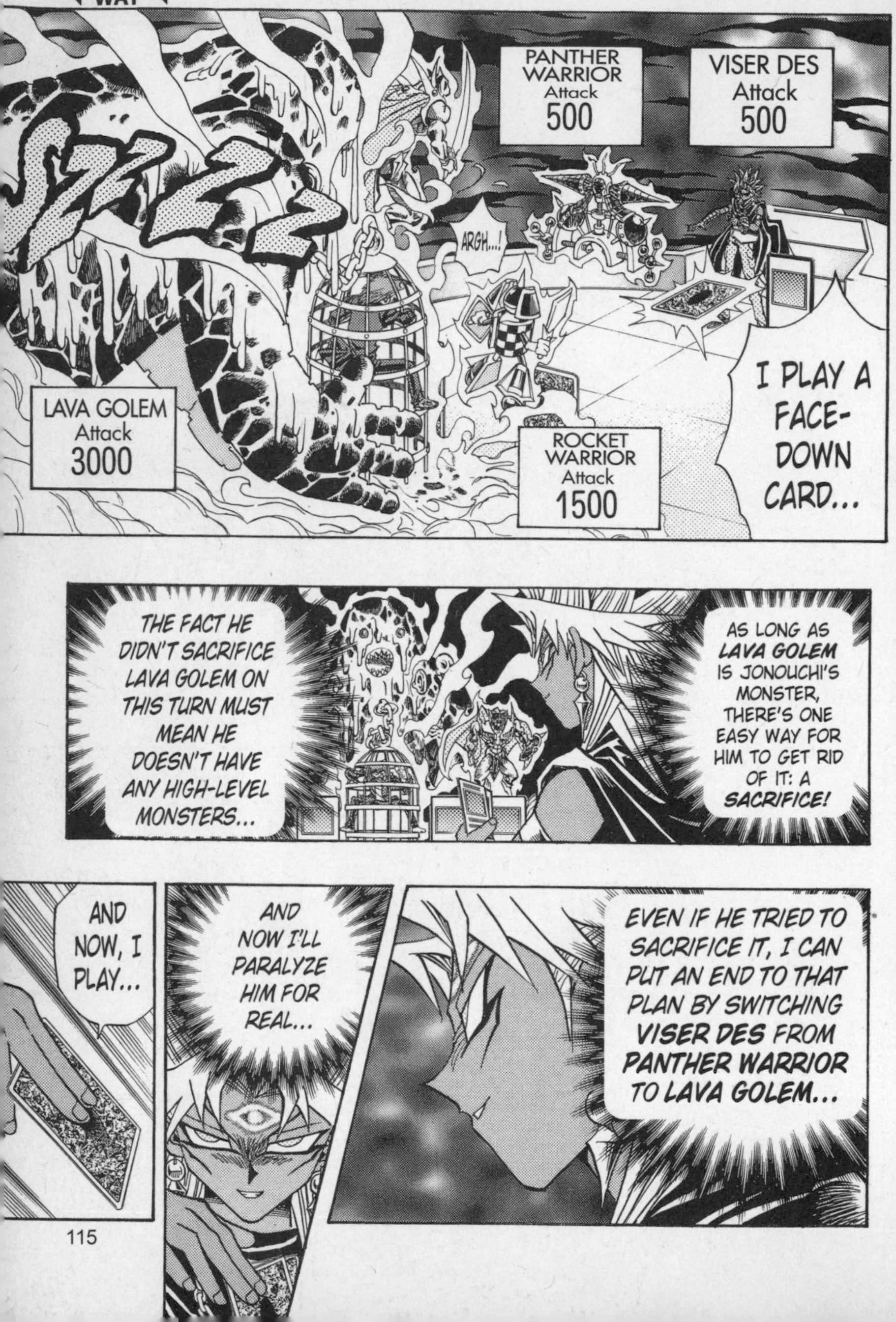

VISER DES Attack 500
PANTHER WARRIOR Attack 500
ARGH...!
I PLAY A FACE-DOWN CARD...
ROCKET WARRIOR Attack 1500
LAVA GOLEM Attack 3000
AS LONG AS **LAVA GOLEM** IS JONOUCHI'S MONSTER, THERE'S ONE EASY WAY FOR HIM TO GET RID OF IT: A **SACRIFICE!**
THE FACT HE DIDN'T SACRIFICE LAVA GOLEM ON THIS TURN MUST MEAN HE DOESN'T HAVE ANY HIGH-LEVEL MONSTERS...
EVEN IF HE TRIED TO SACRIFICE IT, I CAN PUT AN END TO THAT PLAN BY SWITCHING **VISER DES** FROM **PANTHER WARRIOR** TO **LAVA GOLEM...**
AND NOW I'LL PARALYZE HIM FOR REAL...
AND NOW, I PLAY...

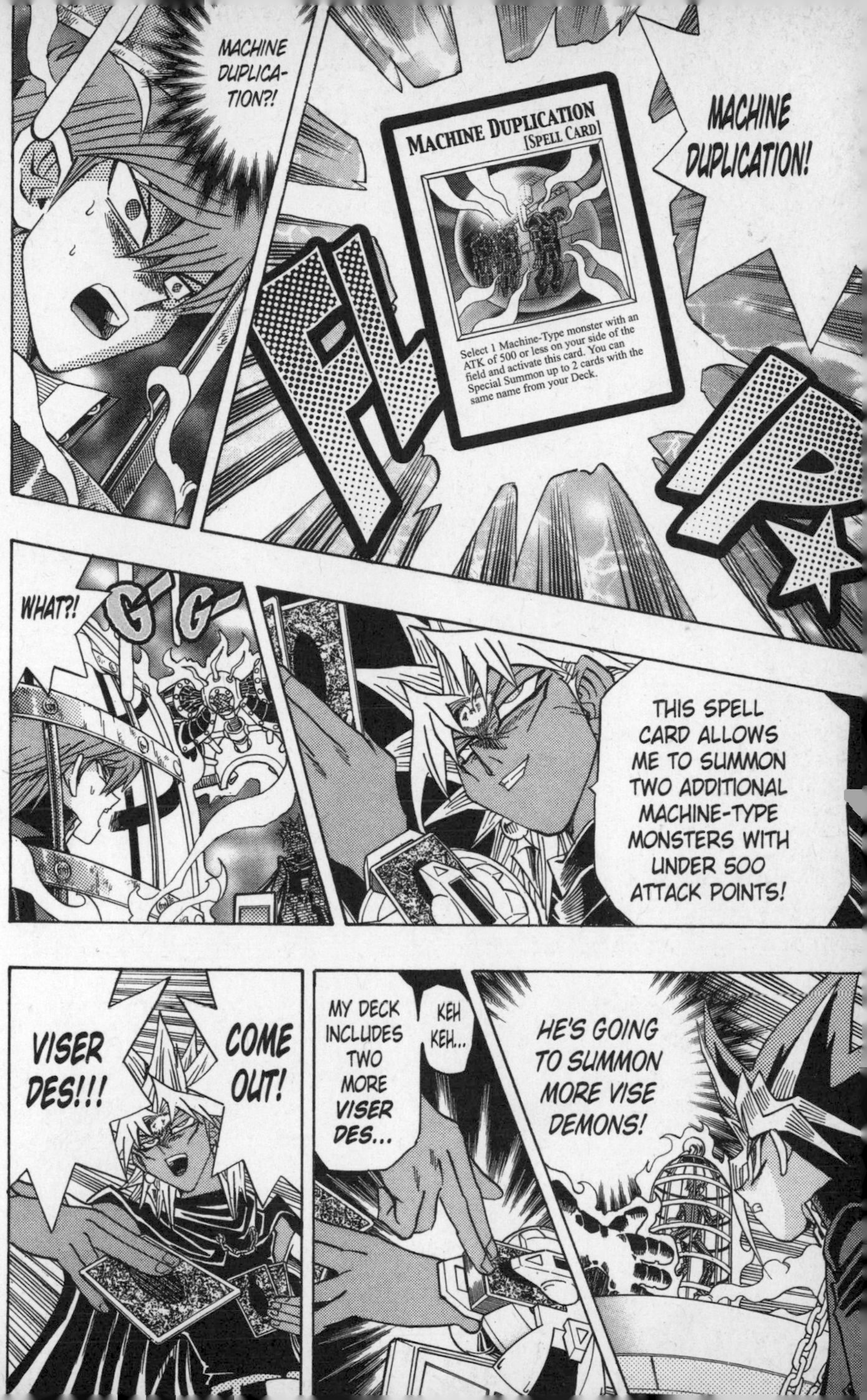

MACHINE DUPLICATION!
MACHINE DUPLICATION
[SPELL CARD]
Select 1 Machine-Type monster with an ATK of 500 or less on your side of the field and activate this card. You can Special Summon up to 2 cards with the same name from your Deck.
MACHINE DUPLICATION?!
THIS SPELL CARD ALLOWS ME TO SUMMON TWO ADDITIONAL MACHINE-TYPE MONSTERS WITH UNDER 500 ATTACK POINTS!
WHAT?!
G-G-
HE'S GOING TO SUMMON MORE VISE DEMONS!
KEH KEH...
MY DECK INCLUDES TWO MORE VISER DES...
COME OUT!
VISER DES!!!

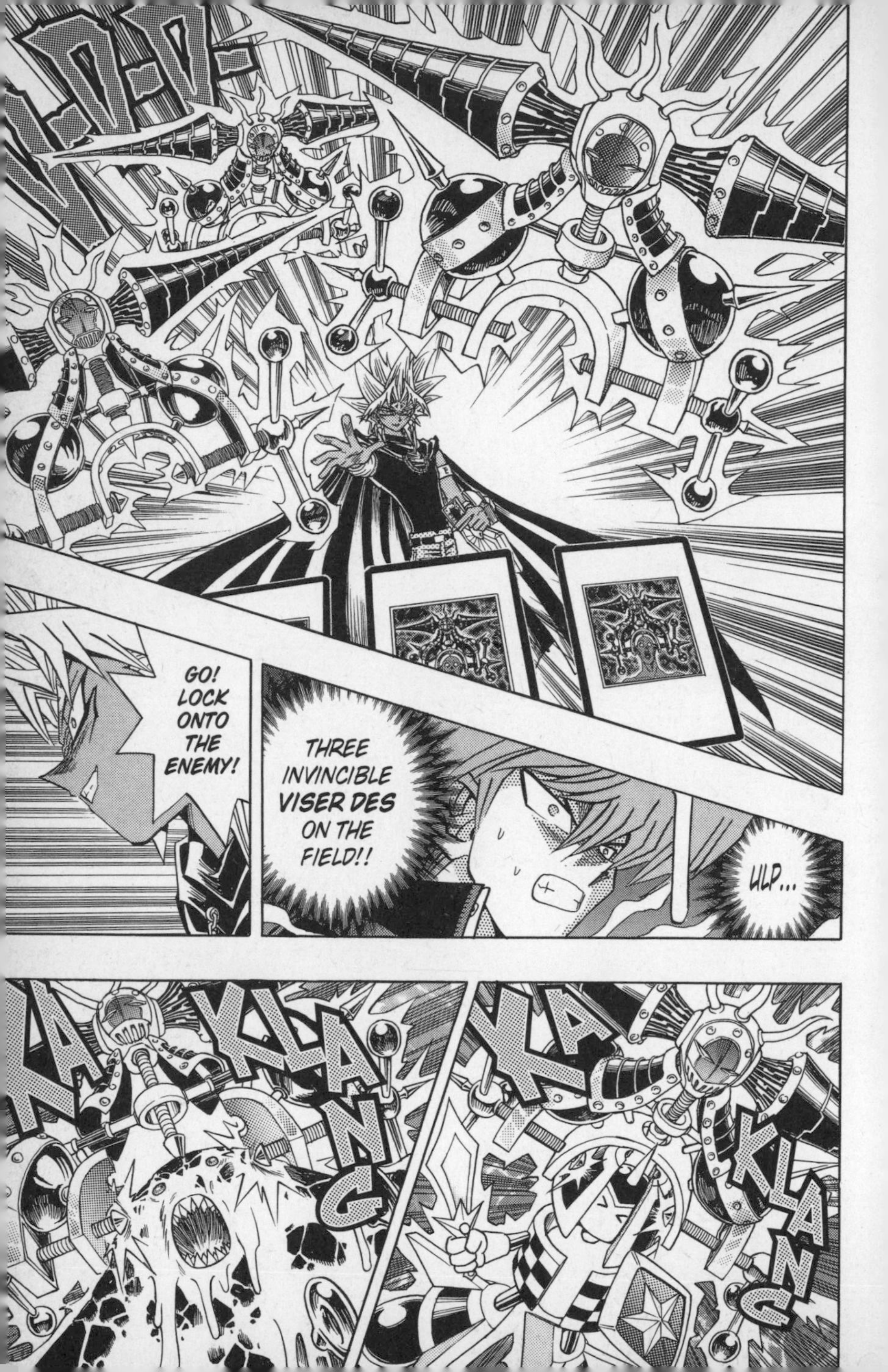
THREE INVINCIBLE VISER DES ON THE FIELD!!
ULP...
GO! LOCK ONTO THE ENEMY!
KA KLANG
KA KLANG

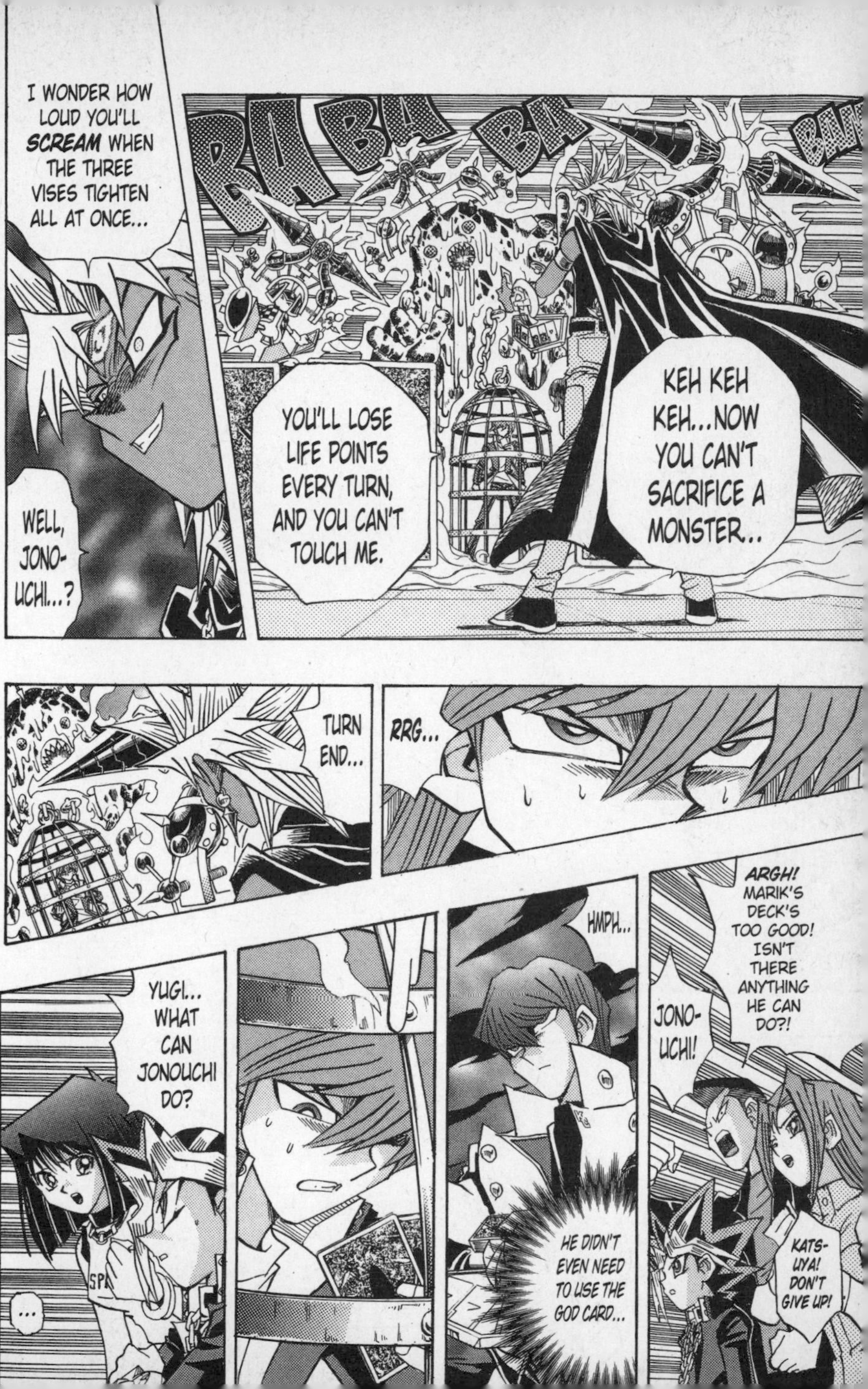
RA BA BA
KEH KEH KEH...NOW YOU CAN'T SACRIFICE A MONSTER...
YOU'LL LOSE LIFE POINTS EVERY TURN, AND YOU CAN'T TOUCH ME.
I WONDER HOW LOUD YOU'LL *SCREAM* WHEN THE THREE VISES TIGHTEN ALL AT ONCE...
WELL, JONO-UCHI...?
RRG...
TURN END...
ARGH! MARIK'S DECK'S TOO GOOD! ISN'T THERE ANYTHING HE CAN DO?!
JONO-UCHI!
KATS-UYA! DON'T GIVE UP!
HMPH...
HE DIDN'T EVEN NEED TO USE THE GOD CARD...
YUGI... WHAT CAN JONOUCHI DO?
...

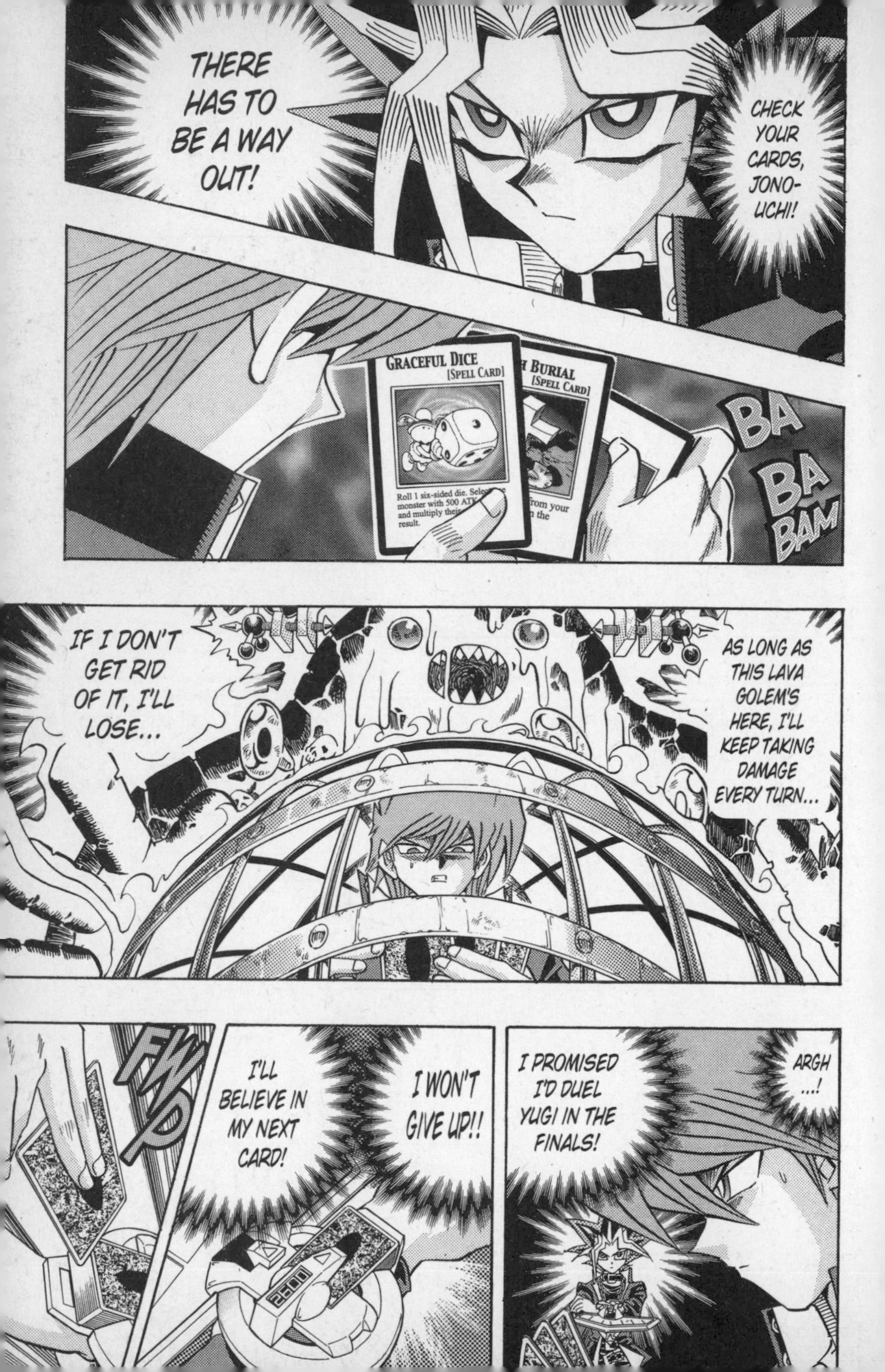
CHECK YOUR CARDS, JONO-UCHI!
THERE HAS TO BE A WAY OUT!
BA BA BAM
GRACEFUL DICE
[SPELL CARD]
H BURIAL
[SPELL CARD]
AS LONG AS THIS LAVA GOLEM'S HERE, I'LL KEEP TAKING DAMAGE EVERY TURN...
IF I DON'T GET RID OF IT, I'LL LOSE...
ARGH ...!
I PROMISED I'D DUEL YUGI IN THE FINALS!
I WON'T GIVE UP!!
I'LL BELIEVE IN MY NEXT CARD!
FWP

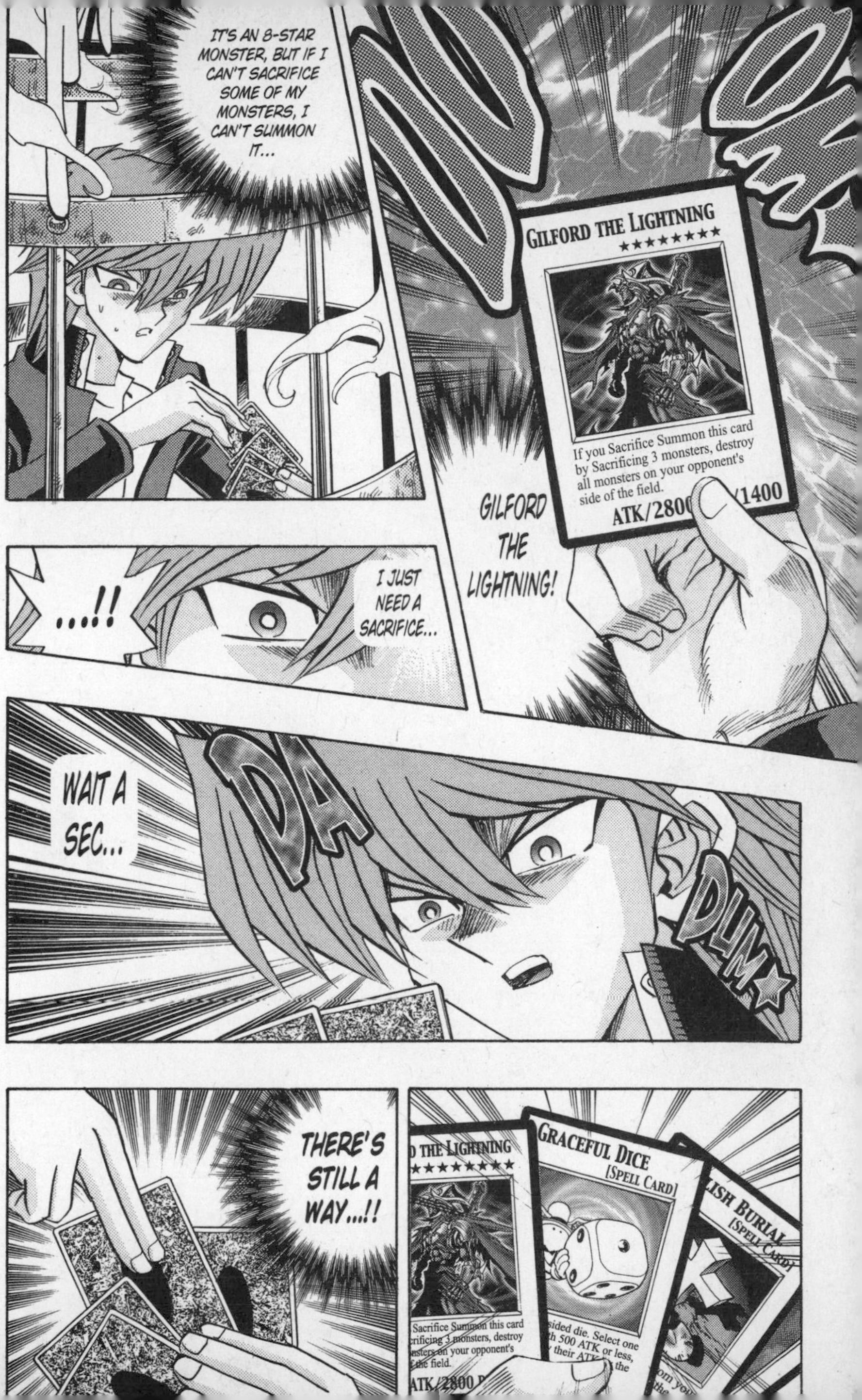
GILFORD THE LIGHTNING
If you Sacrifice Summon this card by Sacrificing 3 monsters, destroy all monsters on your opponent's side of the field.
GILFORD THE LIGHTNING!
IT'S AN 8-STAR MONSTER, BUT IF I CAN'T SACRIFICE SOME OF MY MONSTERS, I CAN'T SUMMON IT...
I JUST NEED A SACRIFICE...
...!!
DA
DUM
WAIT A SEC...
GRACEFUL DICE
[SPELL CARD]
THERE'S STILL A WAY...!!

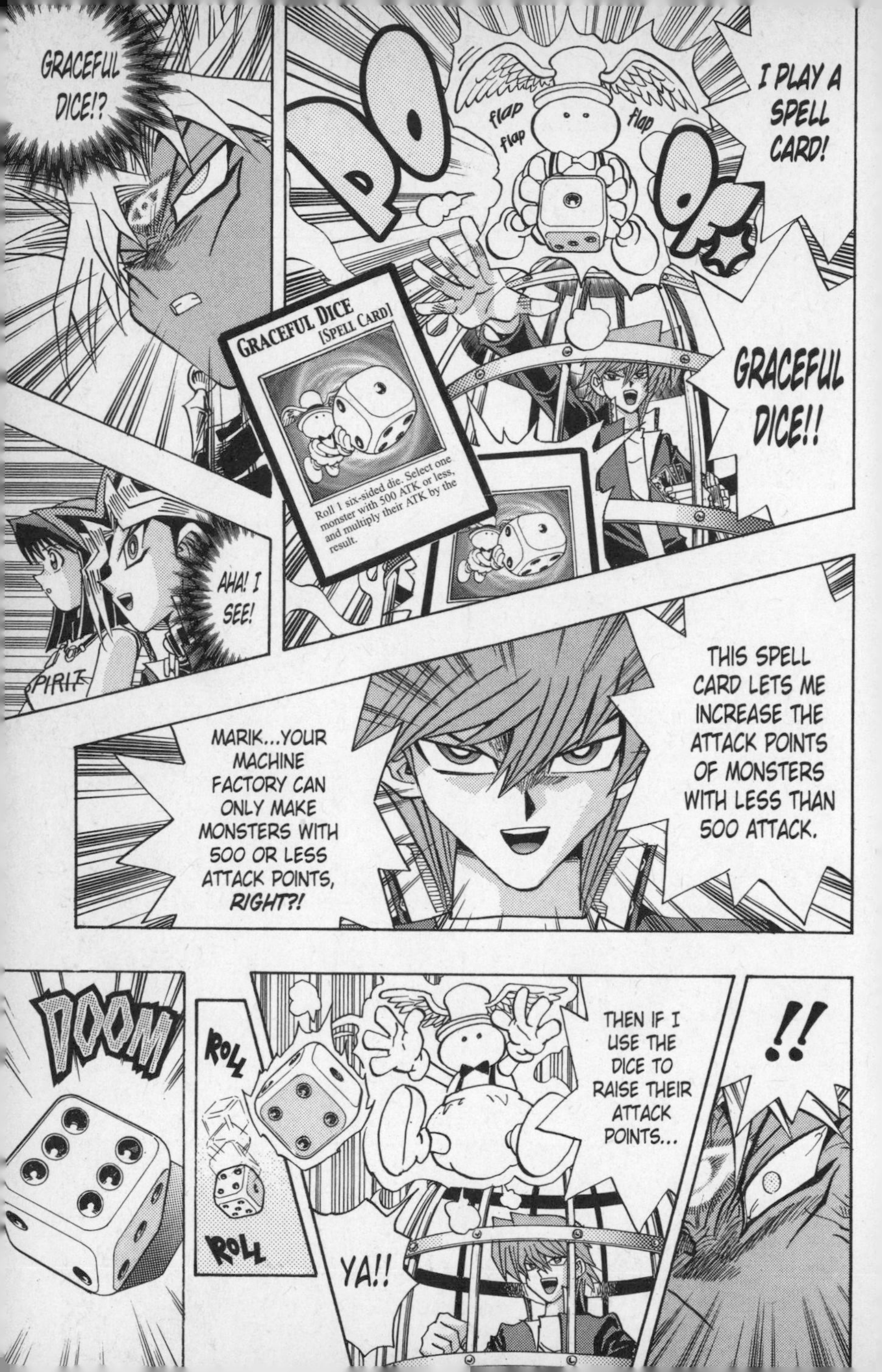
I PLAY A SPELL CARD!
POOF
flap
flap
flap
GRACEFUL DICE
[SPELL CARD]
Roll 1 six-sided die. Select one monster with 500 ATK or less, and multiply their ATK by the result.
GRACEFUL DICE!!
GRACEFUL DICE!?
AHA! I SEE!
THIS SPELL CARD LETS ME INCREASE THE ATTACK POINTS OF MONSTERS WITH LESS THAN 500 ATTACK.
MARIK...YOUR MACHINE FACTORY CAN ONLY MAKE MONSTERS WITH 500 OR LESS ATTACK POINTS, *RIGHT?!*
!!
THEN IF I USE THE DICE TO RAISE THEIR ATTACK POINTS...
YA!!
ROLL
ROLL
DOOM

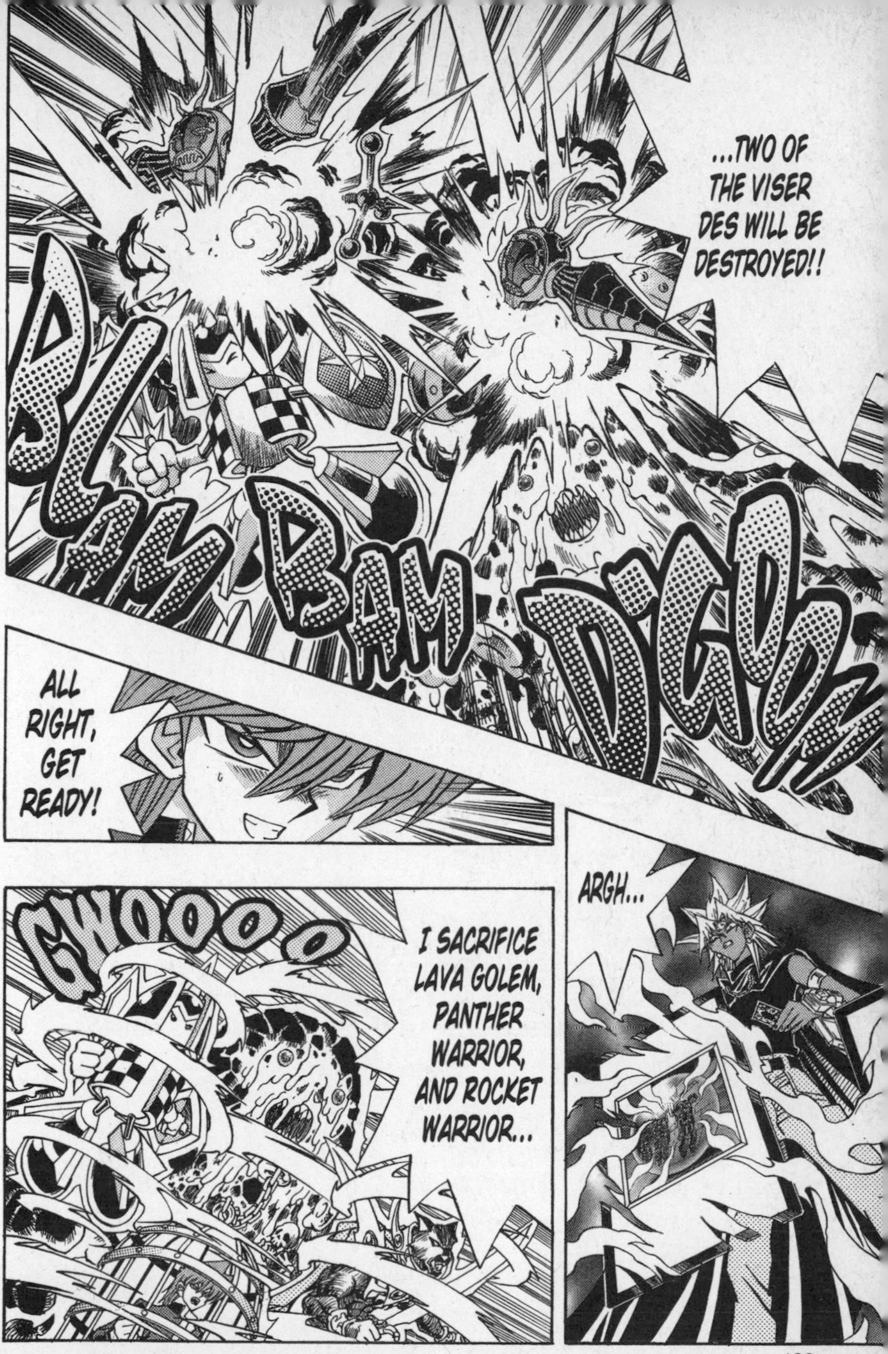
...TWO OF THE VISER DES WILL BE DESTROYED!!
BAM
ALL RIGHT, GET READY!
ARGH...
GWOOOOO
I SACRIFICE LAVA GOLEM, PANTHER WARRIOR, AND ROCKET WARRIOR...

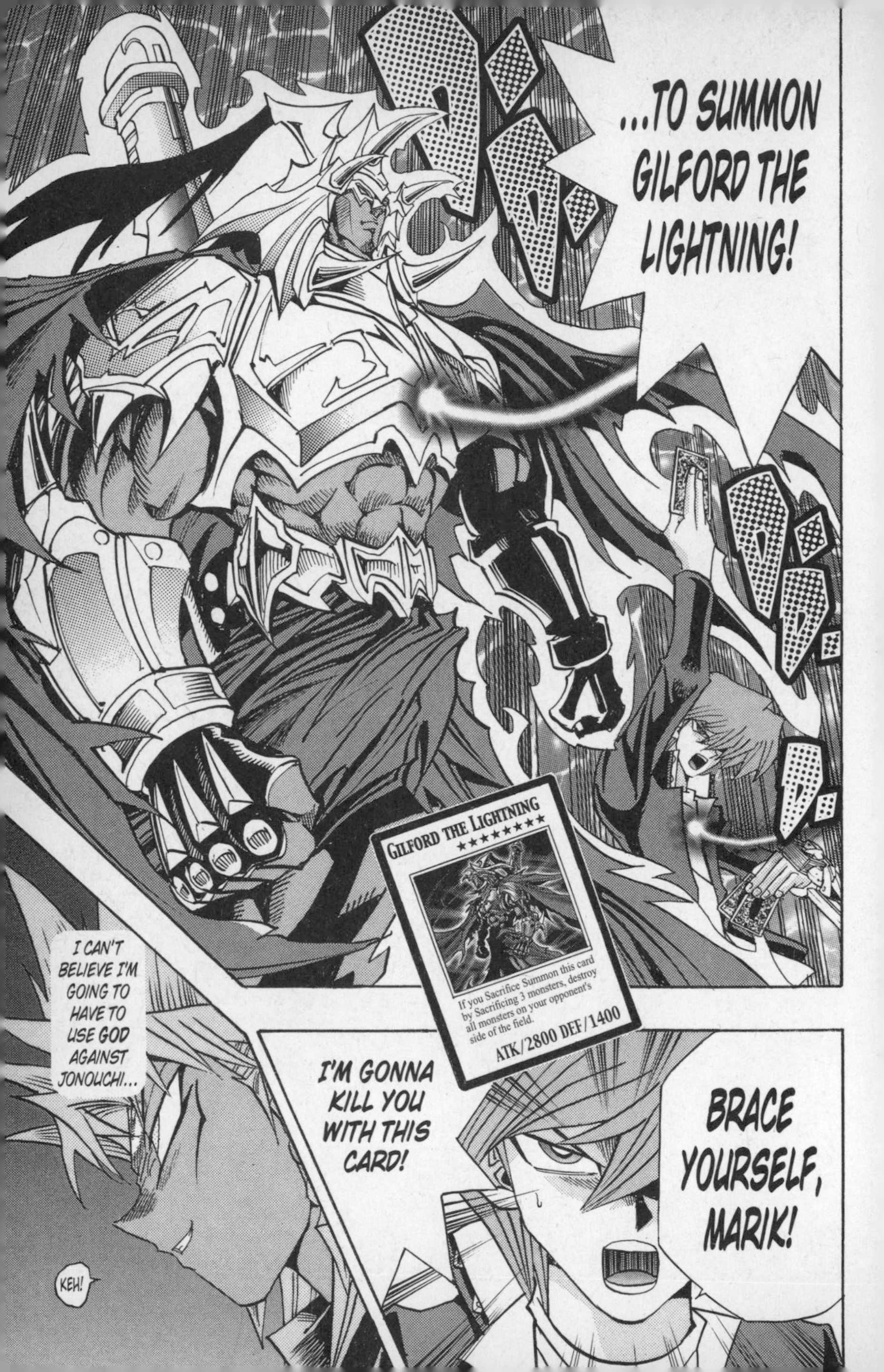
...TO SUMMON GILFORD THE LIGHTNING!
GILFORD THE LIGHTNING
If you Sacrifice Summon this card by Sacrificing 3 monsters, destroy all monsters on your opponent's side of the field.
ATK/2800 DEF/1400
BRACE YOURSELF, MARIK!
I'M GONNA KILL YOU WITH THIS CARD!
I CAN'T BELIEVE I'M GOING TO HAVE TO USE GOD AGAINST JONOUCHI...
KEH!

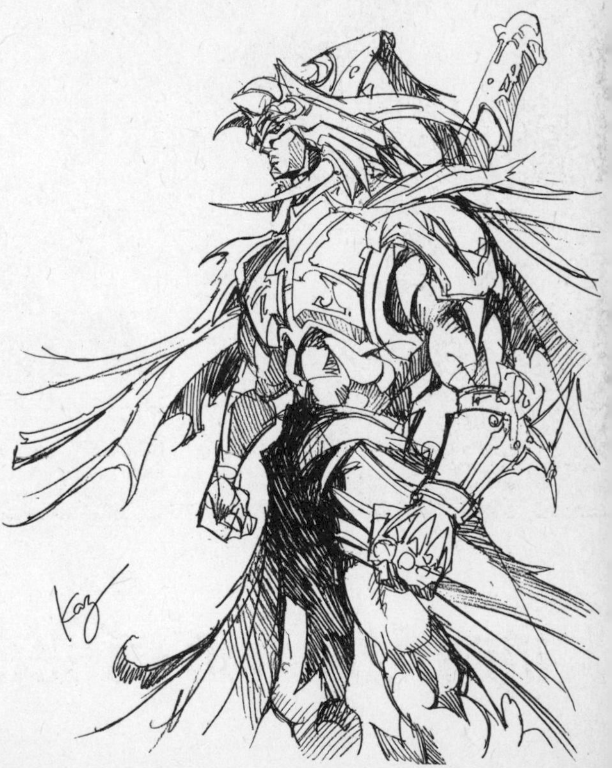
Kaz

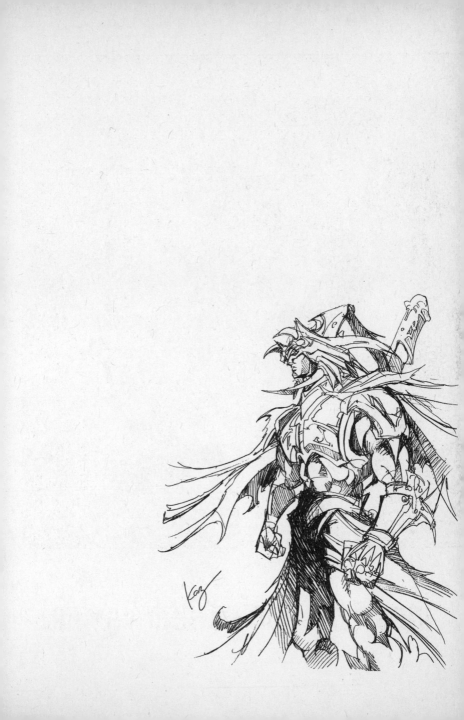

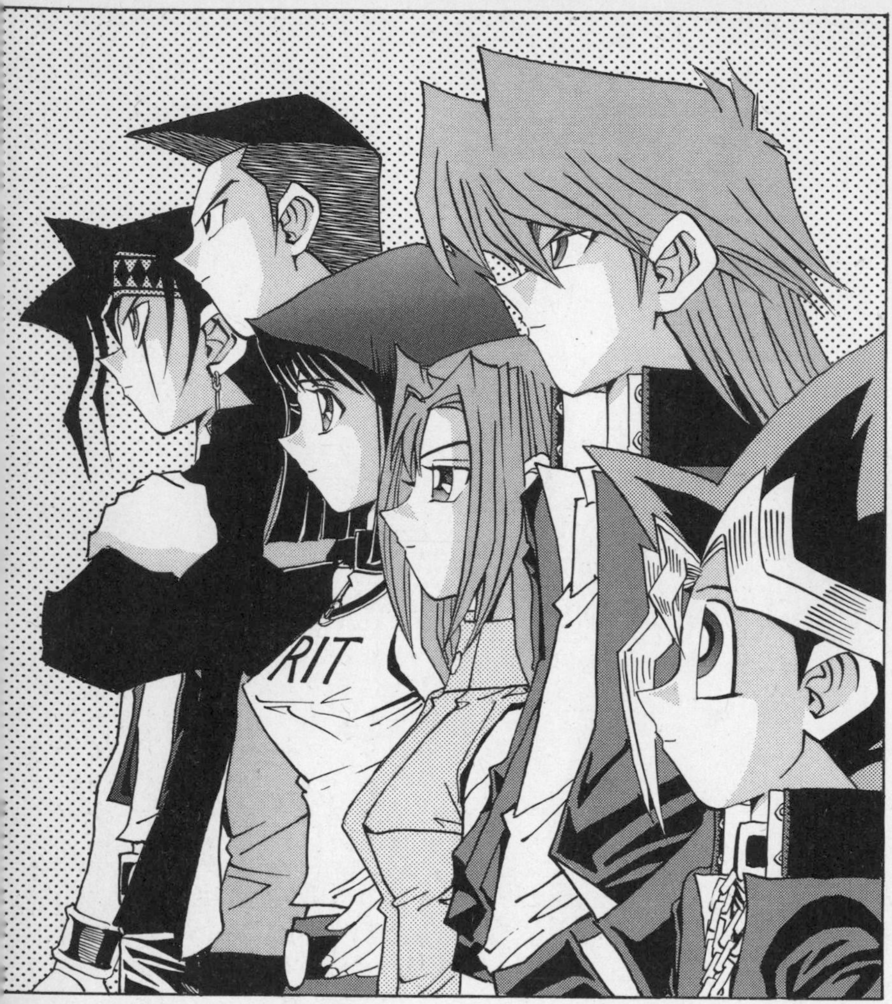
RIT

DUEL 189: GOD'S THIRD POWER!

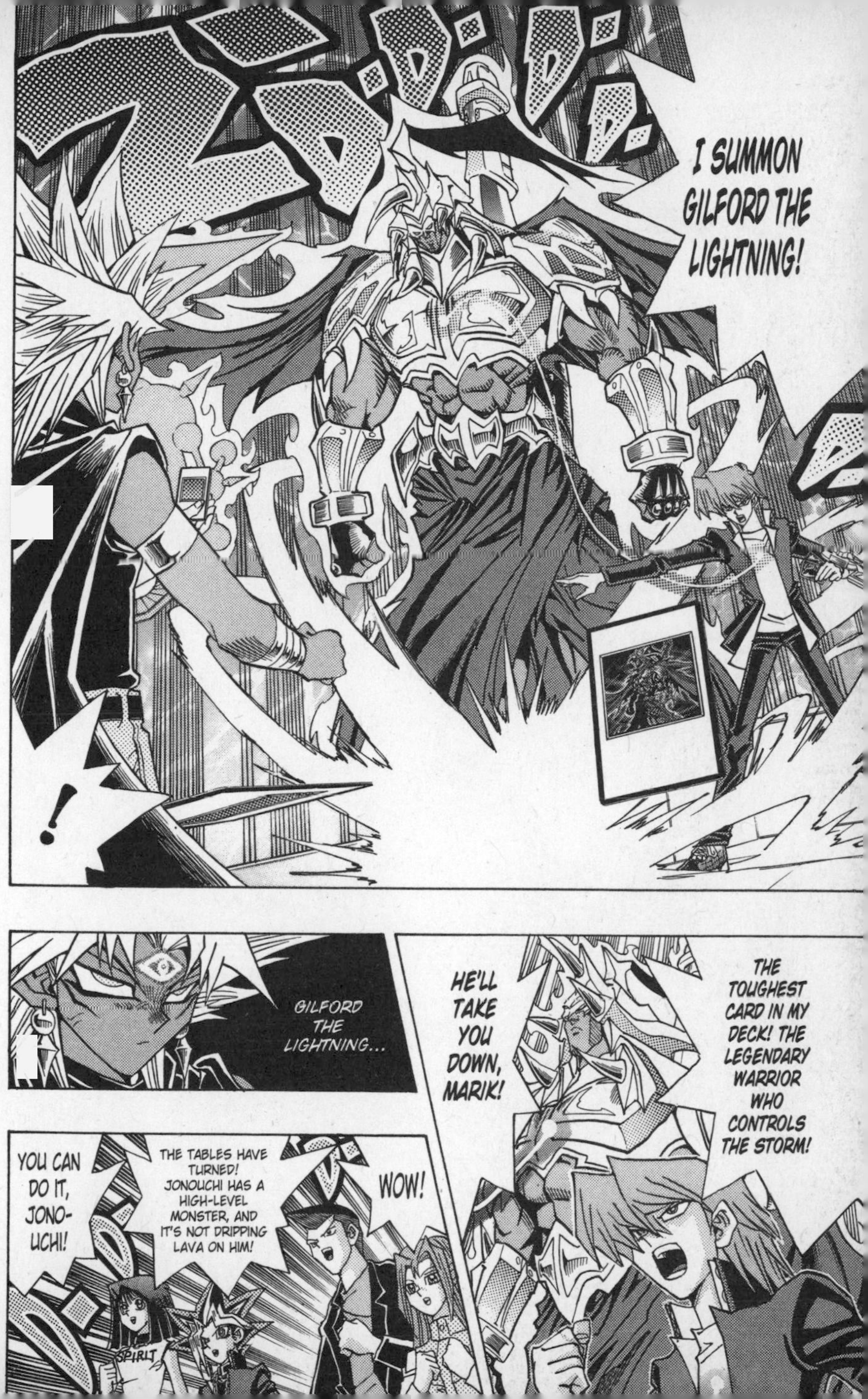
I SUMMON GILFORD THE LIGHTNING!
!
THE TOUGHEST CARD IN MY DECK! THE LEGENDARY WARRIOR WHO CONTROLS THE STORM!
HE'LL TAKE YOU DOWN, MARIK!
GILFORD THE LIGHTNING...
WOW!
THE TABLES HAVE TURNED! JONOUCHI HAS A HIGH-LEVEL MONSTER, AND IT'S NOT DRIPPING LAVA ON HIM!
YOU CAN DO IT, JONO-UCHI!
SPIRIT

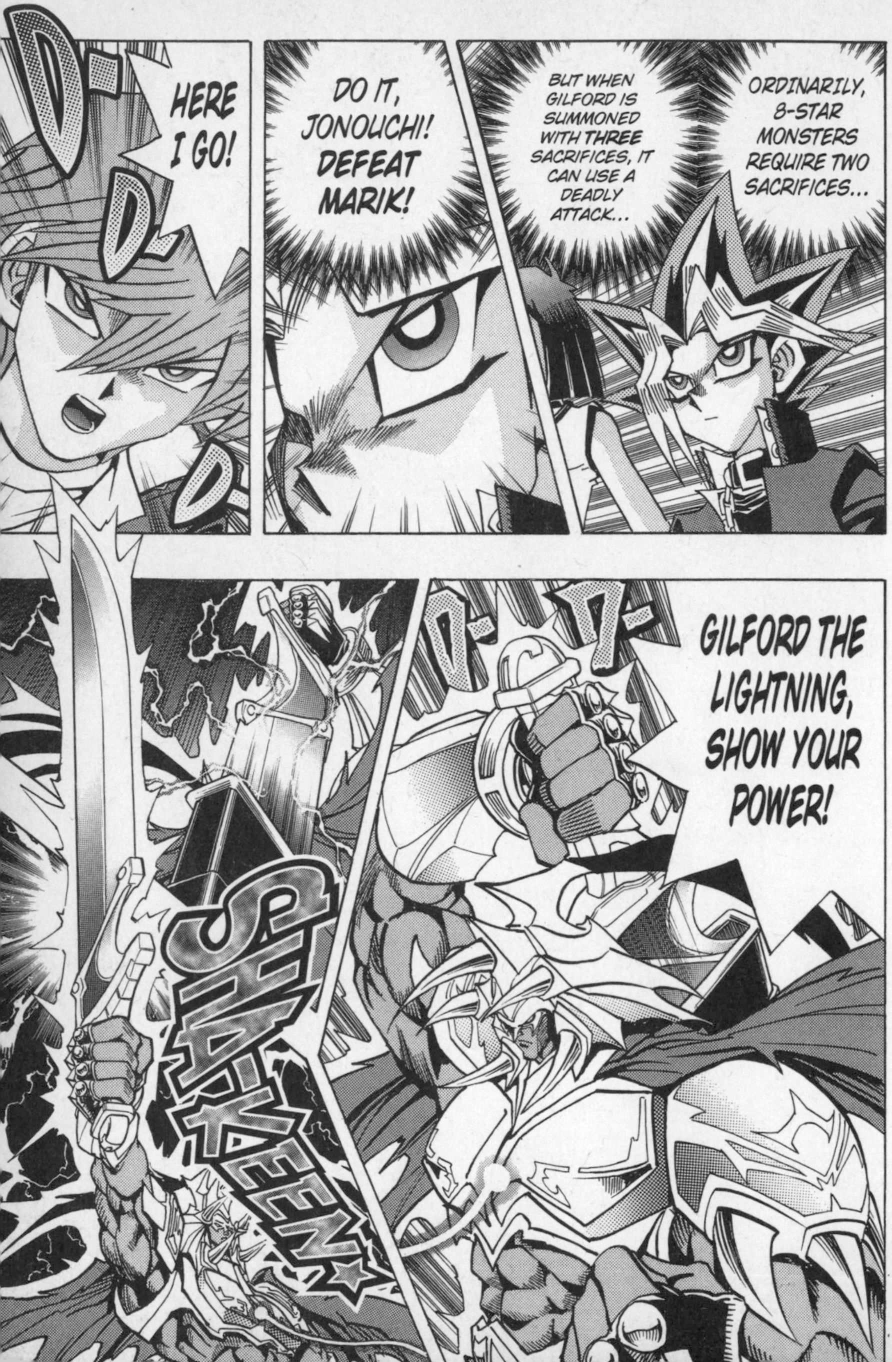
ORDINARILY, 8-STAR MONSTERS REQUIRE TWO SACRIFICES...
BUT WHEN GILFORD IS SUMMONED WITH THREE SACRIFICES, IT CAN USE A DEADLY ATTACK...
DO IT, JONOUCHI! DEFEAT MARIK!
HERE I GO!
D- D- D-
GILFORD THE LIGHTNING, SHOW YOUR POWER!
SHAKEEN

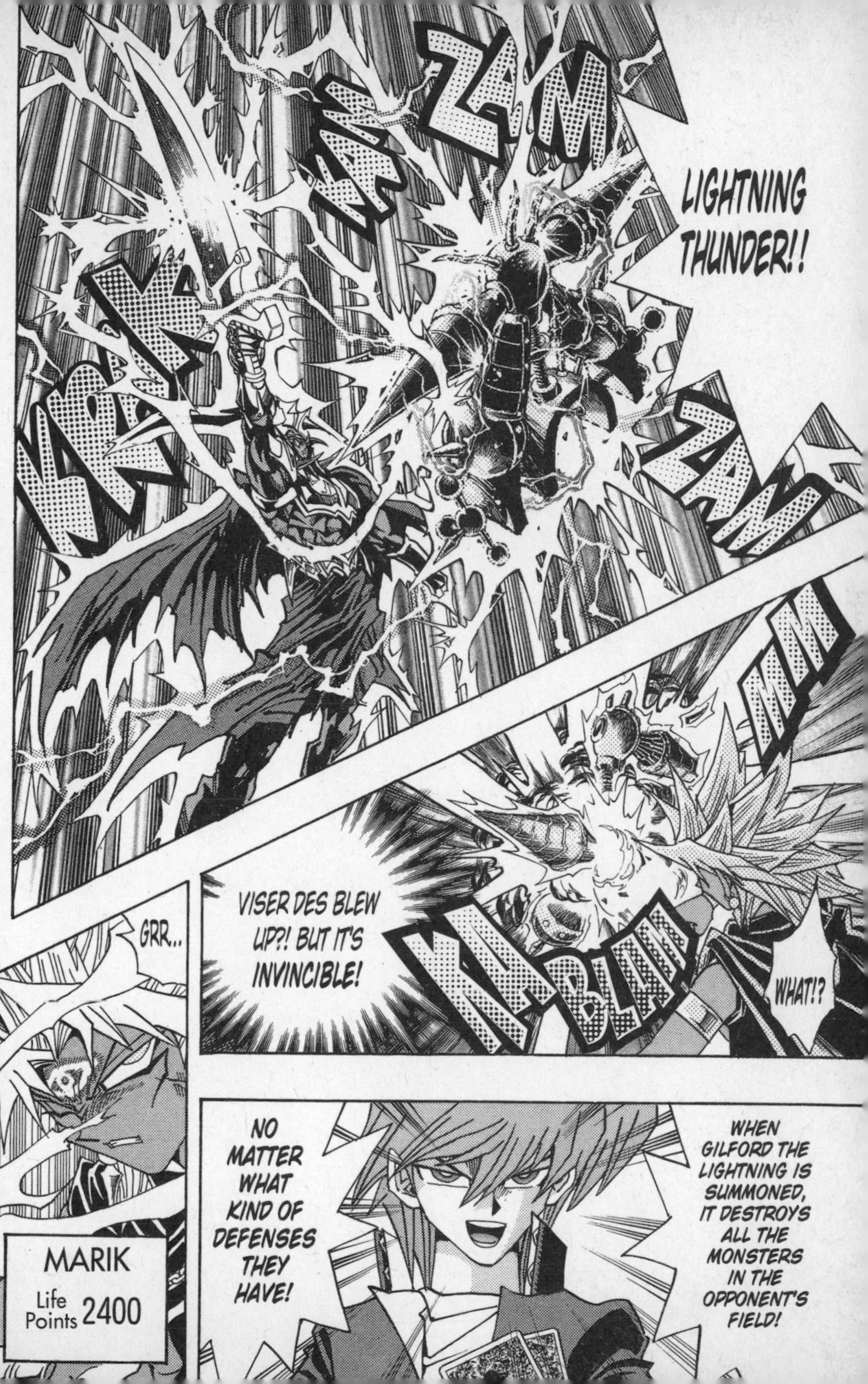

ZAM
LIGHTNING THUNDER!!
ZAM
WHAT!?
VISER DES BLEW UP?! BUT IT'S INVINCIBLE!
BLAM
WHEN GILFORD THE LIGHTNING IS SUMMONED, IT DESTROYS ALL THE MONSTERS IN THE OPPONENT'S FIELD!
NO MATTER WHAT KIND OF DEFENSES THEY HAVE!
GRR...
MARIK
Life Points 2400

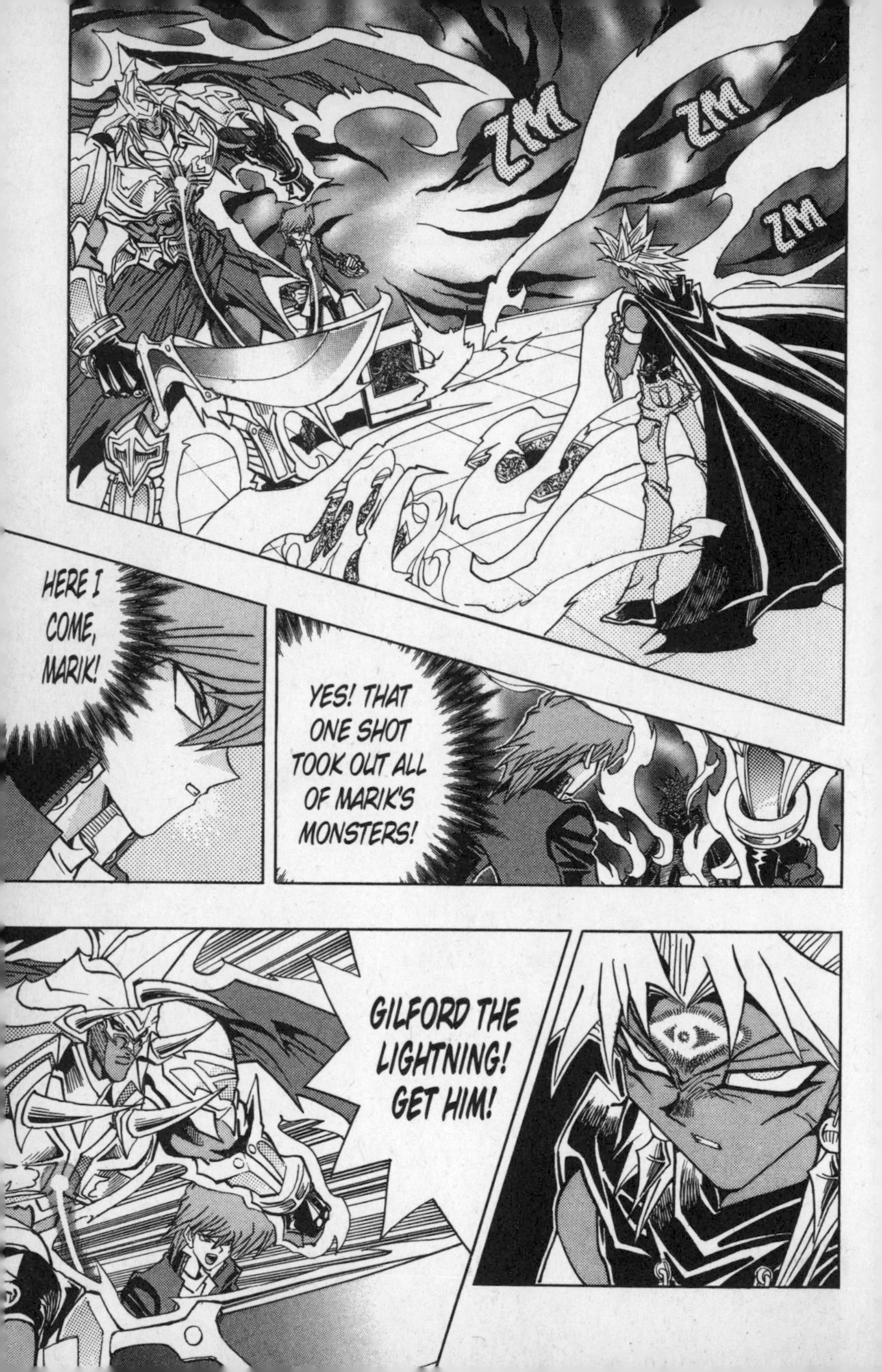
ZM
ZM
ZM
YES! THAT ONE SHOT TOOK OUT ALL OF MARIK'S MONSTERS!
HERE I COME, MARIK!
GILFORD THE LIGHTNING! GET HIM!

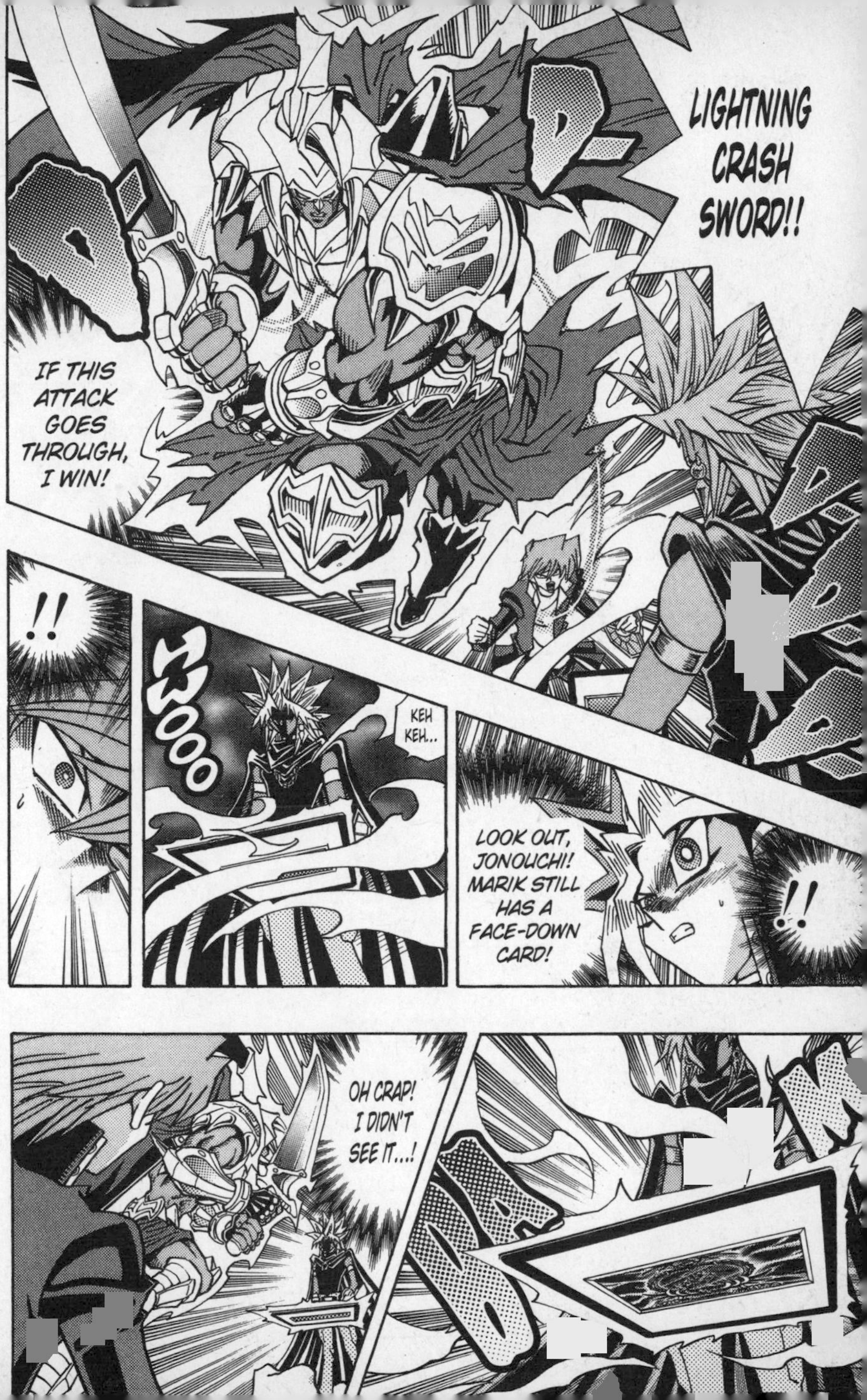
LIGHTNING CRASH SWORD!!
IF THIS ATTACK GOES THROUGH, I WIN!
!!
LOOK OUT, JONOUCHI! MARIK STILL HAS A FACE-DOWN CARD!
KEH KEH...
!!
OH CRAP! I DIDN'T SEE IT...!

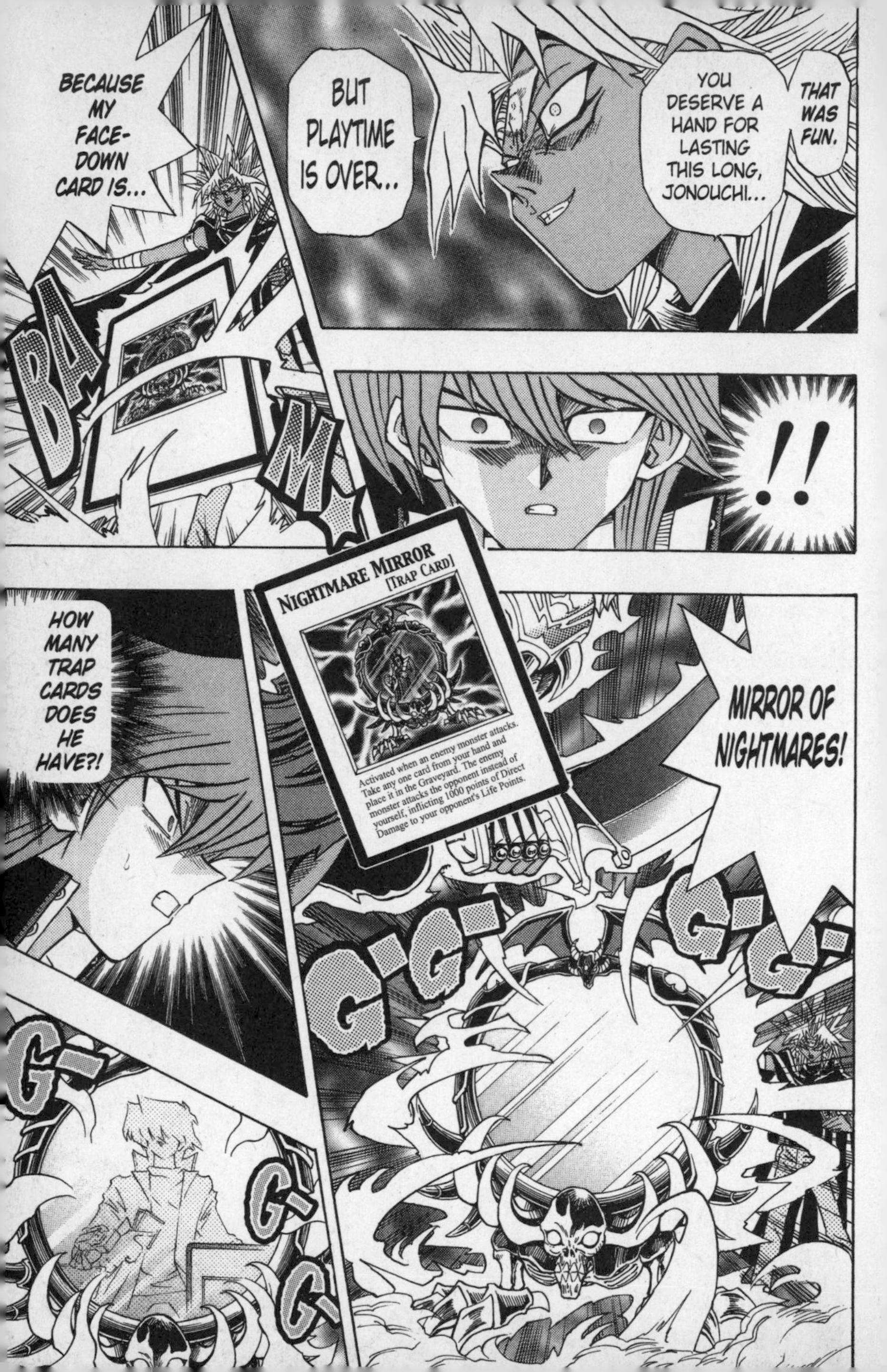
THAT WAS FUN.
YOU DESERVE A HAND FOR LASTING THIS LONG, JONOUCHI...
BUT PLAYTIME IS OVER...
BECAUSE MY FACE-DOWN CARD IS...
BAM
!!
MIRROR OF NIGHTMARES!
NIGHTMARE MIRROR
[TRAP CARD]
Activated when an enemy monster attacks. Take any one card from your hand and place it in the Graveyard. The enemy monster attacks the opponent instead of yourself, inflicting 1000 points of Direct Damage to your opponent's Life Points.
HOW MANY TRAP CARDS DOES HE HAVE?!
G-G-
G-G-
G-
G-
G-

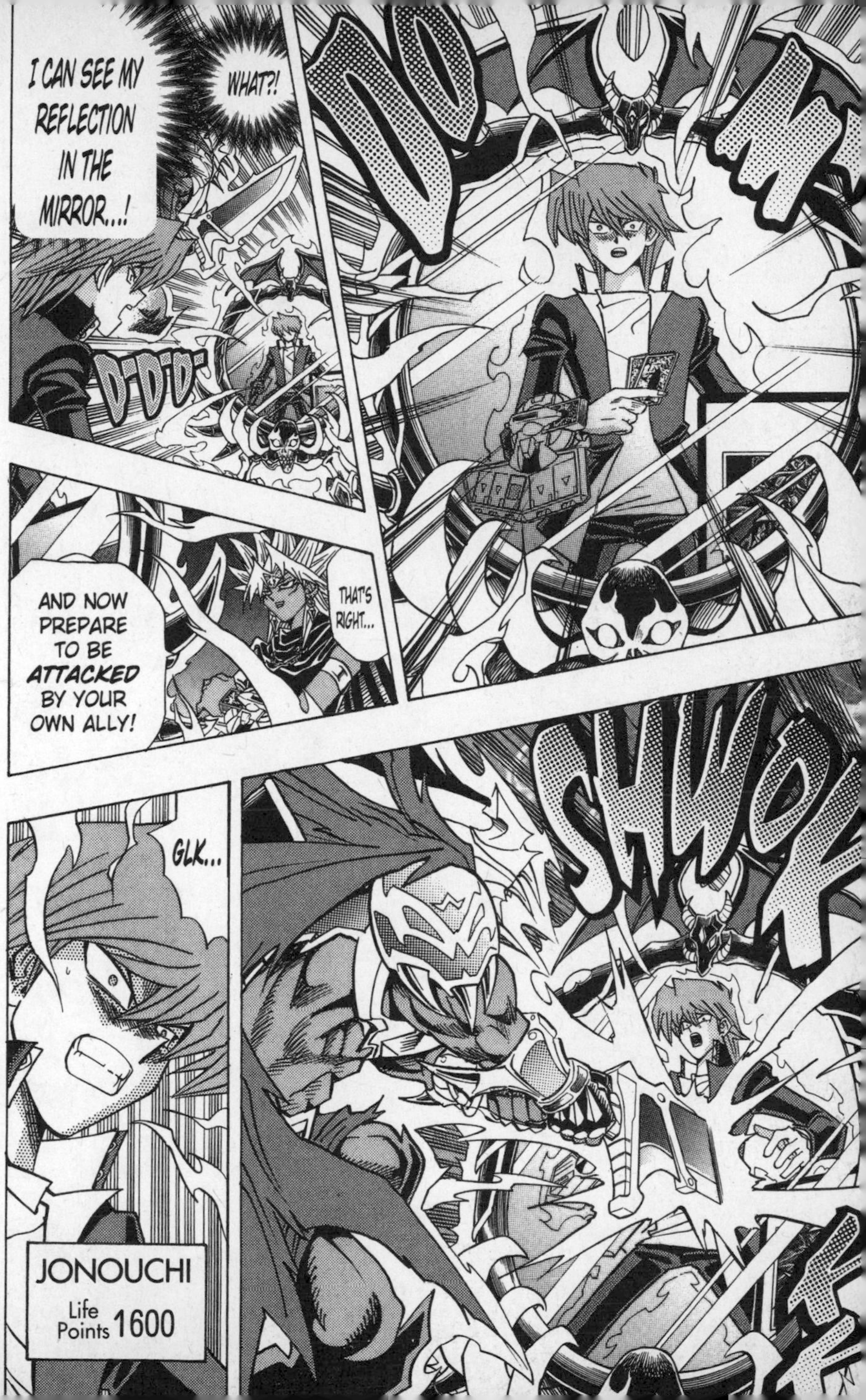
WHAT?!
I CAN SEE MY REFLECTION IN THE MIRROR...!
D-D-D-
THAT'S RIGHT...
AND NOW PREPARE TO BE **ATTACKED** BY YOUR OWN ALLY!
GLK...
JONOUCHI
Life Points 1600

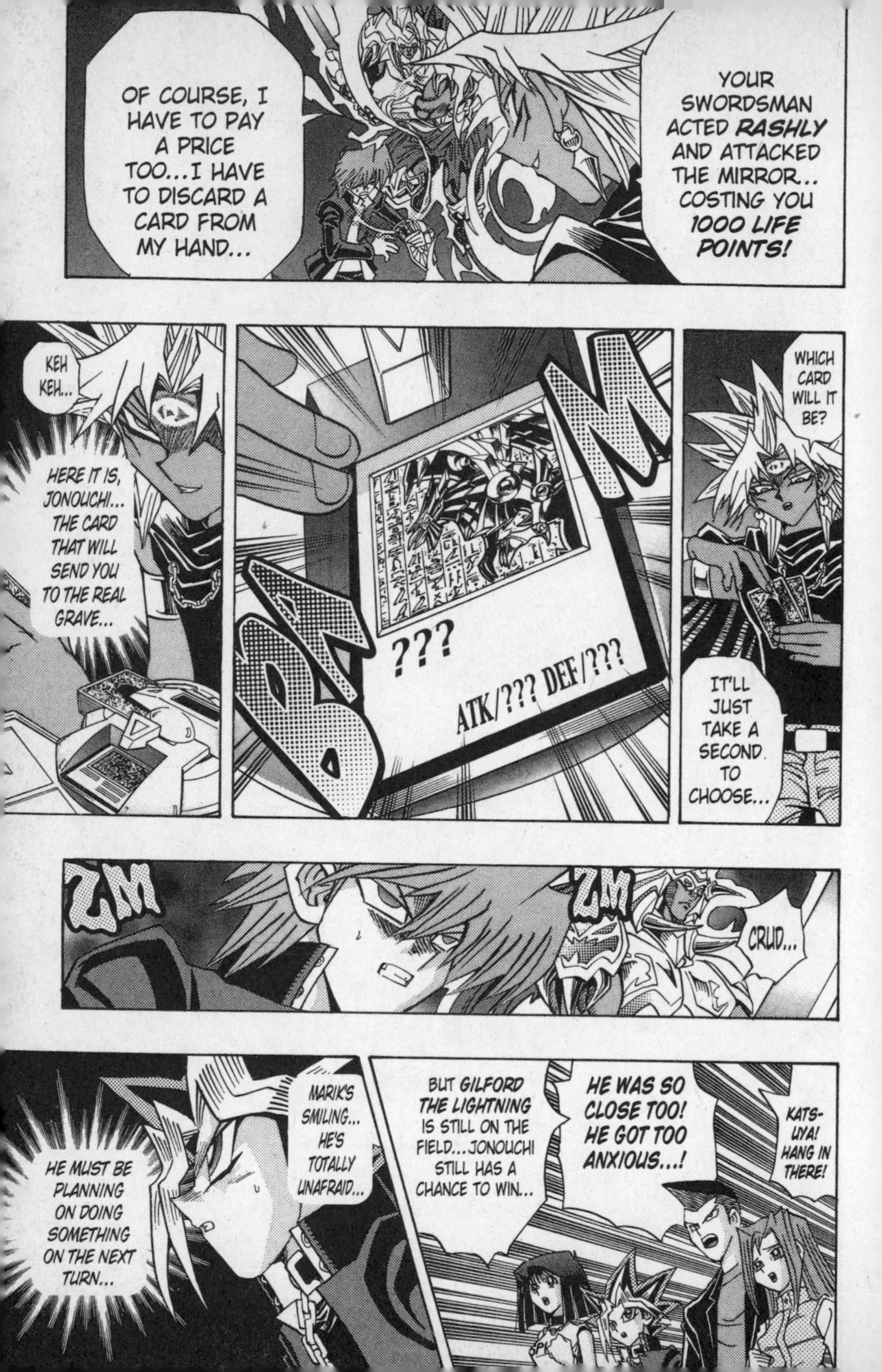
YOUR SWORDSMAN ACTED RASHLY AND ATTACKED THE MIRROR... COSTING YOU 1000 LIFE POINTS!
OF COURSE, I HAVE TO PAY A PRICE TOO...I HAVE TO DISCARD A CARD FROM MY HAND...
WHICH CARD WILL IT BE?
IT'LL JUST TAKE A SECOND TO CHOOSE...
BAM
???
ATK/??? DEF/???
KEH KEH...
HERE IT IS, JONOUCHI... THE CARD THAT WILL SEND YOU TO THE REAL GRAVE...
ZM
ZM
CRUD...
KATSUYA! HANG IN THERE!
HE WAS SO CLOSE TOO! HE GOT TOO ANXIOUS...!
BUT GILFORD THE LIGHTNING IS STILL ON THE FIELD...JONOUCHI STILL HAS A CHANCE TO WIN...
MARIK'S SMILING... HE'S TOTALLY UNAFRAID...
HE MUST BE PLANNING ON DOING SOMETHING ON THE NEXT TURN...

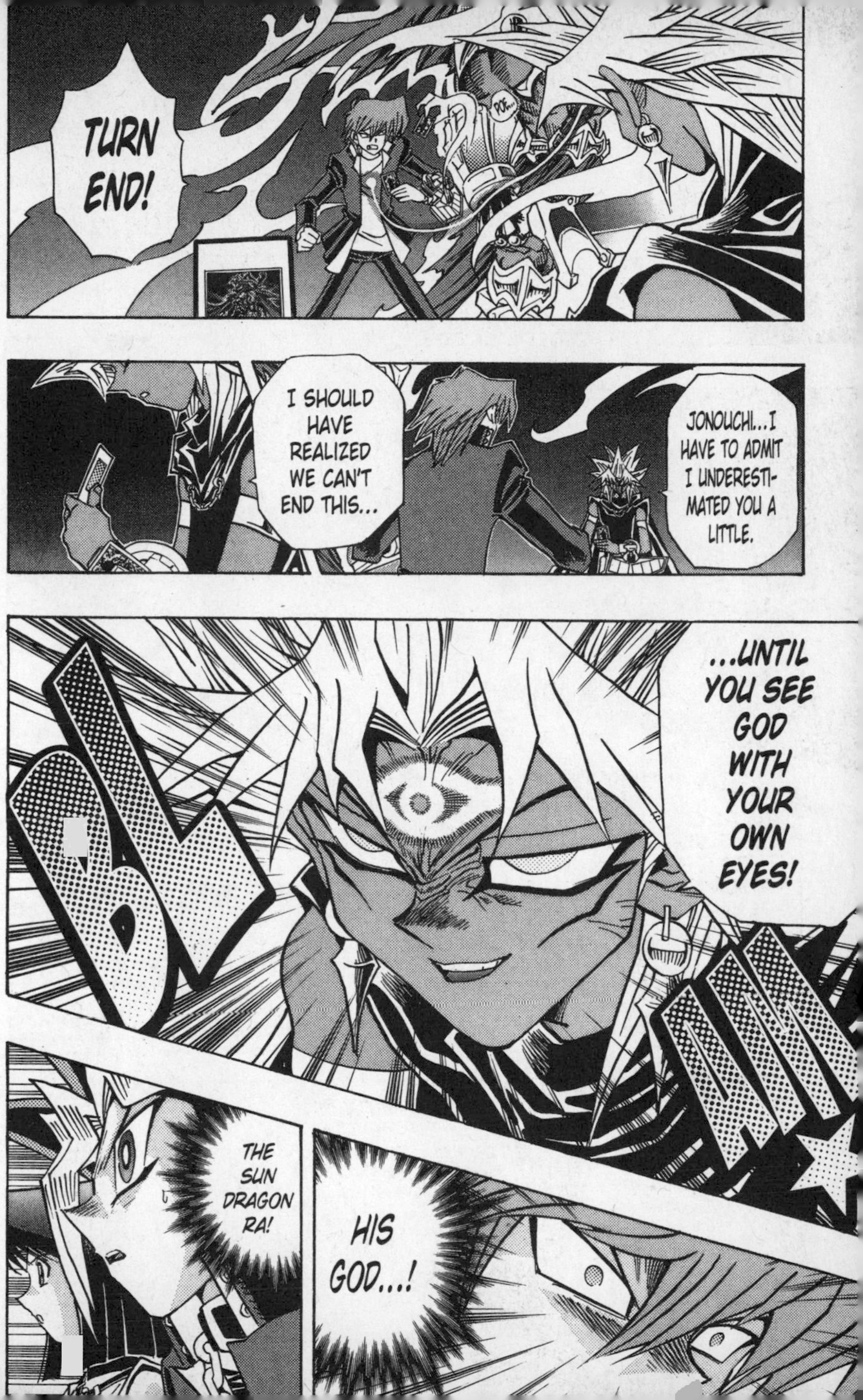
TURN END!
JONOUCHI...I HAVE TO ADMIT I UNDERESTIMATED YOU A LITTLE.
I SHOULD HAVE REALIZED WE CAN'T END THIS...
...UNTIL YOU SEE GOD WITH YOUR OWN EYES!
HIS GOD...!
THE SUN DRAGON RA!

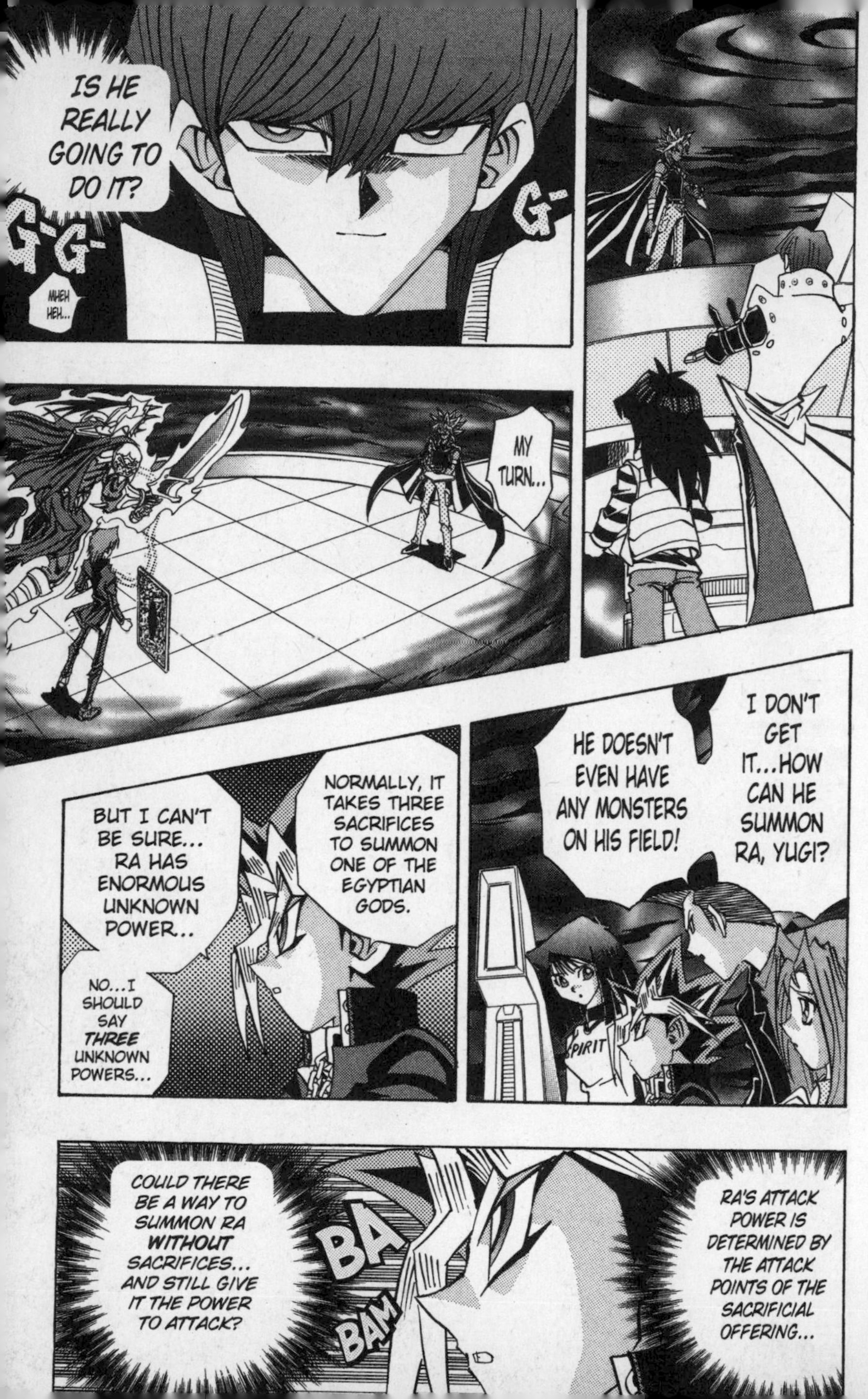
G-
IS HE REALLY GOING TO DO IT?
G-G-
MHEH HEH...
MY TURN...
I DON'T GET IT...HOW CAN HE SUMMON RA, YUGI?
HE DOESN'T EVEN HAVE ANY MONSTERS ON HIS FIELD!
NORMALLY, IT TAKES THREE SACRIFICES TO SUMMON ONE OF THE EGYPTIAN GODS.
BUT I CAN'T BE SURE... RA HAS ENORMOUS UNKNOWN POWER...
NO...I SHOULD SAY *THREE* UNKNOWN POWERS...
RA'S ATTACK POWER IS DETERMINED BY THE ATTACK POINTS OF THE SACRIFICIAL OFFERING...
BA BAM
COULD THERE BE A WAY TO SUMMON RA **WITHOUT** SACRIFICES... AND STILL GIVE IT THE POWER TO ATTACK?

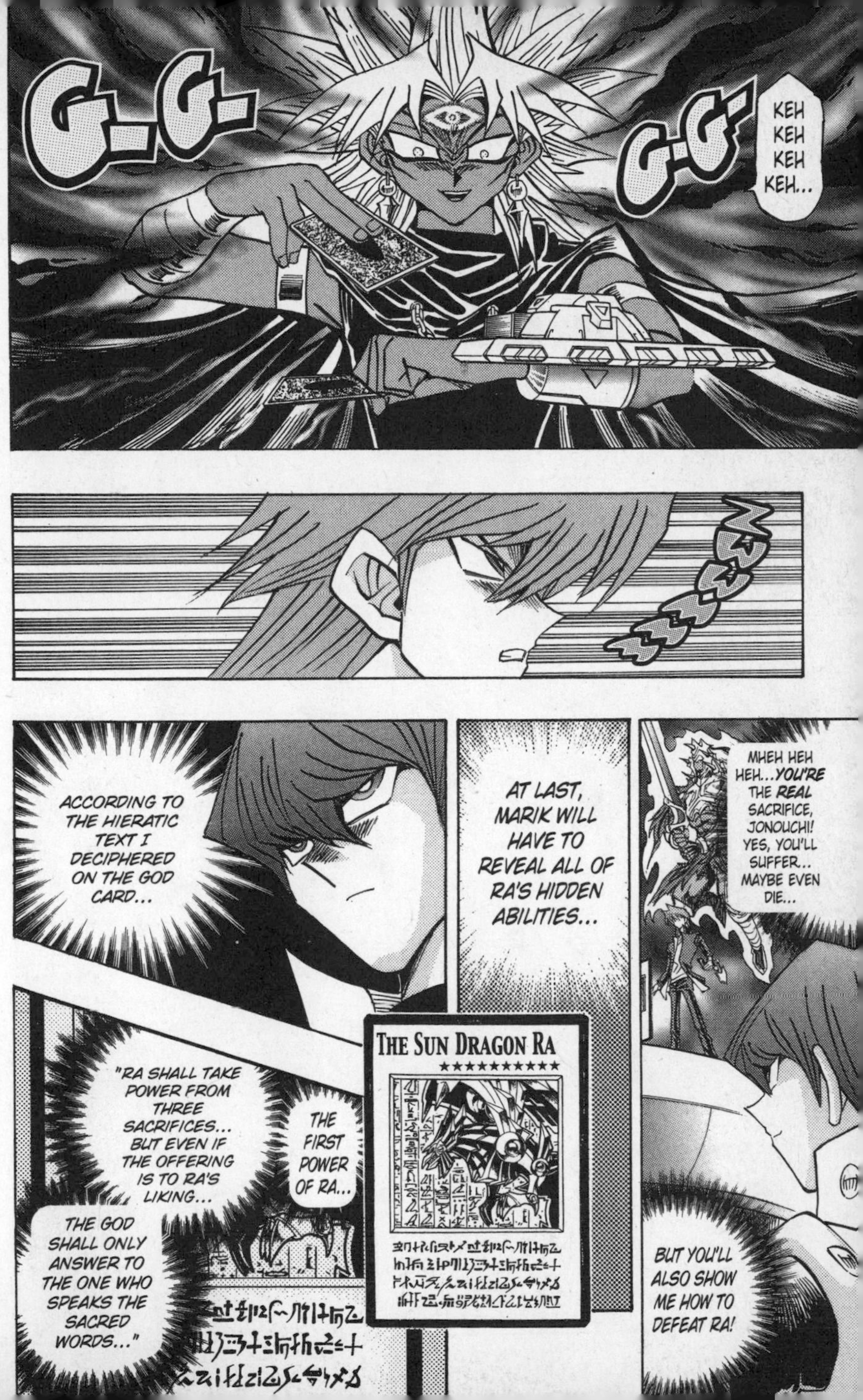
KEH KEH KEH KEH...
G-G-
G-G-
MHEH HEH HEH... YOU'RE THE REAL SACRIFICE, JONOUCHI! YES, YOU'LL SUFFER... MAYBE EVEN DIE...
BUT YOU'LL ALSO SHOW ME HOW TO DEFEAT RA!
AT LAST, MARIK WILL HAVE TO REVEAL ALL OF RA'S HIDDEN ABILITIES...
ACCORDING TO THE HIERATIC TEXT I DECIPHERED ON THE GOD CARD...
THE SUN DRAGON RA
THE FIRST POWER OF RA...
"RA SHALL TAKE POWER FROM THREE SACRIFICES... BUT EVEN IF THE OFFERING IS TO RA'S LIKING...
THE GOD SHALL ONLY ANSWER TO THE ONE WHO SPEAKS THE SACRED WORDS..."

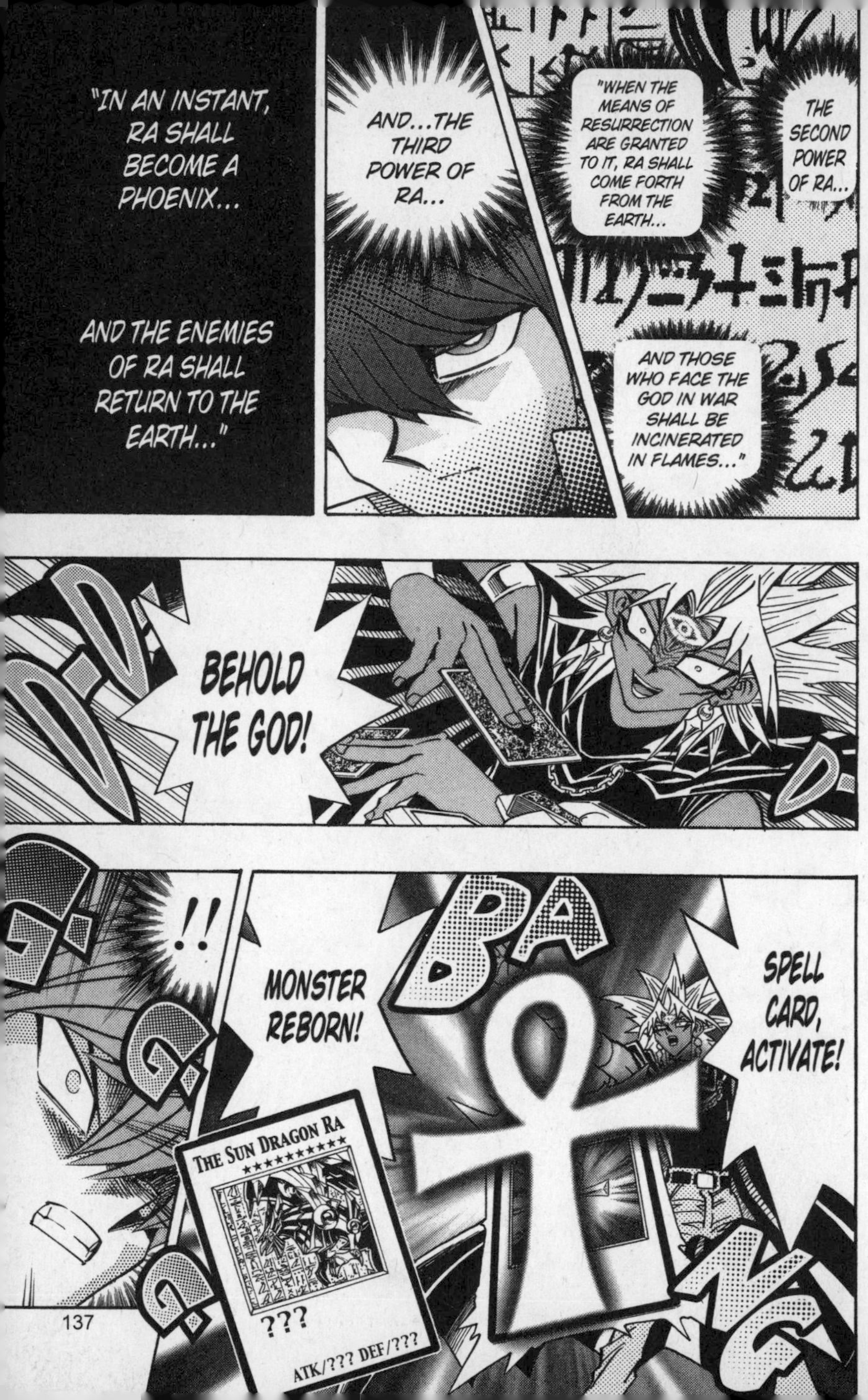
THE SECOND POWER OF RA...
"WHEN THE MEANS OF RESURRECTION ARE GRANTED TO IT, RA SHALL COME FORTH FROM THE EARTH...
AND THOSE WHO FACE THE GOD IN WAR SHALL BE INCINERATED IN FLAMES..."
AND...THE THIRD POWER OF RA...
"IN AN INSTANT, RA SHALL BECOME A PHOENIX...
AND THE ENEMIES OF RA SHALL RETURN TO THE EARTH..."
BEHOLD THE GOD!
BA
SPELL CARD, ACTIVATE!
MONSTER REBORN!
THE SUN DRAGON RA
???
ATK/??? DEF/???
!!

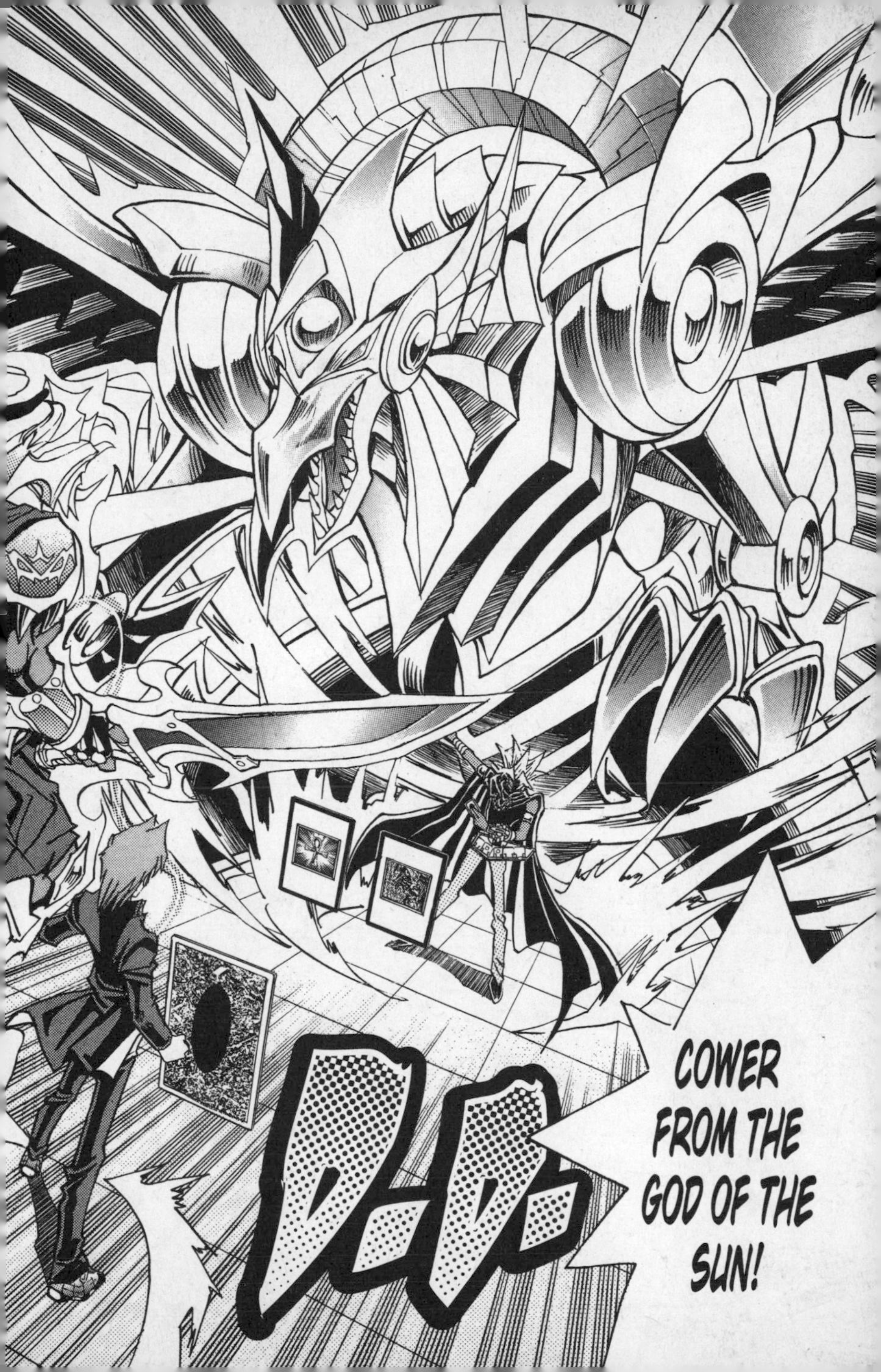
COWER FROM THE GOD OF THE SUN!

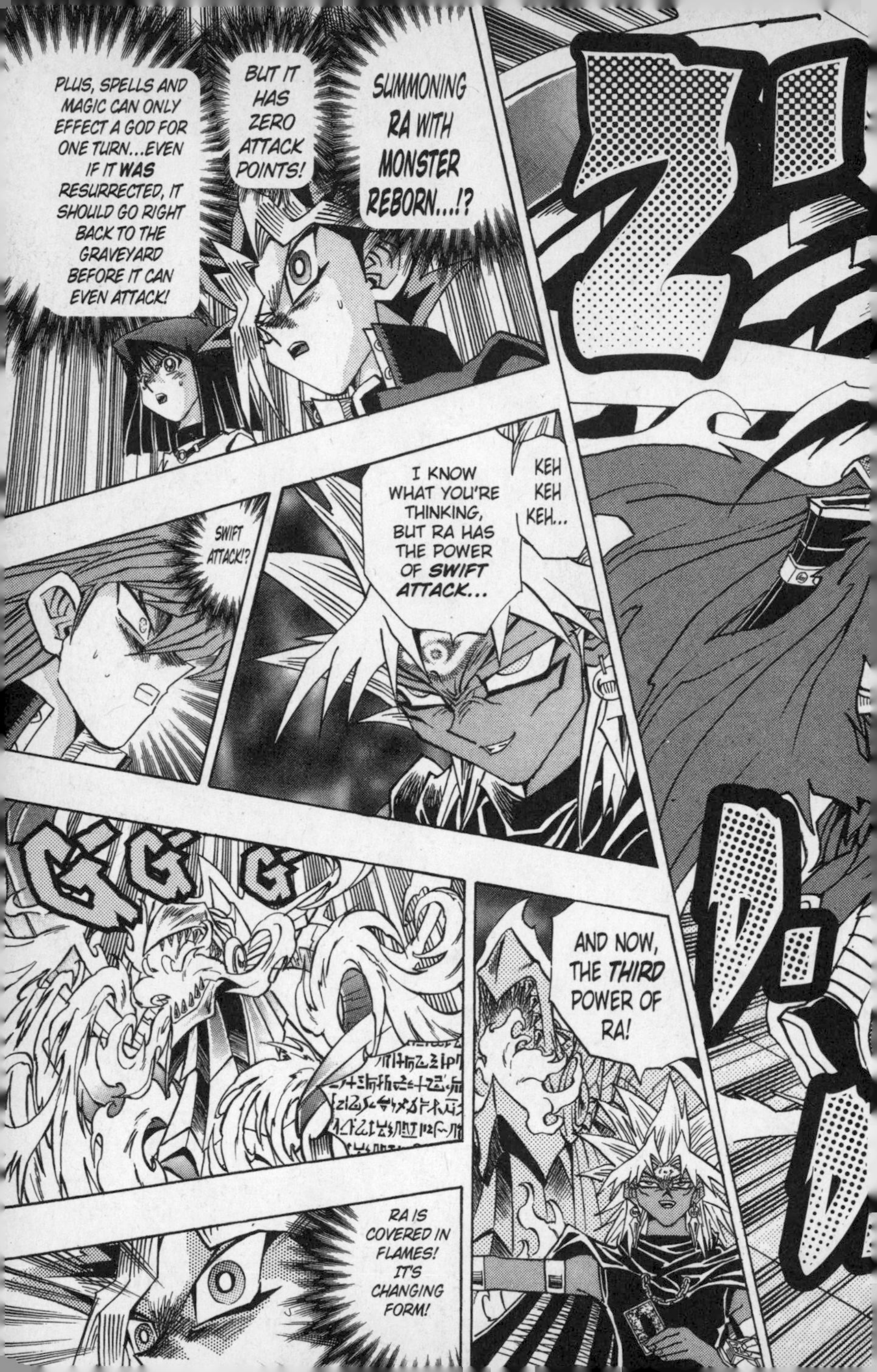
SUMMONING RA WITH MONSTER REBORN...!?
BUT IT HAS ZERO ATTACK POINTS!
PLUS, SPELLS AND MAGIC CAN ONLY EFFECT A GOD FOR ONE TURN...EVEN IF IT **WAS** RESURRECTED, IT SHOULD GO RIGHT BACK TO THE GRAVEYARD BEFORE IT CAN EVEN ATTACK!
KEH KEH KEH...
I KNOW WHAT YOU'RE THINKING, BUT RA HAS THE POWER OF ***SWIFT ATTACK...***
SWIFT ATTACK!?
AND NOW, THE *THIRD* POWER OF RA!
G G G
RA IS COVERED IN FLAMES! IT'S CHANGING FORM!

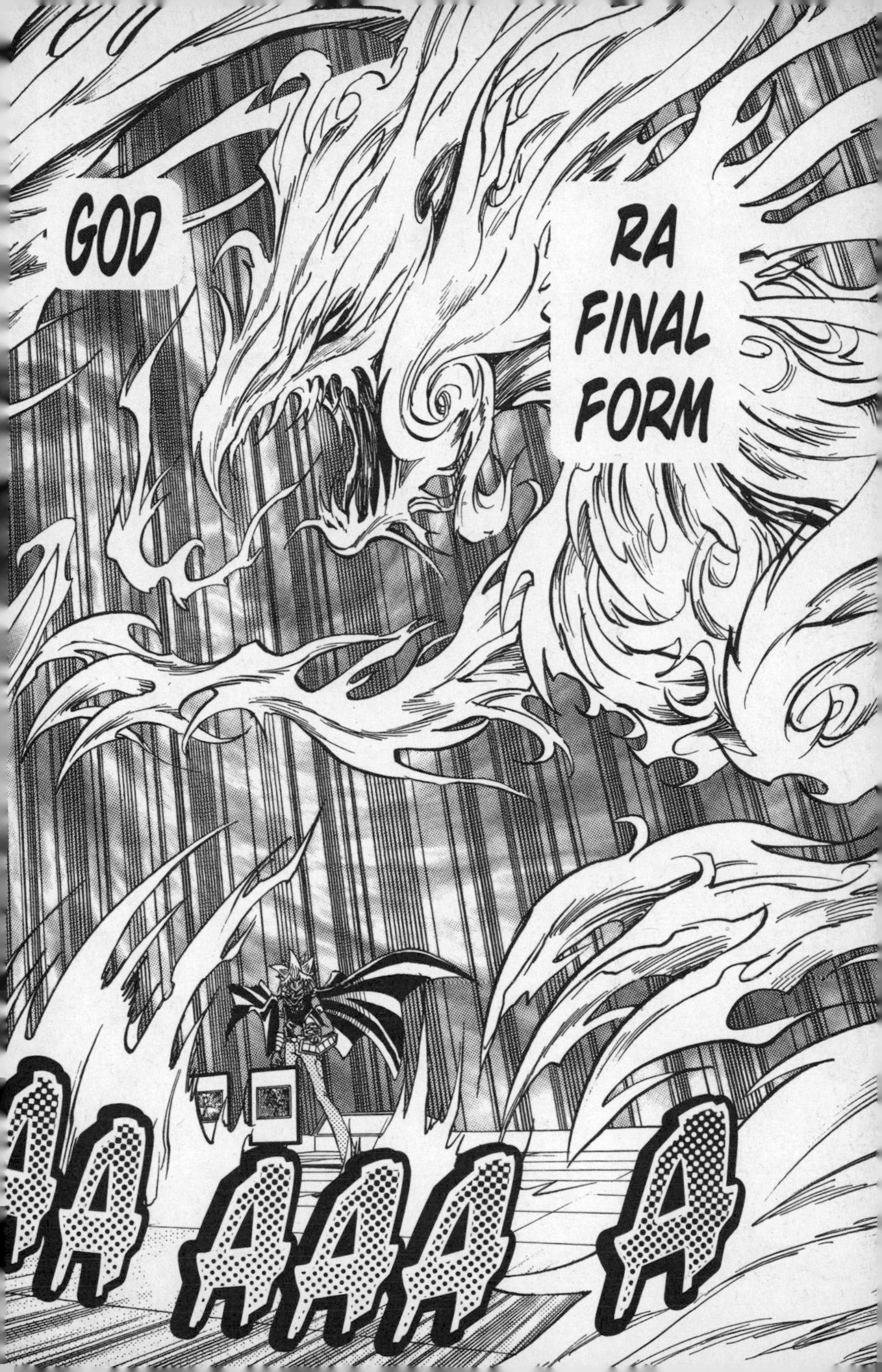
GOD
RA
FINAL
FORM
AAAAAAA

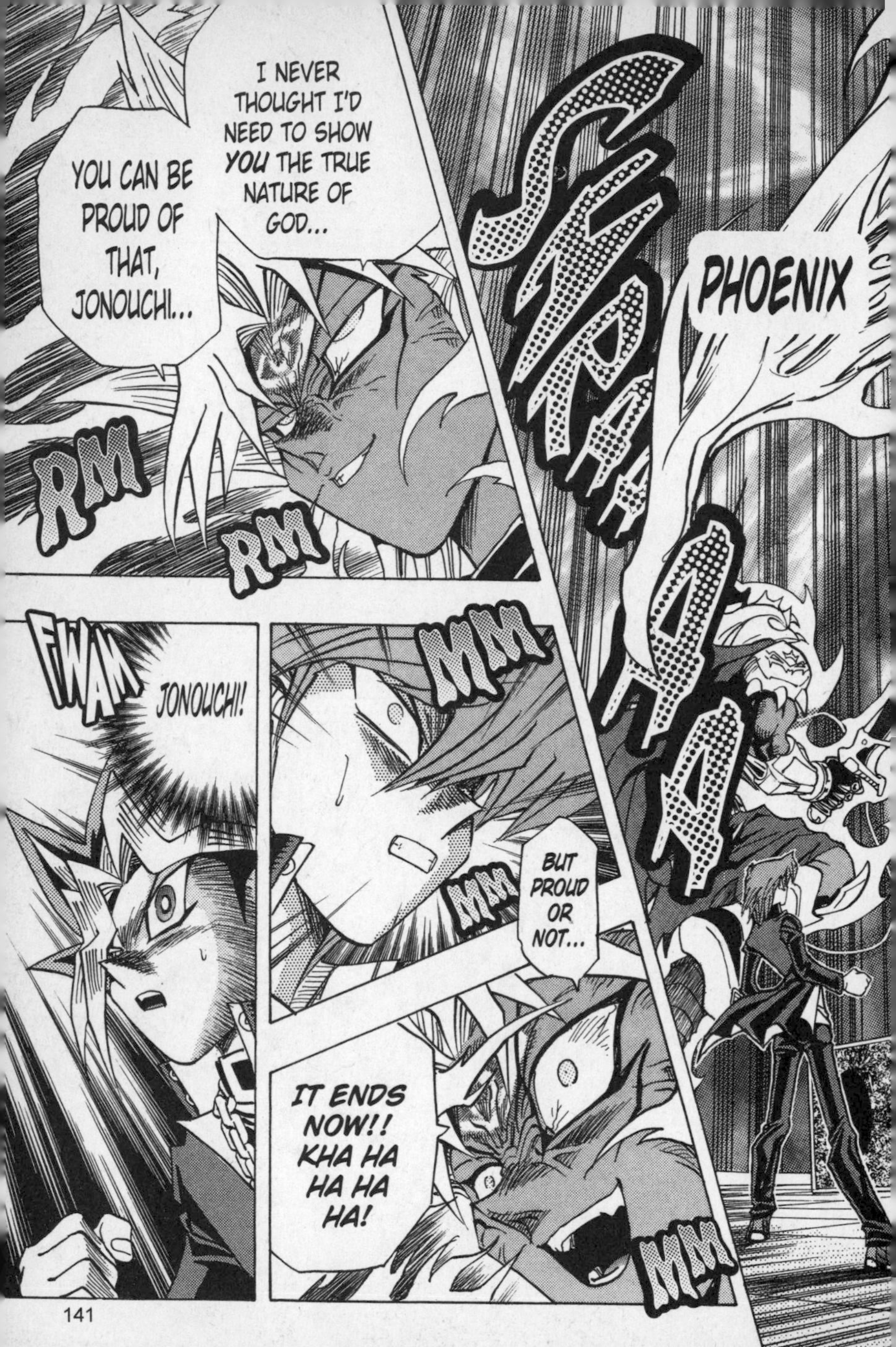

PHOENIX
SHAAAA
I NEVER THOUGHT I'D NEED TO SHOW *YOU* THE TRUE NATURE OF GOD...
YOU CAN BE PROUD OF THAT, JONOUCHI...
RM
RM
MM
MM
BUT PROUD OR NOT...
IT ENDS NOW!! KHA HA HA HA HA!
MM
FWAM
JONOUCHI!

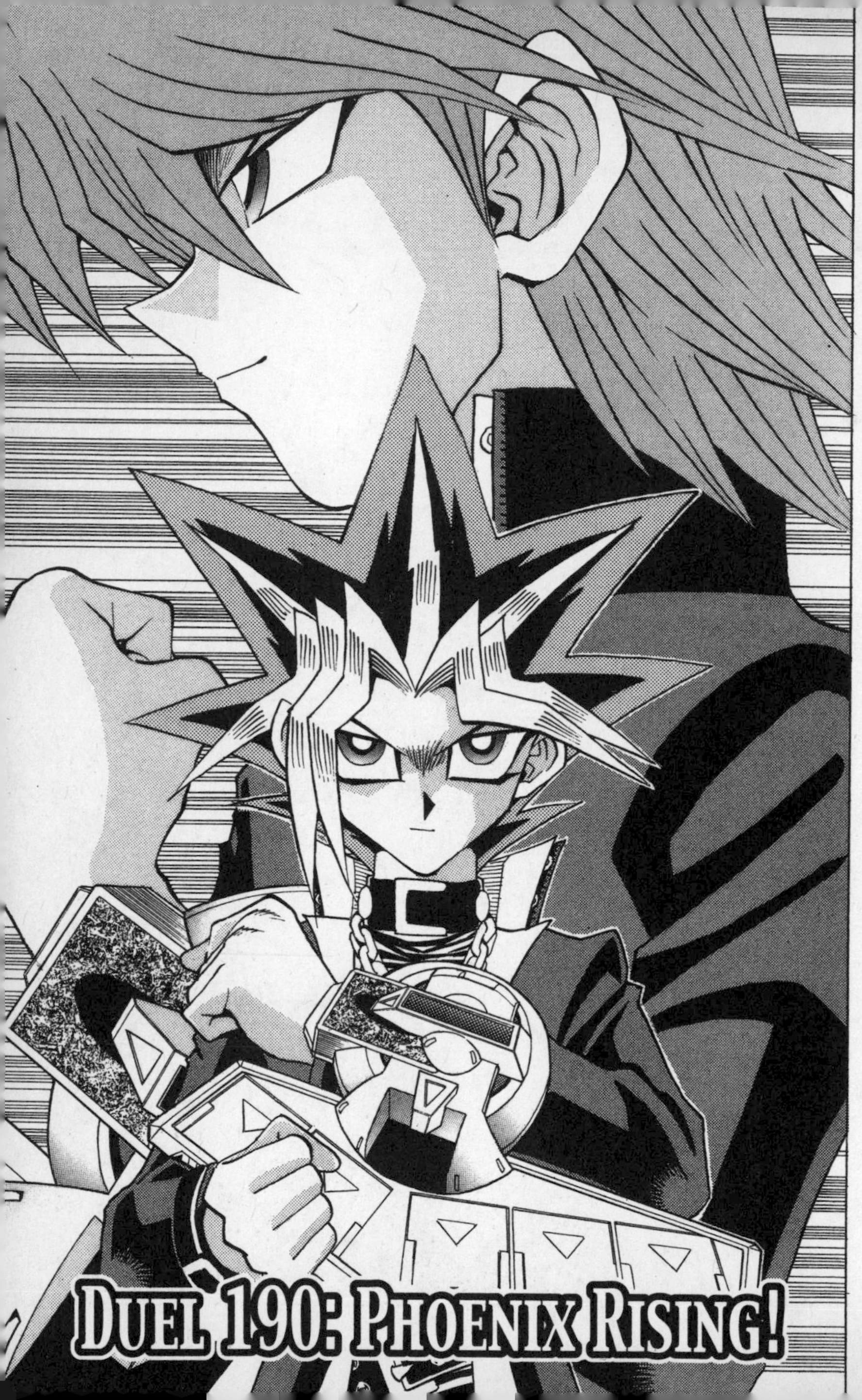
Duel 190: Phoenix Rising!

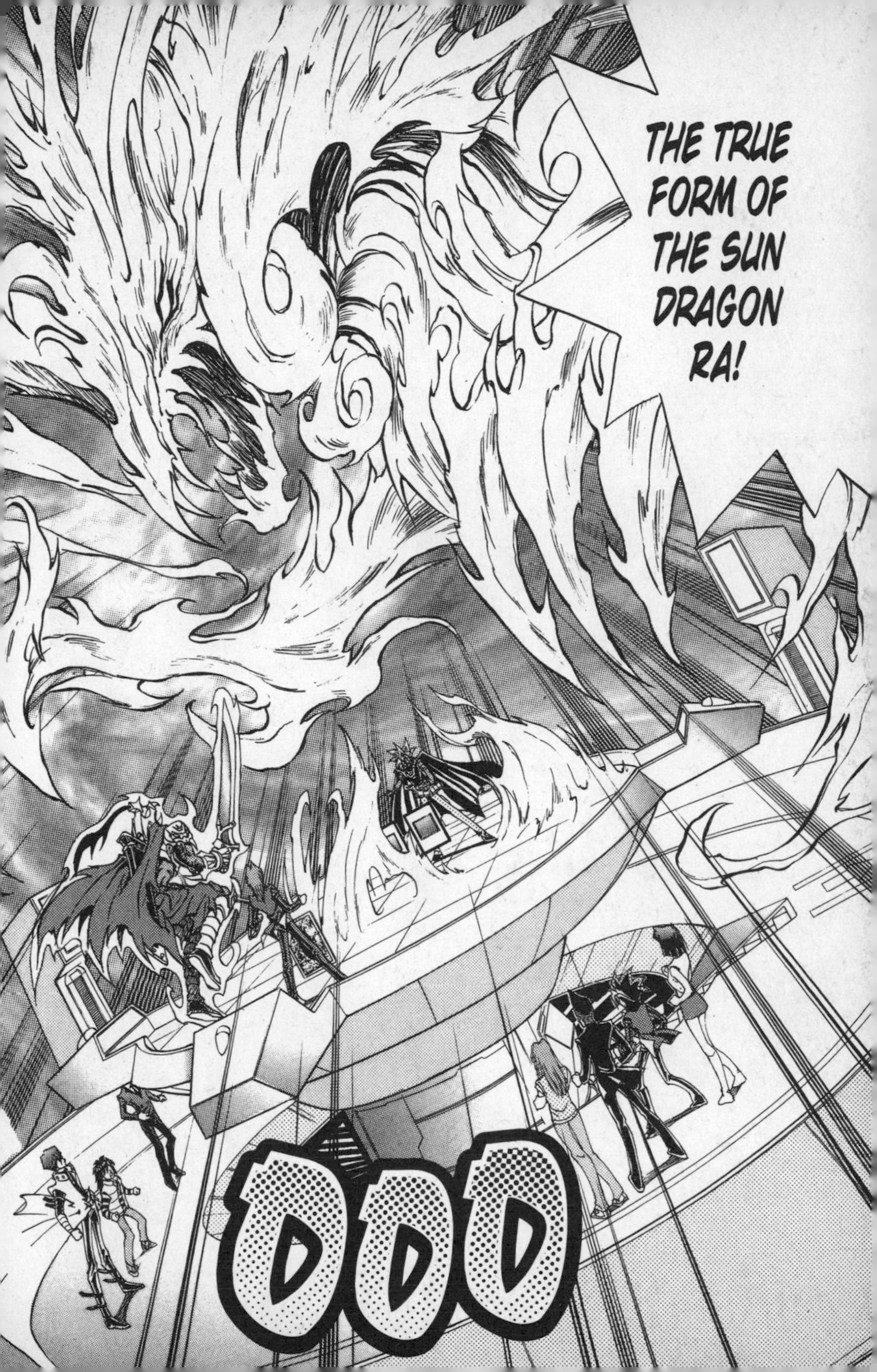
THE TRUE FORM OF THE SUN DRAGON RA!
DDD

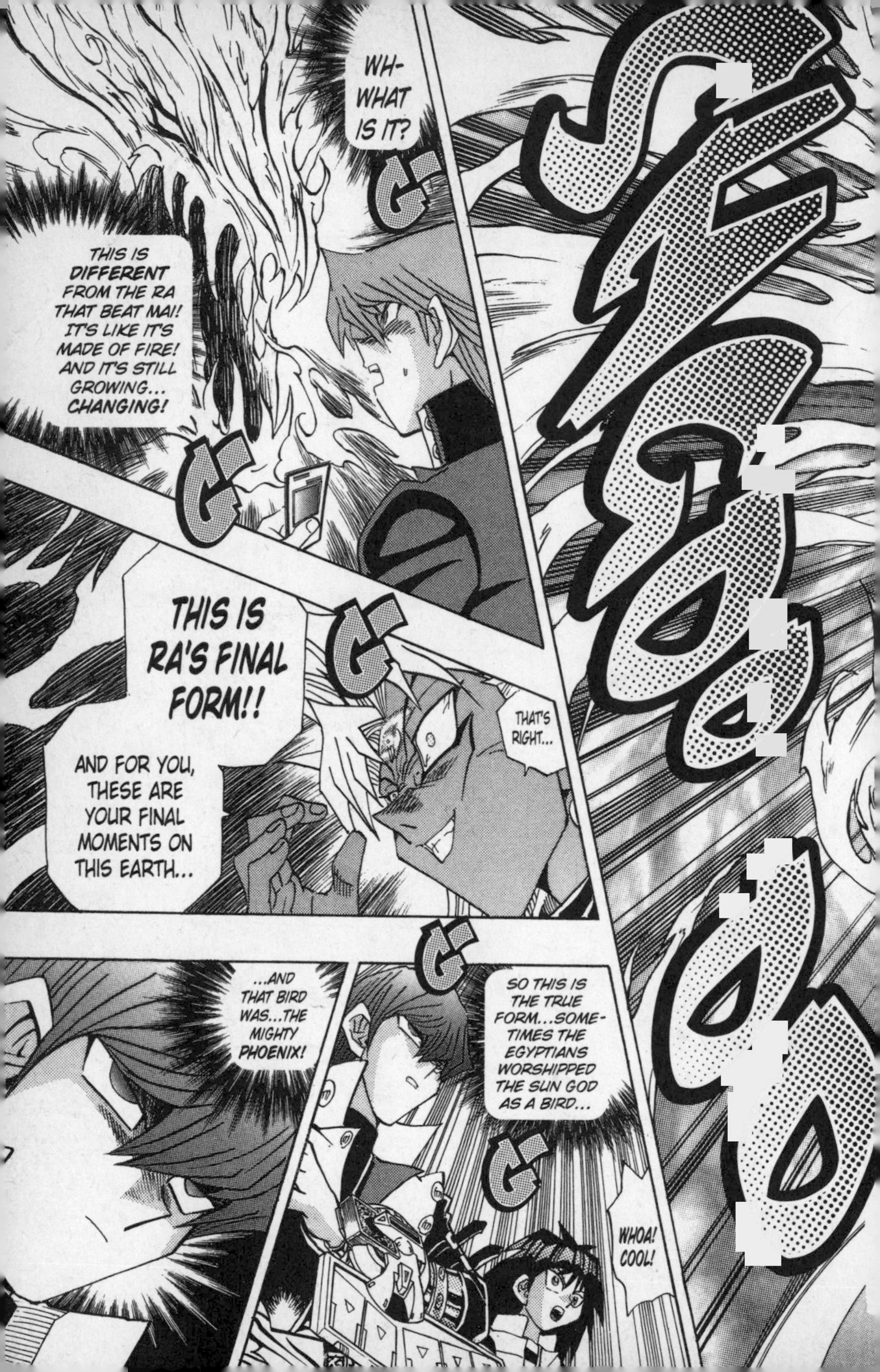
WH- WHAT IS IT?
THIS IS DIFFERENT FROM THE RA THAT BEAT MAI! IT'S LIKE IT'S MADE OF FIRE! AND IT'S STILL GROWING... CHANGING!
THAT'S RIGHT...
THIS IS RA'S FINAL FORM!!
AND FOR YOU, THESE ARE YOUR FINAL MOMENTS ON THIS EARTH...
SO THIS IS THE TRUE FORM...SOME-TIMES THE EGYPTIANS WORSHIPPED THE SUN GOD AS A BIRD...
WHOA! COOL!
...AND THAT BIRD WAS...THE MIGHTY PHOENIX!

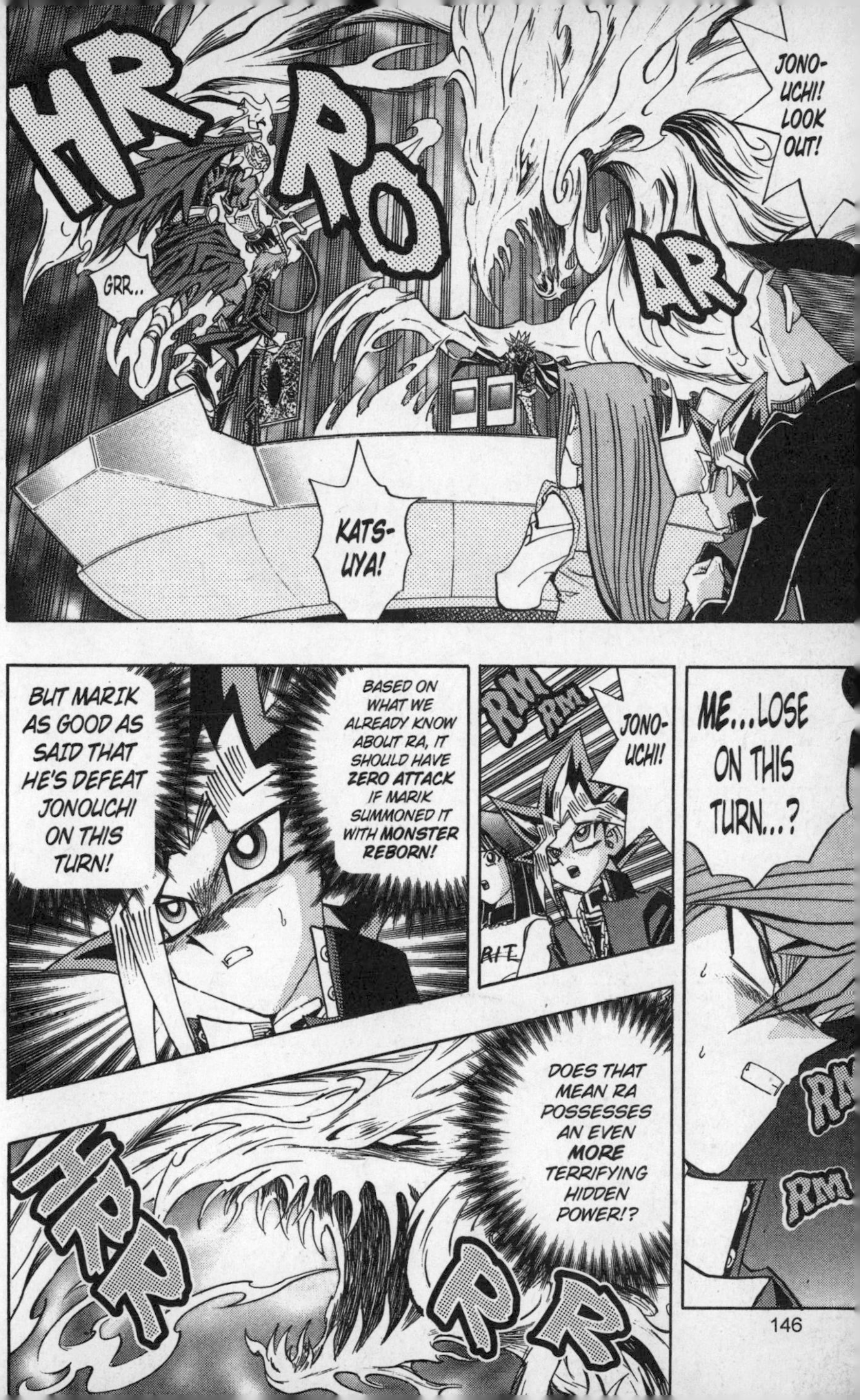
JONO-UCHI! LOOK OUT!
HR RO AR
GRR...
KATS-UYA!
RM RM
ME...LOSE ON THIS TURN...?
RM RM
JONO-UCHI!
BASED ON WHAT WE ALREADY KNOW ABOUT RA, IT SHOULD HAVE ZERO ATTACK IF MARIK SUMMONED IT WITH MONSTER REBORN!
BUT MARIK AS GOOD AS SAID THAT HE'S DEFEAT JONOUCHI ON THIS TURN!
DOES THAT MEAN RA POSSESSES AN EVEN MORE TERRIFYING HIDDEN POWER!?
HRRRR

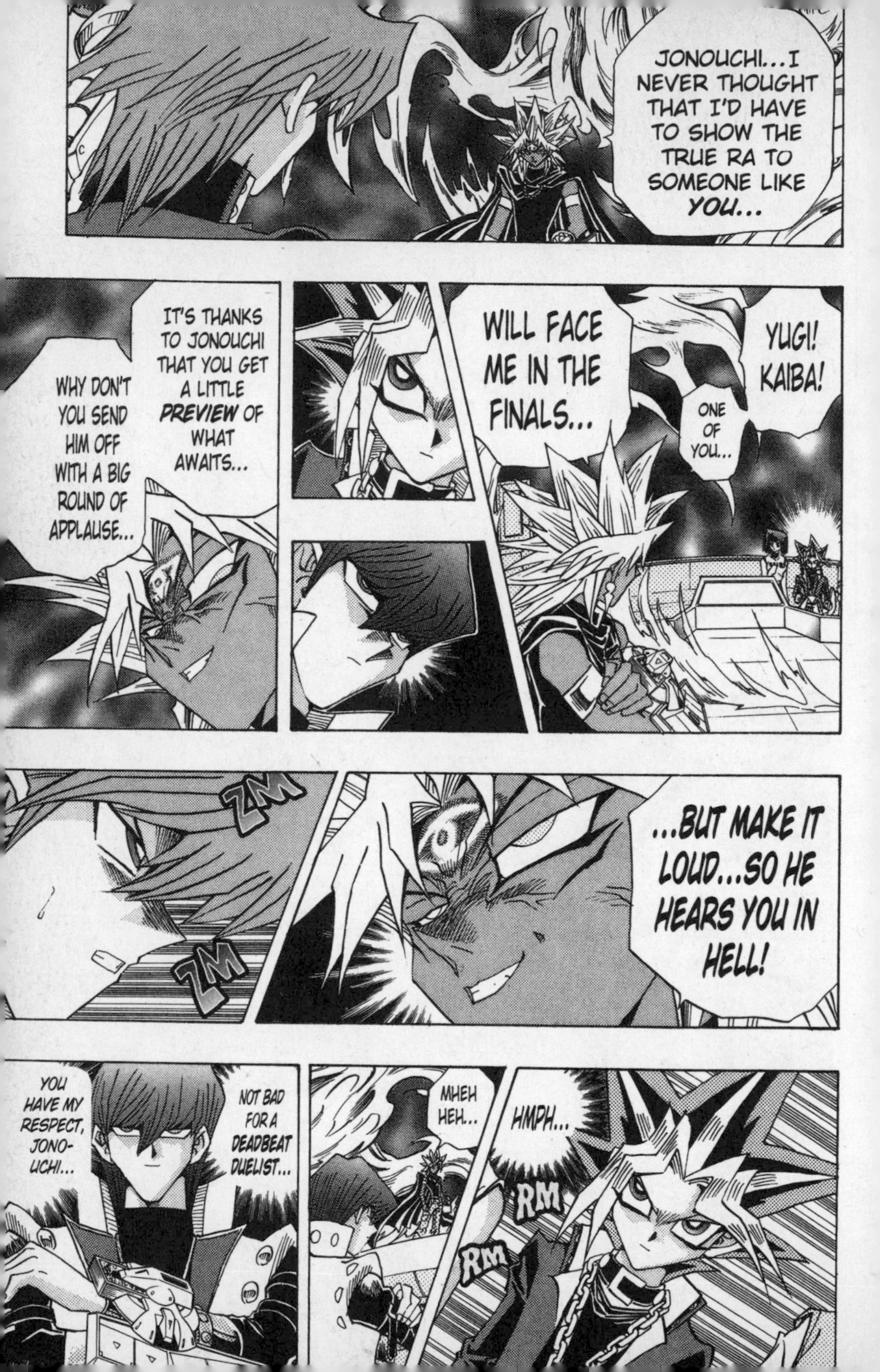
JONOUCHI...I NEVER THOUGHT THAT I'D HAVE TO SHOW THE TRUE RA TO SOMEONE LIKE YOU...
YUGI! KAIBA!
ONE OF YOU...
WILL FACE ME IN THE FINALS...
IT'S THANKS TO JONOUCHI THAT YOU GET A LITTLE PREVIEW OF WHAT AWAITS...
WHY DON'T YOU SEND HIM OFF WITH A BIG ROUND OF APPLAUSE...
...BUT MAKE IT LOUD...SO HE HEARS YOU IN HELL!
ZM
ZM
HMPH...
RM
RM
MHEH HEH...
NOT BAD FOR A DEADBEAT DUELIST...
YOU HAVE MY RESPECT, JONO-UCHI...

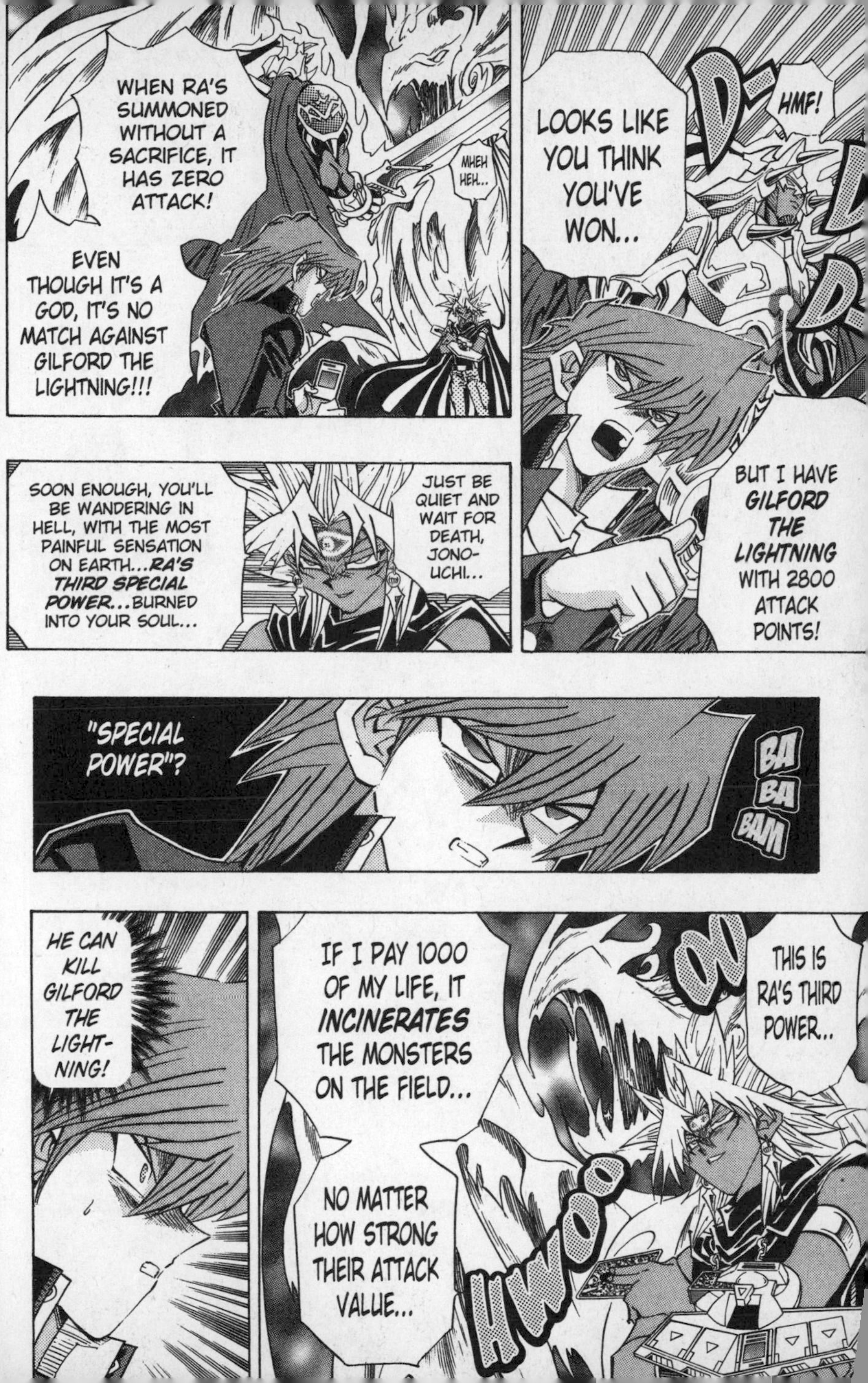
HMF!
D-
LOOKS LIKE YOU THINK YOU'VE WON...
BUT I HAVE *GILFORD THE LIGHTNING* WITH 2800 ATTACK POINTS!
MHEH HEH...
WHEN RA'S SUMMONED WITHOUT A SACRIFICE, IT HAS ZERO ATTACK!
EVEN THOUGH IT'S A GOD, IT'S NO MATCH AGAINST GILFORD THE LIGHTNING!!!
JUST BE QUIET AND WAIT FOR DEATH, JONO-UCHI...
SOON ENOUGH, YOU'LL BE WANDERING IN HELL, WITH THE MOST PAINFUL SENSATION ON EARTH...*RA'S THIRD SPECIAL POWER*...BURNED INTO YOUR SOUL...
BA BA BAM
"SPECIAL POWER"?
THIS IS RA'S THIRD POWER...
OO
IF I PAY 1000 OF MY LIFE, IT *INCINERATES* THE MONSTERS ON THE FIELD...
NO MATTER HOW STRONG THEIR ATTACK VALUE...
HWOO
HE CAN KILL GILFORD THE LIGHT-NING!

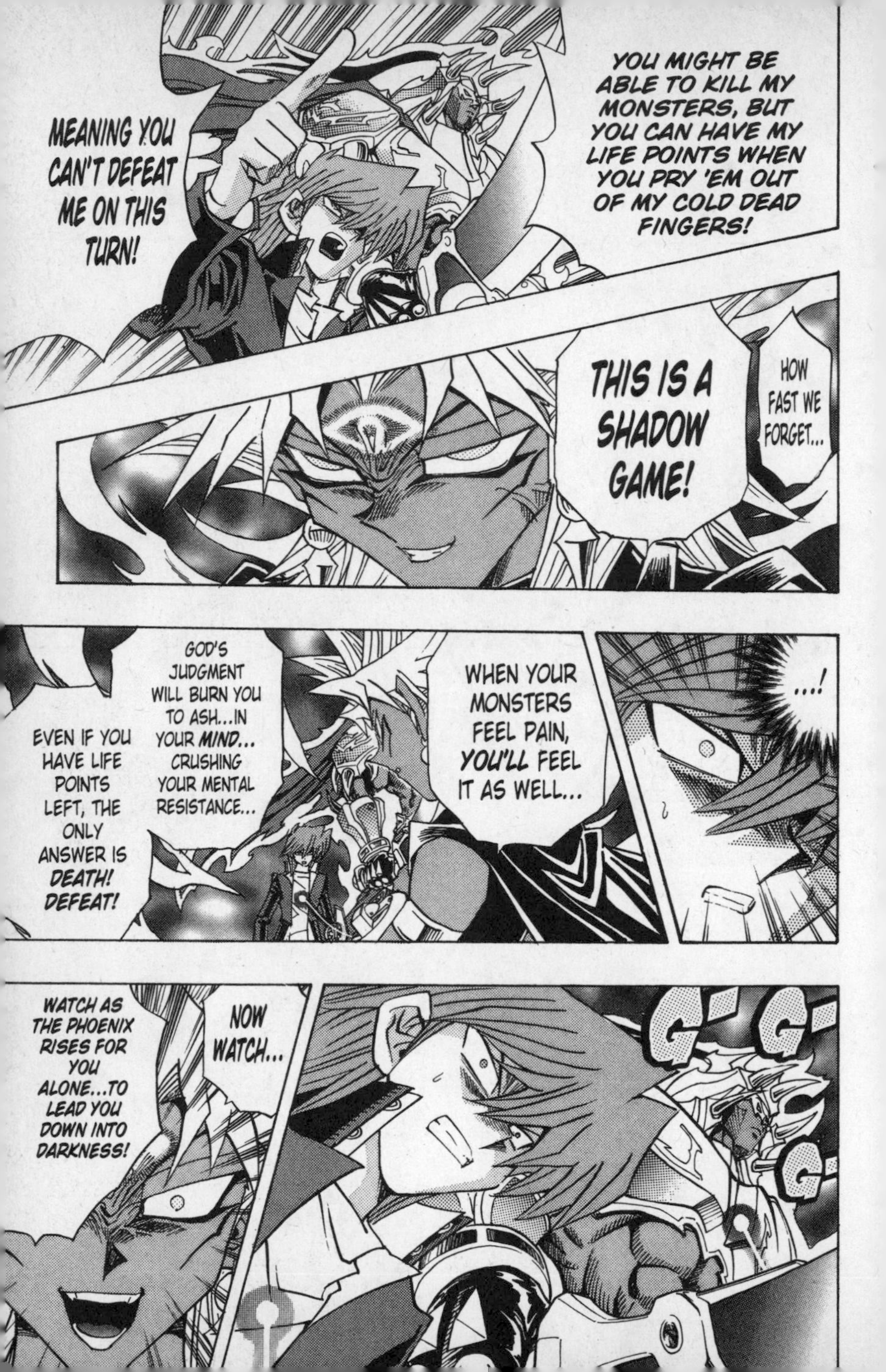
YOU MIGHT BE ABLE TO KILL MY MONSTERS, BUT YOU CAN HAVE MY LIFE POINTS WHEN YOU PRY 'EM OUT OF MY COLD DEAD FINGERS!
MEANING YOU CAN'T DEFEAT ME ON THIS TURN!
HOW FAST WE FORGET...
THIS IS A SHADOW GAME!
...!
WHEN YOUR MONSTERS FEEL PAIN, *YOU'LL* FEEL IT AS WELL...
GOD'S JUDGMENT WILL BURN YOU TO ASH...IN YOUR *MIND*... CRUSHING YOUR MENTAL RESISTANCE...
EVEN IF YOU HAVE LIFE POINTS LEFT, THE ONLY ANSWER IS *DEATH! DEFEAT!*
G-G-G-
NOW WATCH...
WATCH AS THE PHOENIX RISES FOR YOU ALONE...TO LEAD YOU DOWN INTO DARKNESS!

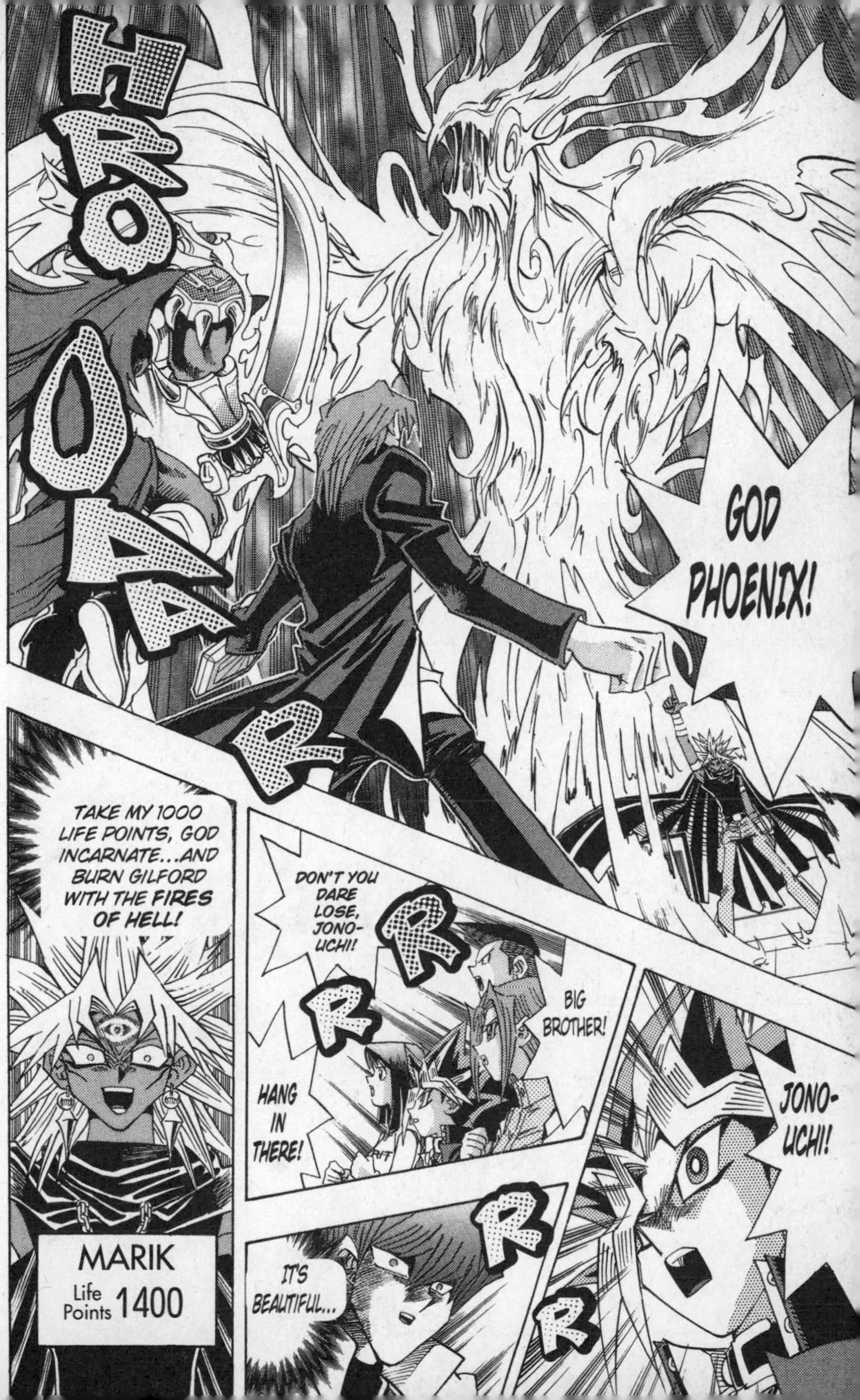
GOD PHOENIX!
HROOAAR
R
DON'T YOU DARE LOSE, JONO-UCHI!
R
R
BIG BROTHER!
HANG IN THERE!
JONO-UCHI!
R
R
IT'S BEAUTIFUL...
TAKE MY 1000 LIFE POINTS, GOD INCARNATE...AND BURN GILFORD WITH THE FIRES OF HELL!
MARIK
Life Points 1400

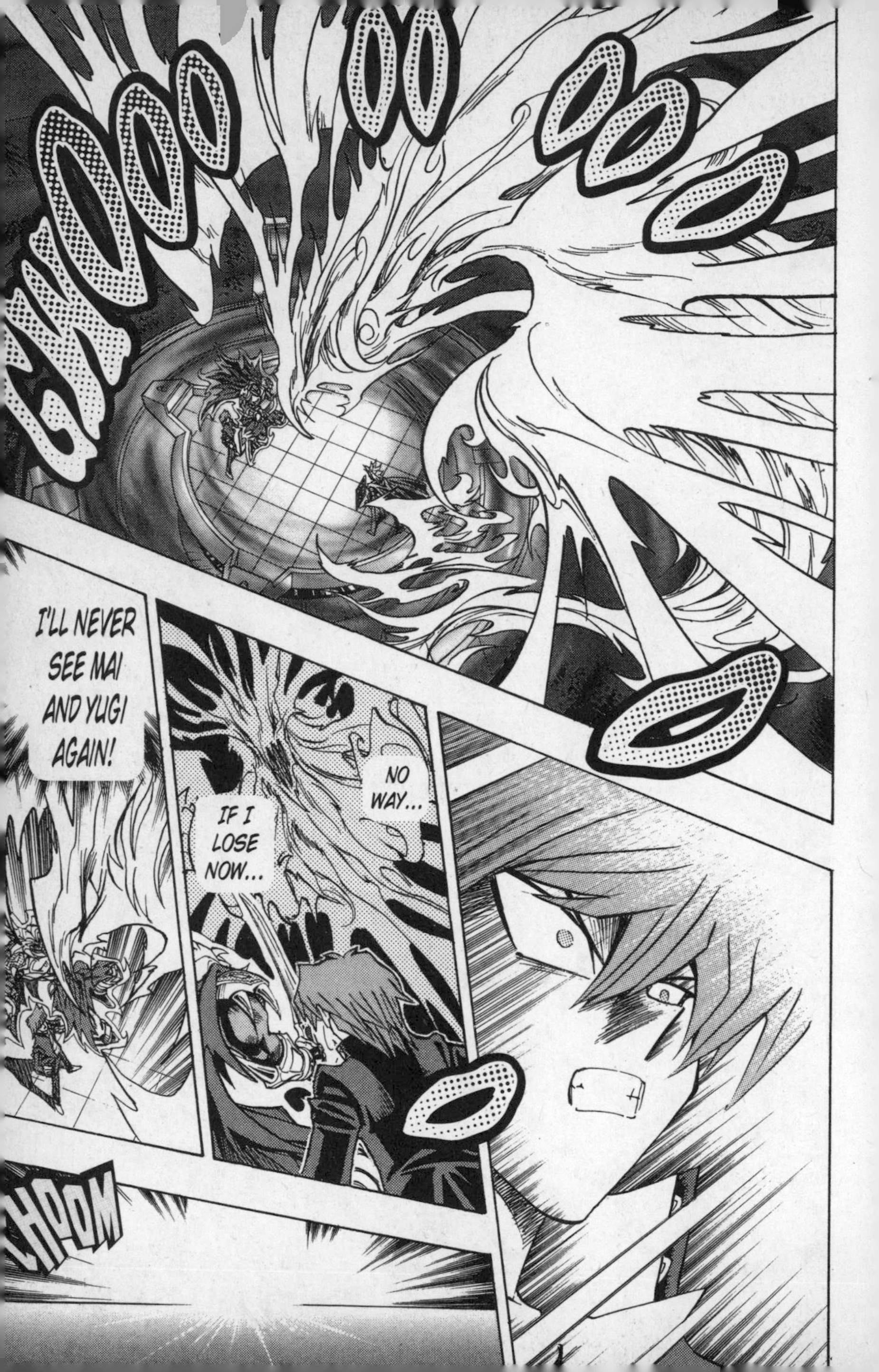
WHOOOOOOOOOO
NO WAY...
IF I LOSE NOW...
I'LL NEVER SEE MAI AND YUGI AGAIN!
HOOM

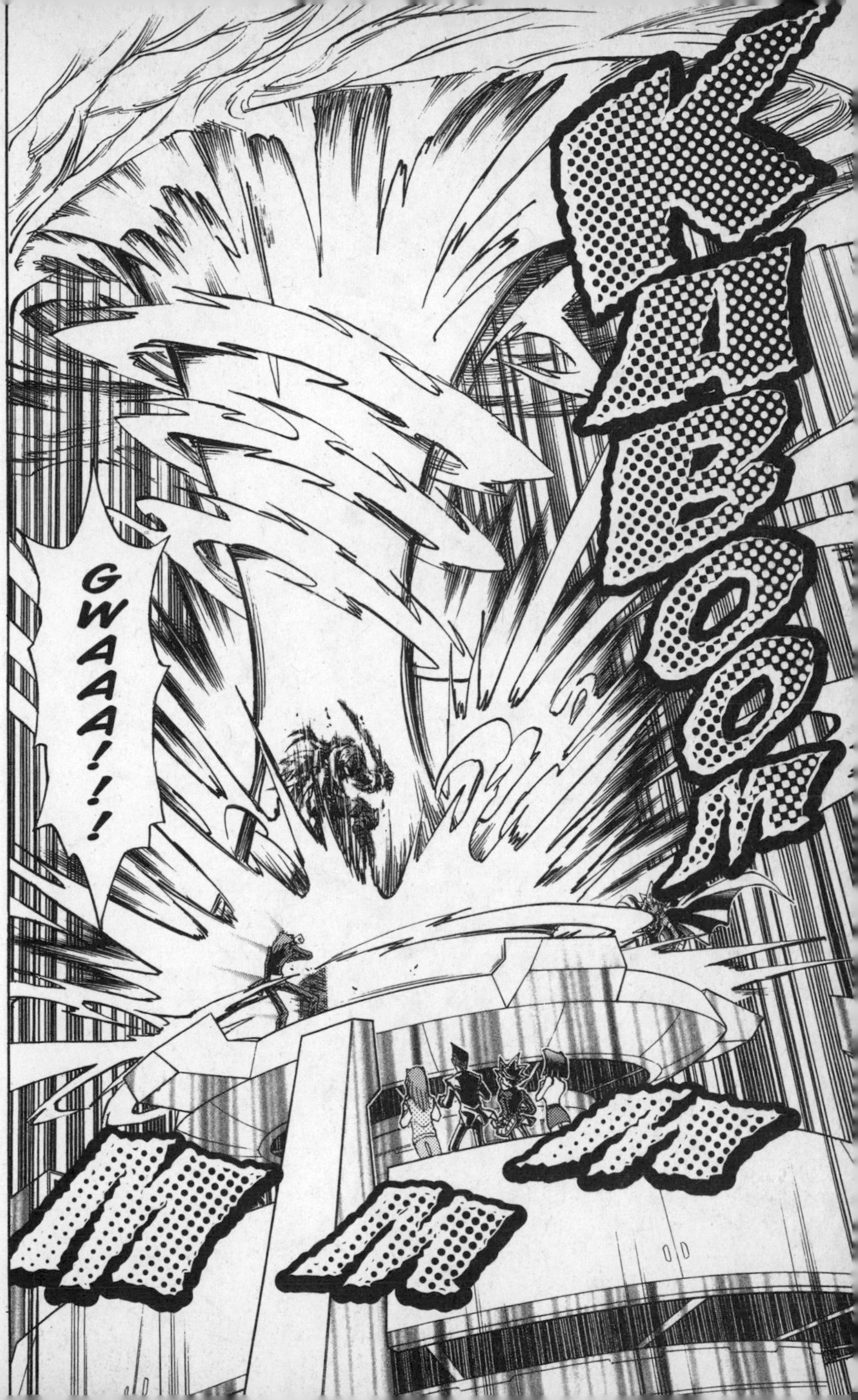
KABOOM
GWAAAA!!!

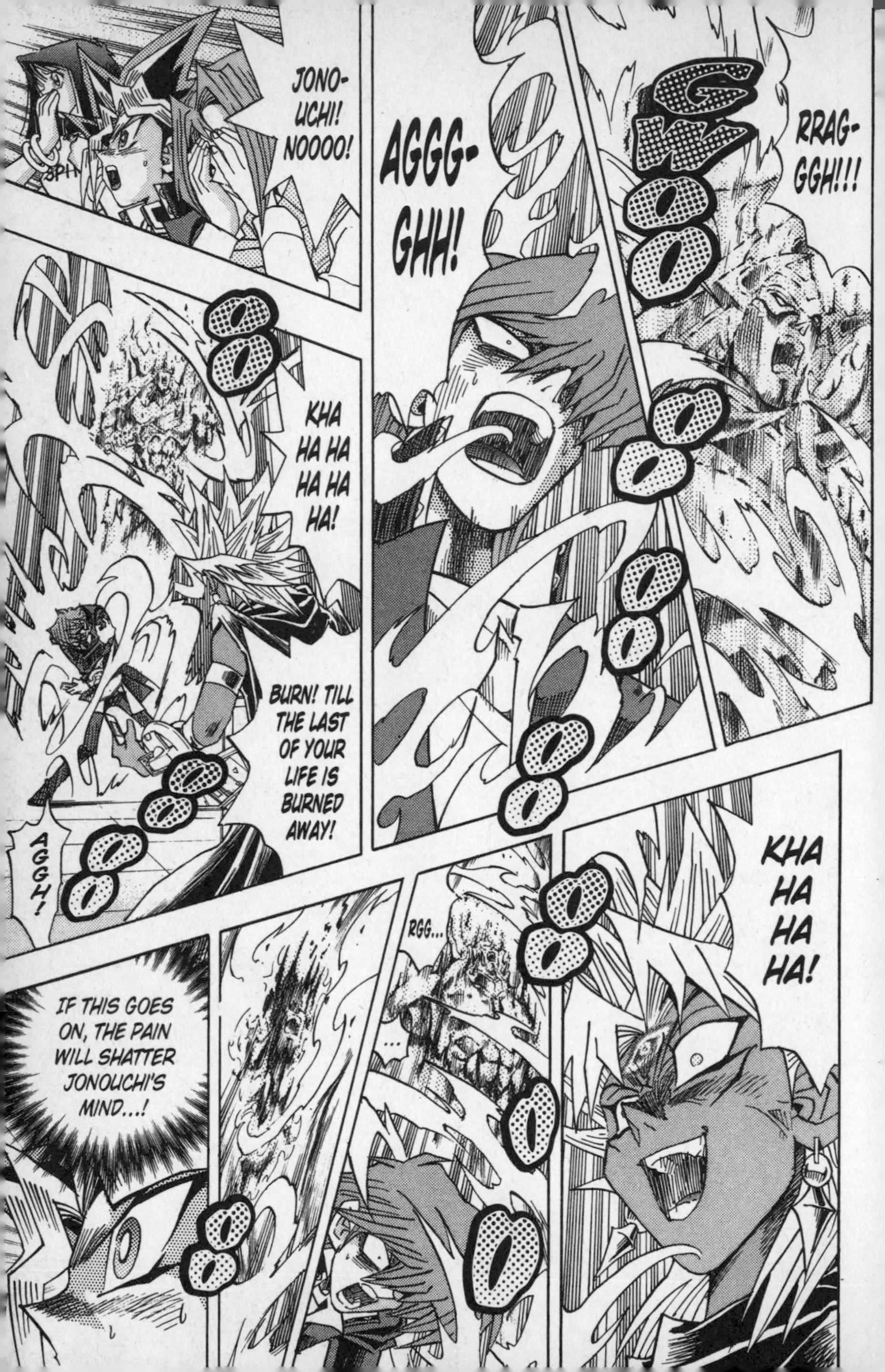
RRAGGGH!!!
AGGG-GHH!
JONO-UCHI! NOOOO!
KHA HA HA HA HA HA!
BURN! TILL THE LAST OF YOUR LIFE IS BURNED AWAY!
AGGH!
KHA HA HA HA HA!
RGG...
...
IF THIS GOES ON, THE PAIN WILL SHATTER JONOUCHI'S MIND...!

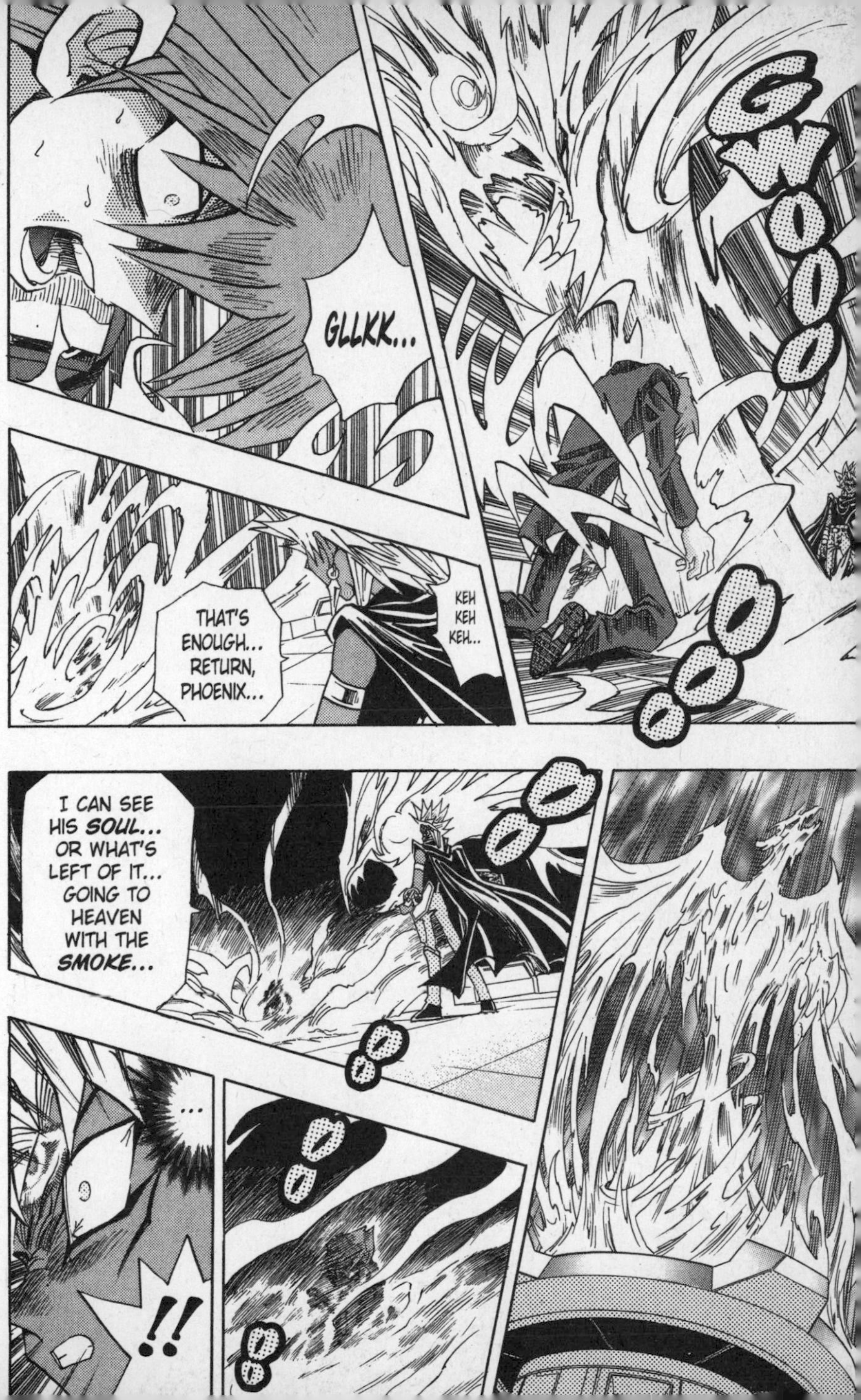
GWOOOO
GLLKK...
KEH KEH KEH...
THAT'S ENOUGH... RETURN, PHOENIX...
I CAN SEE HIS SOUL... OR WHAT'S LEFT OF IT... GOING TO HEAVEN WITH THE SMOKE...
...
!!

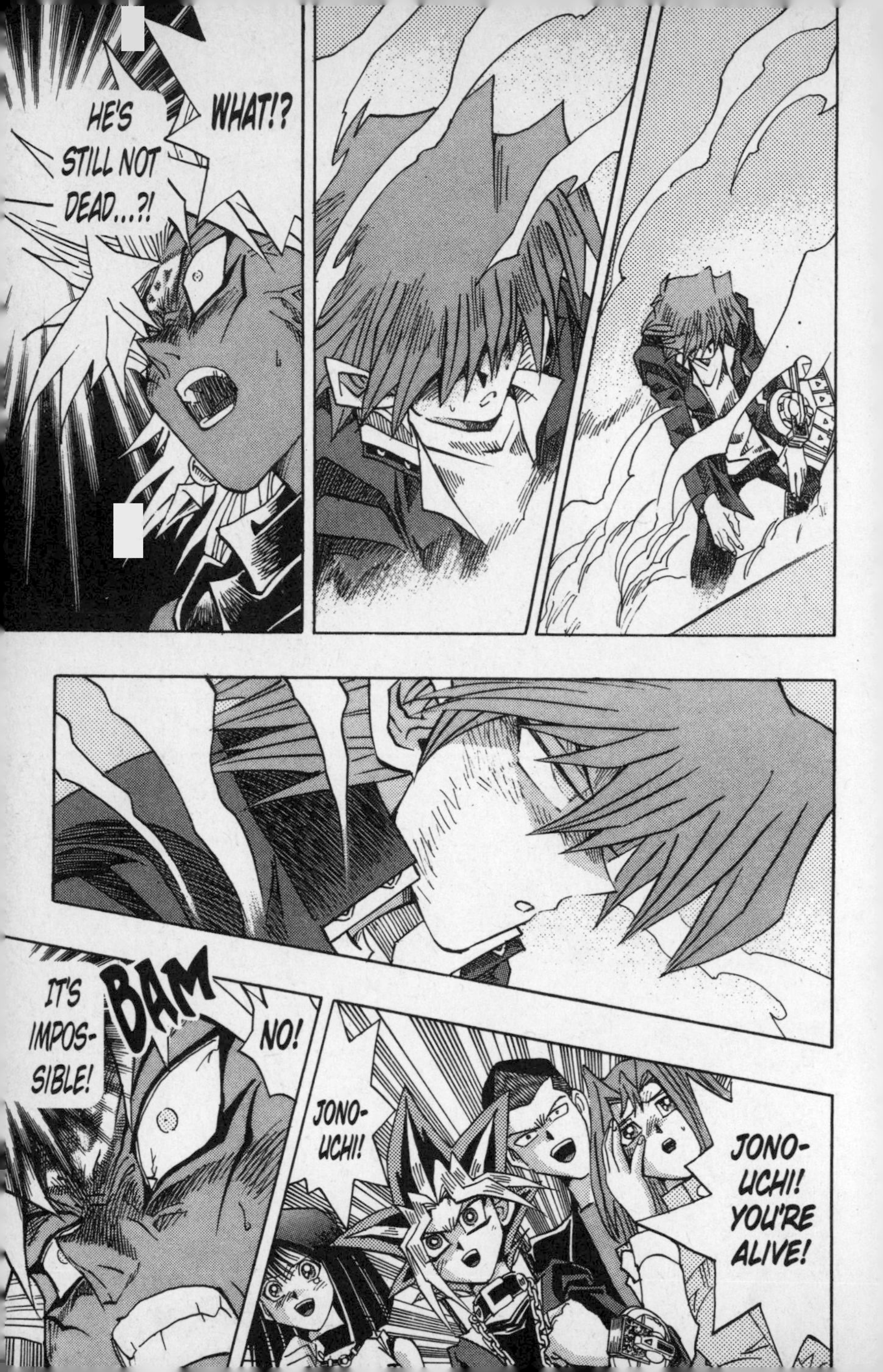
WHAT!?
HE'S STILL NOT DEAD...?!
JONO-UCHI! YOU'RE ALIVE!
JONO-UCHI!
NO!
BAM
IT'S IMPOS-SIBLE!

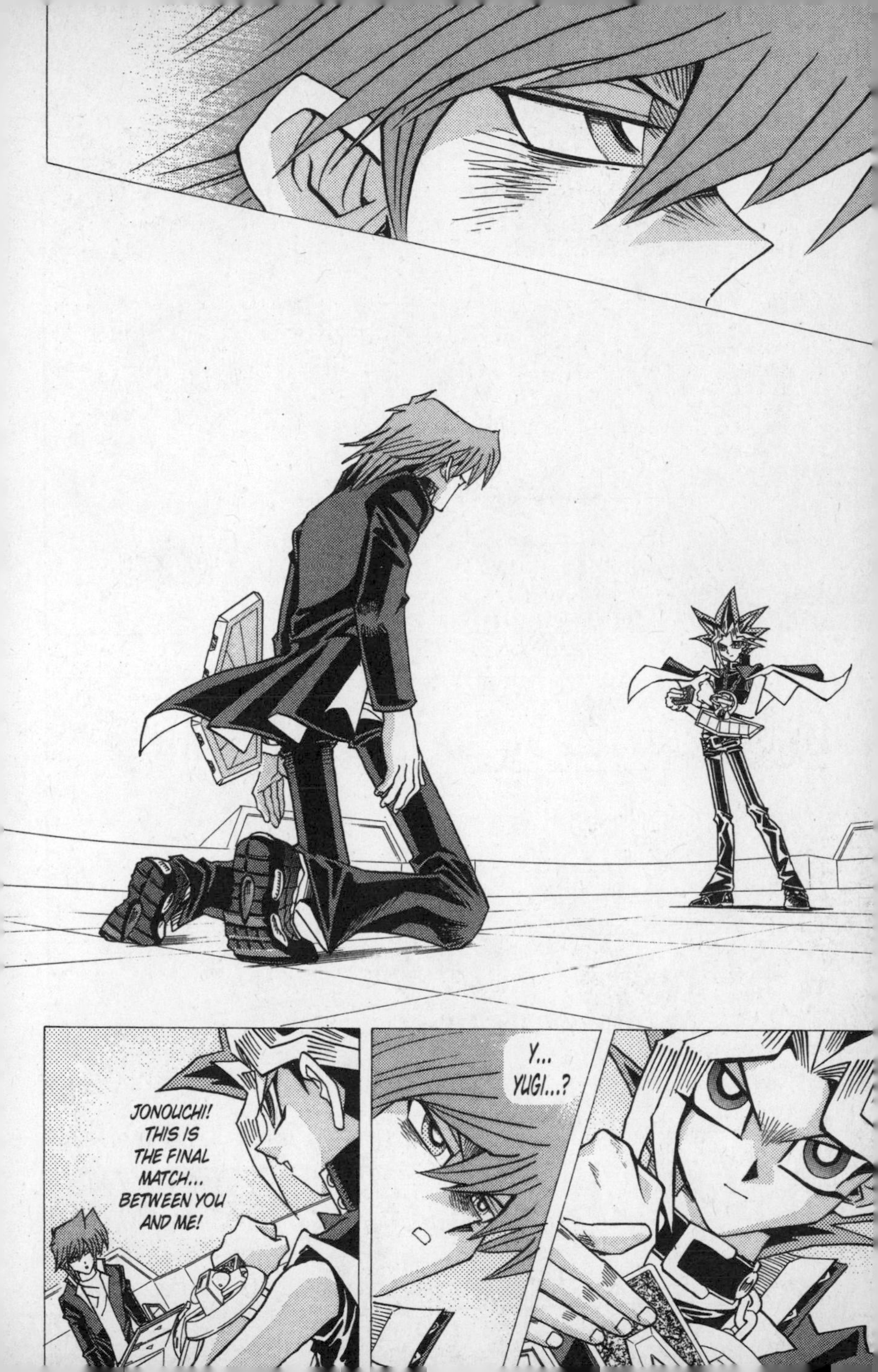
Y... YUGI...?
JONOUCHI! THIS IS THE FINAL MATCH... BETWEEN YOU AND ME!

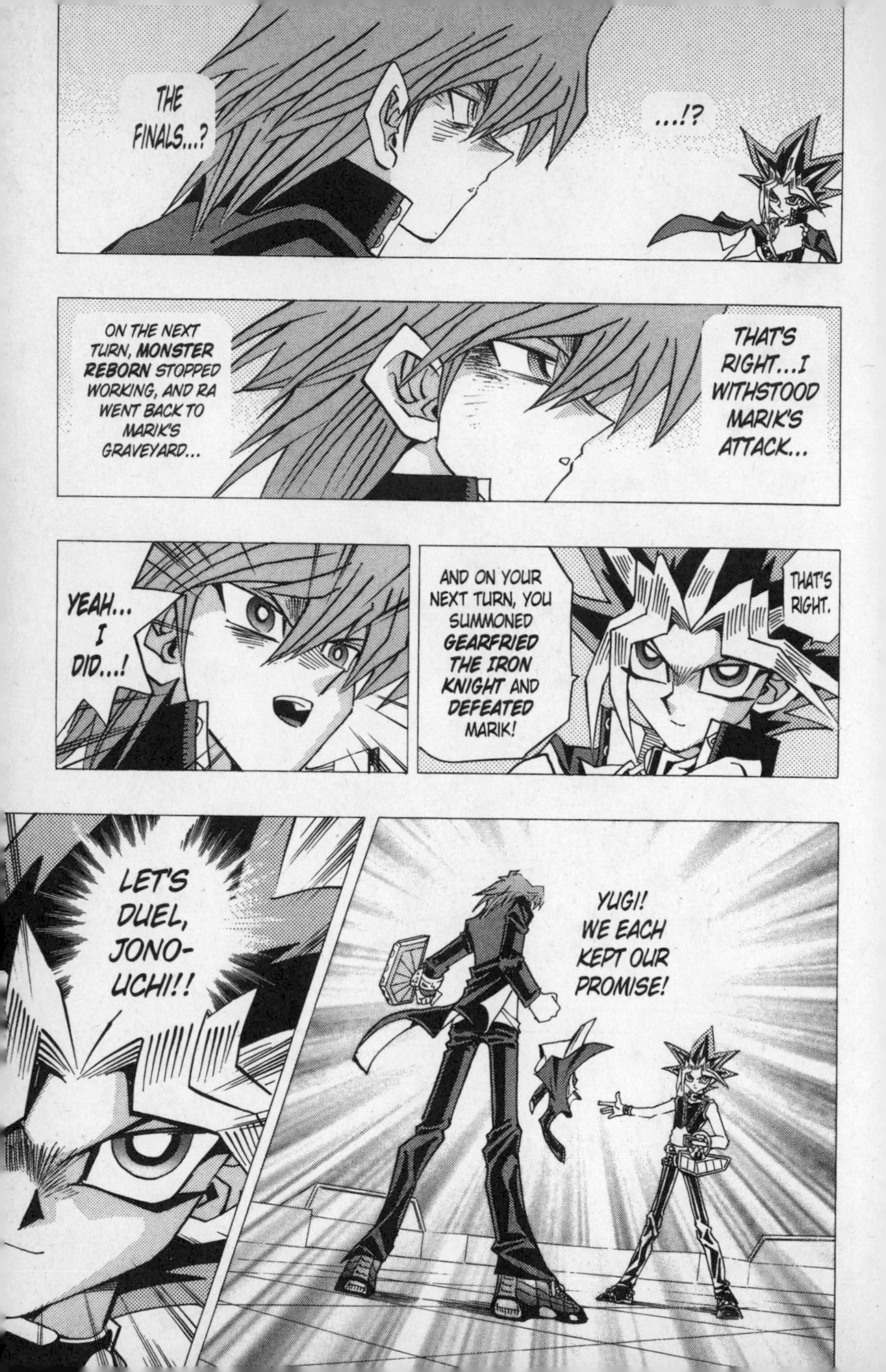

...!?
THE FINALS...?
THAT'S RIGHT...I WITHSTOOD MARIK'S ATTACK...
ON THE NEXT TURN, MONSTER REBORN STOPPED WORKING, AND RA WENT BACK TO MARIK'S GRAVEYARD...
THAT'S RIGHT.
AND ON YOUR NEXT TURN, YOU SUMMONED GEARFRIED THE IRON KNIGHT AND DEFEATED MARIK!
YEAH... I DID...!
YUGI! WE EACH KEPT OUR PROMISE!
LET'S DUEL, JONO-UCHI!!

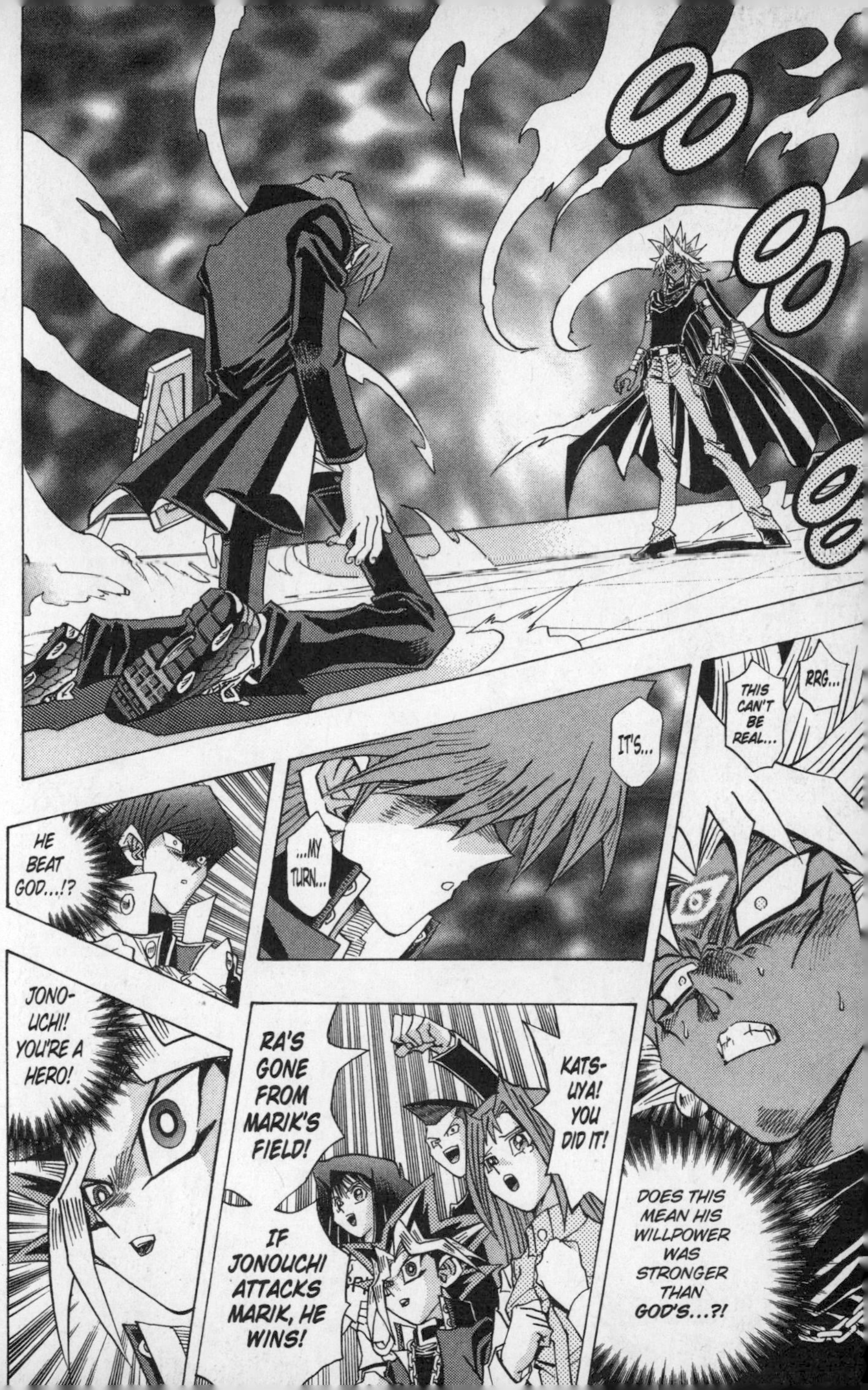
RRG...
THIS CAN'T BE REAL...
DOES THIS MEAN HIS WILLPOWER WAS STRONGER THAN GOD'S...?!
IT'S...
...MY TURN...
HE BEAT GOD...!?
KATSUYA! YOU DID IT!
RA'S GONE FROM MARIK'S FIELD!
IF JONOUCHI ATTACKS MARIK, HE WINS!
JONOUCHI! YOU'RE A HERO!

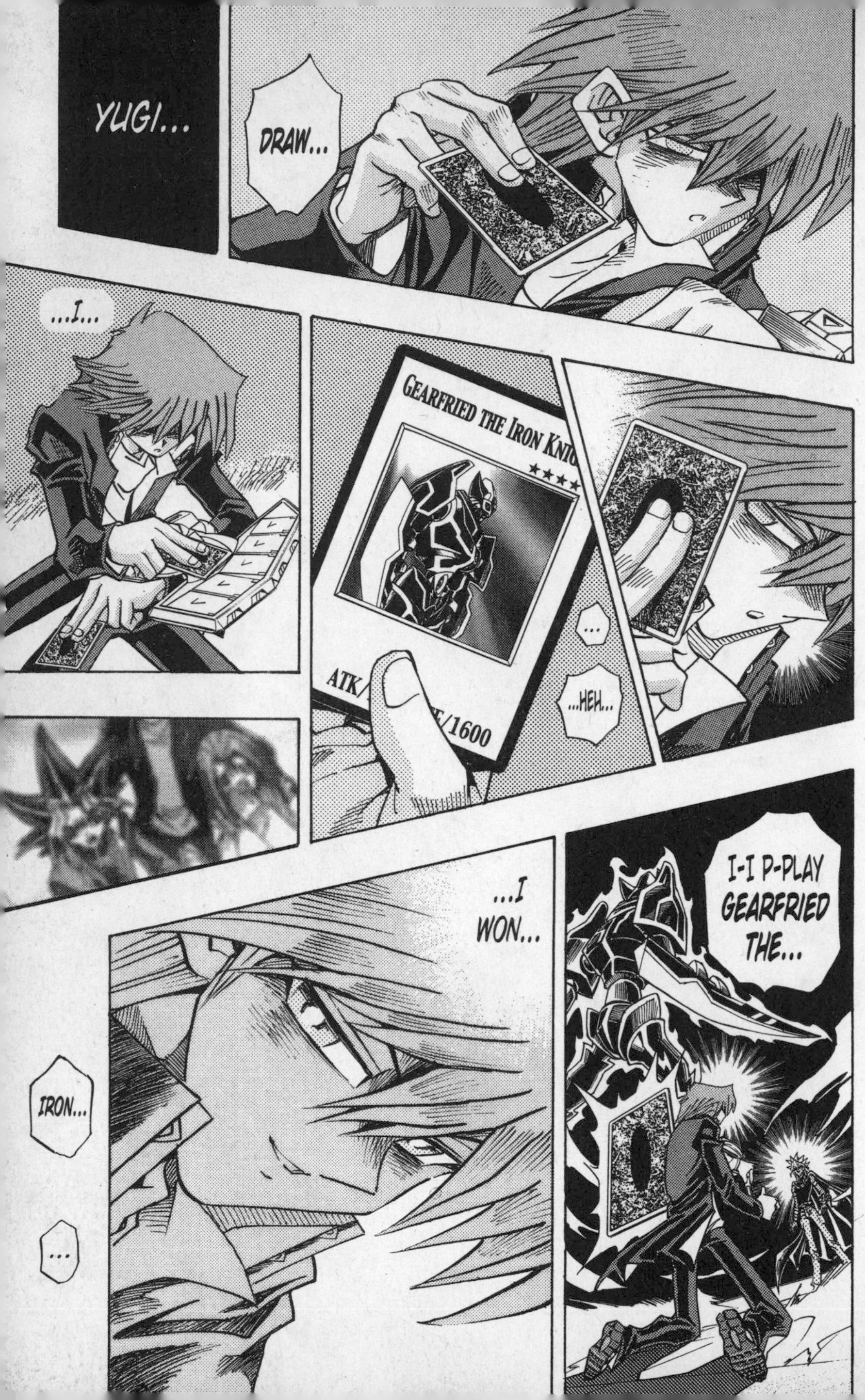
DRAW...
YUGI...
Gearfried the Iron Knig
ATK/
E/1600
...
...HEH...
...I...
I-I P-PLAY GEARFRIED THE...
...I WON...
IRON...
...

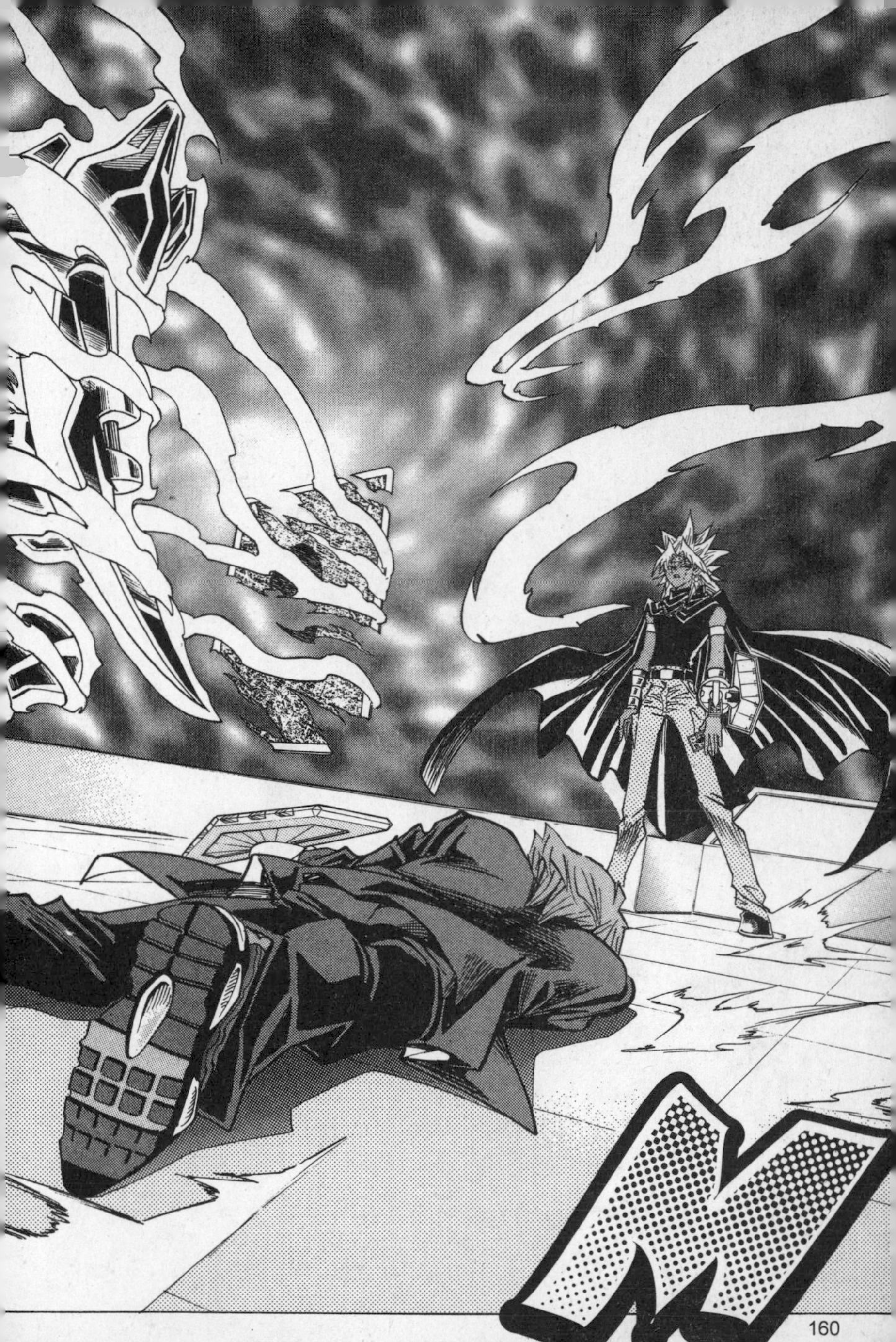
M

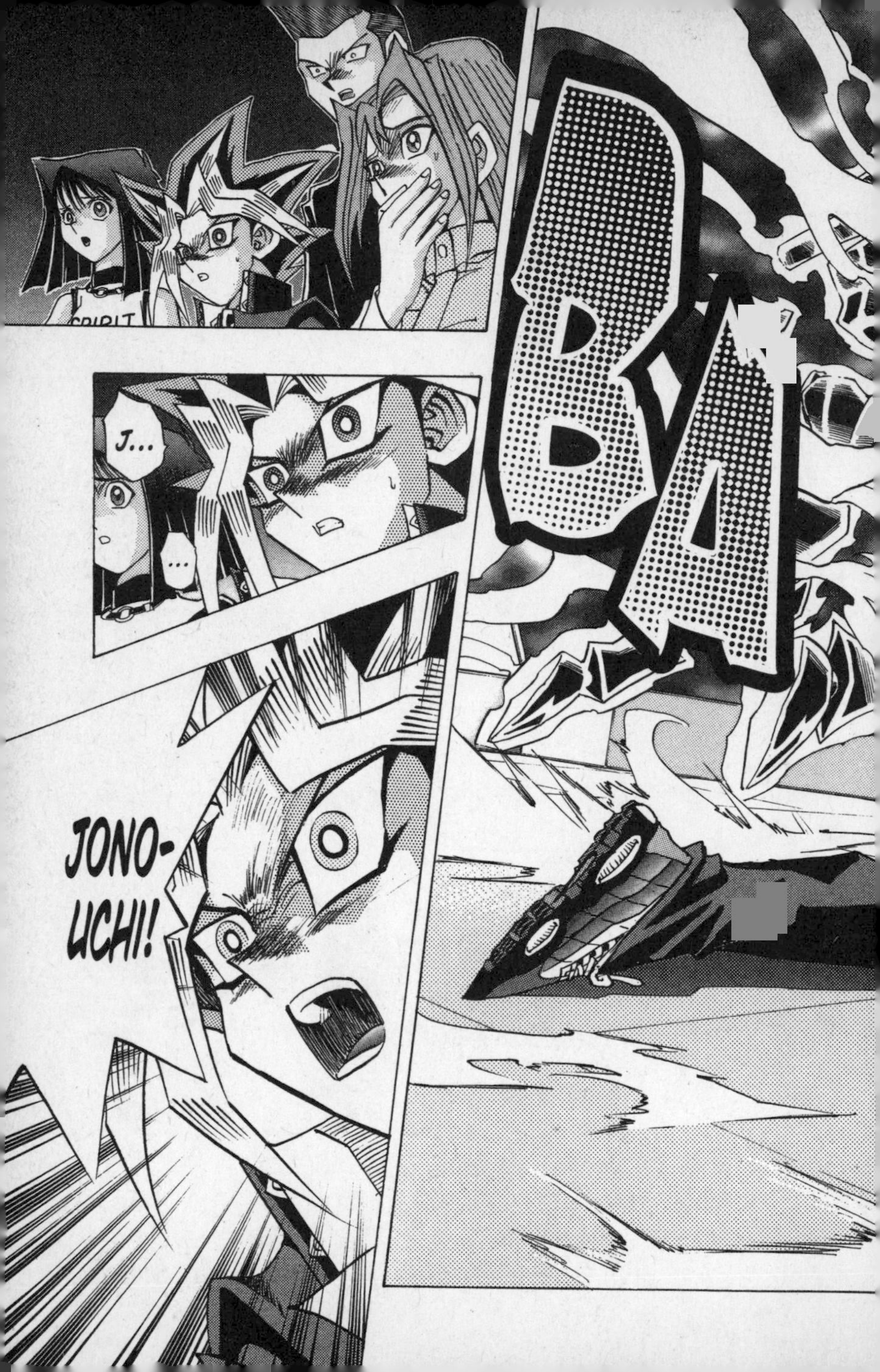
BA
J...
...
JONO-UCHI!

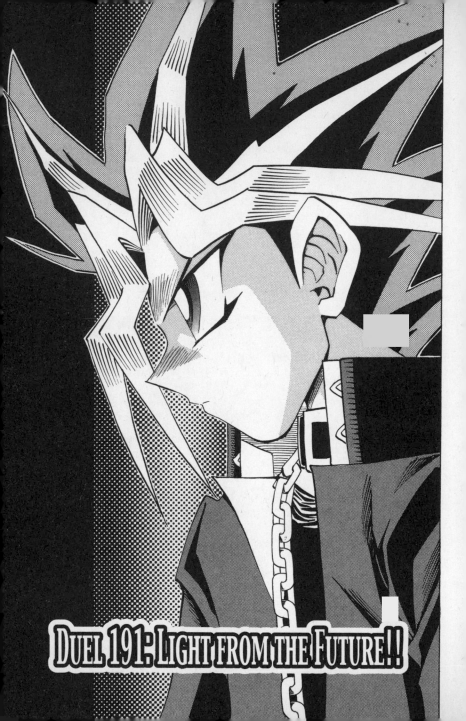

DUEL 191: LIGHT FROM THE FUTURE!!

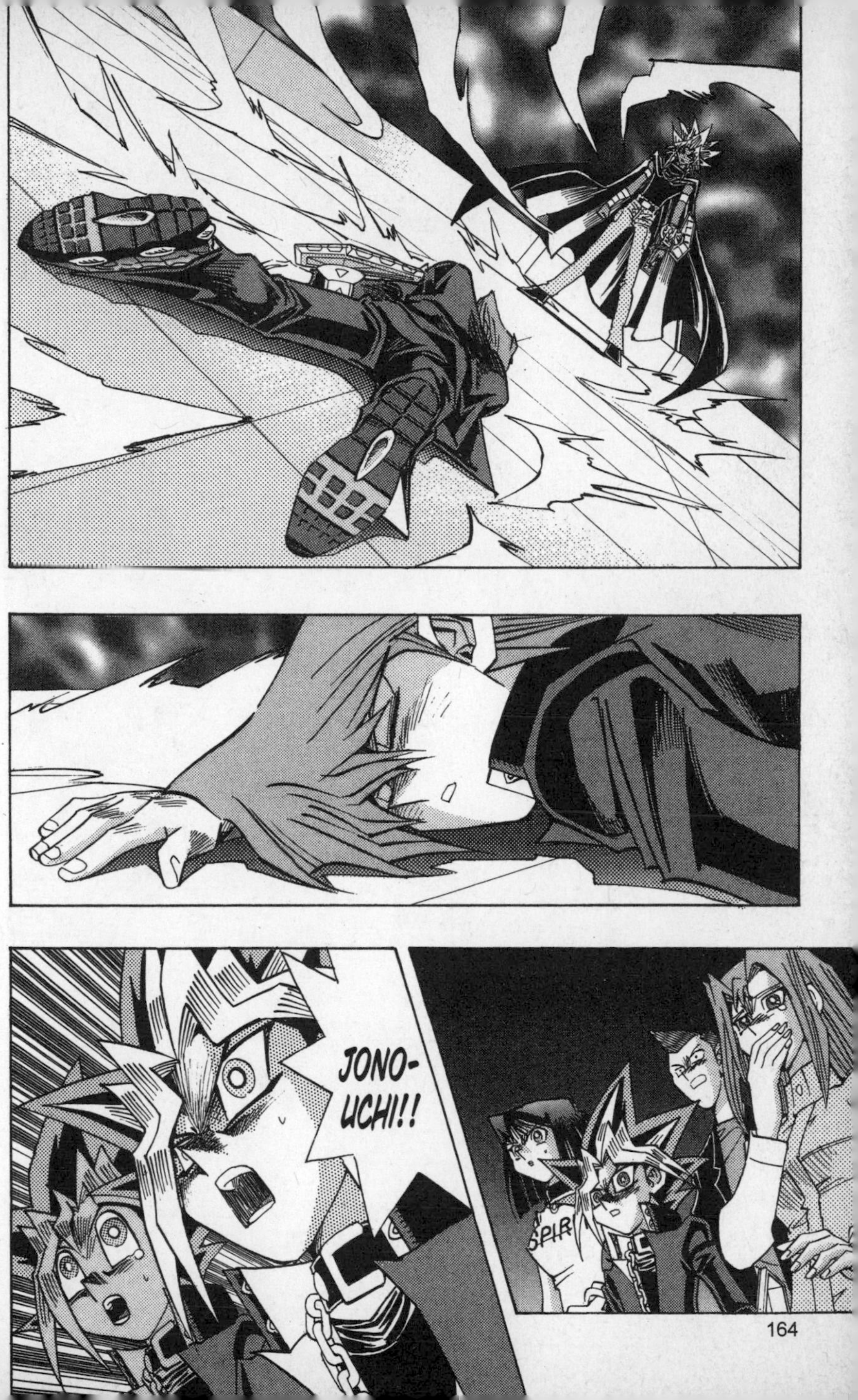
JONO-
UCHI!!

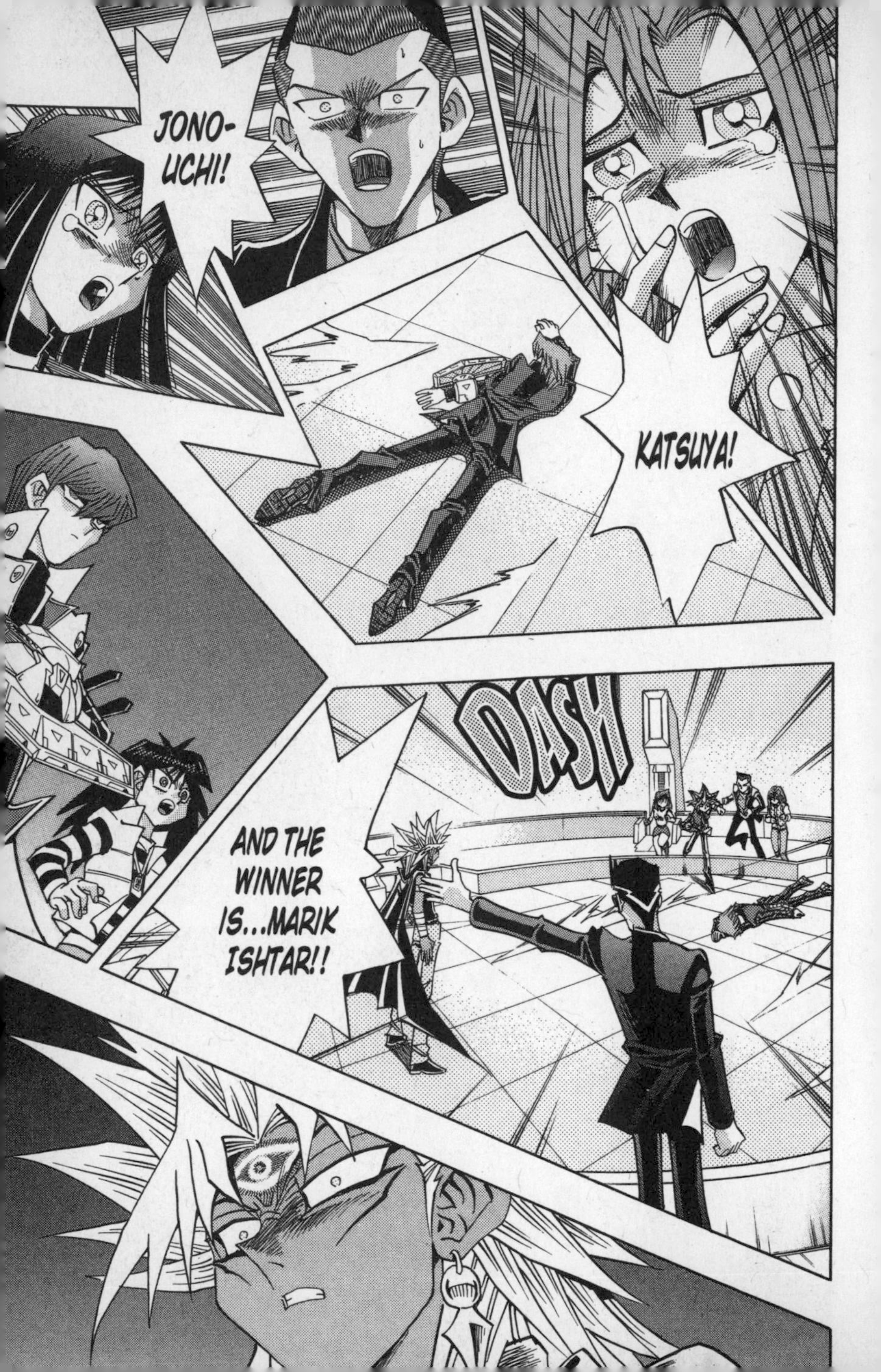
KATSUYA!
JONO-UCHI!
DASH
AND THE WINNER IS...MARIK ISHTAR!!

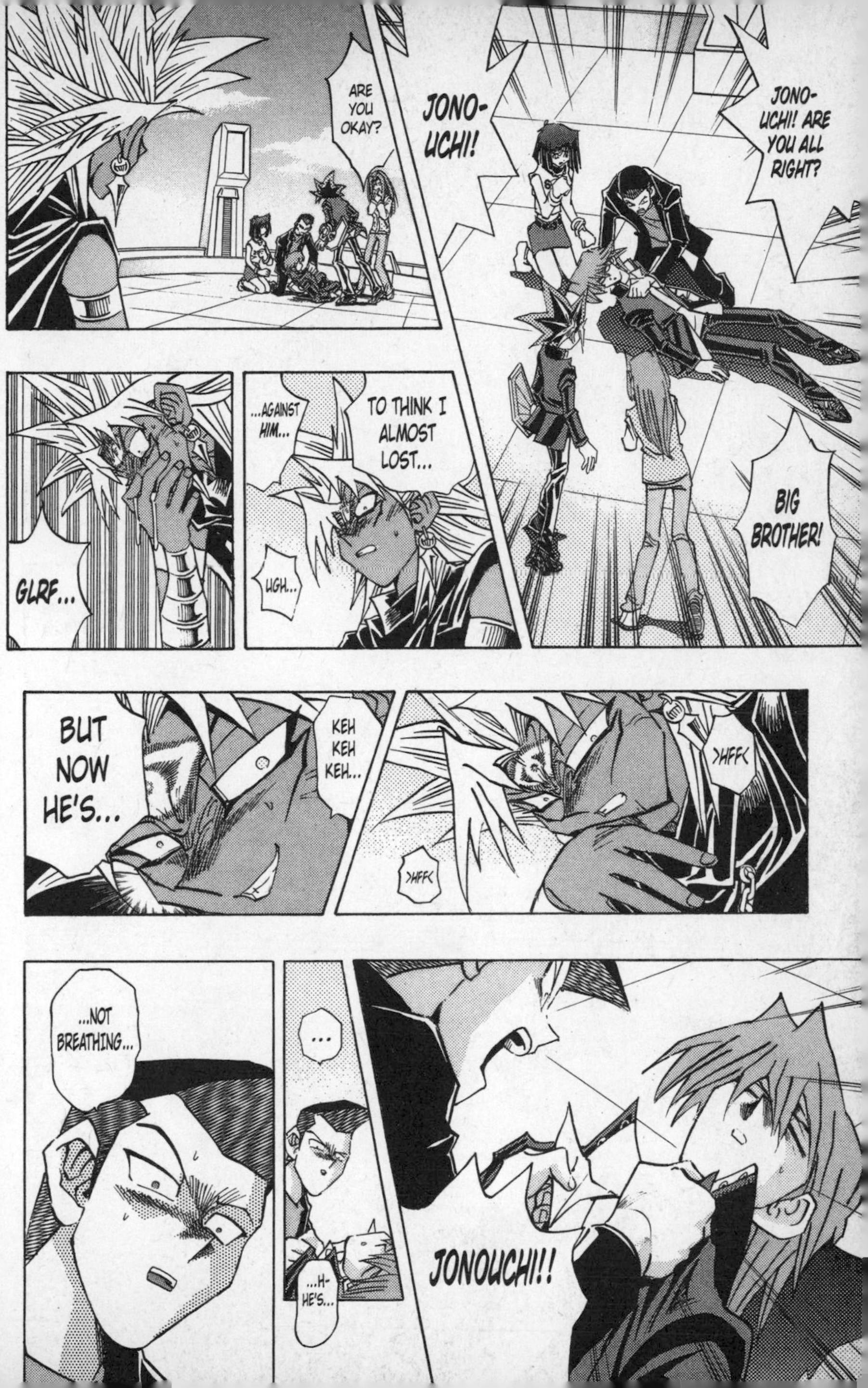
JONO-UCHI! ARE YOU ALL RIGHT?
JONO-UCHI!
BIG BROTHER!
ARE YOU OKAY?
TO THINK I ALMOST LOST...
...AGAINST HIM...
UGH...
GLRF...
>HFF<
>HFF<
KEH KEH KEH...
BUT NOW HE'S...
JONOUCHI!!
...
...H-HE'S...
...NOT BREATHING...

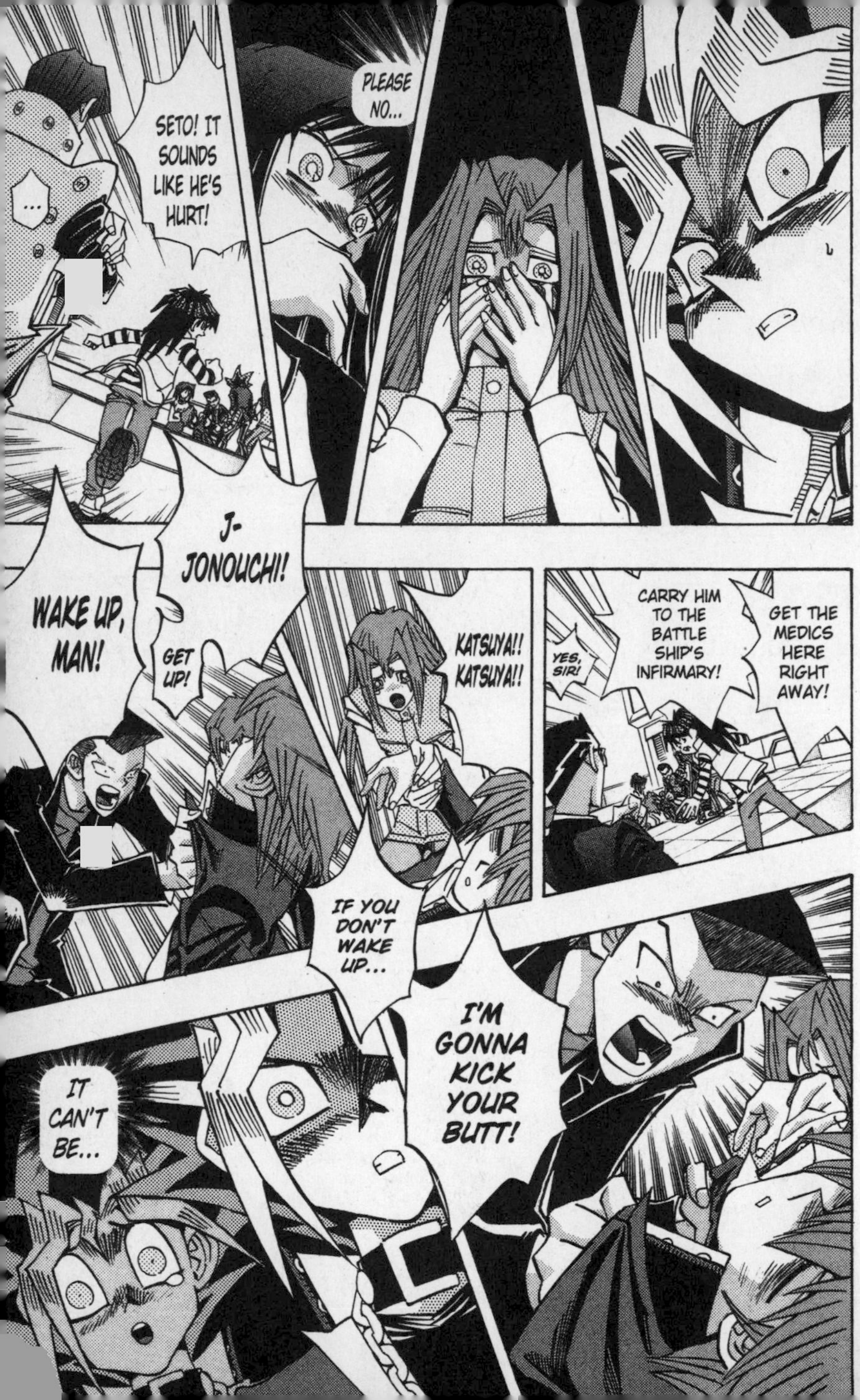
PLEASE NO...
SETO! IT SOUNDS LIKE HE'S HURT!
...
GET THE MEDICS HERE RIGHT AWAY!
CARRY HIM TO THE BATTLE SHIP'S INFIRMARY!
YES, SIR!
J-JONOUCHI!
KATSUYA!! KATSUYA!!
GET UP!
WAKE UP, MAN!
IF YOU DON'T WAKE UP...
I'M GONNA KICK YOUR BUTT!
IT CAN'T BE...

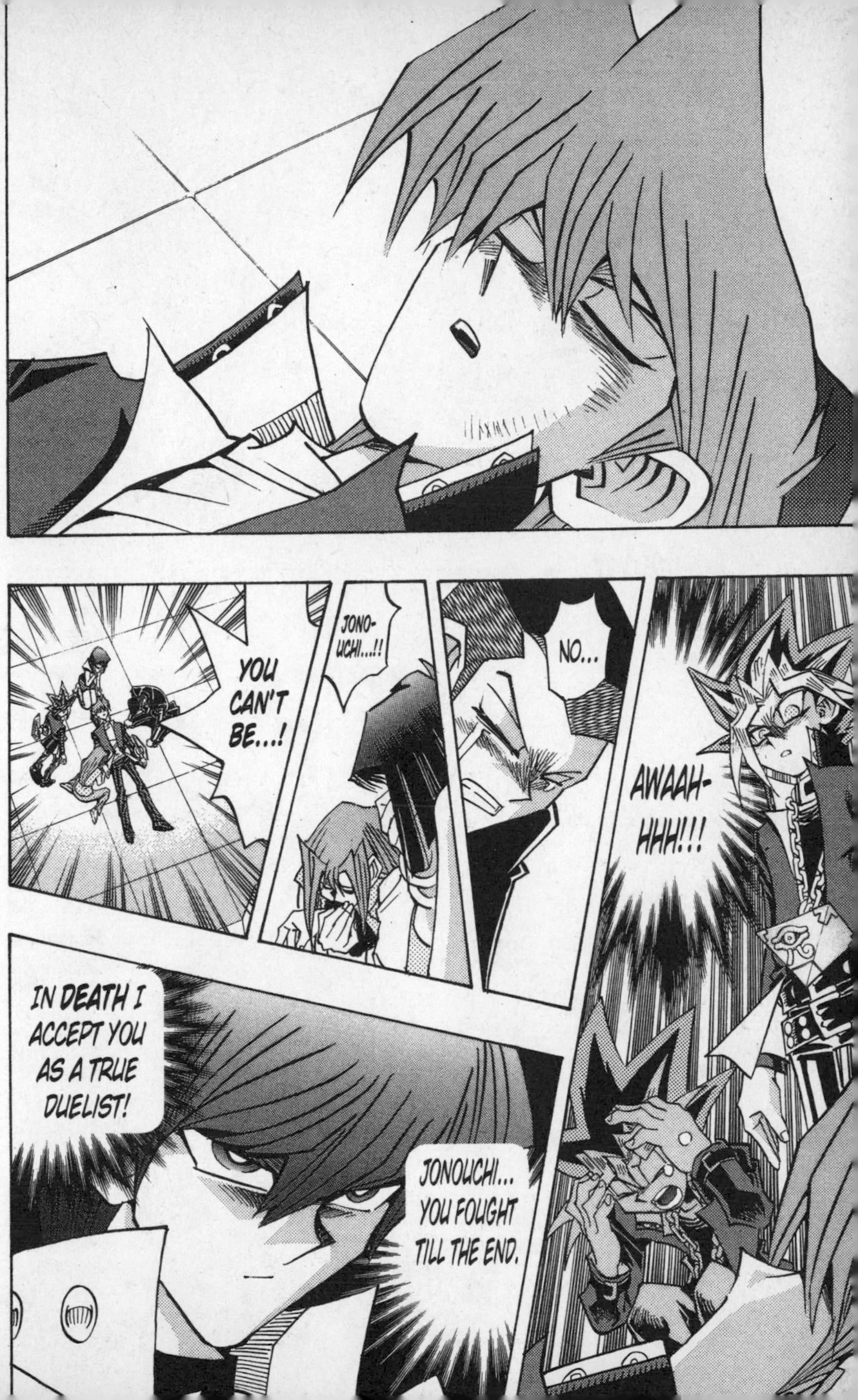
AWAAH-HHH!!!
NO...
JONO-UCHI...!!
YOU CAN'T BE...!
JONOUCHI... YOU FOUGHT TILL THE END.
IN DEATH I ACCEPT YOU AS A TRUE DUELIST!

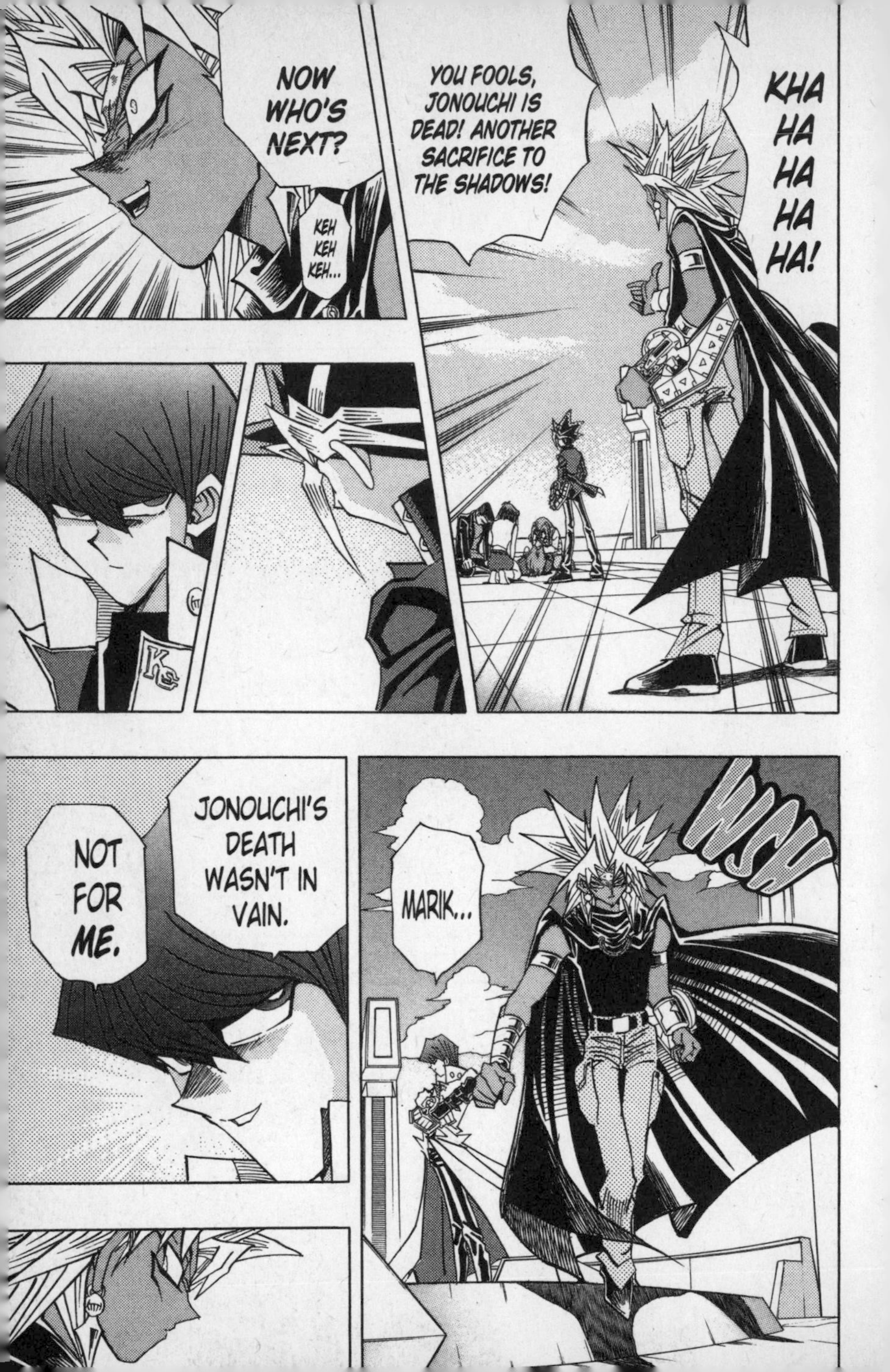
KHA HA HA HA HA!
YOU FOOLS, JONOUCHI IS DEAD! ANOTHER SACRIFICE TO THE SHADOWS!
NOW WHO'S NEXT?
KEH KEH KEH...
WSH
MARIK...
JONOUCHI'S DEATH WASN'T IN VAIN.
NOT FOR ME.

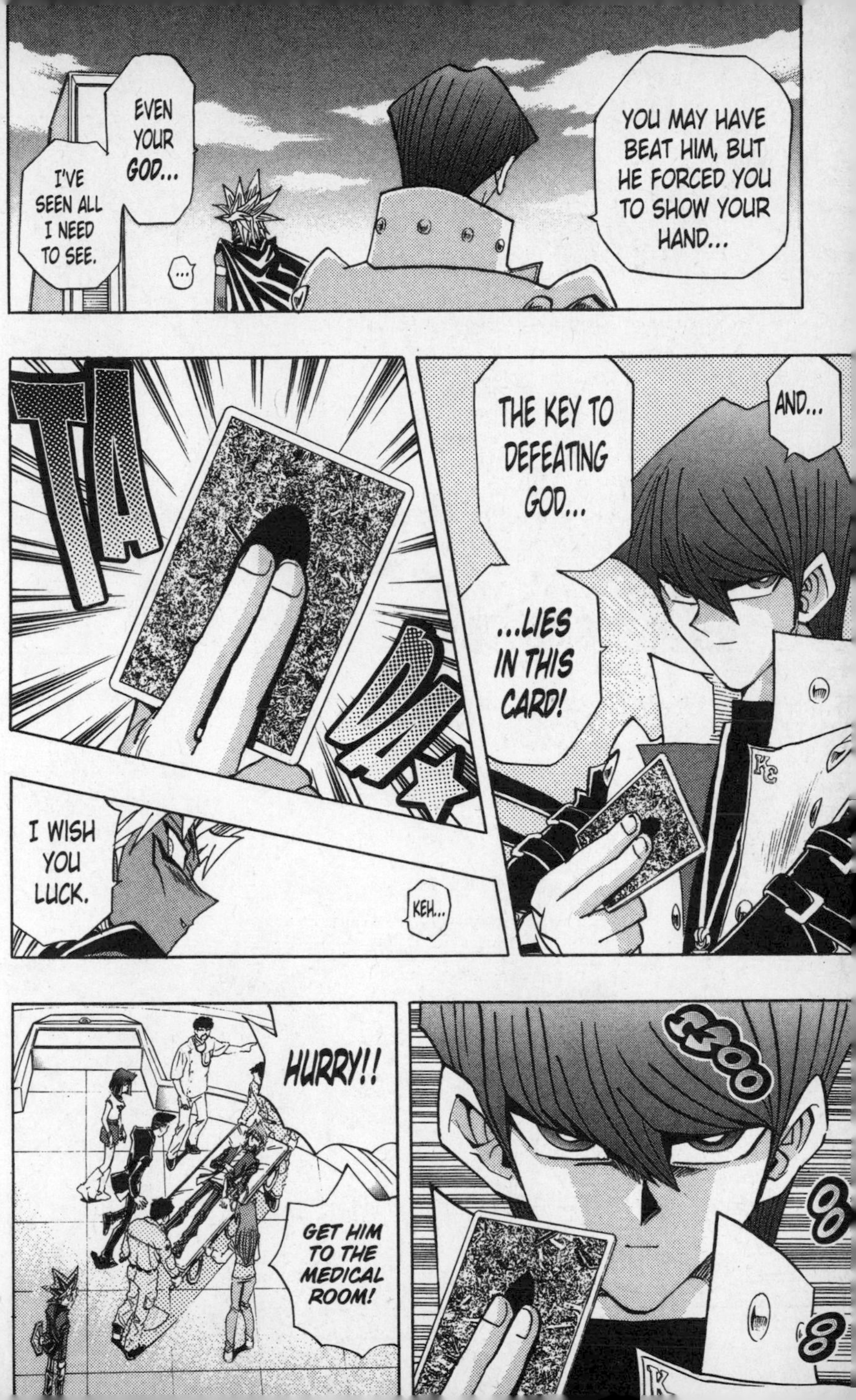
YOU MAY HAVE BEAT HIM, BUT HE FORCED YOU TO SHOW YOUR HAND...
EVEN YOUR GOD...
I'VE SEEN ALL I NEED TO SEE.
...
AND...
THE KEY TO DEFEATING GOD...
...LIES IN THIS CARD!
TA
I WISH YOU LUCK.
KEH...
HURRY!!
GET HIM TO THE MEDICAL ROOM!

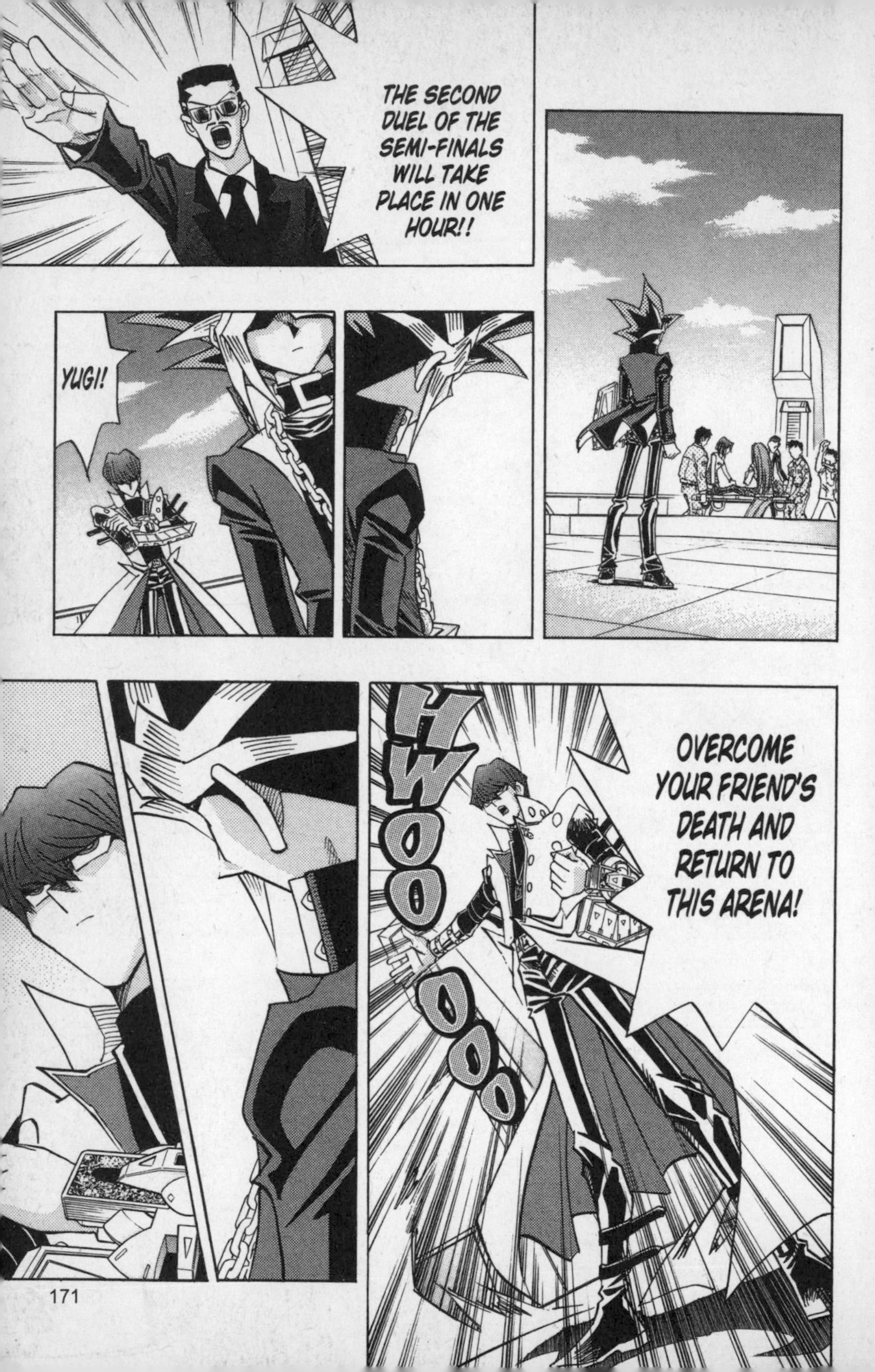
THE SECOND DUEL OF THE SEMI-FINALS WILL TAKE PLACE IN ONE HOUR!!
YUGI!
OVERCOME YOUR FRIEND'S DEATH AND RETURN TO THIS ARENA!
HWOOOOO

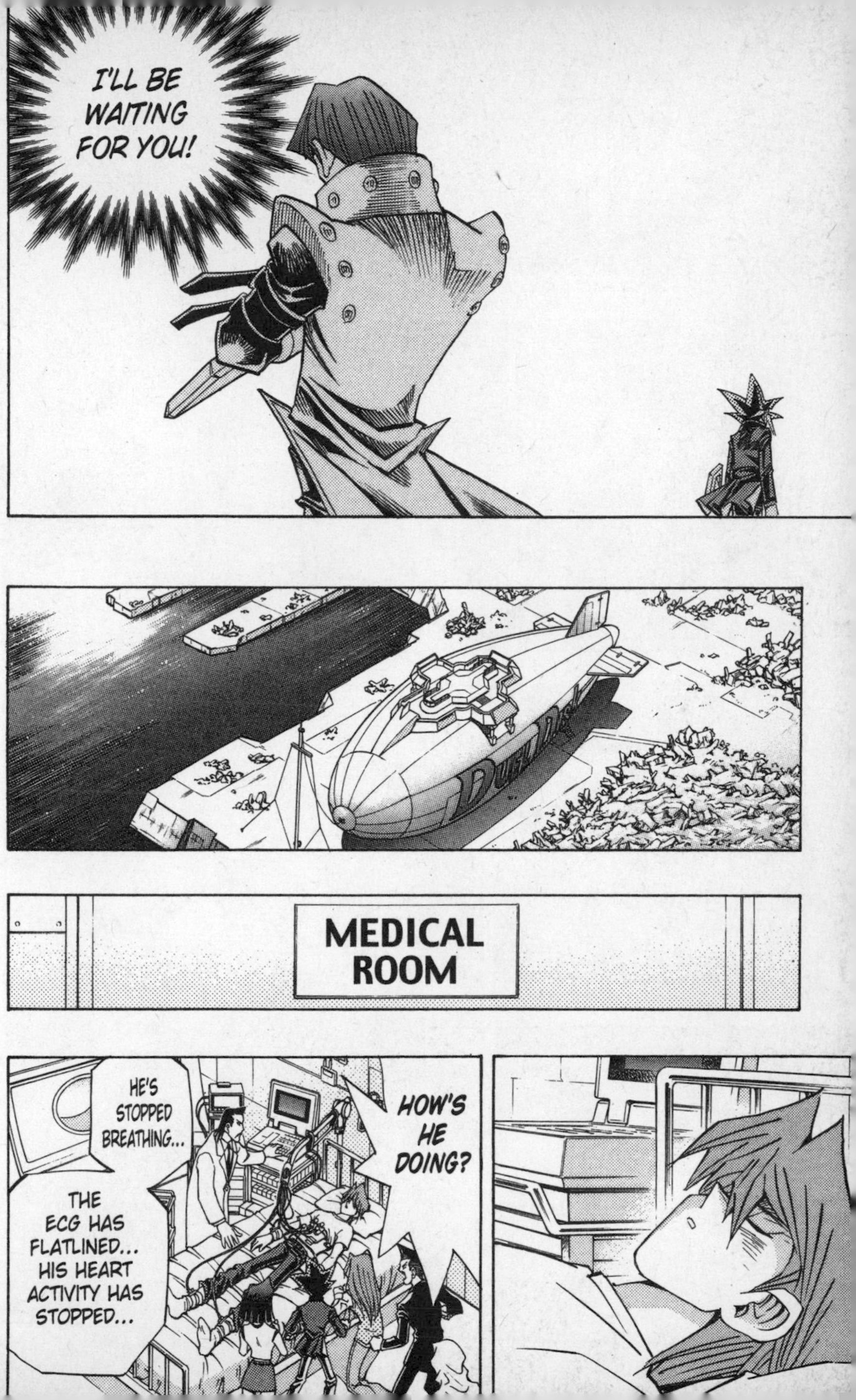
I'LL BE WAITING FOR YOU!
MEDICAL ROOM
HOW'S HE DOING?
HE'S STOPPED BREATHING...
THE ECG HAS FLATLINED... HIS HEART ACTIVITY HAS STOPPED...

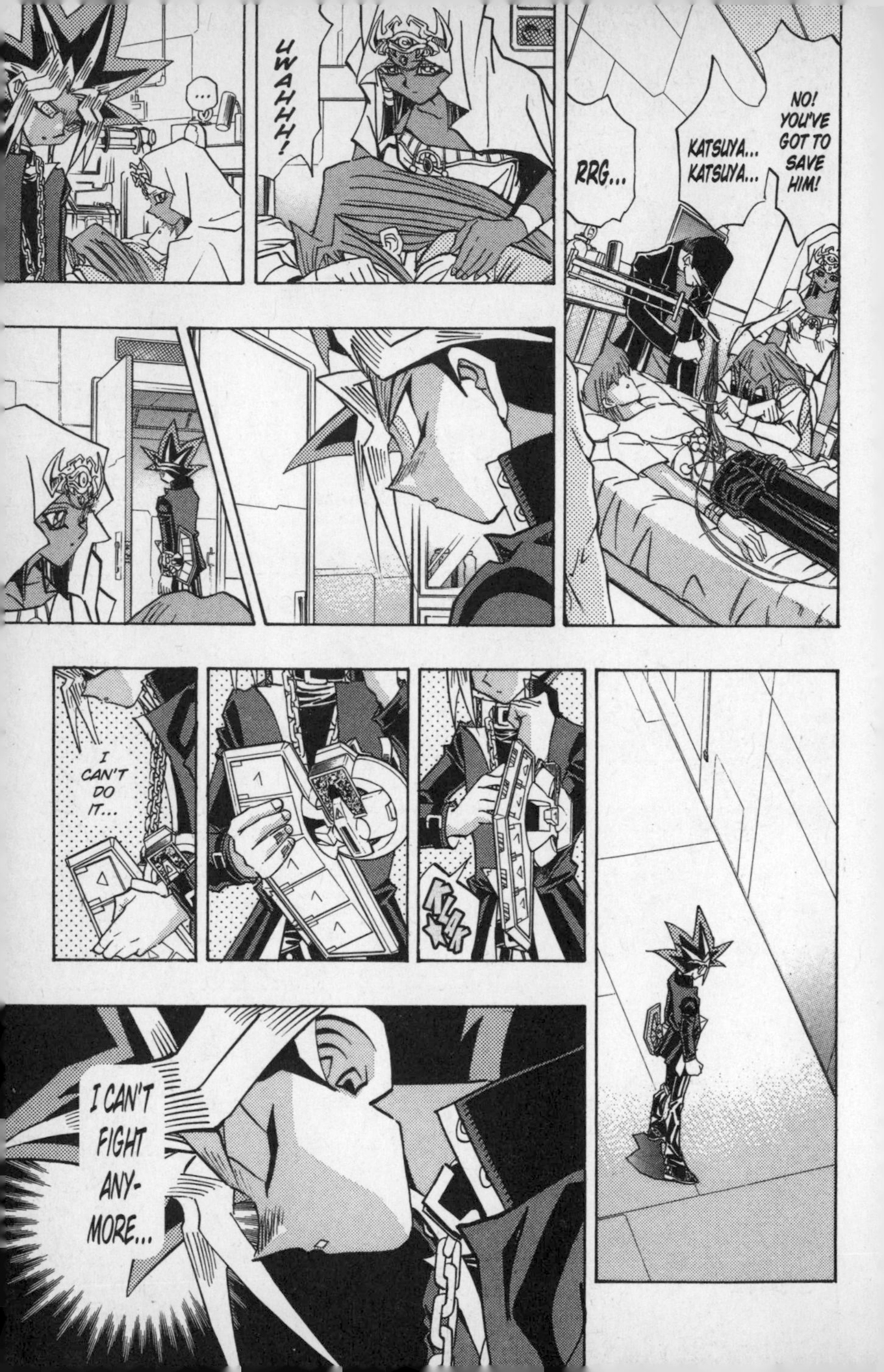
NO! YOU'VE GOT TO SAVE HIM!
KATSUYA... KATSUYA...
RRG...
UWAHHHH!
...
KLAK
I CAN'T DO IT...
I CAN'T FIGHT ANY-MORE...

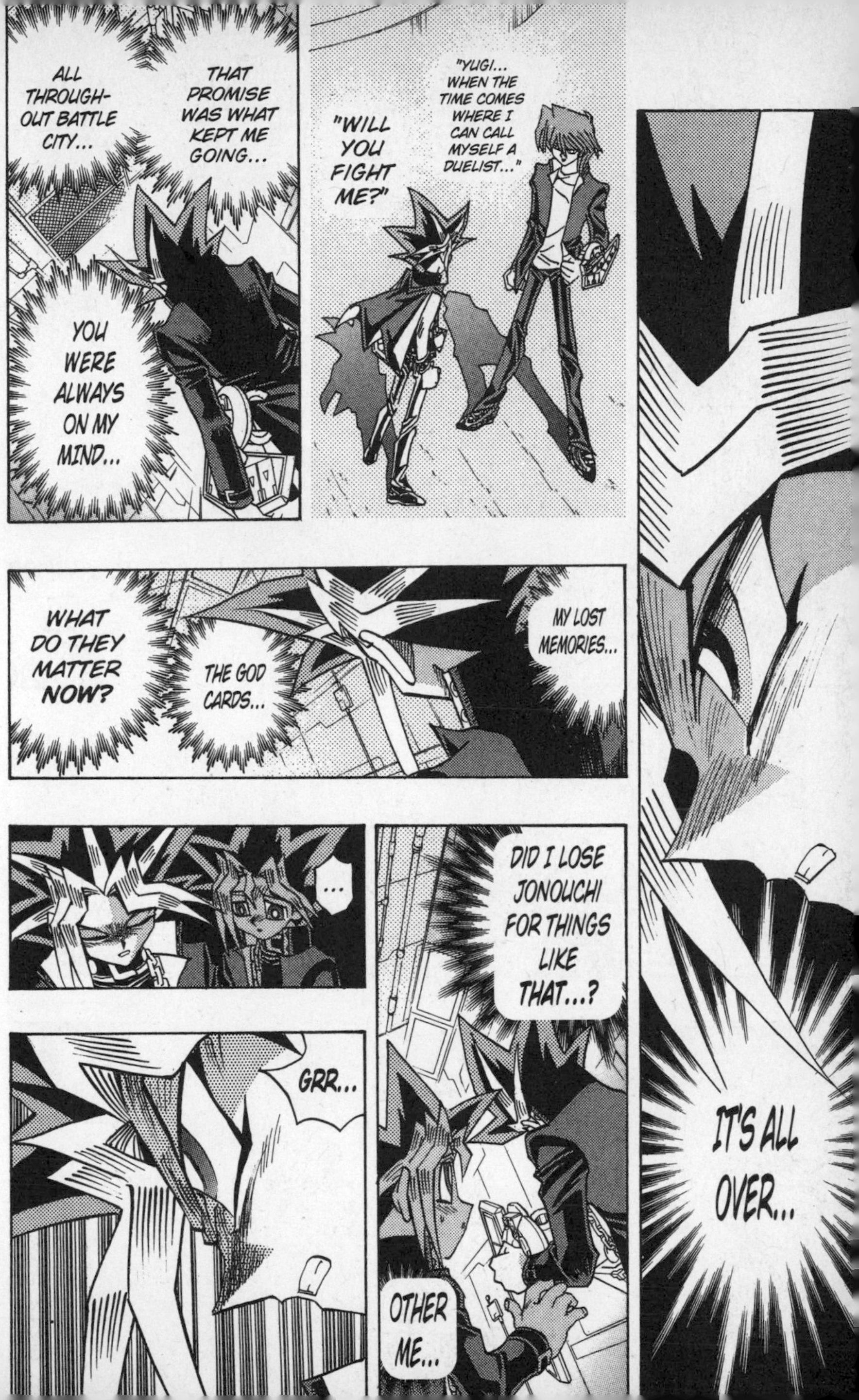
IT'S ALL OVER...
"YUGI... WHEN THE TIME COMES WHERE I CAN CALL MYSELF A DUELIST..."
"WILL YOU FIGHT ME?"
THAT PROMISE WAS WHAT KEPT ME GOING...
ALL THROUGH-OUT BATTLE CITY...
YOU WERE ALWAYS ON MY MIND...
MY LOST MEMORIES...
THE GOD CARDS...
WHAT DO THEY MATTER NOW?
DID I LOSE JONOUCHI FOR THINGS LIKE THAT...?
OTHER ME...
...
GRR...

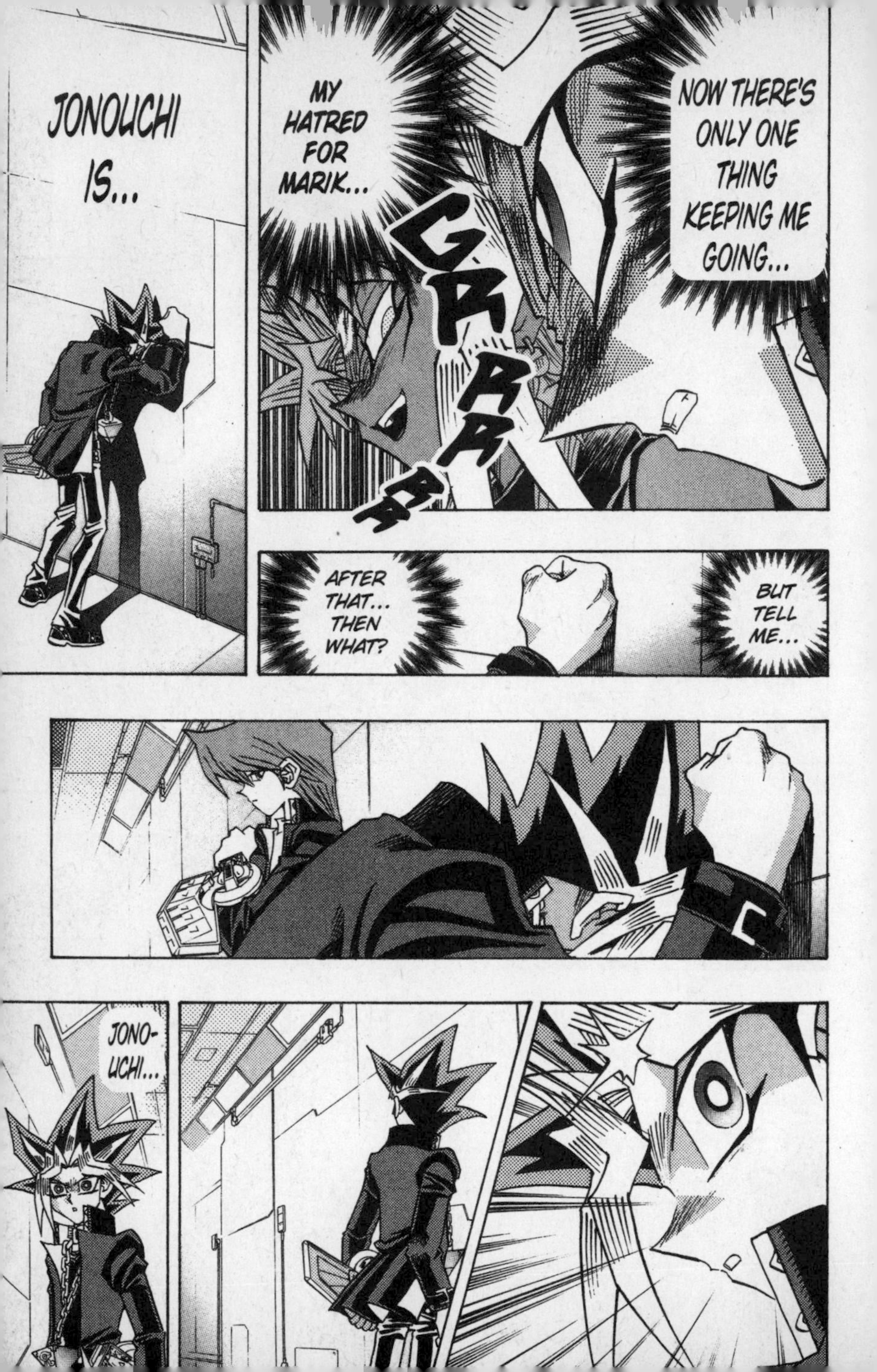
NOW THERE'S ONLY ONE THING KEEPING ME GOING...
MY HATRED FOR MARIK...
GRRRR
BUT TELL ME...
AFTER THAT... THEN WHAT?
JONOUCHI IS...
JONO-UCHI...

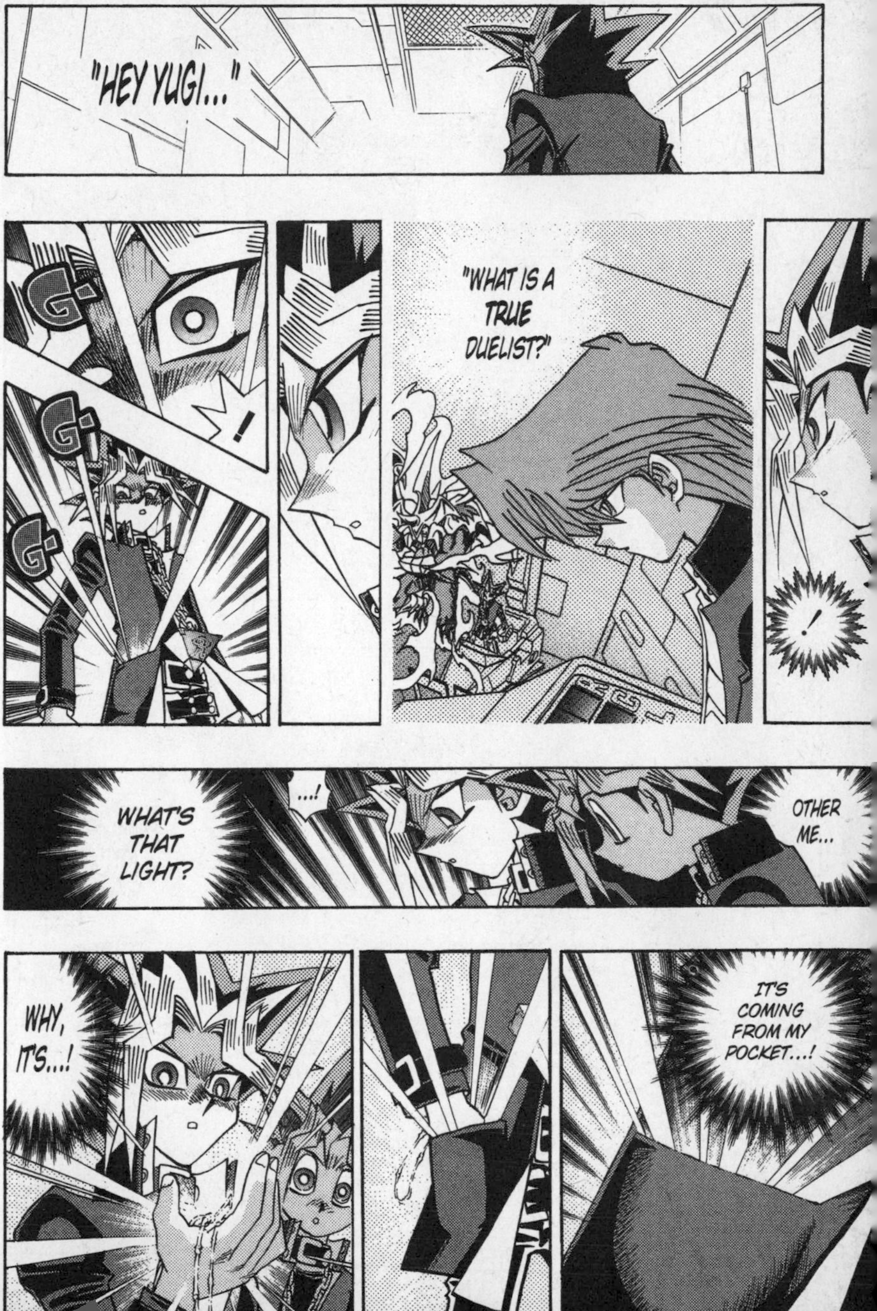
"HEY YUGI..."
!
"WHAT IS A TRUE DUELIST?"
G
!
G
G
OTHER ME...
...!
WHAT'S THAT LIGHT?
IT'S COMING FROM MY POCKET...!
WHY, IT'S...!

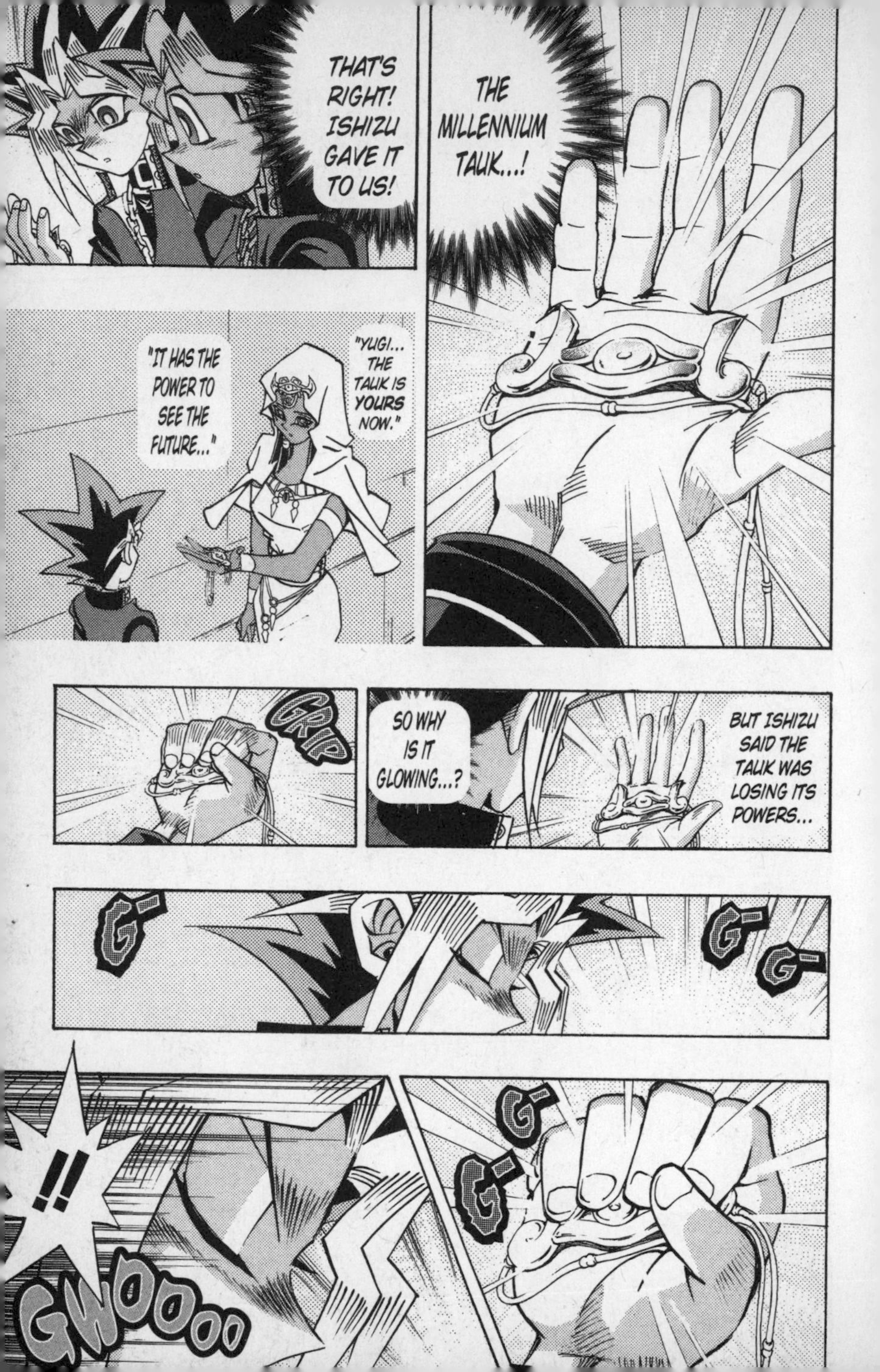
THE MILLENNIUM TAUK...!
THAT'S RIGHT! ISHIZU GAVE IT TO US!
"YUGI... THE TAUK IS YOURS NOW."
"IT HAS THE POWER TO SEE THE FUTURE..."
BUT ISHIZU SAID THE TAUK WAS LOSING ITS POWERS...
SO WHY IS IT GLOWING...?
GRIP
G- G-
G-
G- G-
!!
GWOOOO

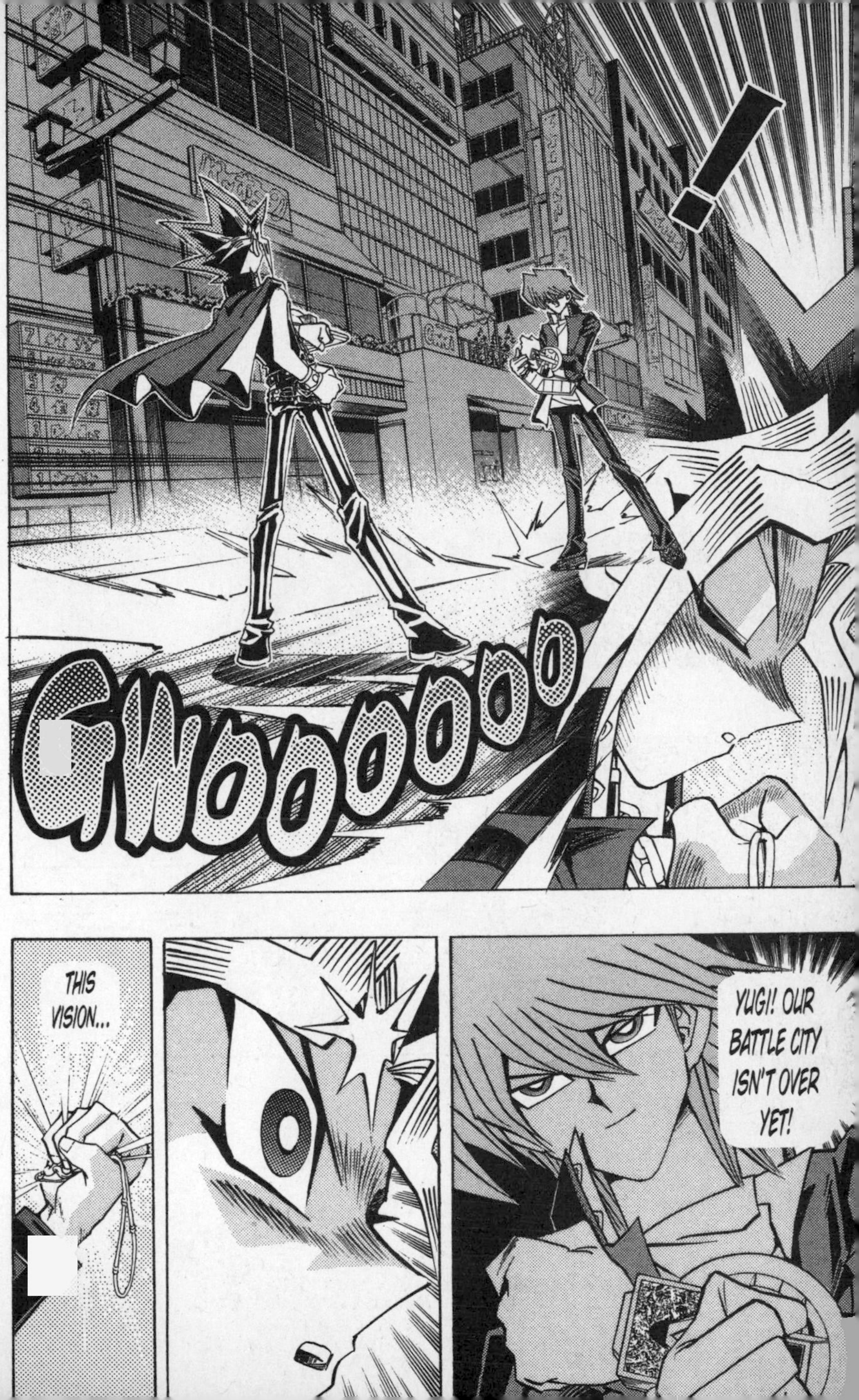
!
YUGI! OUR BATTLE CITY ISN'T OVER YET!
THIS VISION...

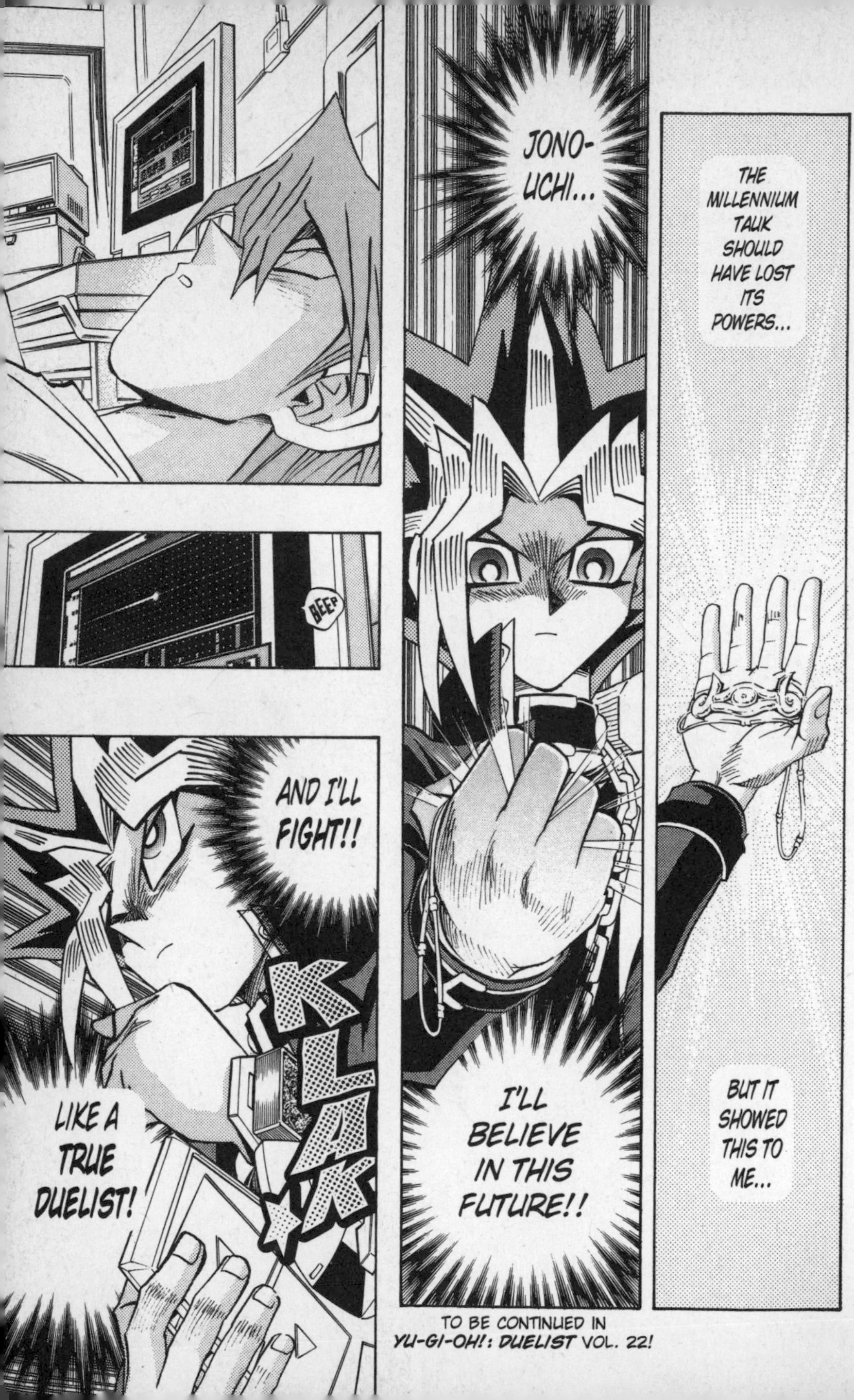
THE MILLENNIUM TAUK SHOULD HAVE LOST ITS POWERS...
BUT IT SHOWED THIS TO ME...
JONO-UCHI...
I'LL BELIEVE IN THIS FUTURE!!
BEEP
AND I'LL FIGHT!!
KLAK
LIKE A TRUE DUELIST!

TO BE CONTINUED IN
YU-GI-OH!: DUELIST VOL. 22!

MASTER OF THE CARDS

The "Duel Monsters" card game first appeared in volume two of the original **Yu-Gi-Oh!** graphic novel series, but it's in **Yu-Gi-Oh!: Duelist** (originally printed in Japan as volumes 8-31 of **Yu-Gi-Oh!**) that it gets really important. As many fans know, some of the card names are different between the English and Japanese versions. In case you play the game, or you're interested in playing, here's a rundown of some of the cards in this graphic novel. Some cards only appear in the **Yu-Gi-Oh!** video games, not in the actual trading card game.

FIRST APPEARANCE IN THIS VOLUME	JAPANESE CARD NAME	ENGLISH CARD NAME
p.7	*Blade Knight*	Blade Knight
p.7	*Dark Jeroid*	Dark Jeroid
p.7	*Gilfer Demon* (Darkness/Black Magic/Demon Clan Gilfer Demon)	Archfiend of Gilfer
p.10	*Kuribo*	Kuriboh
p.19	*Densetsu no Fisherman* (Legendary Fisherman)	The Legendary Fisherman
p.20	*Hakairin* (Destruction Ring/Circle)	Ring of Destruction
p.23	*Tsûkon no Jujutsu* (Spell/Technique of Pain)	Spell of Pain (NOTE: Not a real game card)

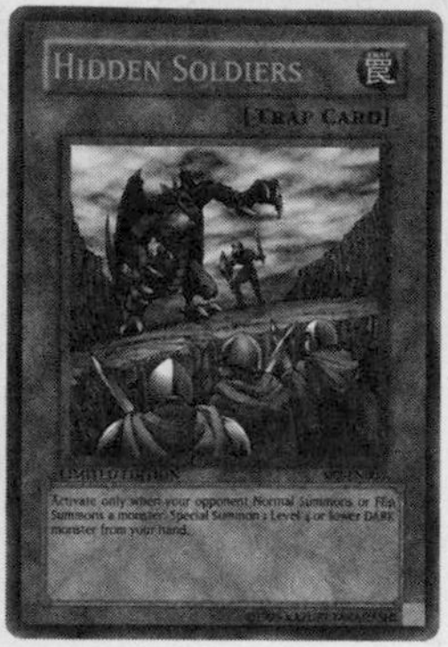
Hidden Soldiers
[Trap Card]
Activate only when your opponent Normal Summons or Flip Summons a monster: Special Summon 1 Level 4 or lower DARK monster from your hand.

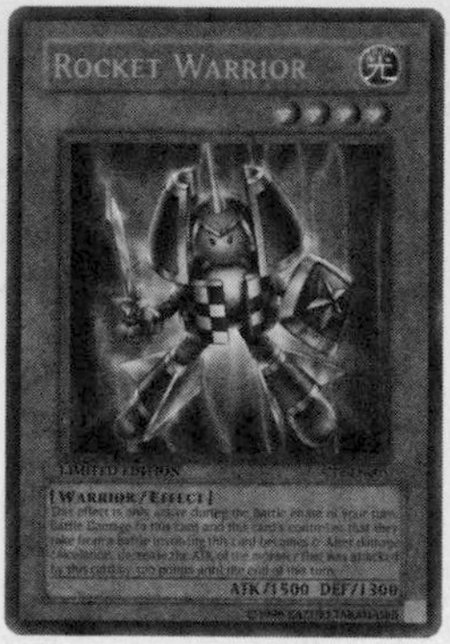
Rocket Warrior
[Warrior / Effect]
ATK/1500 DEF/1300

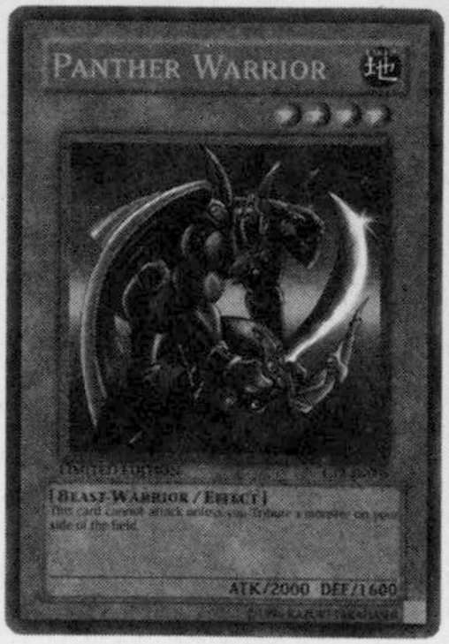
Panther Warrior
[Beast-Warrior / Effect]
This card cannot attack unless you Tribute a monster on your side of the field.
ATK/2000 DEF/1600

FIRST APPEARANCE IN THIS VOLUME	JAPANESE CARD NAME	ENGLISH CARD NAME
p.23	*Haka Arashi* (Graverobber)	Graverobber
p.41	*Shikkoku no Hyôsenshi Panther Warrior* (Jet Black Panther Warrior)	Panther Warrior
p.44	*Jigoku Shijin Helpoemer* (Hell Poet Helpoemer)	Helpoemer
p.51	*Kakure Hei* (Hidden Soldier/Army)	Hidden Soldiers
p.53	*Rocket Senshi* (Rocket Warrior)	Rocket Warrior
p.54	*Manrikimajin Viser Death* (Vise Devil/Demon God/ Genie Viser Death)	Viser Des (NOTE: Not a real game card)
p.69	*Quiz*	Question
p.70	*Gil Garth*	Gil Garth (NOTE: Not a real game card)
p.72	*Tenshi no Saikoro* (Angel Dice)	Graceful Dice

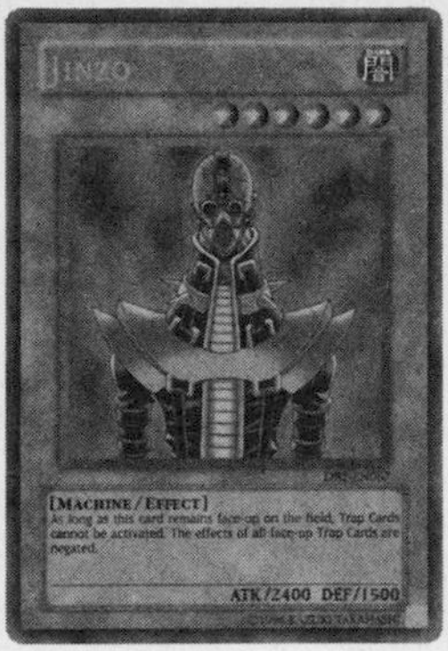
Jinzo
[Machine / Effect]
ATK/2400 DEF/1500

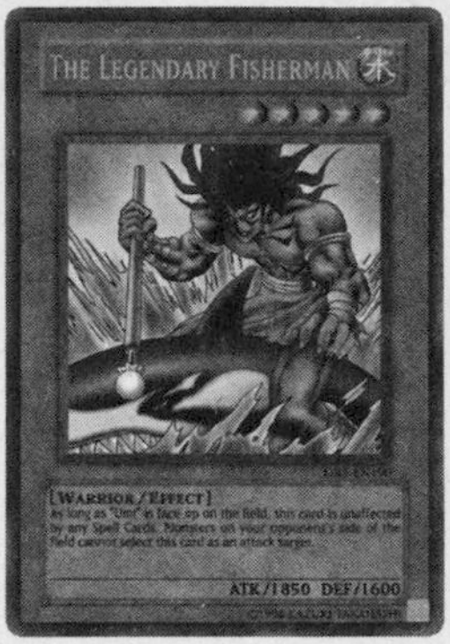
The Legendary Fisherman
[Warrior / Effect]
ATK/1850 DEF/1600

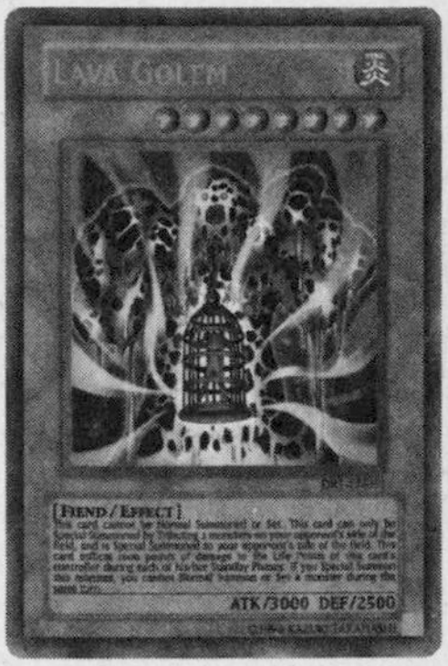
Lava Golem
[Fiend / Effect]
ATK/3000 DEF/2500

FIRST APPEARANCE IN THIS VOLUME	JAPANESE CARD NAME	ENGLISH CARD NAME
p.72	*Jinzô Ningen Psycho Shocker* (Android/Cyborg Psycho Shocker)	Jinzo
p.72	*Baby Dragon*	Baby Dragon
p.75	*Kan'okeuri* (Coffin Seller)	Coffin Seller
p.77	*Jashin no Daisaigai* (Demon/Devil/Evil God's Great Catastrophe)	Malevolent Catastrophe (NOTE: Not a real game card)
p.78	*Legend Devil*	Legend Devil (NOTE: Called "Legendary Fiend" in the anime and video games.)
p.97	*Yami no Gofûheki* (Protective Wind Wall of Darkness)	Dark Wall of Wind (NOTE: Not a real game card)
p.100	*Yôgan Majin Lava Golem* (Lava Demon Lava Golem)	Lava Golem
p.108	*Hurricane*	Giant Trunade
p.109	*Orokana Maisô* (Foolish Burial)	Foolish Burial

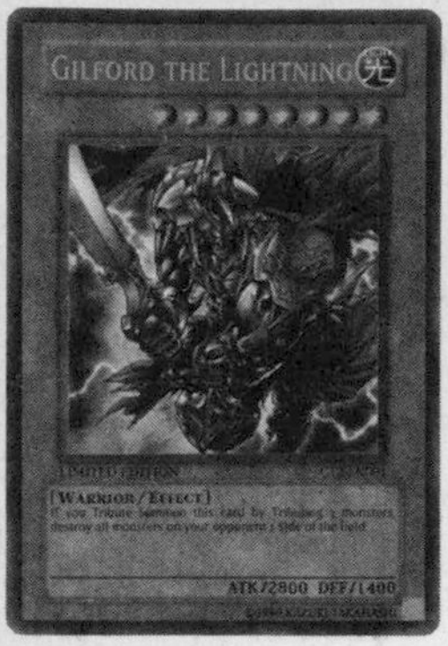
GILFORD THE LIGHTNING
[WARRIOR/EFFECT]
ATK/2800 DEF/1400

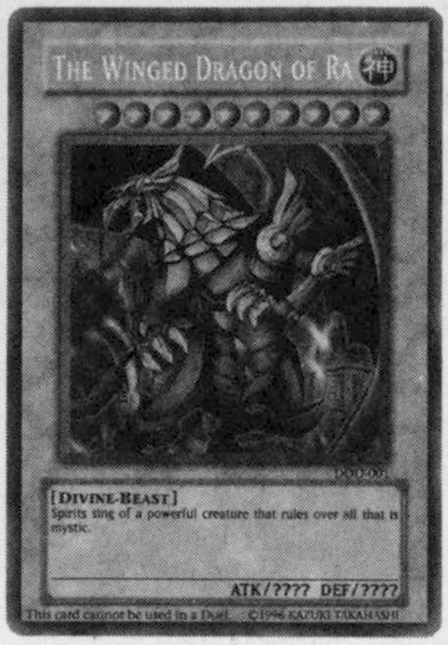
THE WINGED DRAGON OF RA
[DIVINE-BEAST]
Spirits sing of a powerful creature that rules over all that is mystic.
ATK/???? DEF/????
This card cannot be used in a Duel. ©1996 KAZUKI TAKAHASHI

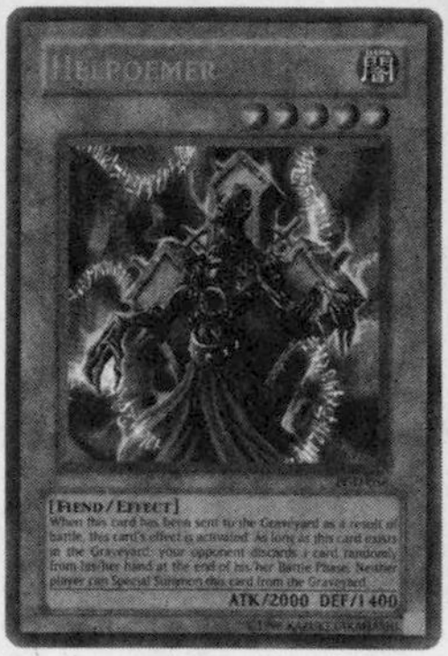
[FIEND/EFFECT]
ATK/2000 DEF/1400

FIRST APPEARANCE IN THIS VOLUME	JAPANESE CARD NAME	ENGLISH CARD NAME
p.112	*Monster Relief*	Monster Relief
p.116	*Kikai Fukuseijutsu* (Machine Proliferation Technique)	Machine Duplication
p.120	*Gilford the Lightning*	Gilford the Lightning
p.131	*Akumu no Makyô* (Demon Mirror of Nightmare)	Nightmare Mirror (NOTE: Not a real game card)
p.133	*Ra no Yokushinryû* (Ra the Winged God Dragon) (NOTE: The kanji for "sun god" is written beside the kanji for "Ra.")	The Sun Dragon Ra (NOTE: Called "The Winged Dragon of Ra" in the English anime and card game.)
p.137	*Shisha Sosei* (Resurrection of the Dead)	Monster Reborn
p.159	*Tetsu no Kishi Gear Fried* (Iron Knight Gear Fried)	Gearfried the Iron Knight

IN THE NEXT VOLUME...

Three thousand years ago, an ancient Egyptian carving predicted the final battle between Yugi and Kaiba...and now that day has finally come! Whose god is stronger: Slifer the Sky Dragon or the God of the Obelisk? And who will go on to face Marik in the finals...?

COMING AUGUST 2007!

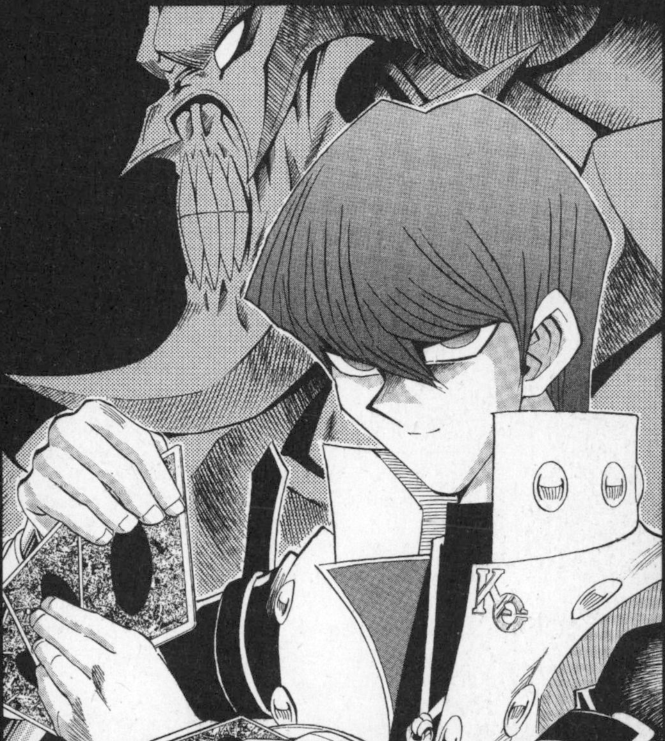

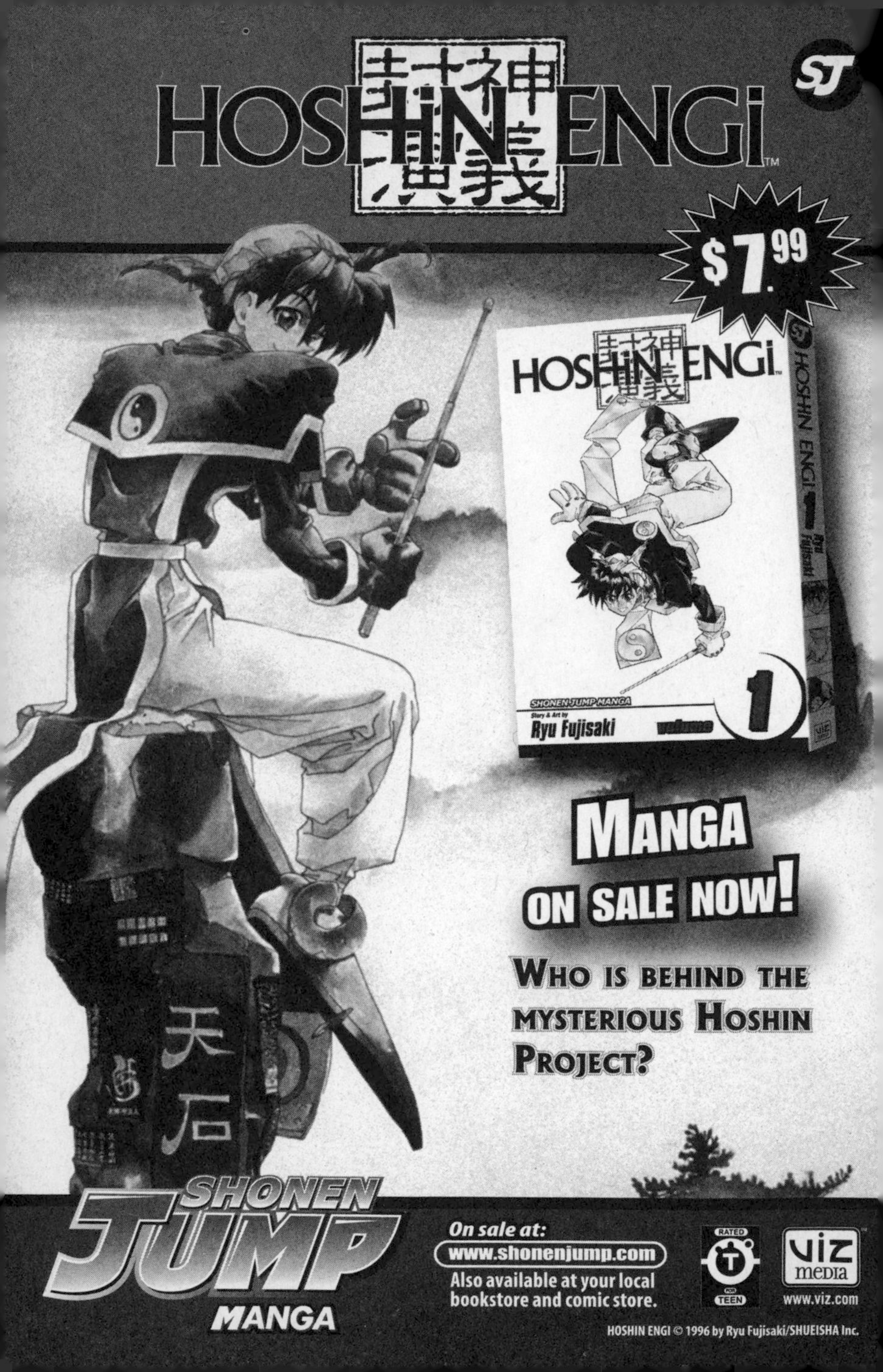

SJ
封神演義
HOSHIN ENGI™
$7.99
HOSHIN ENGI
SHONEN JUMP MANGA
Story & Art by
Ryu Fujisaki
volume 1
MANGA
ON SALE NOW!
WHO IS BEHIND THE MYSTERIOUS HOSHIN PROJECT?
SHONEN JUMP MANGA
On sale at:
www.shonenjump.com
Also available at your local bookstore and comic store.
RATED T FOR TEEN
viz media
www.viz.com
HOSHIN ENGI © 1996 by Ryu Fujisaki/SHUEISHA Inc.

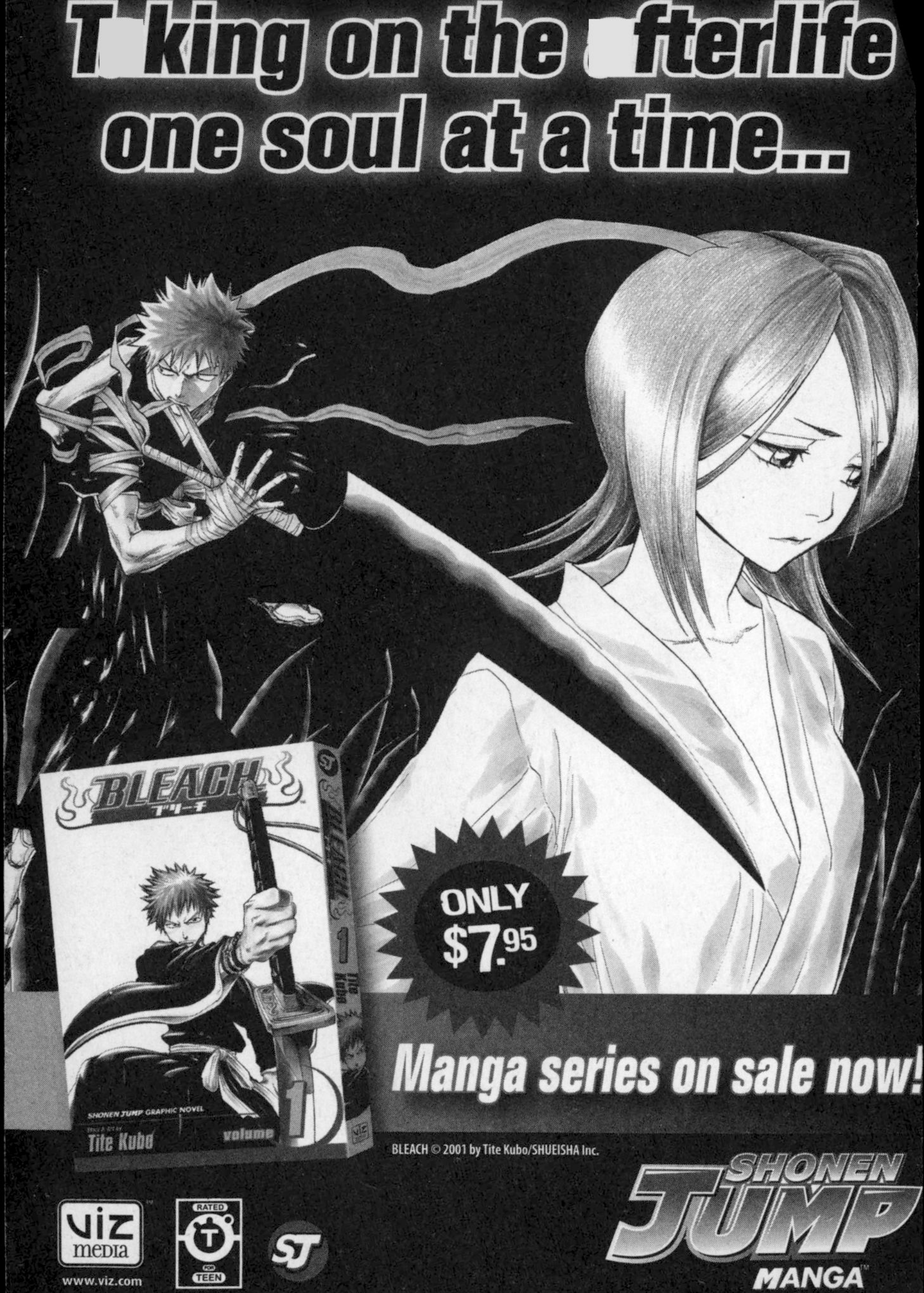
T king on the fterlife
one soul at a time...
BLEACH
ONLY
$7.95
Manga series on sale now!
SHONEN JUMP GRAPHIC NOVEL
Tite Kubo
volume 1
BLEACH © 2001 by Tite Kubo/SHUEISHA Inc.
viz media
www.viz.com
RATED T TEEN
SHONEN JUMP MANGA

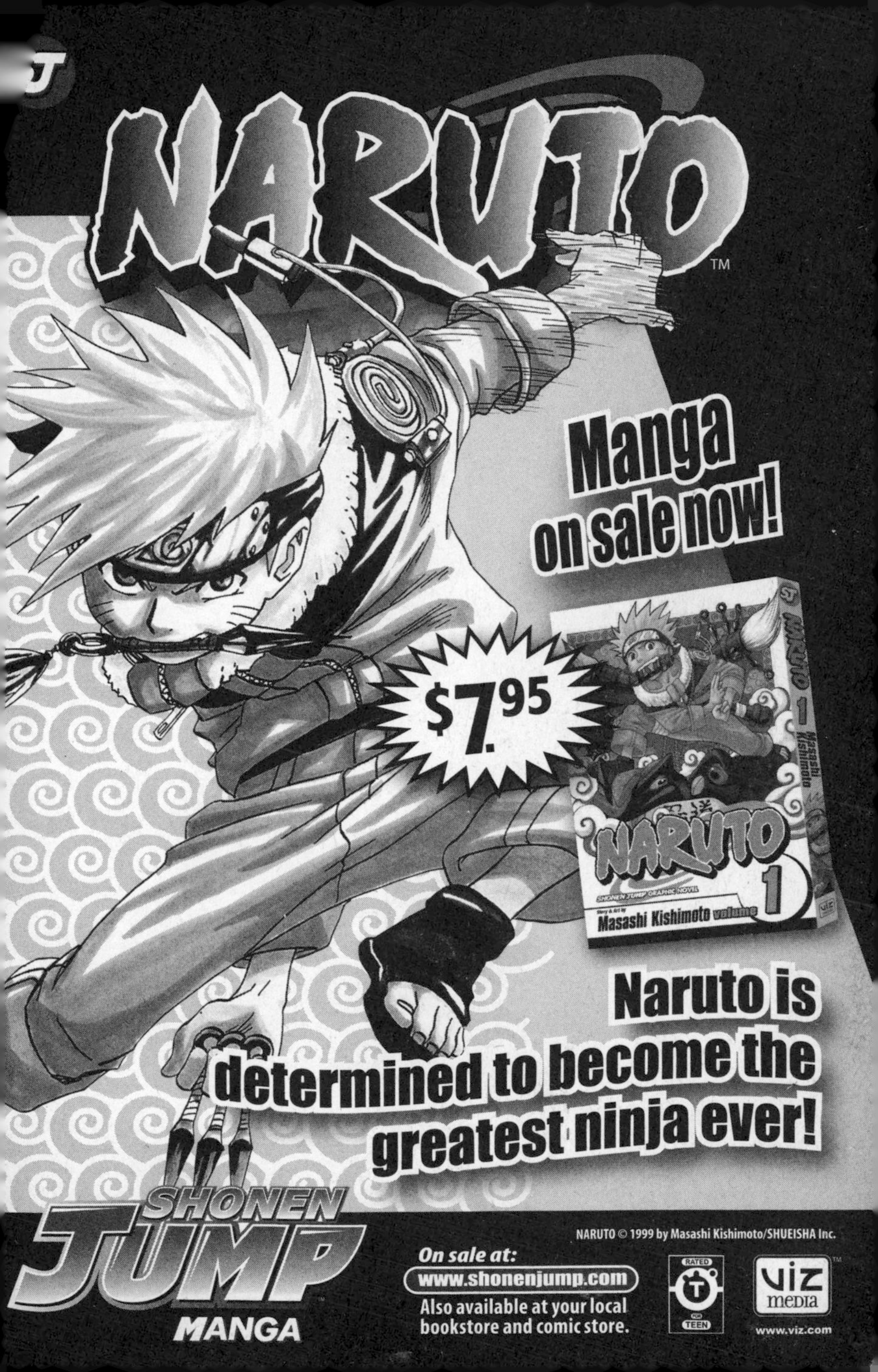

NARUTO™
Manga on sale now!
$7.95
NARUTO
1
Masashi Kishimoto volume 1
Naruto is determined to become the greatest ninja ever!
SHONEN JUMP MANGA
NARUTO © 1999 by Masashi Kishimoto/SHUEISHA Inc.
On sale at:
www.shonenjump.com
Also available at your local bookstore and comic store.
RATED T FOR TEEN
viz media
www.viz.com

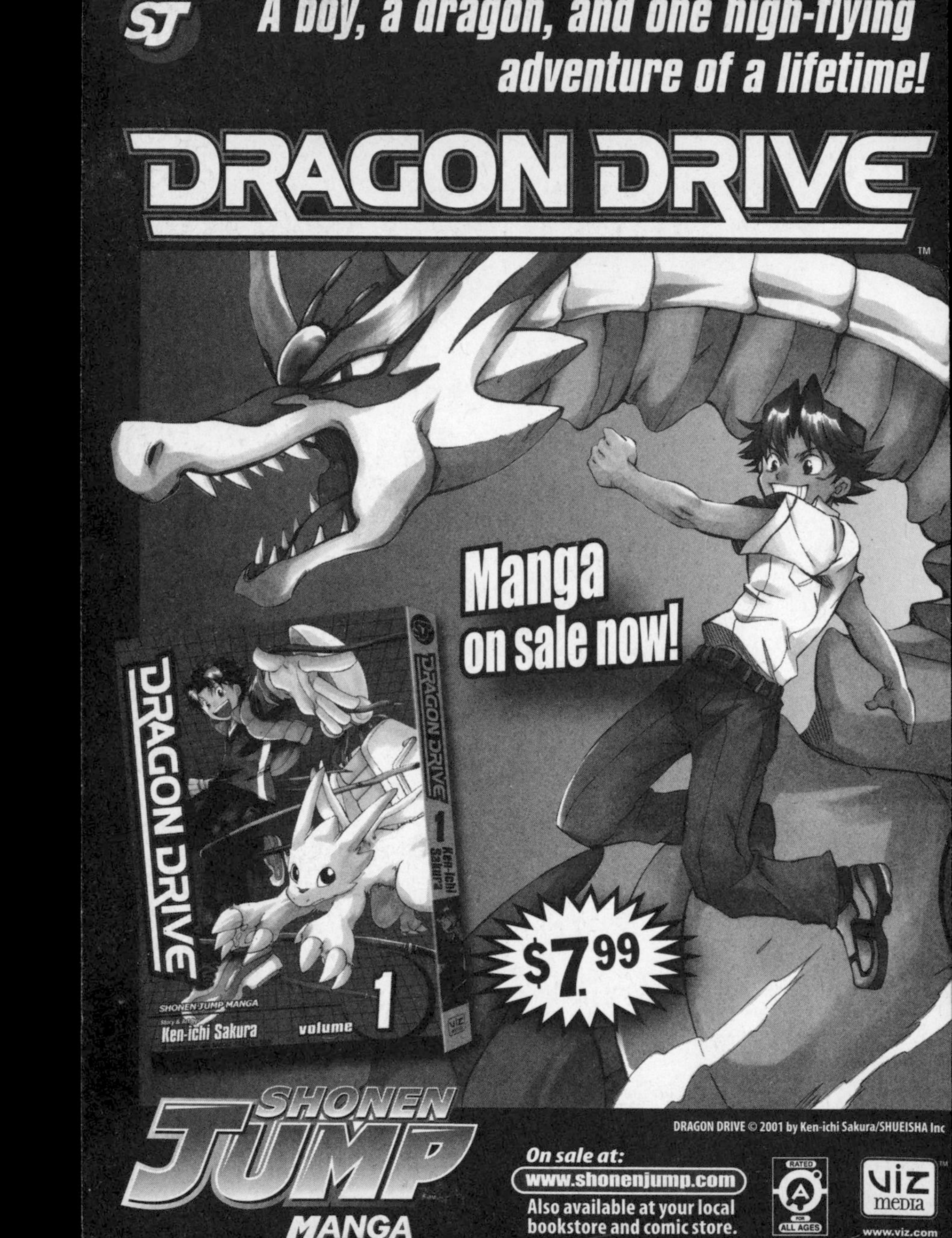
A boy, a dragon, and one high-flying adventure of a lifetime!
DRAGON DRIVE™
Manga on sale now!
DRAGON DRIVE
1 Ken-ichi Sakura
SHONEN JUMP MANGA
Ken-ichi Sakura
volume 1
$7.99
SHONEN JUMP MANGA
DRAGON DRIVE © 2001 by Ken-ichi Sakura/SHUEISHA Inc
On sale at:
www.shonenjump.com
Also available at your local bookstore and comic store.
RATED A FOR ALL AGES
VIZ media
www.viz.com

Tell us what you think about SHONEN JUMP manga!

Our survey is now available online.
Go to: **www.SHONENJUMP.com/mangasurvey**

Help us make our product offering better!

THE REAL ACTION STARTS IN...

THE WORLD'S MOST POPULAR MANGA
www.shonenjump.com

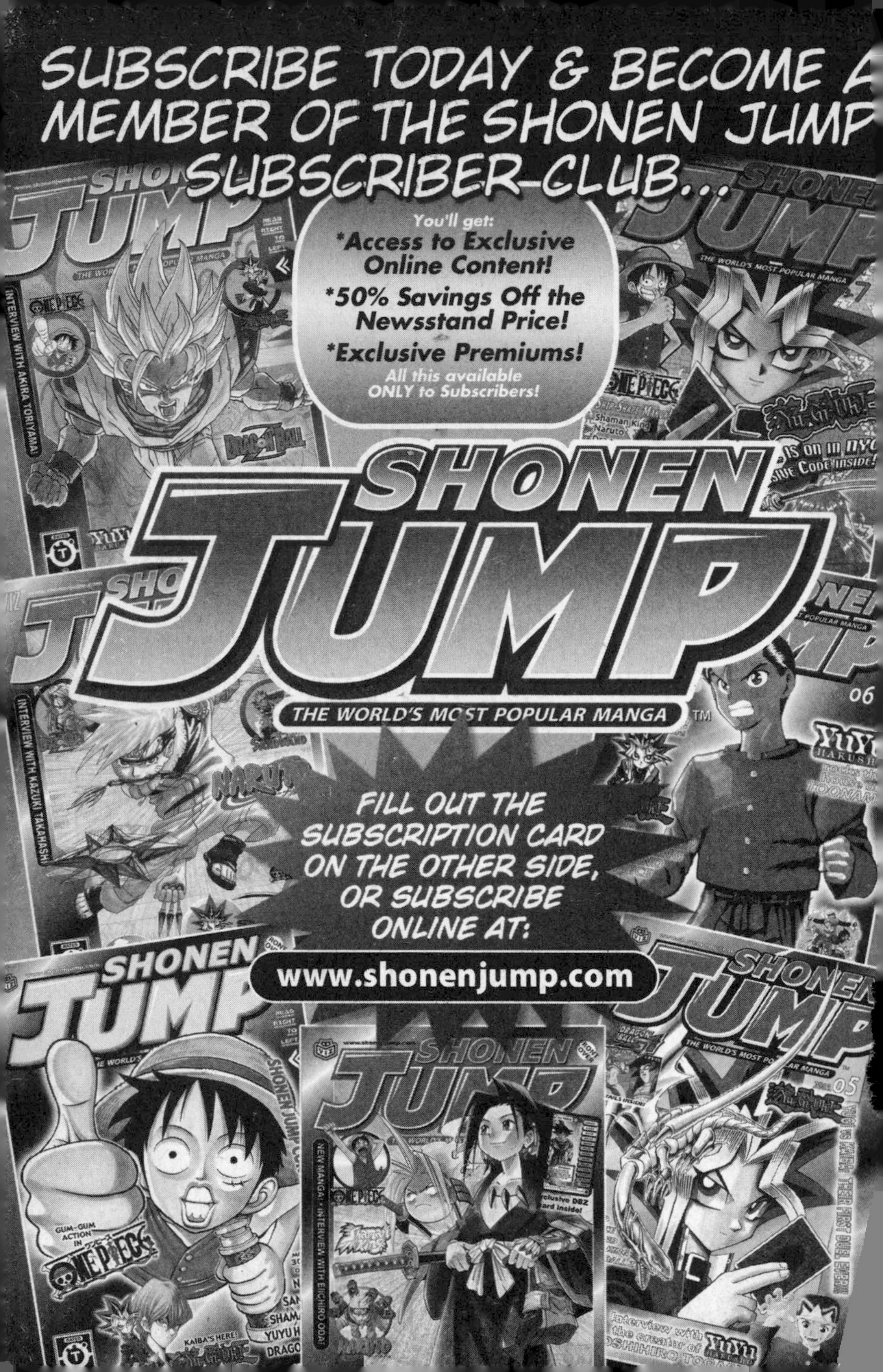
SUBSCRIBE TODAY & BECOME A MEMBER OF THE SHONEN JUMP SUBSCRIBER CLUB...
You'll get:
*Access to Exclusive Online Content!
*50% Savings Off the Newsstand Price!
*Exclusive Premiums!
All this available ONLY to Subscribers!
SHONEN JUMP
THE WORLD'S MOST POPULAR MANGA ™
FILL OUT THE SUBSCRIPTION CARD ON THE OTHER SIDE, OR SUBSCRIBE ONLINE AT:
www.shonenjump.com